LAND CLAIMS IN EAST FLORIDA

1826

Taken from the 19th Congress First Session
House of Representative Report Number 503

LAND CLAIMS IN
EAST FLORIDA

1826

TAKEN FROM THE 19TH CONGRESS FIRST SESSION
HOUSE OF REPRESENTATIVES REPORT NUMBER 503

U.S. CONGRESS

Heritage Books
2025

HERITAGE BOOKS

AN IMPRINT OF HERITAGE BOOKS, INC.

Books, CDs, and more—Worldwide

For our listing of thousands of titles see our website
at
www.HeritageBooks.com

A Facsimile Reprint
Published 2025 by
HERITAGE BOOKS, INC.
Publishing Division
5810 Ruatan Street
Berwyn Heights, MD 20740

Taken from the 19th Congress First Session
House of Representatives Report Number 503
1826

International Standard Book Number
Paperbound: 978-0-7884-9887-9

LAND CLAIMS IN EAST FLORIDA.

COMMUNICATED TO THE HOUSE OF REPRESENTATIVES FEBRUARY 23, 1826

Treasury Department, *February* 21, 1826.

Sir: In obedience to a resolution of the House of Representatives of the 7th instant, directing the Secretary of the Treasury to communicate to the House copies of the registers or abstracts of the claims to lands in East Florida, lately deposited in this department by the commissioners of that district, under the quantity of three thousand five hundred acres, with the general report of said commissioners, containing their reasons for the admission or rejection of the said claims, and full copies, with the evidence and decision of all claims over that quantity which have been made and lately deposited in the Treasury Department, I have the honor to transmit herewith copies of the following documents, to wit:

1. The abstracts of the decisions of the commissioners, numbered from 1 to 10, inclusive.

2. The evidence transmitted in cases exceeding 3,500 acres, referring to abstract No. 3, and numbered 1, 2, 3, 4, 5, 6, 7, 8, 9, 10, 11, 12, 19, 20, 21, 22, 23, 25, 26.

3. The evidence (numbered 11) in the case of Francis P. Fatio *et al.*, lately deposited in the department, but referring to abstract No. 5, printed among the documents of Congress, with the report from this department dated February 21, 1825.*

4. The reports of the commissioners dated January 1, 1826, and 31st of the same month.

I have the honor to be, with great respect, your most obedient servant,

RICHARD RUSH.

Hon. the SPEAKER *of the House of Representatives.*

St. AUGUSTINE, *January* 1, 1826.

SIR: Since my last report the claims to lands in East Florida, accompanying this communication, have been investigated and decided on by the commissioners. With the greatest diligence and industry, our secretary, and the two additional clerks appointed by authority of the law of the 3d of March last, have not been able to translate and copy the whole of the claims filed before us. There now remain to be acted on five hundred and twenty-eight.

From an inspection of the documents now forwarded, you will readily perceive that no want of industry has been manifested by the officers of the board. We last year urged the propriety of our being allowed by Congress the privilege of employing clerks and translators at discretion, at a rate for every hundred words written or translated. This, however, was denied, and hence the business before the commission is not yet completed.

For the principles on which the board have acted, they beg leave to refer to the former reports made by this board, as they have not in any material degree varied from them in the cases now reported.

Register No. 9 embraces a class of cases differently situated in some respects from any yet reported; for at the time of the cession they were not found amongst the records of the government, the only proper place for them. Those circumstances have in some cases been explained, or an effort at explanation has been attempted, that the evidence introduced, although perfectly competent by the legal rules of evidence, we feel bound to say that it has not always been of that clear, disinterested character which is calculated to carry conviction to the mind. Most if not all the witnesses have been interested in the principle to be dicided, although not interested in the particular case before the board. We have forwarded the testimony as nearly in the phraseology of the witnesses as practicable. To that testimony, and that which relates to Tomas de Aguilar, one of the officers of the government, we beg leave particularly to refer. The cases which have been reported as finally acted upon, the commissioners have been as particular as the reason of the cases would justify, and have generally demanded strict proof of the right of the party, so far as the United States are interested; but in the deraignment of title we have not been particular, as our decisions can in no case prejudice the rights of individual claimants; and where a clear, equitable right against the United States has been proved by one claimant, we have considered ourselves at liberty to relax on the rules in behalf of a second claimant for the same land; otherwise (if our decisions be correct) we might have done justice, but would not have given public satisfaction.

We have the honor to remain your most obedient servants,

DAVIS FLOYD.
W. H. ALLEN.

Hon. RICHARD RUSH, *Secretary of the Treasury, Washington.*

STATEMENT.

Claims remaining in the office not yet translated	295
Claims translated, but not prepared, because the claimants have not adduced their testimony	176
Donation claims undecided	37
British claims undecided	20
Total claims in the office	528

Recapitulation of claims acted on this session.

Confirmed, under 1,000 acres	173
Reported for confirmation, over 1,000 acres	10
Reported under the donation act	13
Confirmed under the donation act	10
Rejected	21
	227
Undefined in quantity, and reported	6
	233

* This evidence will be found in No. 454, succeeding said abstract No. 5.

WASHINGTON, *January* 31, 1826.

The undersigned commissioners for ascertaining claims and titles to lands in East Florida report that, in the discharge of the duties assigned them, they have examined and disposed of the claims herein set forth, in the manner and upon the principles exhibited in the following nine classes, numerically arranged.

Number one is a class of claims, as per register transmitted herewith, to lands not exceeding 3,500 acres in quantity, and which have been confirmed by the board. This class of claims is founded on royal titles and on concessions, some of which are unconditional and others conditional. A royal title is the highest order of title known by any law, usage, or principle in the province of East Florida. Titles of this description were designed to convey the fee simple to the grantee; they were usually made by the acting governors of the province in the name of the King; they recited the grant to be in "perpetuity," and also the specific metes and bounds of the land, although it is believed there were a few exceptions. This title may be said to correspond in character with that of a patent issued by our government. Concessions without condition are understood to differ from a royal title only in this, that most of the latter recite the metes and bounds, whereas the unconditional concession, although definite in quantity and location of the land, is still subject to a survey which, when made, was followed up by maturing the concession by a royal title. In concessions with conditions it was always expected by the Spanish authorities that the grantee was to comply with them, and not until then could he obtain a royal title; yet, on proof of conditions performed, it is believed that they were never very rigorous. Orders for survey were generally predicated upon concessions previously granted, yet a few have come before the board that were not, but were made by the deputy governor (as stated in his testimony) by virtue of a verbal order of the governor. In no case, however, has the quantity exceeded 640 acres, which has been confirmed; and then not until the document proved that the grantee had been in the actual possession and cultivation of the land at and before February 22, 1819. In deciding on the cases comprehended in this class the board have, in all cases of royal titles and concessions without condition, where the documents were found amongst the archives of the country, and no allegations on the part of the United States appearing against them, considered themselves bound to grant certificates of confirmation to the claimants; and in all cases exceeding 1,000 acres, and not exceeding 3,500, where the parties, in addition to the preceding qualifications, proved that they were in the actual possession and cultivation of the land at the time of the cession, the board have also considered themselves bound to grant certificates of confirmation, as well as in the cases of concession with condition, where the claimants, in addition to the qualifications mentioned, proved also the conditions to have been substantially performed.

Number two comprises claims not exceeding 3,500 acres, which, although found to be valid Spanish grants, yet have not been confirmed, from the want of proof of actual possession and cultivation at the time of the cession. They consist of royal titles and concessions, as in class No. 1

Number three comprehends claims exceeding 3,500 acres, the titles to which were found amongst the public archives of the country, and are ascertained by the commissioners to be valid Spanish grants, and reported accordingly to Congress for confirmation. On this class the commissioners think it necessary to remark that, although the subject has continued to engage their attention, they have perceived no principle calculated materially to alter their rules of adjudication as set forth in their first report. From the most correct information they have received, they are of opinion that the rules for granting lands were, in East Florida, different from those in the other Spanish provinces. In East Florida the governors seem to have exercised a discretion in granting lands for various purposes to all such as made application for them; but the commissioners have been much perplexed in endeavoring to ascertain the limit of their authority; hitherto their researches have been in vain. That this discretionary power was uniformly exercised by the governors is clearly to be inferred from their own acts; for the first governor after the cession of the province in 1783 made no grants of lands, or but few, and those only in small quantities. The one who succeeded him (Governor Quesada) established and published rules and regulations for the distribution of the public lands, one of which was the appointment of a commissioner, who, with the assistance of a surveyor, was specially intrusted with the distribution of the public lands. This they did in the following proportions: to the heads of family 100 acres, and to each other member, of whatever age, sex, or color, 50 acres. Nevertheless, it is found that Governor Quesada made grants in violation of these rules. His successor (Governor White) established rules differing from those of Quesada, and reduced the quantity to be given to the heads and other members of a family, and added the condition of ten years' possession before the party should be entitled to a royal title, and White also is found to deviate, in some cases, from the rules established by himself, as well as those of Quesada. There is also a peculiarity in the phraseology of a royal title; in all the grants of this nature the legal right to grant the lands is asserted, from which it is clearly to be inferred that the governors considered themselves entitled to and did exercise a discretionary power to grant the public lands to those who might make application for them in such quantities as they conceived might tend most to encourage the population and improvement of the country. By examining the correspondence between the King and the interdants, it will be found that they were particularly charged, and especially in East Florida, to promote the population and improvement of the province by all the prudential means in their power. To this end the commissioners find all the governors giving grants of land for the declared purposes of agriculture, pasturage, grist and saw mills, as well as indemnity for losses, and for military services, each of which seem to be embraced in the discretionary exercise of gubernatorial power. The commissioners trace this exercise, with a few exceptions, up to the year 1814, about which period, whether from a change of policy as applicable exclusively to the province or connected with an expected transfer to the United States, a practice of distribution was introduced differing from the former in the magnitude of the grants. Some of these grants favor the belief that the gratification of individual cupidity may have had some influence in their formation, but how far they comport with the laws of Spain and are entitled to confirmation the commissioners submit to the superior knowledge of Congress. There is one rule which the commissioners suppose it would not be unreasonable to apply in the adjustment of these claims. In cases where an application shall have been made for a grant of land as a remuneration for services, or other object embraced in the policy of the government, and the grant shall have been made accordingly, if the same individual shall have made a second application for remuneration for the same services, it would be no more than just to suppose that the first concession was full and ample, unless otherwise recited in the grant itself, and that the subsequent grant was an assumption of power not warranted by the laws and usages nor the policy of the government.

Number four comprehends claims under the donation act of May, 1824, and not exceeding 640 acres, and which have been confirmed by the board upon satisfactory proof that the claimant was twenty-one years of age, the head of a family, and that he had never received any written evidence of title from either the British or Spanish governments of East Florida; and furthermore, that he was actually settled on and cultivating the land at and previous to February 22, 1819, according to the requirements of the said act.

Number five comprises a class of claims reported to Congress on the ground that the settlements were made between February 27, 1819, and July 17, 1821, the time of the change of government, and originating under the aforesaid donation act.

Number six comprehends claims derived from the Spanish government by written evidence, and which have been ascertained to be valid Spanish grants, and have been reported to Congress on the ground that they were undefined in quantity.

Number seven comprises claims not exceeding 3,500 acres, founded on British grants, which have been recognized by the Spanish authorities, and confirmed by the board upon proof of such recognition; and in cases over 1,000 acres, on proof of actual occupation and cultivation.

Number eight is a register of town lots and out-lots, founded on actual occupation and cultivation previous to February 22, 1819, and which have been confirmed upon proof that they were actually in possession at and previous to the aforesaid day, by and with the consent of the government.

Number nine is a class of claims differing from all the others in an apparent want of formality. The other claims were authenticated by documentary evidence filed in the office, and were entitled to all the legal presumption in their favor which applies to records in our government; but the claims of this class were found in the possession of the claimants, and without any trace of evidence in the archives; and this circumstance, coupled with the equivocal character of the officer who verifies them, casts a shade of suspicion over the whole. In the investigation of these claims the commissioners have required the parties to show reasons why they were not on file in the archives, as well as to prove the execution; but from the interested character of the witnesses produced, the evidence on these points has been hitherto inconclusive. Thinking it probable, however, that some if not many of these claims are good and valid, and being informed by the parties of their ability to remove the suspicion, the commissioners have thought it due to justice that their opinion be suspended, and that a reasonable time should be afforded for the production of testimony.

With the outline afforded by the preceding classification, the commissioners transmit the documentary evidence, and their opinions thereon in each case, in detail. This arrangement of their opinion was suggested by the act by which the board was created, which dictated a minute transcript and investigation of the records, and a periodical accountability to the Secretary of the Treasury; and it was further enforced by the necessity of adjudicating on principles between which no summary can afford an absolute or definitive line of demarcation; and if the documents transmitted should be considered voluminous, it will at the same time be perceived that the features of the claims are various, and that the commissioners, in their operations, have been guided by the injunctions of the law. These operations have been retarded by the labor which was unavoidable in translating and transcribing the original grants and mesne conveyances, and the inadequate assistance afforded by the employment of three clerks, for which number only the law provides.

The operations of the board, independently of those contained in the first report, have resulted in the confirmation of 326 claims, in the rejection of 61, and in a reference to Congress of 88. Besides these claims, there are 528 undetermined, of which 233 are held under advisement for further proof, and 295, although filed, have not been matured to translation; and the commissioners, being sensible that the public interest demands an acceleration of the adjustment of these claims, have to suggest, as a mean of promoting this object, that the work of transcribing and translating be performed for a *pro rata* compensation.

All which is respectfully submitted.

DAVIS FLOYD.
W. H. ALLEN.

Hon. RICHARD RUSH, *Secretary of the Treasury.* .

My friend and colleague, Mr. Floyd, having addressed the above letter to you previous to my arrival at Washington, and approving highly of its remarks in general on the different abstracts, I have signed the letter, without requiring any alteration; but, of course, I should not be considered as participating in such remarks on abstract No. 3 as are only applicable to the cases acted on by him and Mr. Blair previous to my being a member of the board.

Yours, respectfully,

W. H. ALLEN.

Hon. RICHARD RUSH, *Secretary of the Treasury.*

REPORT No. 1.

Register of claims to lands, not exceeding three thousand five hundred acres of land, which have been confirmed by the commissioners for the district of East Florida.

No.	Names of present claimants.	Names of original claimants.	Date of the patent or royal title.	Date of the concession or order of survey.	Quantity of land. (Acres.)	By whom conceded.	Authority or royal order under which the concession was granted.	Conditions.	Date of survey.	By whom surveyed.	Where situated.
1	José Sanchez	Rafael Andrew	July 2, 1817		210	Coppinger	1815		Jan. 22, 1818	Robert McHardy	Mosquito.
2	Robert McHardy	Robert McHardy	July 3, 1815		1,000	Estrada	1790				Tomoka.
3	John Christopher	Spicer Christopher	April 8, 1809		500	White	1790		Feb. 15, 1792	Samuel Eastlake	River Nassau.
4	Farquhar Bethune	Farquhar Bethune	Mar. 4, 1814		1,100	Kindelan	1790		May 18, 1806	Jonathan Purcell	River Halifax.
5	Heirs of Francis Bagley	Francis Bagley	Dec. 24, 1817		300	Coppinger	1790		June 24, 1818	Geo. J. F. Clarke	River St. John's.
6	Prudence Plummer	Samuel Eastlake			300½	Quesada	1790		Jan. 6, 1792	Samuel Eastlake	Do
7	Charles Seton	Charles Seton	Sept. 13, 1816		600	Coppinger	1815		May 18, 1816	Geo. J. F. Clarke	River Nassau.
8	Heirs of John Floyd	Augustin Buyck		Feb. 1, 1793	200	Quesada	1790		May 15, 1793	Josiah Dupont	North river.
9	Heirs of Robert Pritchard	Robert Pritchard		Jan. 3, 1791	450	...do...	1790				Jacksonville, St. John's.
10	Heirs of Theresa Marshall	Theresa Gill		Oct. 10, 1791	533¾	...do...	1790		May 26, 1793	Josiah Dupont	North river.
11	John Houston	Spicer Christopher	April 12, 1809		100	White	1790				Talbot island.
12	Heirs of Pedro de Cala	Thomas Ellerbee		Aug. 4, 1803	200	Quesada	1790				St. Diego swamp.
13	Robert Hutchinson	Robert Hutchinson		Sept. 11, 1811	150	Estrada	1790				Little St. Mary's river.
14	Heirs of E. Waterman	E. Waterman	Feb. 22, 1816		260	Coppinger	1790		Feb. 5, 1816	Geo. J. F. Clarke	Bell's river.
15	John Addison	John Addison	June 8, 1817		1,414	...do...	1790		May 10, 1816	Robert McHardy	Tomoka.
16	Domingo Acosta	Domingo Acosta	Mar. 20, 1817		695	...do...	1815		June 1, 1821 / May 30, 1820 / April 10, 1821	Geo. J. F. Clarke	St. John's river.
17	Widow and heirs of A. Andrew	Lorenzo Capella	April 10, 1804		120	White	1790		May 23, 1793	Josiah Dupont	North river.
18	Heirs of M. O'Neal	Margaret O'Neal	Mar. 12, 1807		307	...do...	1790		April 16, 1792	Samuel Eastlake	Langford creek.
19	Heirs of Samuel Meers	Heirs of Samuel Meers	Oct. 17, 1811		200	Estrada	1790				Tiger island.
20	Andrew Atkinson	Andrew Atkinson	April 5, 1810		450	Coppinger	1815				St. Vincent Ferrer.
21	John Houston	Spicer Christopher	April 12, 1809		100	White	1790				Talbot island.
22	Susannah Cashen	James Cashen	July 11, 1814		700	Kindelan	1790				Amelia island.
23	Heirs of Margaret O'Neal	Margaret O'Neal	June 13, 1810		300	White	1790			John Purcell	Langford creek.
24	Andrew Atkinson	Andrew Atkinson	Nov. 17, 1817		200	Coppinger	1790				St. John's river.
25	Moses Bowden	Moses Bowden		April 5, 1815	250	Kindelan					Do.
26	Robert Andrew's heirs	Robert Andrew	April 6, 1809		500	White	1790		May 12, 1793	Josiah Dupont	St. Diego.
27	Moses Bowden	Uriah Bowden	April 17, 1815		200	Kindelan	1790				South of river St. John's.
28	Heirs of F. Bagley	Heirs of F. Bagley			1,000	Quesada	1790		April 3, 1793	Josiah Dupont	St. John's river.
29	...do...	...do...			248	...do...	1790		April 7, 1793	...do...	Goodman's lake.
30	Francisco Barbe	Francisco Barbe	April 10, 1817		500	Coppinger	1815		Feb. 8, 1817	Geo. J. F. Clarke	Cedar creek, Nassau.
31	William Berrie	Thomas Mann	July 3, 1799		100	White	1790				Turkey island, Nassau.
32	Susannah Cashen	Solomon Miller	June 26, 1802		100	...do...	1790				Amelia island.
33	John Bellamy	Robert Hutchinson	July 31, 1816		300	Coppinger	1790		Mar. 20, 1792	Samuel Eastlake	Little St. Mary's river.

REPORT No. 1.—*Register of claims to lands, not exceeding three thousand five hundred acres, &c.*—Continued

No.	Names of present claimants.	Names of original claimants.	Date of the patent or royal title.	Date of the concession or order of survey.	Quantity of land.	By whom conceded.	Authority or royal order under which the concession was granted.	Conditions.	Date of survey.	By whom surveyed.	Where situated.
					Acres.						
34	Charles Dreward	Charles Dreward	Mar. 18, 1817		250	Coppinger	1790		June 10, 1818	Geo. J. F. Clarke	Cedar creek, St. John's.
35	Farquhar Bethune	Farquhar Bethune	April 22, 1817		425	...do...	1815				Cabbage swamp, St. Mary's.
36	Sarah Bowden	Sarah Bowden		Oct. 1, 1791	149.50	Quesada	1790		Feb. 23, 1793	Josiah Dupont	Julington creek, St. John's.
37	Samuel Harrison	Samuel Harrison	Nov. 12, 1807		600	...do...	1790		Feb. 14, 1792	Samuel Eastlake	Seymour's Point, Nassau river.
38	...do...	...do...			500	White	1790		April 15, 1807	John Purcell	Harrison's Old F...d, J...ia.
39	...do...	...do...		May 16, 1799	500	...do...	1790				West point of Amelia.
40	Heirs of E. Hudnall	José Garcia	Dec. 5, 1817		100	Coppinger	1815		June 8, 1821	George J. F. Clarke	West of river St. John's.
41	William Berrie	William Berrie		June 16, 1801	100	White	1790		Mar. 15, 1807	John Purcell	Northwest of river St. John's.
42	Heirs of William Hobkirk	William Hobkirk	Sept. 24, 1816		335	Coppinger	1815				Banks of river St. Mary's.
43	...do...	...do...	Sept. 24, 1816		350	Coppinger	1815				Bell's creek.
44	Zephaniah Kingsley	Zephaniah Kingsley	Dec. 23, 1815		1,000	Estrada	1790			George J. F. Clarke	South side of St. Mary's river.
45	...do...	...do...	Jan. 18, 1816		300	Coppinger	1790				Saw-mill creek.
46	Anna M. Kingsley	Anna M Kingsley		Jan. 12, 1816	350	...do...	1790				East side of St. John's and Dunn's lake.
47	Zephaniah Kingsley	William Hartley	Dec. 13, 1817		150	...do...	1790		April 10, 1818	A. Burgevin	Orange Grove, Dunn's creek.
48	John Bachelot	John Bachelot	June 10, 1816		300	...do...	1790		Dec. 24, 1807	John Purcell	North point, Amelia island.
49	Heirs of S. Espinosa	Sebastian Espinosa		Sept. 5, 1801	500	White	1790				Ulleridge, Diego plains.
50	George J. F. Clarke	George J. F. Clarke		Dec. 15, 1815	100	Estrada	1790				Amelia island.
51	Sarah Brevard	Francis Brevard's heirs	Feb. 13, 1816		300	Coppinger	1790				Nassau river.
52	John Cavedo	John Cavedo		Jan. 4, 1816	350	Estrada	1815				Black creek.
53	John Bachelot	John Bachelot	June 10, 1816		300	Coppinger	1815				White Point, Amelia island.
54	Charles Seton	William Carney	Aug. 26, 1818		700	...do...	1790		April 14, 1792	Samuel Eastlake	River St. Mary's.
55	Zephaniah Kingsley	Heirs of William Kane	Aug. 19, 1809		300	White	1790		Nov. 30, 1791	...do...	Doctor's creek, St. John's.
56	Heirs of C. Griffin	C. Griffin			450	Quesada	1790		April 8, 1792	...do...	River Nassau.
57	Widow & heirs of N. Sanchez	Nicholas Sanchez	April 24, 1816		365	Coppinger	1815				St. Diego.
58	Joseph Gaunt	Joseph Gaunt		Oct. 12, 1816	335	...do...	1815				Turnbull's swamp.
59	Widow & heirs of N. Sanchez	Nicholas Sanchez	Feb. 3, 1800		300	White	1790		June 23, 1809	John Purcell	Guana creek, Diego plains.
60	John Lowe	John Lowe	Jan. 30, 1812		750	Estrada	1790				Bell's Old Field, Bell's river.
61	Widow and heirs of J. Andrew	Juan Andrew	July 10, 1804		161¾	White	1790		May 24, 1793	Josiah Dupont	North of river, White Oyster bank.
62	Christina Hill	Joseph Sanchez		Nov. 17, 1815	405	Estrada	1815				Diego plains, Casina location.
63	Thomas Napier	Juan B. Entralgo	Nov. 15, 1817		800	Coppinger	1815		Feb. 20, 1818	George J. F. Clarke	Turnbull's swamp.
64	John Middleton	William Garvin	Mar. 29, 1817		200	...do...	1815		April 6, 1817	...do...	Cedar branch, St. John's.
65	William Hartley	William Hartley	Dec. 13, 1817		250	...do...	1790				Goodby's lake, Wells' swamp.
66	Frederick Hartley	Frederick Hartley	May 7, 1803		900	White	1790				St. Nicholas, at Six-mile river.
67	Hannah Nobles	Robert Corwin	April 24, 1817		205	Kindelan	1790		Dec. 20, 1791	Samuel Eastlake	South side of St. John's river.
68	James R. Hanham	José Peso de Burgo			170¾	Quesada	1790		May 26, 1793	Josiah Dupont	North river and Guana creek.
69	Abraham Hannom	Abraham Llanneau		Sept. 18, 1816	50	Coppinger	1790				East side of St. John's river.
70	The guardian of F. Miles	Barbara Hahnham			200	Quesada	1790		June 2, 1793	Josiah Dupont	North river.

REPORT No. 1.—*Register of claims to lands, not exceeding three thousand five hundred acres, &c.—Continued.*

No.	Names of present claimants.	Names of original claimants.	Date of the patent or royal title.	Date of the concession or order of survey.	Quantity of land.	By whom conceded.	Authority or royal order under which the concession was granted.	Conditions.	Date of survey.	By whom surveyed.	Where situated.
					Acres.						
71	The guardian of F. Miles	Francis X. Sanchez	Feb. 4, 1811		300	White	1790		Dec. 13, 1791	Samuel Eastlake	St. John's river.
72	Heirs of E. Hudnall	Daniel Hogans		Mar. 18, 1817	955	Coppinger	1790		May 9, 1817	George J. F. Clarke	North side of St. John's river.
73	...do...	E. Hudnall		Jan. 29, 1802	500	White	1790				Mouth of Nassau river.
74	William Eubanks	William Eubanks		Mar. 18, 1817	150	Coppinger	1790				Burton's island, Nassau river.
75	Robert Harrison	Robert Harris		May 10, 1816	765	...do...	1790		April 20, 1821	George J. F. Clarke	Roundabout, Nassau river.
76	John Bilcock	John Gilcock			300	Querada	1790		Mar. 18, 1792	Samuel Eastlake	Nassau river.
77	Lewis Guibert	Edward M. Wanton		Dec. 23, 1801	400	White	1790		Nov. 17, 1819	George J. F. Clarke	Cedar head, St. John's river.
78	Stephen Fairbanks, jr	Stephen Fairbanks		Mar. 18, 1817	295	Coppinger	1790				Trout creek, St. John's river.
79	Heirs of E. Hudnall	Selby Taylor		April 14, 1817	200	...do...	1790		June 7, 1821	George J. F. Clarke	South head, Pablo creek.
80	John Upegrove	John Upegrove		July 27, 1803	250	White	1790				Peach orchard, Nassau. (See Report No. 9.)
81	José Alvarez	José Alvarez	Sept. 9, 1816		335	Coppinger	1815		Feb. 2, 1817	George J. F. Clarke	Thomas' swamp, Nassau.
82	Zephaniah C. Gibbs	Francis X. Sanchez	Feb. 12, 1811		121	White	1790		Sept. 12, 1818	Robert McHardy	Diego plains, Guana creek.
83	Zephaniah Kingsley	Francis Estacholy	Mar. 15, 1817		50	Coppinger	1790		April 15, 1817	George J. F. Clarke	St. Vincent Ferrer, St. John's.
84	John G. Rushing	John G. Rushing		Nov. 27, 1815	205	Estrada	1790	Complied with	Feb. 1, 1818	...do...	Dunn's creek, St. John's.
85	John Christopher	John Tucker		May 24, 1804	50	White	1790				River Nassau.
86	Zephaniah Kingsley	Manuel Romero	Mar. 17, 1817		100	Coppinger	1790		April 15, 1817	George J. F. Clarke	St. Vincent Ferrer, St. John's.
87	Hannah Nobles	Hannah Nobles		April 23, 1816	100	...do...	1790		May 13, 1817	...do...	Wills' swamp, St. John's.
88	Widow and heirs of L. Capo	Lorenzo Capo		Feb. 24, 1508	175	White	1790	Complied with			Twelve-mile swamp.
89	John Frazer's executors	John Frazer		May 2, 1810	500	...do...	1790				St. Mary's river.
90	John Bellamy	John Mestre		Dec. 3, 1816	50	Coppinger	1790		Feb. 21, 1817	Geo. J. F. Clarke	Cowford, north of St. John's river.
91	Heirs of M. Pons	Mathias Pons	Sept. 17, 1814		400	Kindelan	1790	Complied with	Nov. —, 18..	Juan Purcell	River Matanzas, Casapulla.
92	Susannah Cashen	James Cashen		Oct. 7, 1805	250	White	1790				Amelia island.
93	Pedro Pons	Pedro Pons	June 4, 1817		875	Coppinger	1815				Mills' swamp, Nassau.
94	Heirs of A. Suarez	Thomas Suarez	July 27, 1809		500	White	1790			Juan Purcell	Black Point, Amelia.
95	Domingo Fernandez	James Adamson	April 11, 1817		300	Coppinger	1790		Mar. 1, 1817	Geo. J. F. Clarke	Amelia island.
96	Cornelius Griffith	Cornelius Griffith		Dec. 9, 1802	300	White	1790	Complied with			Banks of St. Mary's river.
97	Geo. J. F. Clarke	Geo. J. F. Clarke		May 9, 1815	1,000	Kindelan	1790				500 acres in Dunn's swamp; 500 acres on Dunn's lake. Surveyed in two tracts of 500 acres each.
98	Domingo Fernandez	Domingo Fernandez	Aug. 19, 1807		150	White	1790				Amelia island.
99	Susannah Cashen	Joseph Reid		July 13, 1804	230	...do...	1790	Complied with			Old Township, St. Mary's.
100	Francis Richard	Francis Richard	Mar. 20, 1815		466	Kindelan	1790				Branchester, St. John's.
101	...do...	...do...	...do...		220	...do...	1790				Pargut, St. John's river.
102	Domingo Fernandez	Domingo Fernandez	Sept. 1, 1813		100	...do...	1790				Amelia island.
103	Jane Murray	Geo. Murray		July 28, 1803	600	White	1790	Complied with			McDougall's swamp.
104	John Christopher	Epicer Christopher	April 8, 1809		500	...do...	1790				Mouth of Nassau river.
105	Domingo Fernandez	Heirs of Maria Mattair	April 25, 1807		200	...do...	1790				Orange grove, Amelia island.

REPORT No. 1.—*Register of claims to lands, not exceeding three thousand five hundred acres, &c.*—Continued.

No.	Names of present claimants.	Names of original claimants.	Date of the patent or royal title.	Date of the concession or order of survey.	Quantity of land. (Acres)	By whom conceded.	Authority or royal order under which the concession was granted.	Conditions.	Date of survey.	By whom surveyed.	Where situated.
106	John Houston	Spicer Christopher	Dec. 2, 1795		600	Quesada	1790		Aug. 10, 1816	Geo. J. F. Clarke	North of Talbot Island.
107	Domingo Fernandez	Domingo Fernandez	April 10, 1817		928	Coppinger	1815		June 8, 1817	....do....	West side of Amelia river.
108	Henry Yonge	Henry Yonge		Mar. 15, 1817	190	....do....	1790				Lofton's swamp.
109	....do....	....do....	Dec. 22, 1815		480	Estrada	1815		April 1, 1816	....do....	St. Mary's river. } These two tracts are in one royal title for 950 acres.
110	....do....	....do....	....do....		500	....do....	1815		April 3, 1816	....do....	St. Mary's river.
111	Francis Richard	Francis Richard		Jan. 9, 1801	110	White	1790		Mar. 1, 1842	Robert McHardy	St. Isabel, St. John's river.
112	Heirs of F. X. Sanchez	F. X. Sanchez		Mar. 4, 1793	1,000	....do....	1790		April 25, 1819	Robert McHardy	Diego plains.
113	....do....	....do....		Aug. 4, 1801	100	....do....	1790		Mar. 30, 1819	A. Burgevin	Do.
114	Daniel Hurlbert	John Tatom	Dec. 15, 1792		200	Quesada	1790				Four miles from St. Augustine.
115	Heirs of Jesse Fish	Jesse Fish		April 1, 1791	500	....do....	1790				Graham's swamp.
116	Heirs of A. Dewees	Andrew Dewees	May 4, 1804		2,290	White	1790		Feb. 8, 1792	Samuel Kastuke	Pablo creek, St. John's.
117	Seymour Picket	Reuben Hogans	May 26, 1815		250	Kindelan	1790		Feb. 29, 1792	....do....	St. John's.
118	Heirs of Con. McFee	Angus Clark	Dec. 10, 1791		446	Quesada	1790	Complied with			Do.
119	A. Clarke and E. Atwater	James W. Lee		Nov. 11, 1794	900	....do....	1790				Do.
120	Elihu Woodruff and others	John Moore	Nov. 9, 1805		350	White	1790				Do.
121	Philip and Mary Dewees	Francis X. Sanchez	Feb. 6, 1811		100	....do....	1790				Guana river.
122	Thomas Moy	Thomas Moy			350	Coppinger	1790		Sept. 21, 1819	Geo. J. F. Clarke	Bell's river.
123	John Wingate	John Wingate			200	....do....	1790		Oct. 4, 1816	....do....	Nassau river.
124	Thomas Prevatt	Thomas Prevatt			550	....do....	1790		May 14, 1818	....do....	St. Mary's river.
125	Frederick Hartley	Frederick Hartley			600	....do....	1790		July 8, 1819	....do....	Julington creek.
126	Peter Sevelly	Peter Sevelly			150	....do....	1790		do		Seven miles from St. Augustine.
127	George Henning	George Henning		Oct. 2, 1805	200	White	1790				Bell's river.
128	George Hartley	George Hartley			400	Coppinger	1790		July 4, 1819	George J. F. Clarke	Julington creek.
129	Martha Dell	Martha Dell			450	....do....	1790		May 26, 1818	....do....	St. Mary's river.
130	William McCully	William McCully			300	....do....	1790		Sept. 8, 1818	....do....	Do.
131	Edward Dixon	Edward Dixon			100	....do....	1790		May 14, 1818	....do....	Do.
132	Wm. and John Lofton	Wm. and John Lofton			300	....do....	1790		July 6, 1819	....do....	Julington creek.
133	Joseph Trevatt	Joseph Trevatt			400	....do....	1790		Oct. 10, 1818	....do....	St. Mary's river.
134	James Plummer	James Plummer			300	....do....	1790		July 18, 1819	....do....	Julington creek.
135	Susannah Cashen	James Cashen	Feb. 22, 1816		1,050	....do....	1815		July 8, 1816	....do....	St. Mary's river.
136	Francis Pellicer	Francis Pellicer	Mar. 30, 1815		1,100	Kindelan	1790				Matanzas.
137	Heirs of Pedro R. de Cala	Pedro R. de Cala		Jan. 24, 1818	500	Coppinger	1815		Sept. 15, 1816	Robert McHardy	Mosquito.
138	Charles Love	Charles Love			300	....do....	1790		Dec. 10, 1817	George J. F. Clarke	St. Mary's river.
139	Pedro Estopa	Pedro Estopa	Sept. 3, 1793		15.3	Quesada	1790		Nov. 28, 1823	G. Darling	Near St. Augustine.
140	Stephen M. Ingersoll	Lewis Scofield	June 16, 1796		100	White	1799				North of St. Augustine.
141	....do....	....do....	Mar. 12, 1799		100	....do....	1790				Twelve-mile swamp.
142	William Lane	William Lane		Feb. 10, 1793	210	Quesada	1790			Josiah Dupont	Trout creek, St. John's.

REPORT No. 1.—*Register of claims to land, not exceeding three thousand five hundred acres, &c.*—Continued.

No.	Names of present claimants.	Names of original claimants.	Date of the patent or royal title.	Date of the concession or order of survey.	Quantity of land. Acres.	By whom conceded	Authority or royal order under which the concession was granted.	Conditions.	Date of survey.	By whom surveyed.	Where situated.
143	Nathaniel Wilds	Nathaniel Wilds			300	Coppinger	1790		Dec. 4, 1817	George J. F. Clarke	Lofton's creek, St. John's.
144	Isaac Hendricks	John Simson			200	Quesada	1790		Oct. 22, 1792	Samuel Eastlake	Potsburg creek, St. John's.
145	...do...	William Hendricks		Dec. 6, 1796	500	White	1790				St. John's, near the Cowford.
146	...do...	John Jones		Feb. 11, 1801	500	...do...	1790				Jacksonville, St. John's.
147	Heirs of C. Griffin	Edward Crosson		Sept 23, 1803	100	...do...	1790				Trout creek, St. John's.
148	Heirs of V. Fitzpatrick	Valentine Fitzpatrick		July 27, 1803	400	...do...	1790				Graham's swamp.
149	...do...	...do...		Dec. 10, 1804	25	...do...	1790				Matanzas.
150	William Gardner	William Gardner		April 5, 1805	150	Kindelan	1790				St. John's river.
151	John Dixon	John Dixon		May 21, 1805	130	White	1790				St. Mary's river.
152	Francis Ferreira	John B. Ferreira		July 27, 1803	14	...do...	1790				One mile and three-quarters from St. Augustine.
153	John Houston	Spicer Christopher	April 12, 1809		92	...do...	1790				Talbot island.
154	Heirs of J. Faulk	John Faulk		Mar. 16, 1803	350	...do...	1790				St. John's river.
155	Isaac Carter	Isaac Carter	June 4, 1806		350	...do...	1790				Nassau river.
156	Fredrick McDonell	William McHenry		Oct. 6, 1790	800	Quesada.	1790				Matanzas bar.
157	William Fitzpatrick	William Fitzpatrick		Nov. 12, 1795	440	...do...	1790		Jan. 24, 1809	John Purcell	St. John's river.
158	Elijah Higginbottom	Elijah Higginbottom			350	Coppinger	1815		Dec. 19, 1818	George J. F. Clarke	St. Mary's river.
159	Joseph Higginbottom	Joseph Higginbottom			300	...do...	1815		Nov. 16, 1817	...do...	Do.
160	Pablo Sabaté	Pablo Sabaté		May 21, 1803	200	White	1790				Diego swamp.
161	Heirs of Elizabeth Cain	Isabel Cain		Dec. 23, 1802	250	...do...	1790				St. John's river.
162	Lazaro Ortega	Lazaro Ortega		June 25, 1819	66	Coppinger	1790		Jan. 30, 1819	A. Burgevin	Guano creek.
163	Heirs of John Tharp	Henry Guibel		Dec. 7, 1802	250	White.	1790				Nassau creek.
164	Joseph Hagens	Joseph Hagens			200	Coppinger	1790		July 15, 1819	George J. F. Clarke	Julington creek.
165	David Scurry	David Scurry			300	...do...	1790		July 26, 1820	...do...	Goodby's lake.
166	Andrew Brennan	Andrew Brennan			400	...do...	1790		Oct. 4, 1819	...do...	Black creek.
167	John Dixon	John Dixon			200	...do...	1790		May 12, 1818	...do...	St. Mary's river.
168	John Mazells	John Mazells			200	...do...	1790		Nov. 10, 1818	...do...	St. Mary's.
169	Wm. Sparkman	John Barding			300	...do...	1790				Boggy swamp.
170	Wm. Nelson	William Nelson			250	Coppinger	1790				St. Mary's.
171	Hartwell Leath	Hartwell Leath			200	...do...	1790		Nov. 11, 1818	George J. F. Clarke	Do.
172	Thos. King	Thos. King			257	...do...	1790		Nov. 26, 1818	...do...	Do.
173	James Bradley	James Bradley			250	...do...	1790		Aug. 16, 1820	...do...	Cedar swamp.

All of which irrespectfully submitted.

DAVIS FLOYD.
W. H. ALLEN.

St. Augustine, *December 31, 1825.*

REPORT No. 2.

Register of claims to land, not exceeding three thousand five hundred acres, which have not been confirmed by the commissioners for East Florida, but which are recommended by them for confirmation by Congress.

No.	Names of present claimants.	Names of original claimants.	Date of the patent or royal title.	Date of the concession or order of survey.	Quantity of land. Acres.	By whom conceded.	Authority or royal order under which the concession was granted.	Conditions.	Date of survey.	By whom surveyed.	Where situated.
1	Charles Seton	Charles Seton	March 1, 1815		1,400	Kindelan	1790	None	May 16, 1816	George J. F. Clarke	Nassau river.
2	Heirs of J. Hutchinson	James Hutchinson		{ Aug. 23, 1803 / April 14, 1807 }	2,000	White	1790	Complied with			St. Lucia.
3	Catalina Hijuelos	Catalina Hijuelos	Dec. 7, 1817		2,000	Coppinger	1815	None	Sept. 9, 1819	A. Burgevin	Okelawha river.
4	Zephaniah Kingsley	William Pengree			2,611	Quesada	1790		Feb. 17, 1799	Dupont & Eastlake	St. John's river.
5	......do.........	Zephaniah Kingsley	Jan. 18, 1816		2,000	Coppinger	1790				Twelve-mile swamp.
6	......do.........	George Sibbald	Jan. 7, 1815		2,000	Kindelan	1790				St. John's river.
7	Domingo Fernandez	Domingo Fernandez	April 10, 1817		1,150	Coppinger	1815				St. John's river.
8	Juan B. Entralgo	Juan B. Entralgo		Dec. 17, 1816	1,000	....do....	1815		April 17, 1821	A. Burgevin	St. John's river.
9	John Bolton	John Atkinson	Dec. 7, 1817		2,000	....do....	1815		May 2, 1818	R. McHardy	Mosquito.
10	Nicholas Estefanopoly	Nicholas Estefanopoly		May 23, 1815	2,500	Kindelan	1815				Savanee.

GENERAL REMARKS.—No. 4. This land was surveyed in four separate tracts.
No. 6. The board ascertain this claim to be covered by a British grant.

Which are respectfully submitted.

DAVIS FLOYD.
GEORGE MURRAY.
W. H. ALLEN.

ST. AUGUSTINE, *December 31, 1825.*

REPORT No. 3.

Register of claims to land, exceeding three thousand five hundred acres, in East Florida, which are founded on patents or royal titles derived from the Spanish government, and which, in the opinion of the commissioners, are valid.

No.	Names of present claimants.	Names of original claimants.	Date of the patent or royal title.	Date of the concession or order of survey.	Quantity of land. (Acres.)	By whom conceded.	Authority or royal order under which the concession was granted.	Conditions.	Date of survey.	By whom surveyed.	Where situated.	Occupation and cultivation. From—	To—
1	Juan B. de Entralgo	F. M. Arredondo		Mar. 20, 1817	4,000	Coppinger	1815	None	July 25, 1820	Andrew Burgevin	5 miles east of Spring Garden		
2	Antonio Huertas	Antonio Huertas		Sept 15, 1817	10,400	...do	1815		April 5, 1821	...do	On a creek near St. John's		
3	William Travers	Philip R. Yonge		Feb. 22, 1817	8,000	...do	1815				40 miles south of Lake George		
4	Juan B. Entralgo	...do		Feb. 22, 1817	12,000	...do	1815				...do		
5	Pedro Miranda	Pedro Miranda		Sept 16, 1817	4,000	...do	1816		April 5, 1821	Andrew Burgevin	Big Spring		
6	Antonio Huertas	Antonio Huertas	July 20, 1816		10,000	...do	1790				Six-mile creek		
7	Juan B. Enralgo	George J. F. Clarke	Dec. 17, 1817		20,000	...do	1815		Aug. 2, 1819	Andrew Burgevin	45 miles west of St. John's		
8	Francis J. Avice	John Huertas	Dec. 24, 1817		6,000	...do	1790		May 31, 1820	...do	St. John's		
9	Joseph M. Arredondo	Joseph M. Arredondo	Mar. 20, 1817		20,000	...do	1815				Big Ham'ck, Alachua		
10	Heirs of Chas. W. Bulow	John Russell		July 30, 1812	4,675	Kindelan	Special		June 25, 1821	G. J. F. Clarke	Timoca		
11	F. M. Arredondo	F. M. Arredondo		Mar. 24, 1817	15,000	Coppinger	1815				West of Lake George		
12	Juan B. Entralgo	F. M. Arredondo		Mar. 20, 1817	4,000	...do	1815		July 25, 1820	Andrew Burgevin	Black creek		
13	F. M. Arredondo & Son	F. M. Arredondo & Son	Dec. 22, 1817		4 leagues of land to each wind.	Intendant of Cuba and Florida	1817	Complied with			Alachua	Nov., 1820	Dec. 24, 1824
14	Peter Mitchel	...do	Dec. 22, 1817		¼ of above.	...do	1817	...do			...do	do.	do.
15	Alex. M. Muir	...do	...do		30,720	...do	1817	...do			...do	do.	do.
16	N. Brush	...do	...do		10,000	...do	1817	...do			...do	do.	do.
17	Elisha Huntington	...do	...do		10,000	...do	1817	...do			...do	do.	do.
18	...do	...do	...do		2,000	...do	1817	...do			...do	do.	do.
19	John Forbes	John Forbes		July 28, 1814	7,000	Kindelan	1790	None	Oct. 23, 1816	G. J. F. Clarke	Little St. Mary's	do.	do.
20	...do	...do		...do	3,000	...do	1790	None	Oct. 20, 1816	...do	Cabbage swamp	do.	do.

The above claims were acted on by the honorables Davis Floyd and W. W. Blair, and reported to Congress on the last session of this board.

CASES REPORTED THIS SESSION.

No.	Names of present claimants.	Names of original claimants.	Date of the patent or royal title.	Date of the concession or order of survey.	Quantity of land. (Acres.)	By whom conceded.	Authority or royal order under which the concession was granted.	Conditions.	Date of survey.	By whom surveyed.	Where situated.	Occupation and cultivation. From—	To—
21	Heirs of Jesse Fish	Jesse Fish		June 19, 1795	10,000	Morales	1790	Complied with			Anastasia island		
22	Teresa Rodriguez	Miguel Mear		Oct. 18, 1815	5,500	Estrada	1815	None			Long Lake		
23	John W. Symington	Juan P. Salas		Aug. 26, 1815	7,000	...do	1815	None			Key West		
24	George Murray	...do		Aug. 26, 1815	7,000	...do	1815	None			New Cape Florida		
25	Archibald Clarke	John X. Arambide		Dec. 4, 1813	80,000	Provincial deputation at Havana	1790				New Cape Florida		
26	Joseph Delespine	...do		Dec. 4, 1813	92,160	...do	1790				...do		

All of which is respectfully submitted.

ST. AUGUSTINE, *December 31, 1825.*

DAVIS FLOYD.
W. H. ALLEN.

REPORT No. 4.

Register of claims to land, not exceeding six hundred and forty acres, founded on actual inhabitation and cultivation previous to February 22, 1819, for which certificates of confirmation have been granted by the undersigned commissioners.

No.	Names of claimants.	Age.	Quantity.	Situation.	Occupation and cultivation.	
					From—	To—
			Acres.			
1	Francis Woods	....	640	North side Mills' swamp	....	....
2	Miguel Papy	....	640	Deep creek, St. John's river	1819	1825
3	George Ginnople	....	640	Headwaters of Boggy swamp	1819	1825
4	John D. Braddock	....	640	Road leading from Rox's Bluff	1810	1824
5	Tolly Lewis	....	640	South of river Miami	1805	1825
6	Pedro Mestre	....	640	Head of the North river	1818	1825
7	James Hagen	....	640	North Miami river, Cape Florida	1810	1825
8	Mrs. Hagen	....	640	South Miami river, Cape Florida	1810	1825
9	Jonathan Lewis	....	640	Near Cape Florida	1813	1825
10	Trankee Lewis	....	640	New river, Cape Florida	1796	1825

All of which is respectfully submitted.

DAVIS FLOYD.
GEORGE MURRAY.
W. H. ALLEN.

St. Augustine, December 31, 1825.

REPORT No. 5.

Register of claims to land, not exceeding six hundred and forty acres, founded on actual inhabitation and cultivation previous to July 17, 1821, which the commissioners report to Congress for confirmation.

No.	Names of claimants.	Age.	Quantity.	Situation.	Occupation and cultivation.	
					From—	To—
			Acres.			
1	Dorcas Black	....	640	On road leading to Jacksonville	1821	1825
2	John R. Hogans	....	640	North side of river St. John's	1820	1825
3	Levi Sparkman	....	640	Little Trout creek	1820	1825
4	John D. Blodworth	....	640	Deadman's swamp	1820	1825
5	Heirs of John Carter	....	640	South side of Trout creek	1820	1825
6	Isaac Carter	....	640	Road from Jacksonville to Camp Pinckney	1820	1825
7	David Scurry*	....	640	North side St. John's river	1819	1825
8	John Brindley	....	640	North side Black creek	1819	1825
9	John Oliver	....	640	East side of Dunn's lake	1818	1825
10	José Papy	....	640	East of Picolata fort, St. John's	1819	1825
11	Andres Papy	....	640	Twelve miles south of St. Augustine	1819	1825
12	Henry Heartly	....	640	St. John's county	1819	1825
13	William Branning	....	640	South side Black creek	1817	1825

* This claim has been rejected, but inserted by mistake.

All of which is respectfully submitted.

DAVIS FLOYD.
GEORGE MURRAY.
W. H. ALLEN.

St. Augustine, December 31, 1825.

REPORT No. 6.

Register of claims derived from the Spanish government by written evidence, undefined in quantity, and are ascertained to be valid, and which are recommended to Congress for confirmation.

No.	Names of present claimants.	Names of original claimants.	Date of patent or royal title.	Date of concession or order of survey.	Quantity of land. (Acres.)	By whom conceded.	Authority or royal order under which the concession was granted.	Conditions.	Date of survey.	By whom surveyed.	Where situated.	Occupation or cultivation. From—	Occupation or cultivation. To—
1	John Bachelot	John Bachelot		Oct. 29, 1800	Undefined	White	1790	None			Doctor's lake		
2	Heirs of Thomas Travers	Migl. Ysnardy		Oct. 19, 1791	do.	Quesada	1791	None	April 5, 1819	A. Burgevin	St. Diego		
3	Bartolome Mestre	Bartolome Mestre		June 28, 1796	do.	White	1790	None			Matanzas river		
4	John Underwood	John Underwood		May 20, 1805	do.	do.	1790	Complied with			Black creek, St. Mary's		
5	Francis F. Bachelot	Raqus Leonardy		19? 1, 1799	An	do.	1770		April 28, 1819	A Burgevin	North river		
6	Gabriel W. Perpall	Thomas Travers			do.						St. Sebastian river		
7	Robert Gibert	Robert Gibert		March 1, 1798	do.	Judicial sale	1798				Matanzas		

No. 7.—This case was omitted, and found in one of the bundles, and added by D. Floyd.

All of which is respectfully submitted.

DAVIS FLOYD,
GEORGE MURRAY,
W. H. ALLEN.

St. Augustine, *December 31, 1825.*

REPORT No. 7.

Register of claims, not exceeding three thousand five hundred acres, founded on patents granted by the British government, and which have been recognized as valid by the Spanish government, and are confirmed by the board of land commissioners for East Florida.

No.	Names of present claimants.	Names of original claimants.	Date of patent or royal order.	Quantity of land. (Acres.)	By whom conceded.	Date of survey.	By whom surveyed.	Where situated.	General remarks.
1	Thomas Travers' heirs	Henry Skinner		420		Aug. 5, 1779	Benjamin Lord	Peavett's swamp	
2	Joseph Peavett's heirs	Joseph Peavett	Feb. 12, 1783	500	Tonyn	March 13, 1782	do.	Durbin's swamp	
3	do.	Robert Payne	April 29, 1771	500	Grant	April 2, 1771	F. G. Mulcaster	Branches Pablo creek	
4	do.	Joseph Peavett	April 14, 1783	250	Tonyn	Sept. 7, 1782	Benjamin Lord	Pablo creek	
5	do.	do.	March 11, 1782	500	do.	June 22, 1781	do.	do.	
6	Charles W. and George J. F. Clarke	Thomas Clarke	April 2, 1770	300	Grant	Jan. 24, 1770	B. Debrahm	Matanzas creek	
7	James and George Clarke	Honoria Clarke	Sept. 29, 1780	500	Tonyn	March 10, 1780	Benjamin Lord	16 miles south St Augustine	
8	Davis Floyd	John E. Tate		1,000				North river	The original documents in this claim were lost, but evidence adduced of 20 years' occupancy was proved.

All of which is respectfully submitted.

DAVIS FLOYD,
GEORGE MURRAY,
W. H. ALLEN.

St. Augustine, *December 31, 1825.*

REPORT No. 8.

Register of claims to town lots and out-lots, founded on actual cultivation and improvement previous to February 22, 1819, for which certificates of confirmation have been granted by the undersigned commissioners.

Number	Names of present claimants	Names of original claimants	Date of patent or royal title	Date of concession or order of survey	Quantity of land	By whom conceded	Conditions	Date of survey	By whom surveyed	Where situated	Occupation From—	To—
1	Farquhar Bethune	George Atkinson	Aug. 16, 1814		Lot No. 7 of square 9, 578 sq. yds.	Kindelan	None	Aug. 11, 1814	George J. F. Clarke	Fernandina	1814	1824
2	....do....	....do....		May 2, 1811	Lot No. 5 of square 9, 578 sq. yds.	Estrada				do	1814	1824
3	Zephaniah Kingsley	Zephaniah Kingsley	July 7, 1815		Lot No. 6 of square 18, 578 sq. yds.	Coppinger		June 23, 1815	George J. F. Clarke	do	1814	1824
4	....do....	....do....	Mar. 27, 1817	Aug. 25, 1815	1,498 square yards	White		Feb. 25, 1817	do	do	1814	1824
5	Farquhar Bethune	F. Entralgo		Jan. 31, 1811	Lot No. 9 of square 9, 578 sq. yds.	White			George J. F. Clarke	do	1814	1824
6	George Fleming's heirs	George Fleming		May 2, 1811	Lot No. 7 of square 7, 578 sq. yds.	Estrada			do	do	1814	1824
7	William Hobkirk	William Hobkirk	Jan. 13, 1816		Lots No. 3 and 4 of square 18, 578 sq. yds.	Coppinger		April 12, 1815	do	do	1814	1824
8	George Atkinson	George Atkinson	May 7, 1817		Lot No. 7 of square 8, 578 sq. yds.	do		April 25, 1817	do	do	1814	1824
9	John Middleton and John Sibley	James Cashen	Mar. 30, 1814		Lot No. 6 of square 1, 578 sq. yds.	Kindelan		Jan. 2, 1814	do	do	1814	1824
10	George Atkinson	George Atkinson	Aug. 16, 1814		Lot No. 11 of square 4, 578 sq. yds.	Coppinger		Jan. 8, 1814	do	do	1814	1824
11	....do....	....do....	May 7, 1817		Lot No. 8 of square 8, 578 sq. yds.	Coppinger		April 25, 1817	do	do	1814	1824
12	Lindsay Todd's executors	Lindsay Todd	June 7, 1814		Lots No. 3 and 4 of square 8, 578 sq. yds.	Kindelan		Oct. 16, 1813	do	do	1814	1824
13	Henry Yonge	Henry Yonge	Jan. 31, 1814		Lot No. 9 of square 1, 1,289 sq. yds.	do		Jan. 3, 1814	do	do	1814	1824
14	Hilberson & Yonge	Hilberson & Yonge		Dec. 4, 1811	A water lot	Estrada			do	do	1814	1824
15	....do....	....do....	Feb. 1, 1816		4½	Coppinger		Oct. 11, 1815	George J. F. Clarke	do		
16	....do....	....do....	Feb. 1, 1816		A marsh lot	do		Oct. 11, 1815	do	do		
17	....do....	....do....	Feb. 1, 1816			do		Oct. 10, 1815	do	do		
18	Domingo Fernandez	Domingo Fernandez	April 10, 1817		Lot No. 4 of square 23, 578 sq. yds.	do			do	do		
19	....do....	....do....	April 10, 1817		Lots No. 5,6,7, & 8 of square 23, 578 sq. yds.	do			do	do		
20	....do....	....do....	Mar. 7, 1819		Lot No. 2 of square 18, 289 sq. yds.	do	Complied with.	June 1, 1817	George J. F. Clarke	do		
21	J. Allen Smith	Widow of José Xeminez	Mar. 9, 1819		95,030 yards	Judicial sale	None	Jan. 3, 1797	José Lorento	St. Augustine		
22	....do....	Martin Floriano			7 acres	Judicial sale			José Lorento	do		
23	Wardens of R. C. Church	Maria Evans			31¼ acres				José Lorento	St. Augustine, Point Esperanza.		
24	....do....	Juana Hambert		Nov. 17, 1792	4,176 square yards	Judicial sale	Complied with.			St. Augustine		
25	Antelm Gay	Bartolome Carrada			644 square yards	Quesada				do		
26	S. Clark	Teresa Marshall	May 21, 1819		5,180 square yds.	Coppinger	None	May 6, 1817	George J. F. Clarke	Fernandina		
27	John Middleton	Benjamin Ayres			Lot No. 8 of square 21, 289 sq. yds.	do		June 26, 1817	do	do		
28	....do....	William Buasou / Anna Wiggins		Mar. 4, 1814 / May 21, 1814	Lot No. 6 of square 14 .... / Lots No. 3 and 4 of square 14	Kindelan				do		

GENERAL REMARKS.—No. 20. Although the royal title in these grants appears after the date, it is evident by claimants' memorial to the governor that they were in possession of said lots according to the surveys.   No. 23. The occupation for many years proven. No. 26. Although the royal title is after the date, the occupation of the lot was proved by the survey.   No. 28. The original grant lost, but occupation proved.   All of which is respectfully submitted.

DAVIS FLOYD.
GEORGE MURRAY.
W. H. ALLEN.

St. AUGUSTINE, *December 31, 1825.*

REPORT No. 9.

Register of claims of which the originals are not found in the office of the keeper of the public archives, and of which there is no proof before the board but the certificates of Thomas de Aguilar, late secretary of the Spanish government.

No.	Names of present claimants.	Names of original claimants.	Date of patent or royal title.	Date of the concession or order of survey.	Quantity of land.	By whom conceded.	Authority or royal order under which the concession was granted.	Conditions.	Date of survey.	By whom surveyed.	Where situated.
					Acres.						
1	Robert McHardy, trustee	Robert McHardy		Nov. 8, 1814	16,000	Kindelan	1790	None	May 10, 1819	A. Burgevin	Old store, St. John's river.
2	Christopher Minchen	Christopher Minchen		Nov. 10, 1817	400	Coppinger	1815				Durbin swamp.
3	José Laroy	José Laroy		Aug. 21, 1815	300	Estrada	1815				Trout creek and Six-mile creek.
4	John Lecount	John Lecount		Aug. 11, 1815	300	Estrada	1815		April 26, 1821	George J. F. Clarke	Dunn's lake.
5	John Uplegrove	John Uplegrove		July 27, 1803	250	White	1790				North side Rose's bluff.

All of which is respectfully submitted.

DAVIS FLOYD.
GEO. MURRAY.
W. H. ALLEN.

St. Augustine, *December* 31, 1825.

REPORT No. 10.

Register of claims ascertained to be valid Spanish grants, but are not confirmed, being covered by British grants.

No.	Claimants.	Original grantees.	By whom granted.	Dates of royal titles.	Dates of concession.	Conditions.	Quantity.	By whom surveyed.	Date of survey.
							Acres.		
1	George F. and O. Palmes	Robert McHardy	Governor White	July 3, 1815	July 21, 1803	None	999.75	See No. 15, report No. 9, of 1824	
2	John Bunch	John Bunch	...do		Aug. 11, 1804	None	2,160.00	See No. 112, report No. 1, of 1824	
3	Zeph. Kingsley	George Sibbald	Governor Kindelan	Jan. 7, 1815	Oct. 6, 1804	None	2,000.00		

All of which is respectfully submitted.

DAVIS FLOYD.
W. H. ALLEN.

Minutes of the board of land commissioners.

DISTRICT OF EAST FLORIDA, ST. AUGUSTINE, *Monday, March 28, 1825.*

Pursuant to an act of Congress entitled "An act to extend the time for the settlement of private land claims in the Territory of Florida," passed March 3, 1825, the board met this day—present, the Hons. Davis Floyd, Geo. Murray, and Will. H. Allen—and proceeded to open their session for the performance of the duties assigned to their office. Whereupon, it was resolved that Thomas Murphy and Lewis Huguon be appointed assistant clerks to this board, pursuant to the said act.

Ordered, That the secretary of this board cause to be inserted in the East Florida Herald an advertisement, stating that the board will meet daily at 10 o'clock a. m. for the transaction of business.

The board having directed the clerks to proceed to the discharge of their duties, adjourned until Tuesday next, the 5th of April, at 10 o'clock a. m.

TUESDAY *April 5, 1825.*

The board met this day pursuant to adjournment. Present: all the members.

The claimants not being sufficiently advised of the reorganization of the board, the same was adjourned until Monday next, the 11th instant, at 10 o'clock a. m.

MONDAY, *April 11, 1825.*

The board met this day pursuant to adjournment. Present: all the members.

The following claims were this day taken up and confirmed by the board, viz:

José Sanchez, two hundred and ten acres of land situated on the west bank of Hilsboro' river, to the south of the old town of Smyrna. R. McHardy's trustee, one thousand acres situated at Tomoka. Jno. Christopher, five hundred acres situated on the river Nassau. Farquhar Bethune, one thousand one hundred acres situated on the Halifax river, Mosquito.

The board adjourned until to-morrow at 10 o'clock a. m.

TUESDAY, *April 12, 1825.*

The board met this day pursuant to adjournment. Present: all the members.

The following claims were this day taken up by the board and confirmed, viz:

Prudence Plummer, three hundred and fifty and a third acres situated on the east side of St. John's river. Charles Seton, six hundred acres situated in Sample's swamp, river Nassau. John Floyd's heirs, two hundred acres situated on the North river. Theresa Marshall's heirs, five hundred and thirty-three and a third acres situated at Santa Teresa, North river. Robert Pritchard's heirs, four hundred and fifty acres situated at Jacksonville, St. John's river. John Houston, one hundred acres situated on Talbot island.

David S. H. Miller *vs.* The United States, for three hundred acres of land situated on the south side of the river S. John's, near the Cowford. This case being called, permission was granted to amend the memorial, and the board confirmed the same to the widow and heirs of Francis Bagley.

Charles Seton *vs.* The United States, for fourteen hundred acres of land situated on Nassau river. The board took up this case, and recommended the same for confirmation.

Manuel Solana presented his memorial to this board, praying confirmation of title to six hundred and forty acres of land situated on McCullough's creek, St. John's river; which is ordered to be filed.

James Plummer presented his memorial to this board, praying confirmation of title to two hundred and sixty-five acres of land situated on Will's creek, with a plat and certificate of survey made for memorialist by Ede Van Evour, dated July 23, 1824, and marked P. Ordered to be filed.

The board adjourned until to-morrow at 10 o'clock a. m.

WEDNESDAY, *April 13, 1825.*

The board met this day pursuant to adjournment. Present: all the members.

Edgar Macon, esq., United States attorney for the district of East Florida, attended the board this day under their order.

Ordered, That John Drysdale, esq., have leave to withdraw his claim for a lot in St. Augustine, filed sometime since.

On motion of Mr. Drysdale, it is ordered that a commission may be issued by the secretary of this board, in blank as to the witnesses, to take testimony, and the testimony so taken may be used in any case in which he is concerned so far as it shall be relevant thereto: provided that interrogatories have been filed in this office five days before the issuing said commission. It is further ordered that two commissioners be named on the part of the claimant in the cause in which the commission may issue, and two commissioners on the part of the United States; and that said commission may be executed by any two of the said commissioners, provided there be one named by each of the said parties.

The board took up the following claims, and confirmed the same, viz:

Pedro R. de Cala's heirs, for two hundred acres of land in St. Diego's swamp, and Robert Hutchinson, for one hundred and fifty acres of land on the banks of Little St. Mary's river.

The board adjourned until to-morrow at 10 o'clock a. m.

THURSDAY, *April 14, 1825.*

The board met this day pursuant to adjournment. Present: all the members.

Edgar Macon, esq., United States attorney for the eastern district of Florida, attended the board this day under their order.

James Riz *vs.* The United States, for five hundred acres of land, part of a grant made to James F. Rattenbury by the Spanish government subsequent to January 24, 1818. This case being called, was rejected by the board.

E. Waterman's heirs vs. The United States, for two hundred and sixty acres of land situated on Bell's river. This case being prepared for trial, was confirmed by the board.

The following cases were ordered to be reported to Congress, being undefined in quantity, viz:

Francis P. Sanchez, for six hundred acres of land situated to the north of St. Augustine, near the road of St. Vincent Ferrer, and G. W. Ferpall, for six hundred and forty acres of land on the river St. Sebastian, one mile south of St. Augustine.

John B. Strong, esq., obtained leave, and amended the memorial of Absalom Beardon and wife, by inserting six hundred and forty in lieu of one hundred and fifty acres of land.

The board adjourned until to-morrow at 10 o'clock a. m.

FRIDAY, *April* 15, 1825.

The board met this day pursuant to adjournment. Present: all the members.

Edgar Macon, esq., United States attorney for the eastern district of Florida, attended the board this day under their order.

The following cases were this day taken up and confirmed by the board, viz:

John Addison, fourteen hundred and fourteen acres of land situated on the river Tomoca, at a place called Carrickfergus; Domingo Acosta, six hundred and ninety-five acres in three tracts—one for two hundred and fifty acres on Caca swamp, the other for one hundred and ninety-five acres on Mount Warter and Mill creek of Rollstown, and two hundred and fifty acres at Mount Tucker, on the east side of St. John's river; the widow and heirs of Antonio Andrew, deceased, one hundred and twenty acres situated on the North river, at a place called Sta. Catalina; Thomas Andrew, for the heirs of Margaret O'Neal, three hundred and seven acres situated on Langford creek; Susannah Cashen, on behalf of the orphans of Samuel Meers, deceased, two hundred acres situated on Tiger island, in East Florida; Andrew Atkinson, four hundred and fifty acres situated at a place known by the name of St. Vincent Ferrer, St. John's river; John Houston, one hundred acres situated on the south end of Talbot island; Susannah Cashen, seven hundred acres situated on Amelia island; Thomas Andrew, for the heirs of Margaret O'Neal, two hundred acres situated on Langford creek.

John Jones, by his attorney, obtained permission from the board, and withdrew his claim for one hundred acres of land.

The Hon. George Murray having retired, the board took up the following claims and confirmed the same, viz:

William Travers, four hundred and twenty acres situated five miles west from St. Augustine; J. Pevett's heirs, five hundred acres situated in Durbin's swamp; J. Pevett's heirs, five hundred acres on Pablo creek.

The board adjourned until to-morrow at 10 o'clock a. m.

SATURDAY, *April* 16, 1825.

The board met this day pursuant to adjournment. Present: all the members.

Edgar Macon, esq., United States attorney for the eastern district of Florida, attended the board this day under their order.

Ordered, That an adjourned meeting of the board of land commissioners be held at Jacksonville, in the county of Duval, on the third Monday of May next, and that the secretary be directed to have fifty handbills printed notifying the same.

The following claims were this day taken up and confirmed by the board, viz: Andrew Atkinson, two hundred acres of land situated between Dunn and Trout creeks; Moses Bowden, two hundred and fifty acres situated on the south side of St. John's river; Thomas Andrew and other heirs of Robert Andrew, deceased, five hundred acres situated at a place called St. Diego.

On motion of claimant's attorney, permission was obtained, and the memorial in the following case, viz: Uriah Bowden, for two hundred acres of land on the south side of St. John's river, was amended by inserting the name "Moses" in lieu of "Uriah;" after which the claim was confirmed by the board.

The honorable George Murray having retired, the board took up the following claims and confirmed the same, viz: J. Pevett's heirs, five hundred acres on the Three Runs of Pablo creek, and J. Pevett's heirs, for two hundred and fifty acres of land situated on the Three Runs.

The board adjourned until Monday next at 10 o'clock a. m.

MONDAY, *April* 18, 1825.

The board met this day pursuant to adjournment. Present: all the members.

Edgar Macon, esq., United States attorney for the eastern district of Florida, attended the board this day under their order.

No business being prepared, the board adjourned until to-morrow at 10 o'clock a. m.

TUESDAY, *April* 19, 1825.

The board met this day pursuant to adjournment. Present: all the members.

Edgar Macon, esq., United States attorney for the eastern district of Florida, attended the board this day under their order.

Samuel Wilson presented his memorial to this board, praying confirmation of title to one hundred and fifty acres of land situated on Trout creek, St. John's river, with a certified copy of plat and certificate of survey made by Pedro Marrot, dated March 2, 1793, herewith filed, and marked exhibit W. Ordered to be filed.

Juan Segui presented his memorial to this board, praying confirmation of title to fifteen acres of land situated at a place called *Macariz*, on the North river, with a certified copy of concession made to Juan Segui by Governor White, dated December 1, 1806. Ordered to be filed.

Juan Gonzalez presented his memorial to this board, praying confirmation of title to one thousand acres of land situated at a place called St. Diego plains, with a plat and certificate of survey made by Andres Burgevin, dated June 28, 1819, marked G; also a certified copy of royal title made to memorialist by Governor Coppinger, and dated June 19, 1818, marked J. Ordered to be filed.

On motion of claimant's attorney, permission was given to amend the memorial in the following case viz: Timothy Hollingsworth, for the heirs of F. Bagley, by inserting "one thousand" in lieu of "nine hundred and ninety" acres, situated at a place called Browns' fort, St. John's river; after which the same was confirmed.

The following cases were also taken up and confirmed by the board, viz: Timothy Hollingsworth for the heirs of F. Bagley, two hundred and forty-eight acres of land situated on Goodman's lake, St. John's river; Francisco Barbé, five hundred acres of land situated in Thomas' swamp, river Nassau; Susannah Cashen, one hundred acres of land situated on Amelia island.

The board adjourned until to-morrow at 10 o'clock a. m.

WEDNESDAY, *April* 20, 1825.

The board met this day pursuant to adjournment. Present: all the members.

Edgar Macon, esq., United States attorney for the eastern district of Florida, attended the board this day under their order.

Pedro Miranda *vs.* The United States, for three hundred and sixty-eight thousand six hundred and forty acres of land situated at Tampa Bay. Permission having been obtained by claimant's attorney, this came on this day to be heard, when G. W. Perpall and John Cavedo were sworn and examined on the the part of United States; after which the case was continued.

The board then adjourned until to-morrow at 10 o'clock a. m.

THURSDAY, *April* 21, 1825.

The board met this day pursuant to adjournment. Present: all the members.

Edgar Macon, esq., United States attorney for the eastern district of Florida, attended the board this day under their order.

William Hobkirk's heirs, for three hundred and twenty-five acres of land situated on the river St. Mary's; Samuel Harrison, five hundred acres of land situated on Amelia island, at a place called Harrison's old fields; and Samuel Harrison, for six hundred acres of land situated on the river Nassau, at a place called Seymour's Point.

On motion of claimants' attorneys, the memorials in the above cases were amended, and they were confirmed.

The following claims were also confirmed this day by the board, viz: John Bellamy, for three hundred acres situated on Little St. Mary's river; Charles Breward, two hundred and fifty acres situated on Cedar creek, St. John's river; Farquhar Bethune, four hundred and twenty-five acres situated on the river St. Mary's, at a place called Cabbage swamp; Sarah Bowden, one hundred and forty-two and a half acres situated on Julington creek, St. John's river; Samuel Harrison, two hundred acres situated on the west point of Amelia island; E. Hudnall's heirs, one hundred acres situated on the east side of St. John's river, at a place called Faulk; William Berrie, one hundred acres situated on St. John's river, at a place called Snelling's old fields; Farquhar Bethune, one lot of land situated in the town of Fernandina, known as lot No. 5, square 9.

On motion, permission was given by the board to the executors of the estate of Sarah Fish, deceased, to amend the memorials in the claims of said Sarah Fish.

The board adjourned until to-morrow at 10 o'clock a. m.

FRIDAY, *April* 22, 1825.

The board met this day pursuant to adjournment. Present: all the members.

Edgar Macon, esq., United States attorney for the eastern district of Florida, attended the board this day, under their order, for the purpose of examining witnesses on the part of the United States in the claim of J. W. Simonton for Key West.

No other business being prepared, the board adjourned until Monday next at 10 o'clock a. m.

MONDAY, *April* 25, 1825.

The board met this day pursuant to adjournment. Present: the Hons. Davis Floyd and W. H. Allen.

Edgar Macon, esq., United States attorney for the eastern district of Florida, attended the board this day under their order.

John W. Simonton *vs.* The United States, for an island called Key West. This day this case came on to be heard, and G. W. Perpall was examined therein on the part of the United States, and the case was submitted.

Henry Sweeny, by his attorney, S. Streeter, presented his memorial to this board, praying confirmation of title to six hundred and forty acres of land situated on the river St. John's, in the county of Duval. Ordered to be filed.

William Hobkirk's heirs, for three hundred and fifty acres of land situated on Bell's creek.

On motion, permission was given to amend the memorial in the said case, and it was confirmed.

The following claims were also confirmed by the board, viz: Zephaniah Kingsley, one thousand acres situated on the south side of St. Mary's river; Zephaniah Kingsley, three hundred acres situated at the head of Saw-mill creek; Anna M. Kingsley, three hundred and fifty acres situated on the east side of Dunn's lake, and east side of St. John's river; Farquhar Bethune, a lot in the town of Fernandina, Amelia island, designated as No. 7 of square 9.

The board adjourned until to-morrow at 10 o'clock a. m.

TUESDAY, *April* 26, 1825.

The board met this day pursuant to adjournment. Present: all the members.

Edgar Macon, esq., United States attorney for the eastern district of Florida, attended the board this day under their order.

The following claims were this day confirmed by the board in favor of claimants, viz: Zephaniah Kingsley, a lot of land situated in the town of Fernandina, designated as No. 6 of the 18th square; Zephaniah Kingsley, one hundred and fifty acres of land situated on the west side of the river St. John's, opposite the mouth of Dunn's lake; John Bachelot, three hundred acres situated on the north point of Amelia island.

The board adjourned until Friday next at 10 o'clock a. m.

FRIDAY, *April* 29, 1825.

The board met this day pursuant to adjournment. Present: all the members.

Edgar Macon, esq., United States attorney for the eastern district of Florida, attended the board this day under their order.

John Cavedo *vs.* The United States, for three hundred acres situated on Black creek, St. John's river.

The board having ascertained this to be a valid grant, made previous to January 24, 1818, to claimant, under the royal order of 1815, confirmed the same, the Hon. George Murray dissenting.

George J. F. Clarke's claim for one hundred acres of land situated on Amelia island.

Permission was given to claimant's attorney to amend the memorial by inserting "Estrada" in lieu of Coppinger; after which it was confirmed.

Archibald Clark and others *vs.* The United States, for two hundred and fifty acres of land situated on St. John's river, at a place called Jolly's old fields.

It appearing to the board that the original memorialist having petitioned the Spanish government for only two hundred acres, and the same being granted by Governor Quesada in his decree bearing date November 11, 1794, and although the same is a valid Spanish grant, the board does not feel itself authorized to confirm the same, but recommends the said two hundred acres of land for confirmation.

NOTE.—This case was reconsidered by the board on September 30, 1825, and confirmed.

Sebastian Espinosa's heirs, claim for five hundred acres of land situated at a place called *Uelleridge,* on the plains of St. Diego.

It appearing to the board that this was a valid Spanish grant, after examining G. W. Perpall therein, the same was confirmed.

The following claims were also confirmed by the board, viz:

Sarah Breward, for three hundred acres of land situated on Nassau river, at a place called Doctor's island.

John Bachelot, for three hundred acres on Amelia island, at a place called White Point.

Zephaniah Kingsley, for a marsh lot in Fernandina, Amelia island.

Farquhar Bethune, for a lot in Fernandina, known as lot No. 9, square 9.

George Fleming's heirs, for a lot in the town of Fernandina, known as lot No. 7, square 7.

The board adjourned until Monday next, May 2, at 10 o'clock a. m.

WEDNESDAY, *May* 4, 1825.

The board met this day. Present: the Hons. Davis Floyd and George Murray.

Edgar Macon, esq., United States attorney for the eastern district of Florida, attended the board this day under their order.

Joseph Gaunt *vs.* The United States, for three hundred and twenty-five acres of land in Turnbull's swamp.

This case being called, and the original concession being exhibited, with the signature of Governor Coppinger attached thereto, Francis J. Fatio was examined as to the validity of said signature; whereupon the said claim was confirmed.

The following claims were also confirmed by the board this day, viz:

Zephaniah Kingsley, for three hundred acres situated on Doctor's creek, St. John's river.

C. Griffith's heirs, for four hundred and fifty acres on the headwaters of Nassau river.

The widow and heirs of N. Sanchez, for three hundred and eighty-five acres at St. Diego.

The widow and heirs of N. Sanchez, for three hundred eighty-five acres on the plains of St. Diego, at a place called Quequi.

John Low, seven hundred and fifty acres at Bell's old fields, Bell's river.

Charles Seton, for seven hundred acres on St. Mary's river.

The following letter was received from William Reynolds, esq., keeper of the public archives:

ST. AUGUSTINE, *May* 2, 1825.

GENTLEMEN: As keeper of the public archives, by appointment of the President of the United States, under an act of Congress passed the 3d of March last, I beg leave to inform you that I am ready to receive that part of the archives now in possession of the secretary of the honorable the board of land commissioners.

With great respect, I remain, gentlemen, your most obedient servant,

WILL. REYNOLDS.

Hon. Messrs. FLOYD, MURRAY, and ALLEN, *Land Commissioners.*

Whereupon, it is ordered that the secretary of this board inform the said William Reynolds that the documents demanded by him were delivered to Messrs. Gibson and Simmons, commissioners appointed by the President of the United States to take possession of the public archives, and that the secretary deliver to the said William Reynolds a copy of the receipt given by said commissioners to this board for said documents.

The board adjourned until Friday next at 10 o'clock a. m.

FRIDAY, *May* 6, 1824.

The board met this day pursuant to adjournment. Present: the Hons. Davis Floyd and William H. Allen.

Edgar Macon, esq., United States attorney for the eastern district of Florida, attended the board this day under their order.

William Hartley, by his attorney, John Drysdale, presented his memorial to this board, praying confirmation of title to two hundred and fifty acres of land situated at the headwaters of Goodby's lake, near Will's swamp, with a certified copy of concession made to memorialist by Governor Coppinger, and dated December 13, 1817. Ordered to be filed.

Lewis Guibert presented his memorial to this board, praying confirmation of title to six hundred and forty acres of land situated in the county of St. John's. Ordered to be filed.

Maria Mabrity, widow, and other heirs of Juan Andrew, vs. The United States, for one hundred and sixty-one and a third acres of land situated on the North river and Guana creek, at a place called White Oyster Bank.

This case being called, and the claimants having produced a royal titte made by Governor White, and dated July 10, 1804, to Juan Andrew, the same was confirmed.

The board adjourned until Thursday next at 10 o'clock a. m.

Thursday, *May* 12, 1825.

The board met this day pursuant to adjournment. Present: the Hons. Davis Floyd and William H. Allen.

Edgar Macon, esq., United States attorney for the eastern district of Florida, attended the board this day under their order.

On motion of claimant's attorney, permission was given to withdraw the following claim, viz: Thomas Napier vs. The United States, for three thousand acres of land.

The board took into consideration the following claim, and confirmed the same to John Middleton and John Sibley, viz: a lot in the town of Fernandina, Amelia island, designated as lot No. 6, 1st square.

The following claims were also confirmed, viz:

John Middleton, two hundred acres of land situated on the west side of St. John's river, at a place called Cedar branch.

Thomas Napier, eight hundred acres situated in the territory of Mosquito, at a place called Turnbulll's west swamp.

Christina Hill, four hundred and five acres situated on Diego plains and at a place called *Casina loca.*

The board adjourned until Saturday at 3 o'clock p. m.

Saturday, *May* 14, 1825.

The board met this day pursuant to adjournment. Present: the Hons. Davis Floyd and George Murray.

Edgar Macon, esq., United States attorney for the eastern district of Florida, attended the board this day under their order.

Testimony being necessary in several cases presented to the board this day for adjudication, and no further business appearing, the same was adjourned to meet on Monday morning next, at the town of Jacksonville, in Duval county.

Jacksonville, Monday, *May* 16, 1825.

The board met this day pursuant to adjournment. Present: the Hons. Davis Floyd and William H. Allen.

Edgar Macon, esq., United States attorney for the eastern district of Florida, attended the board this day under their order.

Dorcas Black vs. The United States, for six hundred and forty acres of land situated at the head of Goodby's lake.

This day this case came on to be heard, and John Black, David Scurry, and James Hall were examined; and it appearing to the board that the same was a valid claim, ordered that the same be reported to Congress.

The board adjourned until to-morrow at 10 o'clock a. m.

Tuesday, *May* 17, 1825.

The board met this day pursuant to adjournment. Present: the Hons. Davis Floyd and William H. Allen.

Edgar Macon, esq., United States attorney for the eastern district of Florida, attended the board this day under their order.

William Nelson presented his memorial to this board, praying confirmation of title to six hundred and forty acres of land situated near Mills' ferry, St. Mary's river; when, on motion of claimant's attorney, the board took up the consideration of the said claim, and, after examining D. C. Hart and J. D. Hart, confirmed the same.

The board adjourned until to-morrow at 10 o'clock a. m.

Wednesday, *May* 18, 1825.

The board met this day pursuant to adjournment. Present: the Hons. Davis Floyd and William H. Allen.

Edgar Macon, esq., United States attorney for the eastern district of Florida, attended the board this day under their order.

Francis Woods presented his memorial to this board, praying confirmation of title to six hundred and forty acres of land situated on the north side of Mills' swamp, and on the east side of the road formerly called the King's road; when, on motion, the board took up the consideration of the said claim, and, after examining John Uptegrove therein, confirmed the same.

John D. Bludworth presented his memorial to this board, praying confirmation of title to six hundred and forty acres of land situated at the head of Dead Man's swamp, near the public road. Ordered to be filed.

Seymour Pickett presented his memorial to this board, praying confirmation of title to six hundred and forty acres of land situated on the north side of St. John's river, on the south prong of Six-mile creek. Ordered to be filed.

Isaac Carter presented his memorial to this board, praying confirmation of title to six hundred and forty acres of land situated on Nine-mile creek. Ordered to be filed.

The heirs of John Carter, deceased, presented their memorial to this board, praying confirmation of title to six hundred and forty acres of land situated on the south side of Trout creek, and at a place called Cold Hill; which is ordered to be filed.

Cotton Rawls, sen., presented his memorial to this board, praying confirmation of title to six hundred and forty acres of land situated near the head of the south prong of Trout creek; which is ordered to be filed.

The board adjourned until to-morrow at 10 o'clock a. m.

THURSDAY, *May* 19, 1825.

The board met this day pursuant to adjournment. Present: the Hons. Davis Floyd and William H. Allen.

Edgar Macon, esq., United States attorney for the eastern district of Florida, attended the board this day under their order.

Levi Sparkman presented his memorial to this board, praying confirmation of title to six hundred and forty acres of land situated on Little Trout creek, and on the public road leading from Jacksonville to Camp Pinkney. Ordered to be filed.

There being no further business before the board, the same was adjourned to meet at St. Augustine.

ST. AUGUSTINE, MONDAY, *May* 30, 1825.

The board met this day. Present: all the members.

José Papy presented his memorial to this board, praying confirmation of title to six hundred and forty acres of land about four miles south of Picolata fort, with an affidavit of Bartolome Solana, dated May 25, 1825. Ordered to be filed.

Miguel Papy presented his memorial to this board, praying confirmation of title to six hundred and forty acres of land situated on Deep creek. Ordered to be filed.

Andrew Papy presented his memorial to this board, praying confirmation of title to six hundred and forty acres of land situated about ten or twelve miles to the south of St. Augustine, with an affidavit of Bartolome Solana, dated May 25, 1825. Ordered to be filed.

Thomas Napier, by his attorney, having obtained permission at a former meeting of this board to withdraw his memorial for three thousand acres of land comprised in separate tracts, this day, by his said attorney, presented three several memorials for one thousand acres each, comprising said three thousand acres, situated as follows:

One thousand acres, situated on the west side of Hillsborough river; one thousand acres, situated on the west side of the river Ys, or Indian river; one thousand acres, situated in the hammock known by the name of Chachala Hammock, on the west side of Payne's savanna; which are ordered to be filed.

William Hartley *vs.* The United States, for two hundred and fifty acres of land situated at the head-waters of Goodby's lake, near Wills' swamp.

It appearing to the board that the above was a valid Spanish concession made by Governor Coppinger to memorialist December 13, 1817, it was found that one hundred and fifty acres thereof had been confirmed to Zephaniah Kingsley; it is therefore ordered that one hundred acres alone be confirmed to claimant.

Frederick Hartley *vs.* The United States, for four hundred and fifty acres of land situated on the opposite side of St. Nicholas, at a place called Six-mile river.

It appearing to the board that the concession made to memorialist by Governor White, dated May 7, 1803, only conceded two hundred acres of land, the board therefore confirm the same two hundred acres to claimant.

The following claims were also confirmed by the board:

Hannah Nobles, for two hundred and eight acres of land situated on St. John's river, at a place called Beauclerk's Point; William Hobkirk, for a town lot in Fernandina, designated as square 18, and lots 3 and 4; James R. Hanham, one hundred and seventy and two-thirds acres situated on the North river and Guana creek; Abraham Hannean, for fifty acres, at Little Grove, St. John's river, and north of Buena Vista the guardian of Francis Miles, for two hundred acres on the North river; the guardian of Francis Miles, for three hundred acres on St. John's river; Ezekiel Hudnall's heirs, for two hundred and fifty-five acres on the north bank of the river St. John's, and on the east side of Hogan's creek; E. Hudnall's heirs, for five hundred acres on the river Nassau, at a place called Pumpkin Bluff.

The board adjourned until Monday next at 10 o'clock a. m.

MONDAY, *June* 6, 1825.

The board met this day. Present: the Hons. Davis Floyd and George Murray.

Edgar Macon, esq., United States attorney for the eastern district of Florida, attended the board this day under their order.

On motion of claimant's attorney, the board ordered the following case to be opened, viz:

William Hartley *vs.* The United States, for two hundred and fifty acres of land; which was laid over for further consideration.

The heirs of Francis Cain presented their memorial to this board, praying confirmation of title to two hundred acres of land situated on the south fork of Nassau river, with a British grant made to John Burnett by Governor Moultrie, dated October 5, 1772; also a plat and warrant of survey by Frederick George Mulcaster, dated October 2, 1781. Ordered to be filed.

William Eubanks *vs.* The United States, for two hundred acres, Burton's island, Nassau river. This case being called, and it appearing to the board that the claimant was only entitled to one hundred and fifty acres of land, by concession made by Governor Coppinger, it is therefore ordered that the said one hundred and fifty acres be confirmed to William Eubanks.

Robert Harrison *vs.* The United States, for seven hundred and sixty-five acres of land on the river Nassau, near the Roundabout.

It appearing to the board by the concession made by Governor Coppinger to memorialist May 10, 1816, was as above described, and not on the south of Dunn's creek, as set forth in the memorial of claimant to the board—it, therefore, appearing to the board that the same was a valid Spanish grant, permission was given to claimant's attorney to amend the said memorial, after which it was confirmed.

Stephen Eubanks, jr., vs. The United States, for three hundred and twenty-five acres of land on the north of Trout creek, St. John's river.

It appearing to the board that this was a valid Spanish grant, made to memorialist by Governor Coppinger March 18, 1817, and the location of said tract being changed contrary to that set forth in the said concession, permission was given to amend the memorial of claimant to this board, and the board confirmed the said tract to claimant under the location as above set forth.

The following claims were also confirmed this day by the board, viz:

John Silcock, three hundred acres of land situated three miles from the head of Nassau river; Lewis Guibert, four hundred acres on the east side of St. John's river, near Picolata; the heirs of E. Hudnall, deceased, two hundred acres at the south head of St. Pablo creek; and George Atkinson, a lot of land in the town of Fernandina, designated as lot No. 7 of the eighth square.

The board adjourned until Wednesday morning next at 10 o'clock a. m.

WEDNESDAY, *June* 8, 1825.

Present: all the members.
There being no business prepared, the board adjourned until to-morrow at 10 o'clock a. m.

THURSDAY, *June* 9, 1825.

The board met this day pursuant to adjournment. Present: all the members.
There being no business prepared, the board adjourned until Monday next, the 13th instant, at 10 o'clock a. m.

MONDAY, *June* 13, 1825.

The board met pursuant to adjournment. Present: the Hons. Davis Floyd and Geo. Murray.

Edgar Macon, esq., United States attorney for the eastern district of Florida, attended the board this day under their order.

The wardens of the Roman Catholic church of St. Augustine presented their memorial to this board, praying confirmation of title to thirty-one and a half acres of land situated at a point called Esperanza, within the limits of the city of St. Augustine. Ordered to be filed.

Andrew Paceti presented his memorial to this board, praying confirmation of title to a lot of land without the gates of this city, with a certificate of concession by Governor White, dated May 10, 1807. Ordered to be filed.

Lorenzo Capella presented his memorial to this board, praying confirmation of title to a lot of land without the gates of this city, with a certificate of concession made to him by Governor Coppinger June 6, 1817. Ordered to be filed.

Jane Murray, by her attorney, B. A. Putnam, presented her memorial to this board, praying confirmation of title to six hundred acres of land situated at a place called McDougal's Plantation, with a certificate of concession made to George Murray by Governor White July 28, 1803. Ordered to be filed.

The attorney of Samuel Fairbanks, assignee of Reuben Charles, obtained permission and withdrew the claim for six hundred and forty acres; and, in place thereof, presented the memorial of Reuben Charles, for six hundred and forty acres of land situated about twelve miles from St. Augustine, and near the Twelve-mile swamp. Ordered to be filed.

On motion of claimant's attorney permission was given to withdraw the papers in the following claim, viz: James Riz, for five hundred acres of land; which was rejected by the board April 14, 1825.

The attorney in the case of Michael Lynch, for three hundred and thirty-five acres, obtained permission and amended the memorial thereof, and introduced, as evidence in the same, Farquhar Bethune.

M. Bethune obtained permission to withdraw the claim of Philip R. Yonge, for five hundred acres of land situated at Chichester, St. John's river.

The attorney in the claim of David Turner, for three hundred and ninety acres of land, obtained permission to amend the memorial thereof by inserting "ninety" in lieu of three hundred and ninety acres of land.

Jno. G. Rushing vs. The United States, for two hundred and five acres of land situated on the north side of St. John's river. This case being called, on motion, the claimant's attorney obtained permission and amended the memorial thereof; and it appearing to the board that the same was a valid concession made by Governor Estrada November 27, 1815, in favor of memorialist, the same was confirmed.

The following claims were also, after due consideration, confirmed by the board, viz:

José Alvarez, for three hundred and fifty-five acres of land situated in Thomas' swamp, Nassau river; Zephaniah Kingsley, for fifty acres situated at St. Vincent Ferrer, (bluff,) St. John's river; Zephaniah C. Gibbs, for one hundred and twenty-one acres situated on the head of the Guana river, to the west, on St. Diego plains; John Uptegrove, for two hundred and fifty acres situated on the river Nassau, at a place called the Peach Orchard.

The board adjourned until to-morrow at 10 o'clock a. m.

TUESDAY, *June* 14, 1825.

The board met this day pursuant to adjournment. Present: all the members.

Edgar Macon, esq., United States attorney for the eastern district of Florida, attended the board this day under their order.

Ann Stallings, by her attorney, John B. Strong, presented her memorial to this board, praying confirmation of title to six hundred and forty acres of land situated on Goodby's lake, with no exhibits; which is ordered to be filed.

Sarah Faulk, widow, and the other heirs of John Faulk, deceased, by their agent, E. R. Gibson, presented their memorial to this board, praying confirmation of title to two hundred and fifty acres of land situated on the east side of the river St Mary's, with no exhibits. Ordered to be filed.

Sarah Faulk, widow, and the other heirs of John Faulk, deceased, by their agent, E. R. Gibson, presented their memorial to this board, praying confirmation of title to one hundred acres of land situated on the east side of St. John's river; which is ordered to be filed.

John Christopher vs. The United States, for fifty acres of land situated on the river Nassau. This case being called, and it appearing to the board that the same was a valid Spanish concession made by Governor White, the board confirmed the same.

Bartolome Mestre, jr., for his mother, Mariana Mestre, vs. The United States, for three hundred acres of land on Thompson's branch, Matanzas river. This case being called, and it appearing to the board that the same was undefined in quantity, after examining John B. Strong therein, it is ordered that the same be reported to Congress with the testimony therein.

Farquhar Bethune and James Hall were this day examined, on the part of the United States, in the claim of Pedro Miranda, for three hundred and sixty-eight thousand six hundred and forty acres of land.

The board adjourned until to-morrow at 10 o'clock a. m.

WEDNESDAY, *June* 15, 1825.

The board met this day pursuant to adjournment. Present: the Hons. Davis Floyd and George Murray.

Edgar Macon, esq., United States attorney for the eastern district of Florida, attended the board this day under their order.

On motion, Pedro Miranda was allowed to withdraw his claim for a lot of land within the city of St. Augustine.

The heirs of Robert Andrews, deceased, by their attorney, John Drysdale, presented their memorial to this board, praying confirmation of title to one hundred acres situated at the head of Guana creek, with a certificate of concession made by Governor White, dated November 18, 1799. Ordered to be filed.

George J. F. Clarke and G. W. Perpall were examined in the following claims, viz:

Farquhar Bethune, for one hundred and seventy acres, and William Ladd, for one thousand five hundred and twenty-five acres of land.

The board adjourned until to-morrow at 10 o'clock a. m.

THURSDAY, *June* 16, 1825.

The board met this day pursuant to adjournment. Present: all the members.

Edgar Macon, esq., United States attorney for the eastern district of Florida, attended the board this day under their order.

The heirs of Gerard Forrester, by their attorney, Farquhar Bethune, presented their memorial to this board, praying confirmation of title to five hundred acres of land situated on the river St. John's, with a certified copy of plat and certificate of survey by Pedro Marrot, December 17, 1791. Ordered to be filed.

José Bonely's heirs, by their attorney John B. Strong, presented their memorial to this board, praying confirmation of title to six hundred and ten acres situated on the river Mosquito, with a certified copy of concession, dated September 24 1796. Ordered to be filed.

Abner Williams' heirs, by their attorney, J. B. Strong, presented their memorial to this board, praying confirmation of title to one hundred and fifty acres of land situated on the south side of the river St. John's, at a place called Rowl's Plantation, with a certified copy of concession by Governor White, dated June 2, 1801. Ordered to be filed.

Zephaniah Kingsley vs. The United States, for one hundred acres of land at St. Vincent Ferrer, south side of St. John's river. This case being called, permission was given to amend the memorial; after which, it appearing to the board that the same was a Spanish grant made previous to January 24, 1818, it was confirmed.

The following claims were also confirmed by the board, viz: Hannah Nobles, one hundred acres, situated on Wills' swamp, south side of St. John's river; Lorenzo Capo's heirs, one hundred and seventy-five acres, situated in Twelve-mile swamp, confirmed in favor of the widow and heirs of Lorenzo Capo.

The board then adjourned until to-morrow at 10 o'clock a. m.

FRIDAY, *June* 17, 1825.

The board met this day pursuant to adjournment. Present: all the members.

Edgar Macon, esq., United States attorney for the eastern district of Florida, attended the board this day under their order.

The following claims, viz: The widow and heirs of Antonio Pons, one hundred and seventy-five acres; José Bonely's heirs, six hundred and ten acres, being called, and not being prepared for trial, were continued.

No further business appearing before the board, the same was adjourned until Monday next at 10 o'clock a. m.

MONDAY, *June* 20, 1825.

The board met this day pursuant to adjournment. Present: all the members.

Edgar Macon, esq., United States attorney for the eastern district of Florida, attended the board this day under their order.

Fernando de la Maza Arredondo, sen., and divers other claimants, vs. The United States. This day the attorney for the above claimants, as well as the attorney for the United States, presented the interrogatories to be propounded to the witnesses to be examined on behalf of the above claimants; and thereupon it was ordered that the commission issued from this board, directed to Messrs. Colin Mitchel and William B. Wallace, of the city of Havana, on the part of the claimants, and Messrs. Charles Drake and John Mountain, of the said city, on the part of the United States, to examine the witnesses aforesaid, agreeable to an order of the board made April 13, 1825.

The board adjourned until to-morrow at 10 o'clock a. m.

WEDNESDAY, *June* 22, 1825.

The board met this day. Present: the Hons. George Murray and W. H. Allen.

Edgar Macon, esq., United States attorney for the eastern district of Florida, attended the board this day under their order.

José Noda presented his memorial to this board, praying confirmation of title to a lot of land situated on the east of the road leading from the city of St. Augustine, with a certified copy of concession made to him by Governor White, dated February 9, 1808. Ordered to be filed.

Pedro Estopa presented his memorial to this board, praying confirmation of title to a lot of land situated on the east side of the road leading from the city of St. Augustine, made by Governor White, dated July 20, 1807. Ordered to be filed.

Francis Triay presented his memorial to this board, praying confirmation of title to a lot of land situated without the gates, and to the north of the city of St. Augustine, on the west side of the road, with a certified copy of concession made to him by Governor Estrada, dated October 3, 1815. Ordered to be filed.

John Frazer's Executors *vs.* The United States, for five hundred acres of land situated on St. Mary's river. This case being called, and it appearing to the board that the same was a valid Spanish concession made to John Frazer May 2, 1810, the same was confirmed.

Susannah Cashen, five hundred acres; same, three hundred acres. These cases being called, permission was given to amend the memorials thereof, and the cases were laid over.

Valentine Fitzpatrick, for twenty-five acres of land. This case being called, and not being prepared for trial, was continued.

The board adjourned until to-morrow at 10 o'clock a. m.

THURSDAY, *June* 23, 1825.

The board met this day pursuant to adjournment. Present: all the members.

No business being prepared, the board adjourned until Saturday next at 10 o'clock a. m.

SATURDAY, *June* 25, 1825.

The board met this day pursuant to adjournment. Present: all the members.

No business being prepared, the board adjourned until Monday next at 10 o'clock a. m.

MONDAY, *June* 27, 1825.

The board met this day pursuant to adjournment. Present: all the members.

No business being prepared, the board adjourned until to-morrow at 10 o'clock a. m.

TUESDAY, *June* 28, 1825.

The board met this day pursuant to adjournment. Present: all the members.

The secretary having informed the board that no business was prepared, on account of his not having access to the public archives, until the same would be arranged for the purpose of examining the translations with the original documents on file in that office, it is therefore ordered that the board adjourn until Tuesday, the 5th of July next.

FRIDAY, *July* 8, 1825.

The board met this day. Present: the Hons. Davis Floyd and W. H. Allen.

Edgar Macon, esq., United States attorney for the eastern district of Florida, attended the board this day under their order.

The following claims being called, and being prepared for trial, were confirmed by the board, viz: George Atkinson, for one lot of land situated in the town of Fernandina, designated as lot No. 11 of the 4th square; George Atkinson, for one lot of land situated in the town of Fernandina, designated as No. 8 of the 8th square; Lindsay Todd's executors for two half lots of land situated in the town of Fernandina, designated as Nos. 3 and 4 of the 8th square.

Permission was given to amend the memorial in the following claims, and the same were laid over, viz: Hibberson and Yonge, one lot in Fernandina; same, one lot in Fernandina; same, four and a quarter acres in Fernandina; same, one lot in Fernandina; same, one lot in Fernandina.

Testimony being required in the following cases, they were continued, viz: Governor Atkinson, one lot in Fernandina; same, one lot in Fernandina; same, one lot in Fernandina; same, one lot in Fernandina.

James Arnau, one hundred and twenty-five acres of land on the North river.

Clara Prates Arnau, one hundred and seventy-five acres of land on the North river.

The board adjourned until to-morrow at 10 o'clock a. m.

SATURDAY, *July* 9, 1825.

The board met this day pursuant to adjournment. Present: the Hons. Davis Floyd and W. H. Allen.

Edgar Macon, esq., United States attorney for the district of Florida, attended the board this day under their order.

The widow and heirs of Antonio Martinez, by their agent, John Cavedo, presented their memorial to this board, praying confirmation of title to seventy acres of land situated at Moultrie, with a concession to Antonio Martinez, dated August 26, 1807. Ordered to be filed.

Joseph Bergallo, by his agent, John Cavedo, presented his memorial to this board, praying confirmation of title to two hundred and thirty acres of land situated on the river Nassau, at a place called Thomas' swamp, with a royal title dated March 18, 1817. Ordered to be filed.

The heirs of Robert Andrew, for one hundred acres of land situated on the plains of Urliche, with a copy of concession made to Robert Andrew, dated October 18, 1793. Ordered to be filed.

Bartolo Solana, by his attorney, John B. Strong, presented his memorial to this board, praying confirmation of title to six hundred and forty acres of land situated near the Big Cypress swamp. Ordered to be filed.

The attorney of claimant obtained permission, and filed a plat and certificate in the following claim, viz: Pedro R. de Cala vs. The United States, for five hundred acres of land.

The board adjourned until Monday next at 10 o'clock a. m.

MONDAY, *July* 11, 1825.

The board met this day pursuant to adjournment. Present: all the members.

Edgar Macon, esq., United States attorney for the eastern district of Florida, attended the board this day under their order.

The following claims being called, and being prepared for trial, were confirmed by the board, viz: Henry Yonge, for a lot of land situated in the town of Fernandina, Amelia island, and designated as number nine of first square; Hibberson and Yonge, for four and a quarter acres of land situated in the town of Fernandina; Hibberson and Yonge, a lot in Fernandina; Hibberson and Yonge, for a marsh lot in Fernandina; Hibberson and Yonge, for a marsh lot in Fernandina.

On motion of claimant's attorney, the board resumed the consideration of the following claim, and confirmed the decree passed thereon the 30th of May last, viz: William Hartley, for two hundred and fifty acres of land.

G. W. Perpall was examined in the claim of Thomas Napier, for three thousand acres of land in three separate tracts of one thousand acres each.

The board adjourned until to-morrow at 10 o'clock a. m.

TUESDAY, *July* 12, 1825.

The board met this day pursuant to adjournment. Present: all the members.

Edgar Macon, esq., United States attorney for the eastern district of Florida, attended the board this day under their order.

John Bellamy vs. The United States, for fifty acres of land situated at Jacksonville, St. John's river. This case being called, and it appearing to the board that the same was a valid Spanish concession made by Governor Coppinger to John Mestre previous to January 24, 1818, and regularly conveyed to claimant, the same is therefore confirmed.

The following claims being called, and not being prepared for trial, were, on motion of their respective attorneys, continued, viz: Zephaniah Kingsley, five hundred acres of land; Charles Edmouston, five hundred acres; Isaac Sasportas, four hundred and twenty-five acres; Ezekiel Haddock, one hundred and fifty acres; Joseph Haddock, two hundred and fifty acres.

The honorable George Murray having retired, Antonio Alvarez was examined on the part of the claimant in the following claim: Pedro Miranda, for three hundred and sixty-eight thousand six hundred and forty acres at Tampa Bay; as also in the claim of Thomas Napier, for three thousand acres of land in three tracts of one thousand acres each.

The board adjourned until to-morrow at 10 o'clock a. m.

THURSDAY, *July* 14, 1825.

The board met this day. Present: all the members.

Edgar Macon, esq., United States attorney for the eastern district of Florida, attended the board this day under their order.

The following claims were, after due consideration, submitted, viz: Thomas Napier, for one thousand acres at Chachala hammock; Thomas Napier, for one thousand acres at Indian river; same, for one thousand acres at Mosquito South lagoon.

The honorable George Murray having retired, Bernardo Segui was examined on the part of the claimant in the following claim, viz: Pedro Miranda, for three hundred and sixty-eight thousand six hundred and forty acres at Tampa Bay.

The board adjourned until to-morrow at 10 o'clock a. m.

TUESDAY, *August* 9, 1825.

The board met this day. Present: the Hons. Davis Floyd and William H. Allen.

This day Samuel King presented his memorial for three hundred acres of land, with a copy of concession dated April 10, 1804, on Nassau river, by his attorney, Belton A. Copp; which was ordered to be filed.

The following claims being called, and being prepared for trial, were confirmed, viz: Mathias Pons' heirs, four hundred acres at Casapulla, on the river Matanzas; Susannah Cashen, two hundred and fifty acres on Amelia island; Pedro Pons, eight hundred and seventy-five acres in Mills' swamp, Nassau river; Domingo Fernandez, one lot in Fernandina, number four, square twenty-three; Domingo Fernandez, four half lots in Fernandina, Nos. 5, 6, 7, and 8, of square 23; heirs of Antonio Suarez, five hundred acres on Amelia island, at a place called Black Point.

The board adjourned.

TUESDAY, *August* 16, 1825.

The board met this day. Present: the Hons. George Murray and William H. Allen.

John Carr presented his memorial to this board, praying confirmation of title to six hundred and forty acres of land situated on Lofton's swamp, one of the waters of Nassau river. Ordered to be filed.

Domingo Fernandez vs. The United States, for three hundred acres of land situated on Amelia island. This case being called, and it appearing to the board that the same was a valid Spanish grant made by Governor Coppinger to James Adamson previous to January 24, 1818, and by him conveyed to memorialist, the same was confirmed.

On motion of claimant's attorney, the following claims were, after due consideration, confirmed by the board, viz: C. Griffith's heirs, for three hundred acres of land situated on the banks of the river St. Mary's.

Miguel Papy, for six hundred and forty acres of land situated on Deep creek, near St. John's river.

The board adjourned until to-morrow at 10 o'clock a. m.

WEDNESDAY, *August* 17, 1825.

The board met this day pursuant to adjournment. Present: the Hons. George Murray and William H. Allen.

George J. F. Clarke *vs.* The United States, for one thousand acres of land in two tracts, viz: five hundred acres situated or Durbin's swamp, to the north of the bridge crossing the creek of said swamp; and five hundred acres on the east bank of Dunn's lake. The board having ascertained this to be a valid Spanish concession, confirmed the same to claimant in the situations pointed out as above.

The following claims were also confirmed by the board, viz: Domingo Fernandez, one hundred and fifty acres on Amelia island; Susannah Cashen, two hundred and thirty acres on the banks of the river St. Mary's, at a place called Old Township; Francis Richard, four hundred and sixty-six acres on St. John's river, at a place called Branchester; Francis Richard, two hundred and thirty acres on St. John's river, at a place called Parque; Domingo Fernandez, one hundred acres on Amelia island.

The following cases being called, and not being prepared for trial, were continued, viz: William Drummond, five hundred acres; Samuel and George Brennan, three hundred acres; José Youngblood, six hundred acres; George J. F. Clarke, one thousand acres; John H. McIntosh, eight hundred acres; Duncan L. Clinch, one thousand acres; Elizabeth Wiggins, three hundred acres.

The board adjourned.

TUESDAY, *August* 23, 1825.

The board met this day. Present: the Hons. Davis Floyd and George Murray.

Edgar Macon, esq., United States attorney for the eastern district of Florida, attended the board this day under their order.

The following claims being called, and being prepared for trial, were severally confirmed by the board, viz:

Jane Murray, six hundred acres of land situated at a place called McDougal's Plantation.

John Christopher, five hundred acres situated on and near the mouth of Nassau river.

Domingo Fernandez, two hundred acres situated on the main, opposite Amelia island.

The board having ascertained that the following claims were made subsequent to January 24, 1818, were, after due consideration, rejected, viz:

McDowell & Black, one thousand acres of land on Dunn's lake.

Belton A. Copp, one thousand acres on the east side of the river St. John's, near Lake George.

The following claims being called, and not being prepared for trial, were continued, viz:

Nathaniel Wilds, for one hundred and eighty-four acres.

William Frink, three hundred and twenty-one acres.

George Morrison, one hundred and fifty acres.

Louisa H. Christopher, one hundred and eighty acres.

The board adjourned until Thursday morning next at 10 o'clock.

THURSDAY, *August* 25, 1825.

The board met this day pursuant to adjournment. Present: the Hons. Davis Floyd and William H. Allen.

Edgar Macon, esq., United States attorney for the eastern district of Florida, attended the board this day under their order.

John Houston *vs.* The United States, for six hundred acres on Talbot island. This case being called, and it appearing to the board that the same was a valid Spanish grant made to Spicer Christopher, deceased, by Governor Quesada, and it also appearing of record that the said John Houston is one of the heirs of said Christopher, the same is therefore confirmed to claimant.

The following claims being called, and not being prepared for trial, were continued, viz: Zachariah Hogans, for fifty acres; John Houston, Little Talbot island.

On motion of John Drysdale, esq., the order of rejection was set aside on the following claims, and they were accordingly reopened: Belton A. Copp, one thousand acres; McDowell & Black, one thousand acres.

The board adjourned until Saturday next at 10 o'clock a. m.

SATURDAY, *August* 27, 1825.

The board met this day pursuant to adjournment. Present: the Hons. Davis Floyd and George Murray.

Edgar Macon, esq., United States attorney for the eastern district of Fl ·ida, attended the board this day under their order.

Charles F. Sibbald, by his attorney, John Rodman, presented his memorial to this board, praying confirmation of title to ten thousand acres of land situated on Trout creek. Ordered to be filed.

Charles F. Sibbald, by his attorney, John Rodman, presented his memorial to this board, praying confirmation of title for four thousand acres of land situated in Turnbull's swamp. Ordered to be filed.

Charles F. Sibbald, by his attorney, John Rodman, presented his memorial to this board, praying confirmation of title to two thousand acres of land situated at Rowley's hammock. Ordered to be filed.

The following claims being prepared for trial were confirmed, viz:

Domingo Fernandez, two hundred and twenty-eight acres situated on the west side of Amelia river.

Henry Yonge, one hundred and ninety acres situated in Lofton's swamp.

William P. Yonge, four hundred and eighty acres situated on St. Mary's river.

William P. Yonge, five hundred acres situated on St. Mary's and Little St. Mary's rivers.

On application of claimant's attorney, permission was given to amend the memorial as to the location of the land in the following claim, viz:

Antonio Alvarez vs. The United States, for fifteen hundred acres of land, which was recommended for confirmation September 8, 1824.

The board adjourned until Monday next at 10 o'clock a. m.

MONDAY, August 29, 1825.

The board met this day pursuant to adjournment. Present: all the members.

Edgar Macon, esq., United States attorney for the eastern district of Florida, attended the board this day under their order.

Andrew Branning vs. The United States, for six hundred and forty acres of land, under the donation act, situated on Black creek. This case being called, and it appearing to the board from the evidence produced therein that the claimant was entitled to said land, confirmed the same.

The board also reported to Congress the following claims under the said act, viz:

John D. Bludworth, six hundred and forty acres situated near the public road, at the head of Deadman's swamp.

William Branning, six hundred and forty acres on the south side of Black creek.

John Brindly, six hundred and forty acres on the north side of Black creek.

Isaac Carter, six hundred and forty acres on Nine-mile creek, on the road leading to Camp Pinkney.

The heirs of John Carter, deceased, six hundred and forty acres on the south side of Trout creek.

The testimony in the following claims not being sufficient, and it being the opinion of the board that the claimants were not entitled to the land set forth in said claims, rejected the same, viz:

Jesse Carlisle, six hundred and forty acres on the east side of Little Black creek, at a place called Ferguson's Neck, at the head of Doctor's lake

Hardy Ellanier, six hundred and forty acres on the waters of Little Black creek, in the county of Duval.

William Evins, six hundred and forty acres on Durbin's creek and the road leading from St. Augustine to the Cowford.

The board adjourned until to-morrow at 10 o'clock a. m.

TUESDAY, August 30, 1825.

The board met this day pursuant to adjournment. Present: the Hons. Davis Floyd and W. H. Allen.

Edgar Macon, esq., United States attorney for the eastern district of Florida, attended the board this day under their order.

Philip Solana, by his agent, Antonio Alvarez, presented his memorial to this board, praying confirmation of title to a lot of land without the gates of St. Augustine, containing three hundred and sixty and a quarter yards. Ordered to be filed.

The following claims being called, and it appearing to the board, from the evidence therein, that the claimants were entitled to the land set forth in said claims, confirmed the same, viz:

James Sparkman, six hundred and forty acres on the headwaters of Boggy swamp and east of public road.

William Sparkman, six hundred and forty acres on the headwaters of Boggy swamp and west of public road.

The board also reported to Congress the following claims, viz:

John R. Hogans, six hundred and forty acres on the north side of St. John's river.

Levi Sparkman, six hundred and forty acres on Little Trout creek, on the road leading to Camp Pinkney.

The board adjourned until to-morrow at 10 o'clock a m.

WEDNESDAY, August 31, 1825.

The board met this day pursuant to adjournment. Present: all the members.

Edgar Macon, esq., United States attorney for the eastern district of Florida, attended the board this day under their order.

On motion of A. Bellamy, esq., it is ordered that a commission issue to any two of the United States officers at Tampa Bay to take the evidence of any witnesses on any cases which may arise under the donation act of Congress.

On motion of John Drysdale, esq., it is ordered that the claim of Robert Mitchel, trustee to a section and a half of Alachua, be submitted.

Horatio S. Dexter was this day examined, on the part of the United States, in the following claims, viz:

William Williamson, six hundred and forty acres of land at Hogtown, Alachua.

John Oliver, six hundred and forty acres of land on the east side of Dunn's lake.

The board adjourned until Friday next at 10 o'clock a. m.

FRIDAY September 2, 1825.

The board met this day pursuant to adjournment. Present: all the members.

Edgar Macon, esq., United States attorney for the eastern district of Florida, attended the board this day under their order.

Paul Dupon, by his attorney, John Rodman, presented his memorial to this board, praying confirmation of title to three thousand acres of land situated at Spring Garden. Ordered to be filed.

The following cases being called, and being prepared for trial, were confirmed by the board, viz:

Francis Richard, one hundred and ten acres of land situated on the southern side of St. John's river, at Point St. Isabel.

Domingo Fernandez, a lot of land in Fernandina, Amelia island, designated as No. 2, of square 18.

McDowell & Black vs. The United States, one thousand acres of land.

This case being called, the United States attorney objected to any further proceeding being had in the same, and that it be dismissed from the docket, inasmuch as it appeared that the written evidence of the claimants' title bore date subsequent to January 24, 1818, and claimants praying to be heard by counsel; whereupon an argument was had thereon, but the board not being sufficiently advised of and concerning the same, it was held over until to-morrow; and

The board adjourned until to-morrow at 10 o'clock a. m.

SATURDAY, *September* 3, 1825.

The board met this day pursuant to adjournment. Present: all the members.

Edgar Macon, esq., United States attorney for the eastern district of Florida, attended the board this day under their order.

McDowell & Black *vs.* The United States, one thousand acres of land.

The board not being prepared to give its decision in this case, it was held over till Monday next at 10 o'clock a. m.; and the board adjourned.

MONDAY, *September* 5, 1825.

The board met this day pursuant to adjournment. Present: all the members.

Edgar Macon, esq., United States attorney for the eastern district of Florida, attended the board this day under their order.

McDowell & Black *vs.* The United States, one thousand acres of land.

The board not being prepared to give its decision in this case, it was held over until to-morrow, and the board adjourned until to-morrow.

TUESDAY, *September* 6, 1825.

The board met this day pursuant to adjournment. Present: all the members.

Edgar Macon, esq., United States attorney for the eastern district of Florida, attended the board this day under their order.

McDowell & Black *vs.* The United States, one thousand acres of land.

The board having minutely considered and deliberated on the above case, this day decided that the same must be rejected.

J. Allen Smith *vs.* The United States, for a lot of land in the city of St. Augustine.

This case being called, and it appearing to the board that the same was a valid Spanish grant, confirmed the same.

The board adjourned until Saturday next at 10 o'clock a. m.

SATURDAY, *September* 10, 1825.

The board met this day pursuant to adjournment. Present: all the members.

Edgar Macon, esq., United States attorney for the eastern district of Florida, attended the board this day under their order.

No business being prepared, the board adjourned until Wednesday next at 10 o'clock a. m.

WEDNESDAY, *September* 14, 1825.

The board met this day pursuant to adjournment. Present: all the members.

Edgar Macon, esq., United States attorney for the eastern district of Florida, attended the board this day under their order.

The wardens of the Roman Catholic church of St. Augustine presented their memorial to this board, praying confirmation of title to two lots of land in the city. Ordered to be filed.

Frankee Lewis presented his memorial to this board, praying confirmation of title to six hundred and forty acres of land, under the donation act, situated on New river, near Cape Florida. Ordered to be filed.

The following claims being called, and it appearing to the board that they were valid Spanish grants made previous to January 24, 1818, confirmed the same, viz:

Heirs of Francis X. Sanchez, for one thousand acres of land situated on St. Diego plains, at a place called *Montes de San Diego.*

Heirs of Francis X. Sanchez, one hundred acres of land situated on Diego plains, at a place called *Montes de Puercos.*

J. Allen Smith, for a lot of land situated in the city of St. Augustine.

Daniel Hulbert, for two hundred acres of land situated four miles north of the city of St. Augustine.

The following claims were, on motion of their respective attorneys, confirmed by the board, viz:

George Gianople, for six hundred and forty acres of land, under the donation act, situated about twelve miles northwest from St. Augustine.

The heirs of Jesse Fish, for five hundred acres of land situated in Graham's swamp.

The board adjourned until Friday next at 10 o'clock a. m.

TUESDAY, *September* 20, 1825.

The board met this day. Present: all the members.

Edgar Macon, esq., United States attorney for the eastern district of Florida, attended the board this day under their order.

The following claim was recommended for confirmation, viz:

The heirs of James Hutchinson, two thousand acres of land on Jupiter island.

The board adjourned until to-morrow at 10 o'clock a. m.

FRIDAY, *September* 23, 1825.

The board met this day. Present: the Hons. Davis Floyd and George Murray.

Edgar Macon, esq., United States attorney for the eastern district of Florida, attended the board this day under their order.

Charles W. Clarke was examined in the claim of Horatio S. Dexter *vs.* The United States, for sixteen thousand acres of land on Indian river.

The board adjourned until to-morrow at 10 o'clock a. m.

MONDAY, *September* 26, 1825.

The board met this day. Present: the Hons. Davis Floyd and George Murray.

Edgar Macon, esq., United States attorney for the eastern district of Florida, attended the board this day under their order.

John Andrew presented his memorial to this board, praying confirmation of title to six hundred and forty acres of land, under the donation act, situated on Tocoy creek, St. John's river. Ordered to be filed.

Emanuel Crespo presented his memorial to this board, praying confirmation of title to six hundred and forty acres of land situated about a mile from the mouth of Tocoy creek, near St. John's river. Ordered to be filed.

The heirs of Andrew Dewees *vs.* The United States, for two thousand six hundred and thirty-three and a third acres of land situated on the south side of St. John's river, and east side of Pablo creek. This case being called, permission was given to amend the memorial thereof; and it appearing to the board that the same was a valid Spanish grant made previous to January 24, 1818, and also in evidence that the whole or part of said grant has been cultivated by the said heirs for many years, the same is therefore confirmed to them.

Seymour Pickett *vs.* The United States, for two hundred and fifty acres of land at a place called Hodguins, on St. John's river. This claim being called, and claimant having produced a royal title made to R. Hogans by Governor Kindelan May 26, 1815, and conveyance from said Hogans to him, the board confirmed the same.

Constance McFee *vs.* The United States, for four hundred and forty-six acres of land on St. John's river. It appearing to the board that claimant was a British subject, and that she resided without the jurisdiction of the United States, rejected the same.

[NOTE.—This case was reconsidered by the board September 30, 1825, and confirmed.]

On motion of Mr. Putnam, permission was given to file an affidavit in the claim of José Papy, for six hundred and forty acres of land.

The board adjourned until to-morrow at 10 o'clock a. m.

TUESDAY, *September* 27, 1825.

The board met this day pursuant to adjournment. Present: the Hons. Davis Floyd and W. H. Allen.

Edgar Macon, esq., United States attorney for the eastern district of Florida, attended the board this day under their order.

Maria R. Scott presented her memorial to this board, praying confirmation of title to a lot of land situated in the town of Fernandina, Amelia island, designated as lot No. 8 of eighth square. Ordered to be filed.

The widow of Juan Lorenzo presented her memorial to this board, praying confirmation of title to a lot of land situated without the gates of St. Augustine and within the fifteen hundred yards. Ordered to be filed.

Antonio Rogero presented her memorial to this board, praying confirmation of title to a lot of land situated without the gates of St. Augustine and within the fifteen hundred yards. Ordered to be filed.

José Hernandez presented his memorial to this board, praying confirmation of title to a lot of land situated without the gates of St. Augustine and within the fifteen hundred yards. Ordered to be filed.

The following claims being called, and the same being undefined in quantity, were reported to Congress, viz:

William Travers, for one thousand acres of land situated at a place called the Old Savannas, North river.

Jehu Underwood, for six hundred acres of land situated on Black creek, Duval county.

Francis P. Sanchez *vs.* The United States for one thousand acres of land situated at the head of Indian river. This case being called, and it appearing to the board that it was made subsequent to January 24, 1818, rejected the same.

The board then adjourned until to-morrow at 10 o'clock a. m.

WEDNESDAY, *September* 28, 1825.

The board met this day pursuant to adjournment. Present: the Hons. Davis Floyd and William H. Allen.

Edgar Macon, esq., United States attorney for the eastern district of Florida, attended the board this day under their order.

A number of cases being called, and not being prepared for trial, on motion of their respective attorneys they were continued; and there being no further business, the board adjourned until to-morrow at 10 o'clock a. m.

THURSDAY, *September* 29, 1825.

The board met this day pursuant to adjournment. Present: the Hons. Davis Floyd and George Murray.

The heirs of William O'Neal presented their memorial to this board, praying confirmation of title to three hundred acres of land situated on the river St. Mary's and Lanford creek. Ordered to be filed.

The following claim being called, and being undefined in quantity, was reported to Congress, viz:

John Bachelot, for a marsh island situated near Doctor's island.

The board adjourned until to-morrow at 10 o'clock a. m.

FRIDAY, *September* 30, 1825.

The board met this day pursuant to adjournment. Present: all the members.

Edgar Macon, esq., United States attorney for the eastern district of Florida, attended the board this day under their order.

On motion of claimants' attorney, the following claim was reopened, viz:

Archibald Clark and others, for two hundred and fifty acres of land, and permission was given to amend the memorial thereof by inserting "two hundred" in place of two hundred and fifty acres; whereupon it was moved that the decree of the 29th of April last be set aside and said claim be confirmed, which is allowed and ordered by the board.

Constance McFee *vs.* The United States, for four hundred and forty-six acres of land on St. John's river. In this case G. W. Perpall, attorney in fact for Constance McFee, moved the board to open the same, and that the order of rejection be set aside, and that he have leave to amend the memorial in behalf of the heirs of Constance McFee, she having lately died, which was granted; and the same was also confirmed to said heirs upon the affidavit of G. W. Perpall, stating that he, as attorney for Mrs. McFee, had held possession of said land for the last twelve years.

The board adjourned until to-morrow at 10 o'clock a. m.

SATURDAY, *October* 1, 1825.

There being no business prepared, the board adjourned until Friday next, the 7th instant, at 10 o'clock a. m.

Edgar Macon, esq., United States attorney for the eastern district of Florida, attended the board this day for the purpose of collecting testimony in various cases before the board.

FRIDAY, *October* 7, 1825.

The board met this day pursuant to adjournment. Present: the Hons. George Murray and William H. Allen.

Edgar Macon, esq., United States attorney for the eastern district of Florida, attended the board this day under their order.

Francis Paz, by his attorney, J. N. Cox, presented his memorial to this board, praying confirmation of title to fifteen hundred acres of land on Pellicer's creek, with a certified copy of concession made to him by Governor Estrada, dated November 12, 1815. Ordered to be filed.

Philip and Mary Dewees *vs.* The United States, for one hundred acres of land on Guana river. This case being called, and it appearing to the board that the same was a valid Spanish grant made to Francis X. Sanchez February 6, 1811, who was father to claimants, confirmed the same.

The board adjourned until Monday next at 10 o'clock a. m.

MONDAY, *October* 10, 1825.

The board met this day pursuant to adjournment. Present: the Hons. Davis Floyd and George Murray.

Edgar Macon, esq., United States attorney for the eastern district of Florida, attended the board this day under their order.

Juan Garcia, by his attorney, B. A. Putnam, presented his memorial to this board, praying confirmation of title to six hundred and forty acres of land situated near St. John's river. Ordered to be filed.

James and George Clarke, for five hundred acres of land situated on the west of Matanzas river.

Charles W. and George J. F. Clarke, for three hundred acres of land situated on Matanzas river, at a place called Worcester.

The above claims being taken up, and it appearing to the board that the same were British grants made in favor of the ancestors of claimants, confirmed the same.

The board adjourned until to-morrow at 10 o'clock a. m.

TUESDAY, *October* 11, 1825.

The board met this day pursuant to adjournment. Present: the Hons. Davis Floyd and W. H. Allen.

Edgar Macon, esq., United States attorney for the eastern district of Florida, attended the board this day under their order.

There being no business prepared, the board adjourned until to-morrow at 10 o'clock a. m.

WEDNESDAY, *October* 12, 1825.

The board met this day pursuant to adjournment. Present: the Hons. Davis Floyd and W. H. Allen.

Edgar Macon, esq., United States attorney for the eastern district of Florida, attended the board this day under their order.

No business being prepared, the board adjourned until Friday next at 10 o'clock a. m.

FRIDAY, *October* 14, 1825.

There being no business prepared, the board was adjourned until Friday next, the 21st instant, at 10 o'clock a. m.

Edgar Macon, esq., United States attorney for the eastern district of Florida, attended this day under their order.

FRIDAY, *October* 21, 1825.

There being no business prepared, and the secretary being occupied in making out the report of the board for Congress, the same was adjourned until Monday next at 10 o'clock a. m.

Edgar Macon, esq., United States attorney for the eastern district of Florida, attended the board this day under their order.

MONDAY, October 24, 1825.

The board met this day, but there being no business on hand, it adjourned until to-morrow at 10 o'clock a. m.

Edgar Macon, esq., United States attorney for the eastern district of Florida, attended the board this day under their order.

WEDNESDAY, October 26, 1825.

The board met this day. Present: all the members.

Edgar Macon, esq., United States attorney for the eastern district of Florida, attended the board this day under their order.

The heirs of Thomas Fitch, deceased, presented their memorial to this board, praying confirmation of title to four thousand five hundred acres of land situated in the territory of Mosquito. Ordered to be filed.

The heirs of Thomas Fitch, deceased, presented their memorial to this board, praying confirmation of title to one thousand acres of land situated at a place called Berresford, St. John's river. Ordered to be filed.

The heirs of Thomas Fitch, deceased, presented their memorial to this board, praying confirmation of title to nineteen hundred acres of land situated at a place called Mount Oswald, Mosquito. Ordered to be filed.

Davis Floyd presented his memorial to this board, praying confirmation of title to one thousand acres of land situated between the North river and Guana creek. Ordered to be filed.

Margaret Cook presented her memorial to this board, praying confirmation of title to a lot of land situated without the gates of St. Augustine and within the fifteen hundred yards. Ordered to be filed.

Margaret Cook presented her memorial to this board, praying confirmation of title to a lot of land situated without the gates of St. Augustine and within the fifteen hundred yards. Ordered to be filed.

Ralph King, by his attorney, John Drysdale, presented his memorial to this board, praying confirmation of title to five thousand acres of land situated in Turnbull's swamp. Ordered to be filed.

The heirs of John Faulk, by their agent, E. R. Gibson, presented their memorial to this board, praying confirmation of title to two hundred and fifty acres of land at a place called Anderson's cowpen, on the river St. Mary's, with a certified copy of concession made to John Faulk June 22, 1792, by Governor Quesada. Ordered to be filed.

The heirs of James McGirt, by their agent, E. R. Gibson, presented their memorial to this board, praying confirmation of title to three hundred acres of land situated about nine miles north from St. Augustine, with a certified copy of concession made to James McGirt, and dated February 24, 1792. Ordered to be filed.

The heirs of James McGirt, by their agent, E. R. Gibson, presented their memorial to this board, praying confirmation of title to three hundred acres of land situated on Nassau river, with a copy of concession by Governor Quesada, dated February 24, 1792. Ordered to be filed.

The heirs of James McGirt, by their agent, E. R. Gibson, presented their memorial to this board, praying confirmation of title to five hundred acres of land situated on St. Mary's river, with a copy of concession made to James McGirt by Governor White June 15, 1790. Ordered to be filed.

The heirs of James McGirt, by their agent, E. R. Gibson, presented their memorial to this board, praying confirmation of title to three hundred acres of land situated on St. Mary's river, with a copy of concession made to James McGirt by Governor Quesada January 24, 1793. Ordered to be filed.

The heirs of James McGirt, by their agent, E. R. Gibson, presented their memorial to this board, praying confirmation of title to three hundred acres of land situated on St. John's river, with a certified copy of permission to exchange lands between John McQueen and James McGirt, by Governor Quesada, dated March 8, 1792. Ordered to be filed.

The heirs of James McGirt, by their agent, E. R. Gibson, presented their memorial to this board, praying confirmation of title to a small island called Martin's island, on St. Mary's river, containing about eighty acres, with a certified copy of concession to James McGirt, dated April 26, 1793. Ordered to be filed.

The heirs of James McGirt, by their agent, E. R. Gibson, presented their memorial to this board, praying confirmation of title to eighteen caballerias, or six hundred acres of land, situated on the west side of St. John's river, with a plat and certificate of survey by Don Pedro Marrot, dated January 17, 1792. Ordered to be filed.

On motion, the claim of William Ovington, as executor of James Alexander, for seven acres of land situated in the city of St. Augustine, rejected by the board March 29, 1824, was reopened and ordered to be filed.

On motion of the claimant's attorney, the order of rejection of April 20, 1824, on the following claim, viz: Elihu Woodruff and others, for three hundred and fifty acres of land on St. John's river, was set aside; and the board taking into consideration said claim, and finding the same a valid Spanish grant made to John Moore, and by him regularly conveyed to claimants, confirmed the same.

The wardens of the Roman Catholic church of St. Augustine vs. The United States, for a tract of land containing thirty-one and a half acres situated at the point called Esperanza, within the limits of the said city. The board took up the consideration of said claim, and confirmed the same.

Nicholas Estefanopoly vs. The United States, for two thousand five hundred acres of land situated on the west of the river Suwannee. On motion of claimant's attorney, this claim was taken up, and the board not being fully advised therein, the same was submitted and held under consideration.

On motion of B. A. Putnam, esq., permission was given to withdraw the following claim, viz.: Samuel and George Brennan, for three hundred acres of land; the Hon. Davis Floyd dissenting.

Joseph M. Hernandez was this day examined in the claim of George J. F. Clarke for sixteen thousand acres of land.

The board adjourned until to-morrow at 10 o'clock a. m.

THURSDAY, October 27, 1825.

The board met this day pursuant to adjournment. Present: the Hons. Davis Floyd and W. H. Allen.

Edgar Macon esq., United States attorney for the eastern district of Florida, attended the board this day under their order.

Thomas Jones, by his attorney, A. Bellamy, presented his memorial to this board, praying confirmation of title to six hundred and forty acres of land, under the donation act, situated in the county of Alachua, near the Gulf of Mexico. Ordered to be filed.

Peter Nichols, by his attorney, A. Bellamy, presented his memorial to this board, praying confirmation of title to six hundred and forty acres of land, under the donation act, situated in the county of Alachua, near the Gulf of Mexico. Ordered to be filed.

Francis Durant, by his attorney, A. Bellamy, presented his memorial to this board, praying confirmation of title to six hundred and forty acres of land, under the donation act, situated in the county of Alachua, near the Gulf of Mexico. Ordered to be filed.

John Toy, by his attorney, A. Bellamy, presented his memorial to this board, praying confirmation of title to six hundred and forty acres of land, under the donation act, situated in the county of Alachua, near the Gulf of Mexico. Ordered to be filed.

Richard D. Ford, by his attorney, A. Bellamy, presented his memorial to this board, praying confirmation of title to six hundred and forty acres of land, under the donation act, situated in the county of Alachua, near the Gulf of Mexico. Ordered to be filed.

Nathaniel Tanner, by his attorney, A. Bellamy, presented his memorial to this board, praying confirmation of title to six hundred and forty acres of land, under the donation act, situated in the county of Alachua, near the Gulf of Mexico. Ordered to be filed.

The heirs of Thomas Fitch presented their memorial to this board, praying confirmation of title to one thousand acres of land situated on the river St. John's, at a place called Spring Garden. Ordered to be filed.

The heirs of Thomas Fitch presented their memorial to this board, praying confirmation of title to eight hundred acres of land situated at a place called Pengree's old field. Ordered to be filed.

Thomas Reynolds, administrator of Wm. G. Christopher, by his attorney, John Rodman, presented his memorial to this board, praying confirmation of title to five hundred acres of land situated on Santa Juana creek, in the county of Nassau. Ordered to be filed.

On motion of B. A. Putnam, esq., permission was given to withdraw the following claim, to wit: Domingo Fernandez, for nine hundred acres of land, and in place thereof presented the following claim: Juan McClure, for nine hundred acres of land situated on Amelia island; which was ordered to be filed.

On motion, permission was given to John Rodman, esq., to file a deposition of Farquhar Bethune in the claim of Charles Sibbald, for sixteen thousand acres of land.

G. W. Perpall, Geo. J. F. Clarke, and Joseph S. Sanchez were this day examined by the board in the following claims, to wit: Davis Floyd, one thousand acres of land; Geo. J. F. Clarke, sixteen thousand acres of land; the wardens of the Roman Catholic church of St. Augustine, one lot of land; and Ralph King, five thousand acres of land.

The board adjourned until to-morrow at 10 o'clock a. m.

FRIDAY, *October* 28, 1825.

The board met this day, but there being no business prepared, it was adjourned until to-morrow at 10 o'clock a. m.

Edgar Macon, esq., United States attorney for the eastern district of Florida, attended the board this day under their order.

SATURDAY, *October* 29, 1825.

The board met this day pursuant to adjournment. Present: all the members.

Edgar Macon, esq., United States attorney for the eastern district of Florida, attended the board this day under their order.

The heirs of Thomas Fitch presented their memorial to this board, praying confirmation of title to one thousand one hundred acres of land situated on Diego plains. Ordered to be filed.

The heirs of Thomas Fitch presented their memorial to this board, praying confirmation of title to four hundred acres of land situated on the plains of Diego. Ordered to be filed.

The heirs of Thomas Fitch presented their memorial to this board, praying confirmation of title to three thousand acres of land situated on the plains and swamp of Diego, at a place known by the name of Chacaras. Ordered to be filed.

The heirs of Thomas Fitch presented their memorial to this board, praying confirmation of title to two hundred and fifty-five acres of land situated on Diego plains. Ordered to be filed.

The heirs of Thomas Fitch presented their memorial to this board, praying confirmation of title to four hundred acres of land situated on Diego plains. Ordered to be filed.

The wardens of the Roman Catholic church of St. Augustine *vs.* The United States, for one lot of land in St. Augustine on which the church and school-house stand. This came by its attorney, who obtained permission and amended the memorial thereof; and it appearing from the evidence produced therein that the same is a valid Spanish grant, the board confirmed the same.

Antelm Gay *vs.* The United States, for two lots of land situated in St. Augustine.

It appearing to the board that the above was a valid Spanish grant made to the original grantee, and regularly conveyed to claimant, the same was confirmed.

The board adjourned until Monday next at 10 o'clock a. m.

MONDAY, *October* 31, 1825.

The board met this day, but there being no business prepared, it was adjourned until to-morrow at 10 o'clock a. m.

Edgar Macon, esq., United States attorney for the eastern district of Florida, attended the board this day under their order.

List of claims received this day at the office of the Board of Land Commissioners, and are ordered to be filed.

Pedro Mestre's memorial for six hundred and forty acres of land, under the donation act, situated on the north of the head of the North river.

James Rouse's memorial for six hundred and forty acres of land, under the donation act, situated on the river St. Mary's.

McCully's memorial for six hundred and forty acres, under the donation act, situated on the river St. Mary's.

Thomas Prevatt's memorial for six hundred and forty acres of land, under the donation act, situated on the river St. Mary's.

Will. Haddock's memorial for six hundred and forty acres of land, under the donation act, situated on the river St. Mary's.

Joseph R. Prevatt's memorial for six hundred and forty acres of land, under the donation act, situated on the river St. Mary's.

Achilles Murat's memorial for one thousand two hundred acres of land, situated about nine miles south of St. Augustine.

Joseph Fenwick's memorial for six hundred acres of land situated on the north side of Trout creek.

Susannah Rollin's memorial for two hundred acres of land situated on the river Nassau, with a copy of concession by Governor White, dated December 6, 1799.

Charles Deshon's memorial for three hundred and fifty acres of land situated on St. John's river, with a copy of concession made to Waltero Drumer by Governor Quesada, dated April 5, 1793; also a plat and certificate of survey in favor of William Drummond, dated July 20, 1819, by George J. F. Clarke; also a deed of conveyance from William Drummond to Charles Deshon, dated May 6, 1822.

The heirs of Margaritta O'Neal's memorial for two tracts of land: one for nine caballerias and seven acres of land, or three hundred and seven acres of land, lying on Lansford creek, with a copy of plat and certificate of survey by Pedro Marrot, dated April 16, 1792; and the other for seven caballerias and ten acres of land, or two hundred and forty-three and a third acres, lying on Lansford creek, with a copy of plat and certificate of survey by Pedro Marrot, dated April 17, 1792; also a royal title to the said Margaritta O'Neal, dated March 13, 1807, by Governor White.

The board adjourned until to-morrow at 10 o'clock a. m.

TUESDAY, *November* 1, 1825.

The board met this day, but there being no business prepared, the same was adjourned until to-morrow at 10 o'clock a. m.

Edgar Macon, esq., United States attorney for the eastern district of Florida, attended the board this day under their order.

WEDNESDAY, *November* 2, 1825.

The board met this day, but there being no business prepared, the same was adjourned until to-morrow at 10 o'clock a. m.

Edgar Macon, esq., United States attorney for the eastern district of Florida, attended the board this day under their order.

THURSDAY, *November* 3, 1825.

The board met this day pursuant to adjournment. Present: the Hons. Davis Floyd and Wm. H. Allen.

Edgar Macon, esq., United States attorney for the eastern district of Florida, attended the board this day under their order.

Blake Williamson, through Wm. H. Allen, esq., presented his memorial to this board for six hundred and forty acres of land situated on the river Nassau, in the county of Duval; and the said Wm. H. Allen, esq., having declared that he received said memorial from the claimant, who resides in the country, previous to November 1, 1825, the same was therefore ordered to be filed.

On motion, the following claims, viz: William P. Yonge, for five hundred acres; and the same, for four hundred and eighty acres of land, confirmed by the board August 27, 1825, were reopened, and permission given to amend the memorials thereof, and they were reconfirmed to Henry Yonge, the original grantee.

The following claims were, after due examination, submitted, viz:

George J. F. Clarke, for ten thousand acres of land; and same, for four thousand five hundred acres of land.

The board adjourned until to-morrow at 10 o'clock a. m.

FRIDAY, *November* 4, 1825.

The board met this day pursuant to adjournment. Present: all the members.

Edgar Macon, esq., United States attorney for the eastern district of Florida, attended the board this day under their order.

The following claims were, after due examination, submitted, viz:

George J. F. Clarke, two thousand acres of land; and same, for two thousand acres of land.

Full and sufficient testimony having been taken in the following claims as to the occupation and cultivation thereof, they were confirmed to claimants, viz:

Peter Sevelly, one hundred and fifty acres of land on Long bay, about seven miles to the northwest of St. Augustine.

William and John Lofton, three hundred acres of land on the north of Julington creek, St. John's river.

George Henning, two hundred acres on Bell's river, near Row's bluff.

John Wingate, two hundred acres on Lofton's swamp, Nassau river.

James Plummer, three hundred acres on the north of Julington creek, St. John's river.

Thomas Moy, three hundred and fifty acres at Row's bluff, on Bell's river.

Martha Dell, four hundred and fifty acres on St. Mary's river.

William McCully, three hundred acres high up St. Mary's river.

Joseph Prevatt, four hundred acres on Turner's swamp, St. Mary's river.

Thomas Prevatt, five hundred and fifty acres on St. Mary's river.

Edward Dixon, one hundred acres on Pigeon creek, St. Mary's river.

George Hartley, four hundred acres on Old Field branch, Julington creek, St. John's river.

Frederick Hartley, six hundred acres on Old Field branch, Julington creek, St. John's river.

The board adjourned until to-morrow at 10 o'clock a. m.

Saturday, *November* 5, 1825.

The board met this day pursuant to adjournment, but no business being prepared, the same was adjourned.

Edgar Macon, esq., United States attorney for the eastern district of Florida, attended the board this day under their order.

Tuesday, *November* 8, 1825.

The board met this day, but no business being prepared, the same was adjourned until to-morrow at 3 o'clock p. m.

Edgar Macon, esq., United States attorney for the eastern district of Florida, attended the board this day under their order.

Wednesday, *November* 9, 1825.

The board met this day pursuant to adjournment. Present: the Hons. D. Floyd and W. H. Allen.

Edgar Macon, esq., United States attorney for the eastern district of Florida, attended the board this day under their order.

Richard D. Curtis presented his bill to the board, amounting to twelve dollars, for carpenter's work, which was approved and ordered to be audited and certified.

Francis R. Sanchez was this day examined, on the part of the United States, in the claim of William Branning, for six hundred and forty acres of land.

The board adjourned until to-morrow at 3 o'clock p. m.

Thursday, *November* 10, 1825.

The board met this day pursuant to adjournment. Present: the Hons. Davis Floyd and W. H. Allen.

Edgar Macon, esq., United States attorney for the eastern district of Florida, attended the board this day under their order.

On motion, the following claims were taken up, and permission given to amend the memorials thereof, and James Bradley, Lewis P. Fatio, and Horatio S. Dexter were examined as witnesses therein; after which they were submitted, viz: Francis R. Sanchez, five hundred acres; Simeon Sanchez, four hundred acres; John Sanchez, four hundred acres.

Permission being given, the following claim was presented to the board for adjudication, when Francis R. Sanchez was examined therein; and the board being satisfied as to the occupation and cultivation of the land according to law, reported the same to Congress, viz: David Scurry, for 640 acres of land situated on the south side of St. John's river.

The board adjourned until to-morrow at 3 o'clock p. m.

Friday, *December* 2, 1825.

The board met this day. Present: the Hons. Davis Floyd and W. H. Allen.

Pedro Mestre *vs.* The United States, for six hundred and forty acres of land situated on the north of the head of the North river, under the donation act. This case was taken up, and it appearing by the evidence adduced therein that claimant was entitled to said land, the board confirmed the same.

The board adjourned.

Wednesday, *December* 14, 1825.

The board met this day. Present: the Hons. Davis Floyd and William H. Allen.

Joseph Delespine *vs.* The United States, for ninety-two thousand one hundred and sixty acres of land. This case being called, was, after due consideration, reported to Congress for confirmation.

The following claims were also reported for confirmation, viz: John W. Simonton, for an island called Key West (Cayo Hueso) or Thompson's island; Catalina Hijuelos, for two thousand acres situated at a place called Big Grove.

The following claim was, after due consideration, rejected by the board, viz: Peter Mitchell, for himself and others, for three thousand five hundred acres of land at a place called Volusia, St. John's river.

The board adjourned until to-morrow at 10 o'clock a. m.

Thursday, *December* 15, 1825.

The board met this day. Present: all the members.

Nicholas Estefanopoly *vs.* The United States, for two thousand five hundred acres. This case being called, was, after due consideration, ordered to be reported to Congress for their determination.

Zephaniah Kingsley *vs.* The United States, for two thousand acres of land. The board in this case having ascertained that this claim is covered by a British grant, the same is ordered to be reported to Congress.

The following claims were called up, and it appearing to the board that they are valid Spanish grants, they are therefore reported to Congress for confirmation, viz: Zephaniah Kingsley, for two thousand acres; Zephaniah Kingsley, for two thousand six hundred and eleven acres; Archibald Clark, for eighty thousand acres of land.

The board adjourned until to-morrow at 10 o'clock a. m.

Friday, *December* 16, 1825.

The board met this day pursuant to adjournment. Present: the Hons. Davis Floyd and William H. Allen.

The following claims were this day reported to Congress for confirmation, viz: Teresa Rodriguez, for five thousand five hundred acres; Wiggins' estate, for twelve hundred acres; Sarah Fish's heirs, for ten thousand acres; Domingo Fernandez, for one thousand one hundred and fifty acres.

Susannah Cashen's claim, for one thousand and fifty acres of land situated on St. Mary's river, was taken up and confirmed by the board.

The board adjourned until to-morrow at 10 o'clock a. m.

MONDAY, *December* 19, 1825.

The board met this day. Present: all the members.

The following claims were this day confirmed by the board, viz: the heirs of Pedro R. de Cala, for five hundred acres; Davis Floyd, one thousand acres of land; Francis Pellicer, one thousand one hundred acres of land.

John Bolton *vs.* The United States, for two thousand acres of land situated in Turnbull's back swamp. The board having ascertained the above to be a valid Spanish grant made previous to January 24, 1818, report the same to Congress for confirmation.

There appearing no evidence before the board as to the actual occupation and cultivation of the following tracts previous to January 24, 1818, and July 17, 1821, they therefore reject the same, viz: Francis R. Sanchez, five hundred acres; Simeon Sanchez, four hundred acres; John Sanchez, four hundred acres of land situated on Hogtown creek, Alachua.

On motion, permission was given to amend the memorial in the following claim, viz: Francis de Medicis, for eighty-three and a third acres of land situated on St. John's river.

The board adjourned until to-morrow at 10 o'clock.

TUESDAY, *December* 20, 1825.

The board met this day pursuant to adjournment. Present: the Hons. Davis Floyd and W. H. Allen.

John B. Entralgo *vs.* The United States, for one thousand acres of land on the east side of the St. John's river, at a place called Rollstown. The board having ascertained this to be a valid Spanish grant made previous to January 24, 1818, do therefore report the same to Congress for confirmation.

On motion of claimant's attorney, permission was given to amend the memorial in the claim of Sarah Faulk, for two hundred and fifty acres of land, and to file two affidavits in the following claim, viz: George Branning, for six hundred and forty acres of land.

The board adjourned until to-morrow at 10 o'clock a. m.

THURSDAY, *December* 22, 1825.

The board met this day. Present: the Hons. Davis Floyd and William H. Allen.

The following claims being called, and the evidence produced therein being satisfactory to the board as to the occupation and cultivation thereof, confirmed the same, viz: Charles Love, for three hundred acres; Pedro Estopa, for fifteen and three-tenths acres.

Robert Miller *vs.* The United States, for an island situated between Jupiter and Indian rivers. The board having ascertained this claim to be undefined in quantity, and there appearing no evidence to prove the compliance of the conditions set forth in the concession thereof, do reject the same.

Permission was given to amend the memorial of John K. S. Holzendorf, for four hundred acres of land, by inserting "the heirs of Valentine Fitzpatrick, deceased," in place of said Holzendorf.

The board adjourned until to-morrow at 10 o'clock a. m.

FRIDAY, *December* 23, 1825.

The board met this day pursuant to adjournment. Present: the Hons. Davis Floyd and William H. Allen.

Full and sufficient testimony having been adduced in the following claims, the board confirmed the same, viz: Stephen M. Ingersoll, for one hundred acres of land situated north of St. Augustine; Stephen M. Ingersoll, one hundred acres of land situated in the Twelve-mile swamp; William Lain, two hundred and ten acres on Trout creek, a branch of St. John's; Nathaniel Wilds, three hundred acres on Lofton's creek, a branch of St. John's; Isaac Hendricks, two hundred acres on Pottsburg creek, St. John's river; Isaac Hendricks two hundred acres on south side of river St. John's, near the Cowford; Isaac Hendricks, five hundred acres on the north side of St. John's river, near Jacksonville; Cornelius Griffith's heirs, one hundred acres on the east side of one of the branches of Trout creek, St. John's river; the heirs of Valentine Fitzpatrick, for four hundred acres on Graham's swamp; the heirs of Valentine Fitzpatrick, twenty-five acres on Sam's hammock, Matanzas river; William Gardner, one hundred and fifty acres on the south side of the river St. John's; S. Clarke, a lot of land in Fernandina; John Dixon, one hundred and thirty acres, river St. Mary's, at Faulk's swamp; Francis Ferreira, fourteen acres without the old lines, and about one and three-quarter mile north of the city of St. Augustine; John Houston, ninety-two acres on Talbot island; Polly Lewis, six hundred and forty acres, under the donation act, on the east side of Miami river, near Key Biscaino; John D. Braddock six hundred and forty acres, under the donation act, in the county of Duval, on the road from Rose's bluff; John Faulk's heirs for three hundred and fifty acres, Mulberry Grove, St. John's river.

Permission having been given to amend the memorials in the following claims, and claimants having produced sufficient testimony therein, they were confirmed, viz: Isaac Carter, three hundred and fifty acres on river Nassau; Ferdinand D. McDonell, eight hundred acres on Matanzas river; William Fitzpatrick, four hundred and forty acres, Cedar Point, north side St. John's river.

The board adjourned until to-morrow at 10 o'clock a. m.

SATURDAY, *December* 24, 1825.

The board met this day pursuant to adjournment. Present: all the members.

The following claims were this day taken up and confirmed by the board, viz:

Elijah Higginbottom, three hundred and fifty acres on Little St. Mary's river; Joseph Higginbottom, three hundred acres on Spell's swamp, Nassau river; Pablo Sabaté, two hundred acres at St. Diego; heirs of Elizabeth Cain, two hundred and fifty acres east side of river St. John's, north of Picolata fort; Lazaro Ortega, eighty-eight acres, North river and Guana creek.

Permission was given to amend the memorial of James Smith's heirs for two hundred and fifty acres of land, by inserting "John Tharp's heirs" in place of Smith's heirs, and the board confirmed the same.

The board adjourned until Monday next, the 26th instant.

TUESDAY, December 27, 1825.

The board met this day. Present: all the members.

The following claims under the donation act were taken up and confirmed by the board, if on public lands, viz:

Jonathan Lewis, six hundred and forty acres, river Miami, near Cape Florida; Frankee Lewis, six hundred and forty acres, New river, near Cape Florida; Mrs. Hagens, six hundred and forty acres, river Miami, near Cape Florida; James Hagens, six hundred and forty acres, river Miami, near Cape Florida.

Sufficient testimony being adduced as to the occupation and cultivation of the land previous to July 17, 1821, the board, therefore, report the following claims to Congress under the donation act, viz:

John Oliver, six hundred and forty acres situated on the east side of Dunn's lake, St. John's river; José Papy, six hundred and forty acres, east of Picolata fort, St. John's river; Andres Papy, six hundred and forty acres, south of St. Augustine, on Moses' creek; Henry Heartley, six hundred and forty acres, St. John's county.

The following claims were rejected by the board, viz:

Seymour Pickett, six hundred and forty acres, and Lewis Guibert, six hundred and forty acres of land.

The board adjourned until to-morrow at four o'clock p. m.

WEDNESDAY, December 28, 1825.

The board met this day pursuant to adjournment. Present: all the members.

The following claims being prepared, were confirmed by the board:

John Middleton, two half and one lot in the town of Fernandina, Amelia island; same, for a lot in said town.

The board having examined the following claim, reported the same to Congress, viz:

George Murray, for an island called Cayo Hueso or Thompson's island.

The board adjourned until to-morrow at 4 o'clock p. m.

THURSDAY, December 29, 1825.

The board met this day pursuant to adjournment. Present: all the members.

It being ascertained that the following individuals had grants before the board for 640 acres, under the donation act, rejected the said 640 acres, and confirmed to them as follows, viz:

David Scurry, 300 acres; William Nelson, 350 acres; William Sparkman, 300 acres; Andrew Brennan, 400 acres.

The following claims were also confirmed by the board on actual settlement and cultivation:

Joseph Hagens, 200 acres on Julington creek; Hartwell Leath, 200 acres, Big Creek; Jno. Dixon, 200 acres, St. Mary's river; Thomas, 257 acres, Live-oak landing; James Bradley, 250 acres, Cedar swamp; Jehu Mezells, 200 acres, St. Mary's river.

The following claims were, after due consideration, rejected by the board, viz:

Frederick Hartley, 400 acres; Thomas Higginbottom, 200 acres; Charles Hovey, 400 acres; N. Wilds, 184 acres; Maxey Dell, 700 acres; Stephen Eubanks, 450; Theophilus Woods, sen., 370 acres; James Woods, 75 acres.

The board adjourned until to-morrow at 4 o'clock p. m.

FRIDAY, December 30, 1825.

The board met this day pursuant to adjournment. Present: all the members.

The following accounts were presented to the board, and were, after due investigation, ordered to be passed and certified, viz:

Joseph M. Sanchez, for $518 for house rent.

Waters Smith, United States marshal, for services, &c., $239.

Francis J. Fatio, for contingent expenses of said board, $113.

The honorable Davis Floyd moved to dismiss all the cases which have been translated and laid over, from time to time, for testimony; which motion was overruled by the majority of the board.

The board adjourned *sine die*.

DAVIS FLOYD.
W. H. ALLEN.

Attest:

F. J. FATIO, *S. B. L. C.*

THIRD SESSION.

No. 2.—See REPORT No. 1.

José Sanchez vs. The United States. For two hundred and ten acres of land.

MEMORIAL.

To the honorable the commissioners appointed to ascertain claims and titles to lands in East Florida:

The petition of José Sanchez respectfully showeth: That your memorialist claims title to a tract of land consisting of two hundred and ten acres, situated upon the west bank of Hillsborough, or south Mosquito river, to the south of the old town of Smeyrand north by an artificial canal called Gabardy canal, and fronting upon Hillsborough river aforesaid. A copy of plat and certificate of survey is herewith exhibited, dated January 22, 1818, marked Z; which title your memorialist derives from a royal title made to *Rafael* Andrew, dated June 2, 1817, by Governor Coppinger, in virtue of the royal order of March 29, 1815, who sold the same to Fernando de la Maza Arredondo, jr., by conveyance dated April 2, 1820, who conveyed the same to your memorialist by deed dated March 25, 1822, exhibited, &c., marked A. And your memorialist further showeth that he is legally seized and possessed of said lands; that he is a citizen of the United States and resident of East Florida, and has been ever since the cession of the same to the United States. He prays confirmation of title, &c. All of which is submitted, &c.

JOSÉ SANCHEZ.

[Here follows the translation of the royal title made by Governor Coppinger to Rafael Andrew of the 210 acres, dated July 2, 1817, in virtue of the royal order of 1815.]

[Here follows the translation of the plat and certificate of survey of the land by Robert McHardy, dated January 22, 1818.]

[Here follows a deed of conveyance from Fernando de la Maza Arredondo to claimant. By said deed it appears that Andrew conveyed the 210 acres to Arredondo, reference being made to the public archives for the conveyance.]

DECREE BY THE BOARD.

In this case the claimant exhibited a royal title for the land described in his memorial made by Governor Coppinger to one Rafael Andrew July 2, 1817, in virtue of the royal order of March 29, 1815; a certificate of survey and plat made by Robert McHardy January 22, 1818; a conveyance for the said land from Andrew to Fernando de la Maza Arredondo, and a deed from Arredondo to him. The title of the claimant is confirmed, so far as the United States is concerned. April 11.

No. 1.—See REPORT No. 1.

Robert McHardy's trustee vs. The United States. For one thousand acres of land.

MEMORIAL.

To the honorable the commissioners appointed to ascertain claims and titles to lands in East Florida:

The memorial of John Rodman, assignee of all the estate, real and personal, of Robert McHardy, deceased, in trust for the benefit of his creditors, respectfully showeth: That your memorialist claims title, as the assignee of the said McHardy, to a tract of land consisting of 1,000 acres, situated at Tomoka, bounded as follows: on the north by lands of the heirs of James Ormond, on the east by the river Tomoka, on the south by lands of John Burch, and on the west by the public road; which said land was granted to the said Robert McHardy, in full title, July 3, 1815, by Governor Estrada, founded upon a previous grant made to him September 5, 1808, in virtue of the royal order of October 29, 1790. And your memorialist further showeth that the said Robert McHardy remained in possession of the said land until his death, on December 12, 1822; that said land was much cultivated by him, and very valuable buildings erected thereon; that he was a resident inhabitant of Florida at the time of the cession of the country to the United States. In confirmation of the title of the said McHardy to the aforesaid land, your memorialist herewith presents a certified copy of the absolute title and grant from the Spanish government, dated July 3, 1815. The deed of assignment from the said McHardy to your memorialist of all his estate, real and personal, in trust for the benefit of his creditors, is dated December 1, 1822, and is recorded in the office of the clerk of the county of St. John's. St. Augustine, October 23, 1823.

JOHN RODMAN.

N. B.—The original survey of the said land has been lost.

[Here follows the translation of the royal title made by Governor Estrada to Robert McHardy of the 1,000 acres, dated July 3, 1815, in virtue of the royal order of 1790.]

DECREE BY THE BOARD.

In this case the claimant filed a royal title made to Robert McHardy for the land claimed by Governor Estrada, July 3, 1815. It appearing to the satisfaction of the board that the grant was made in conformity with the Spanish laws and royal orders previous to January 24, 1818, the land is confirmed to the claimant as assignee of Robert McHardy. April 11.

No. 3.—See REPORT No. 1.

John Christopher vs. The United States. For five hundred acres of land.

MEMORIAL.

To the honorable the commissioners appointed to ascertain claims and titles to lands in East Florida:

The memorial of John Christopher, by his attorney, Farquhar Bethune, respectfully showeth: That your memorialist claims title to a tract of land consisting of five hundred acres, situated on the river Nassau, and contained within the following lines and boundaries: the first line runs south 43° west, beginning at a pine tree marked with a cross on the banks of St. Juana creek, and terminating at another pine with the same mark, and is in length one hundred and twenty-nine chains; the second line runs south 32° east, beginning at the same pine and ends at another on the edge of a marsh in the river Nassau, and is in measure forty chains; the front runs partly on the edge of said marsh, and partly on the bank of St. Juana creek, which divides this tract from the lands of Francis Deaz Teran; which title your memorialist derives from a grant originally made to his deceased father, Spicer Christopher, under the orders of Governor Quesada, by Don Pedro Marrot, judge commissioned for that purpose, February 15, 1792, and surveyed by Eastlake, as appears from a certified copy of their certificate, hereunto annexed, and marked A, in pursuance of the royal order of October 29, 1790, and for which tract the full or royal title annexed, marked B, was obtained by said Spicer from Governor White, under date of April 8, 1809, and which tract your memorialist inherits as one of the co-heirs of said Spicer Christopher, deceased. Your memorialist further showeth that he is now in actual possession of said land, and was so at the time of the cession, and for many years preceding; that he is a citizen of the United States and resident on the said tract, now in Duval county. All of which is respectfully submitted.

JOHN CHRISTOPHER,
Per his attorney, FARQ. BETHUNE.

[Here follows the translation of the certificate and plat of survey by Pedro Marrot, commissioned judge for the distribution of lands, of 15 caballerias, (500 acres,) dated February 15, 1792, surveyed for Spicer Christopher.]

[Here follows the translation of the royal title by Governor White to Spicer Christopher for the land, dated April 8, 1809, in virtue of the royal order of 1790.]

DECREE BY THE BOARD.

The claimant exhibited a royal title for the land claimed, made by Governor White, April 8, 1809, to Spicer Christopher, deceased, from whom the claimant derives title by devise; the said devise is on file in this office, in the case of ——— ——— vs. The United States. The title of the claimant is confirmed. April 11.

No. 4.—See REPORT No. 1.

Farquhar Bethune vs. *The United States. For eleven hundred acres of land.*

MEMORIAL.

To the honorable the commissioners appointed to ascertain claims and titles to lands in East Florida:

The memorial of Farquhar Bethune respectfully showeth: That your memorialist claims title to a tract of land consisting of eleven hundred acres of land, situated on the Halifax river, Mosquito, bounded as follows: on the north by lands granted to Samuel Williams; on the east by the river Halifax; on the south and west by vacant lands at the time of the survey; which title your memorialist derives from a grant made to him by Governor White September 5, 1805, in lieu of an equal number of acres granted to him August 5, 1803, and retroceded to government by your memorialist for the above tract, and which grant was made to him in virtue of the royal order of October 29, 1790; and for which tract, after complying with the conditions imposed by said royal order, your memorialist obtained the title in fee simple, hereto annexed, dated March 4, 1814, granted by Governor Kindelan. Your memorialist further showeth that he is now in actual possession of said lands, and was at the time of the cession, and from the year 1805; that he is an inhabitant of Florida and a resident of Amelia island, Duval county; the survey of said tract by John Purcell is also annexed to this memorial. All of which is respectfully submitted, &c.

FARQUHAR BETHUNE.

[Here follows the translation of the certificate and plat of survey by Juan Purcell of 1,100 acres of land, surveyed for claimant, dated May 18, 1806.]

[Here follows the translation of the royal title made by Governor Kindelan to claimant for the 1,100 acres, dated March 4, 1814, in virtue of the royal order of 1790.]

DECREE BY THE BOARD.

A royal grant made to claimant for the land claimed by Governor Kindelan March 4, 1814, and a certificate and plat of survey by John Purcell May 18, 1806, being submitted as evidence of title, the claim is confirmed. April 11.

No. 5.—See REPORT No. 1.

Widow and heirs of Bagley vs. *The United States. For three hundred acres of land.*

MEMORIAL.

To the honorable the commissioners appointed to ascertain claims and titles to lands in East Florida:

The petition of Anna Hogans, widow, and the other heirs of Francis Bagley, deceased, respectfully showeth: That your memorialist claims title to a tract of land consisting of three hundred acres, situated on the south side of the river St. John's; on the north by said river; south by public lands; east by lands granted to Reuben Hogans; and west by lands granted to William Hendricks; which title your memorialist derives from a royal grant made to Francis Bagley in 1816 by Governor Coppinger, in virtue of the royal order of 1790; which title your memorialist derives from having married the widow of said Francis Bagley. And your memorialist further showeth that he is in actual possession of said lands, and was so at the time of the cession; that he is a citizen of the United States and resident of the Territory of Florida.

A. BELLAMY, *Attorney for Memorialists.*

[Here follows the translation of the royal title made by Governor Coppinger to Francisco Bagley of the three hundred acres, dated December 24, 1817, in virtue of the royal order of 1790.]

[Here follows the translation of the certificate and plat of survey by George Clarke of the three hundred acres surveyed for Anna Hogans, widow of Bagley, dated June 24, 1818.]

DECREE BY THE BOARD.

A royal title made by Governor Coppinger to Francis Bagley, deceased, under whom the claimants derive their title to the land in question, dated December 24, 1817, and a certificate of survey and plat by George J. F. Clarke, having been produced as evidence of title, and being satisfactory, the board confirm the title.   April 12.

No. 6.—See Report No. 1.

Prudence Plummer vs. The United States.   For three hundred and fifty and one-third acres of land.

MEMORIAL.

To the honorable the commissioners appointed to ascertain claims and titles to lands in East Florida:

The memorial of Prudence Plummer, widow of Daniel Plummer, deceased, respectfully showeth: That your memorialist claims title to a tract of land known by the name of Montpelier, consisting of three hundred and fifty and one-third acres, situated on the east side of the river St. John's, the boundaries of which said tract commence at a gum tree marked with a cross on the side of a cove or creek of the said river, and terminates where a pine tree is marked with the same sign; this line being bounded by the lands of Isaac Bowden, measuring 56 chains; the second line runs 22° east, beginning at the aforesaid pine tree and terminating with the other mark before mentioned, measuring 180 chains; the third line runs north 70° west, beginning at the aforesaid pine tree and terminating by a cypress tree marked with a cross on the shore of the river St. John's, this line being bounded by lands of Ann Travers, measuring 41 chains; and which said tract of land was originally granted to one Samuel Eastlake, in the year 1792, in virtue of the royal order of October 29, 1790; but he not having fulfilled the conditions required, your memorialist took possession of the said land, and the ownership and possession thereof were confirmed to your memorialist by a decree of the Spanish government in East Florida under Governor White, September 17, 1800, as appear by the said decree, a copy of which is herewith presented. And your memorialist further showeth that she has ever since been in quiet possession of the said land, and cultivated and improved it and now actually resides on it; that she was an inhabitant resident on said land at the time of the cession of Florida to the United States.   All which is respectfully submitted, &c.   St. Augustine, October 23, 1823.

PRUDENCE PLUMMER,
By her attorney JOHN RODMAN.

[Here follows the translation of the certificate and plat of survey of ten caballerias and seventeen acres of land (350 acres) by Pedro Marrot surveyed for Samuel Eastlake, dated January 6, 1792.]
[Here follows a judicial proceeding, by which it appears that the late government confirmed to Mrs. Plummer her right to the land.   Said proceeding is dated September 7, 1800.]

DECREE BY THE BOARD.

The claimant in this case exhibited a certificate and plat of survey made by Pedro Marrot to Samuel Eastlake for the land claimed, dated January 6, 1792.   By a proceeding which was also exhibited, it appeared that the claimant took possession of the land, which was confirmed to her by a decree of the government.   Being of opinion that this claim would have been valid had Florida remained a dominion of Spain, we confirm the title.   April 12.

No. 7.—See Report No. 1.

Charles Seton vs. The United States.   For six hundred acres of land.

MEMORIAL.

To Messrs. Alexander Hamilton, W. W. Blair, and Davis Floyd, land commissioners, now sitting in St. Augustine, East Florida:

Memorial of Charles Seton, merchant and planter, residing in Fernandina, stating his right to the following tract of land granted by authority of his Catholic Majesty Ferdinand VII.

Grant No. 3. Royal titles in fee simple for 600 acres of land in Sample swamp, on the river Nassau, as per plat annexed.   The first line commencing at a pine tree, running south 22° east, 100 chains, to a pine; second line, from that south 68° west, 60 chains, to a pine; third line, from that north 22° west, 100 chains, to a pine; fourth line, from that 68° east, 60 chains, until it strikes the first line; vacant land all around.   Granted by Governor Coppinger, September 13, 1816, for my services during the revolution of 1812 and 1813, in which I was dangerously wounded.   A full grant without any conditions.   Fernandina, October 15, 1823.

CHARLES SETON.

[Here follows the translation of the certificate and plat of survey by G. J. F. Clarke of the six hundred acres, dated May 18, 1816.]
[Here follows the translation of the royal title made by Governor Coppinger to claimant of the six hundred acres, dated September 13, 1816, in virtue of the royal order of 1815.]

DECREE BY THE BOARD.

In this case the claimant exhibited a certificate and plat of survey for the land described in his memorial, dated May 18, 1816; also a royal title made by Governor Coppinger to him on September 13, 1816, in virtue of the royal order of 1815.   We ascertain this to be a valid Spanish grant, and confirm to the claimant the title thereof.   April 12.

No. 8.—See Report No. 1.

John Floyd's heirs vs. The United States. For two hundred acres of land.

MEMORIAL.

To the honorable the commissioners appointed to ascertain claims and titles to lands in East Florida:

The memorial of Catharine Hall, Margaret Floyd, Mary D. Floyd, John Floyd, and Andrew Floyd, children and heirs of John Floyd, otherwise called José Juaneda, deceased, respectfully showeth: That your memorialists claim title to a tract of two hundred acres of land situated on the North river, about twenty miles from the city of St. Augustine, bounded as follows: the first line runs north 65°, beginning at a pine tree marked with the sign of the cross, on the border of the marsh of the North river, and terminates at a stake with the same mark at the border of the marsh of Guana creek, containing 75 chains; the second line runs south 75° west, beginning at a stake marked with the same sign, planted at the border of a marsh of Guana creek, and terminates at a pine tree with the same sign, at the border of a marsh of the North river, containing 70 chains, as appears by the certificate of survey and plat, dated May 15, 1793, a copy of which is herewith presented. The said tract of land was granted by Governor Quesada on February 1, 1793, to Augustine Buyck, under the royal order of October 29, 1790, and by the said Augustine Buyck transferred to the said José Juaneda on April 30, 1799, the father of your memorialists; and the said land was held and cultivated by your memorialists' father until his death, about five years ago, and since his death has been in the uninterrupted possession of your memorialists, who were resident inhabitants of East Florida at the time of the cession of Florida to the United States. In confirmation of the title of your memorialists the following documents are herewith presented:

1. Grant from Governor Quesada, dated February 1, 1793.
2. Transfer by Governor White of the land to José Juaneda, April 30, 1799.
3. Survey and plat.

All which is respectfully submitted. St. Augustine, October 23, 1823.

J. RODMAN, *Attorney for the Memorialists.*

[Here follows the translation of the concession by Governor Quesada of the land to Augustine Buyck, dated February 1, 1793.]

[Here follows the translation of the certificate and plat of survey by Pedro Marrot of six caballerias, (equal to 200 acres,) surveyed for Augustine Buyck, dated May 15, 1793.]

[Here follows the translation of the permission given by Governor White to Augustine Buyck to transfer the 200 acres to José Juaneda, dated April 30, 1799.]

DECREE BY THE BOARD.

The claimants, as heirs of John Floyd, deceased, (alias José Juaneda,) produced to the board the grant to Augustine Buyck for the land claimed, dated February 1, 1793, together with a certificate and plat of survey by Marrot. Buyck, by permission of Governor White, transferred the land to the father of claimants April 30, 1799. The title is confirmed. April 12.

No. 9.—See Report No. 1.

Robert Pritchard's heirs vs. The United States. For four hundred and fifty acres of land.

MEMORIAL.

To the honorable the commissioners appointed to ascertain claims and titles to lands in East Florida:

The memorial of James Hall and Eleanor Hall, his wife, formerly wife of Robert Pritchard, deceased, John Creighton and Mary Creighton, daughter of the said Robert Pritchard, Ann Stallings, widow of Elias Stallings, also daughter of the said Robert Pritchard, Robert Pritchard, son of the said Robert Pritchard, and Amelia Pritchard, daughter of the said Robert Pritchard, respectfully showeth: That your memorialists, the said James Hall and Eleanor Hall, his wife, were residents in Florida, and your other memorialists in the States of Georgia and South Carolina, at the period of the cession of Florida to the United States; that your memorialists, James Hall and Eleanor Hall, and Ann Stallings, are now actual residents in East Florida, and your other memorialists in the United States; that your memorialists claim title to a tract of land consisting of four hundred and fifty acres, situated in Jacksonville, comprising the town of Jacksonville, on the west side of the river St. John's, in the county of Duval, formerly called the ferry of St. Nicholas, which said tract of land is part of a grant from the Spanish government, made in virtue of the royal order of October 29, 1790, by Governor Queseda to the said Robert Pritchard, on January 3, 1791, as appears by a certified copy of the original grant herewith presented. Your memorialists further show that immediately after the aforesaid grant was delivered a regular survey of the same was duly made, but which survey has been lost in consequence of the troubles which took place in this country in the years 1811 and 1812; the making of the said survey and the running of the lines can, however, be proved by living witnesses residing near the said tract of land. That the said Robert Pritchard, immediately on receiving the grant in the year 1791, took possession of said land, planted it, and erected buildings thereon, and the agents of the heirs, under their authority, remained in possession of the same until compelled by the troubles and insurrection in the country in 1811 and 1812 to quit the same, and that since then they have been unlawfully kept out of possession by different persons, some of whom are now on the premises. All of which is respectfully submitted. St Augustine, October 23, 1823.

JOHN RODMAN, *Attorney for Memorialists.*

[Here follows the translation of a grant by Governor Quesada of the land, dated January 3, 1791.]

TERRITORY OF FLORIDA, *St. John's County:*

Personally appeared before me John Jones, who, being duly sworn, deposeth and saith, that twenty years ago or upwards he was well acquainted with Robert Pritchard, and that one Lain settled a tract of land for Robert Pritchard, on which Zachariah Hogans now lives, and that Lain settled said tract for the express purpose to fulfil the conditions of the proclamation of the Spanish government.

JOHN JONES.

Sworn to before me this 19th June, 1824.

SAMUEL FAIRBANKS, J. P.

TERRITORY OF FLORIDA, <i>St. John's County</i>:

Personally appeared before me, Samuel Fairbanks, justice of the peace, Joseph Hogans, who, being duly sworn, deposeth and saith that, in the year 1803 or 1804, he knew John Joseph Lain did cultivate a certain tract of land for Robert Pritchard, deceased, said to have been a part of the tract of land granted him as his headrights, now in possession of Lewis Hogans.

JOSEPH HOGANS.

Sworn to and subscribed before me this 19th June, 1824.

SAMUEL FAIRBANKS, J. P.

TERRITORY OF FLORIDA, <i>St. John's County</i>:

Personally appeared before me, Samuel Fairbanks, justice of the peace for said county, James Plummer, who, being duly sworn, deposeth and saith that about three or four months ago Isaac Hendricks told this deponent that he, Isaac Hendricks, went to the Spanish office and took out two papers, and that he carried them both to George J. F. Clarke, and that Clarke picked out the papers that belonged to Hendricks, and that he, Hendricks, carried the other paper back to the office, not knowing what paper it was.

JAMES PLUMMER.

Sworn to and subscribed before me this 22d June, 1824.

SAMUEL FAIRBANKS, J. P.

TERRITORY OF FLORIDA, <i>St. John's County</i>:

Personally appeared before me, Samuel Fairbanks, justice of the peace, Daniel Hogans, who, being duly sworn, deposeth and saith that about eighteen or twenty years ago this deponent called at a place on the other side of St. John's river, near Jacksonville, and that a man by the name of Lain lived there, and said he was put there by Mr. Robert Pritchard, and that there was a small crop of corn on the place, and one or two small buildings; and about twenty years ago this deponent saith that his father showed him a tree which he told this deponent was the corner tree of Mr. Pritchard's tract, which answered with Vanever's late plat and survey on that place, which I saw at Jacksonville court in April last.

DANIEL HOGANS.

Sworn to and subscribed to this 23d June, 1824.

SAMUEL FAIRBANKS, J. P.

TERRITORY OF FLORIDA, <i>County of St. John's</i>:

Personally appeared before me, S. Fairbanks, justice of the peace for the said county, David Scurry, who, being duly sworn, deposeth and saith that in the year 1818 this deponent was in company with Isaac Hendricks, and he, Hendricks, told this deponent he had taken two plats out of the Spanish office of Pritchard and carried them to George J. F. Clarke, and Mr. Clarke gave him the one for the land this side the river St. John's, where said Hendricks lives. The plat for the other side he put back into the office, and told this deponent he had traced out his lines by Pritchard's plats, and he found everything to answer according to what he had been told; and found the stump of the corner tree near the garrison, on the river side, which the soldiers had cut down, a short leaf pine, and said he would hew a light wood post and set down at the corner. Hendricks wished to <i>know</i> whether this deponent thought if there was more land in the lines than the plat called for, whether the American law would take it from him, as the plat called for 215 acres, to the best of my recollection. Hendricks said he thought there were near 300 acres. Hendricks further told this deponent he had got all his papers in his own name, and that he could go on with his buildings in safety, and that Doctor Stiles had told him so to do, as he had more sense than half the men in Florida.

           ^{his}
DAVID ⋈ SCURRY.
      _{mark.}

Sworn to and subscribed this 24th June, 1824.

SAMUEL FAIRBANKS, J. P.

TERRITORY OF FLORIDA, <i>St. John's County</i>:

Personally appeared before me, S. Fairbanks, one of the justices of the peace for said county, Joseph Summerall, who, being duly sworn, deposeth and saith that he was well acquainted with the late Robert Pritchard when he was settled and cultivated a certain tract of land now in the possession of Isaac Hendricks, at the Old St. Nicholas, said to contain 650 acres, on both sides of the river.

JOSEPH SUMMERALL.

Sworn to and subscribed before me this 19th day of June, 1824.

SAMUEL FAIRBANKS, J. P.

TERRITORY OF FLORIDA, <i>County of St. John's</i>:

Personally appeared before me, S. Fairbanks, Joseph Hogans, who, being duly sworn, deposeth and saith that he was acquainted with the late Robert Pritchard when he was settled on and cultivated a certain tract of land now in the possession of Isaac Hendricks, at the Old St. Nicholas, said to contain 650 acres, on both sides of the river.

JOSEPH HOGANS.

Sworn and subscribed to before me this 19th June, 1824.

SAMUEL FAIRBANKS, J. P.

DECREE BY THE BOARD.

The board having ascertained that the foregoing claim of Pritchard's heirs was a valid one under the late Spanish government, they therefore confirm it to the heirs aforesaid.   April 12.

No. 10.—See Report No. 1.

Teresa Marshall's heirs vs. The United States.   For five hundred and thirty-three and a third acres of land.

MEMORIAL.

To the honorable the commissioners appointed to ascertain claims and titles to lands in East Florida:

The memorial of Eliza Burnett, for herself and the other heirs of Teresa Marshall, deceased, respectfully showeth: That your memorialist, as one of the heirs of the said Teresa Marshall, *as such heirs, and also in their own rights,* claims title in and to a certain tract or parcel of land containing five hundred and thirty-three and one-third acres, situated and being in East Florida aforesaid; that the said land was granted without any condition, and in absolute property, on the tenth day of October, in the year 1791, by the governor of East Florida to the said Teresa Marshall, then Teresa Hills, the widow and relict of one Lodowick Hills.   Your memorialist and the other heirs of the said Teresa Marshall, being children of the said Teresa Marshall by the said Lodowick Hills, as the headrights of her, said Teresa Marshall, then Teresa Hills, and of her children, and upon the joint property of herself and her said children, under the order of the King of Spain of October 29, 1790, as will more fully and at large appear by a reference to a certified copy of the original grant to the said Teresa Marshall, herewith submitted and filed, and marked exhibit A.   Your memorialist further showeth that the said tract of land was surveyed, by order of the government, by Josiah Dupont, a surveyor regularly authorized for that purpose, and under the superintendence and direction of one Pedro Marrot, an officer appointed by the government to make a special delivery of this land to the said Teresa Marshall, then Teresa Hills; and that the said tract or parcel of land was formally delivered to her, after the survey thereof by the said Pedro Marrot, on May 28, 1793, as will appear by a reference to the exhibit B, herewith submitted and filed.   Your memorialist further shows that the said tract or parcel of land is situated on the North river, on the west side thereof, about nine miles from the city of St. Augustine, and is known by the name of Santa Teresa, and has the following lines and dimensions, that is to say: the first line begins at the stake marked with a cross on the margin of the marsh of a branch called the Sweet Water branch, and runs north 78 degrees west, 45 chains, to another stake with the same mark; the second line runs thence north 32 degrees east, 25 chains, to a live-oak marked with a cross; the said two lines were, at the time of the said survey of the said land, bounded by vacant lands; the third line runs from the said live-oak north 58 degrees west, 62 chains, to a pine also marked with a cross, and was bounded at the time of survey by lands of one Roque Leonardy; the fourth runs south 10 degrees east, 87 chains, to another pine marked with a cross; the fifth line runs thence south 37 degrees east, 43 chains, to a pine marked with a cross; the sixth line runs thence north 78 degrees east, 53 chains, to another pine marked also with a cross, which said last-mentioned pine is on the margin of the said Sweet Water branch; all which will more fully and distinctly appear by a reference to a copy of the original plat of the survey thereof, being part of exhibit B. Your memorialist further shows that the said Teresa Marshall occupied and cultivated the said land for many years after the grant thereof, and that she departed this life about the year ——, leaving your memorialist and her other children her heirs.   Your memorialist further shows that she and the other children of the said Teresa Marshall were, before and at the time of the cession of this Territory to the United States, and are now, inhabitants and settlers of East Florida; and that the said Teresa Marshall was, when the said land was granted to her as aforesaid, and at the time of her death, a resident and settler of East Florida, and a subject of the King of Spain.   Wherefore, your memorialist prays a confirmation of the title of the heirs of the said Teresa Marshall in and to the said tract of land and its appurtenances, conformably to the acts of Congress in such cases made and provided.

ELIZA BURNETT,
By JOHN DRYSDALE, *her Attorney.*

[Here follows the translation of a concession by Governor Quesada of the land, dated October 10, 1791, to Teresa Marshall.]

[Here follows the translation of certificate and plat of survey by Pedro Marrot of sixteen caballerias, (equal to 533⅓ acres,) dated May 28, 1793, surveyed for Teresa Marshall.]

DECREE BY THE BOARD.

The claimants, as heirs of Teresa Marshall, deceased, produced in evidence an unconditional grant for the land described in their memorial to this board, made by Governor Quesada to the aforesaid Teresa Marshall, dated October 10, 1791; also a certificate and plat of survey of the same.   In consideration whereof, we confirm the same.   April 12.

No. 11.—See Report No. 1.

John Houston vs. The United States.   For one hundred acres of land.

MEMORIAL.

To the honorable the commissioners appointed to ascertain claims and titles to lands in East Florida:

The petition of John Houston respectfully showeth: That your memorialist claims title to a tract of land consisting of one hundred acres, situated on the island of Talbot, bounded north and south by lands of your memorialist, east and west by marshes; which title your memorialist derives from a royal grant made to William Hendricks, June 13, 1809, by Governor White, in virtue of the royal order of 1790, who sold the same to Spicer Christopher, as will be seen by the royal grant which is herewith presented, who, by his last will, conveyed the same to your memorialist.   And your memorialist further showeth that he is in actual possession of said lands, and was so at the time of the cession; that he is a citizen of the United States and resident of the Territory of Florida.

A. BELLAMY, *Memorialist's Attorney.*

[Here follows the translation of the royal title made by Governor White to Spicer Christopher of the hundred acres, dated April 12, 1809; said title specifying that William Hendricks had ceded the land to Christopher.]

DECREE BY THE BOARD.

The royal title made by Governor White to Spicer Christopher, dated April 12, 1809, being submitted as evidence of title for the hundred acres, and being satisfactory, the board confirm the claim to Houston and his heirs.   April 12.

No. 12.—See REPORT No. 1.

Pedro R. de Cala vs. *The United States.   For two hundred acres.*

MEMORIAL.

To the honorable the commissioners appointed to ascertain claims and titles to lands in East Florida:

The petition of the heirs of Pedro R. de Cala respectfully showeth: That your memorialists claim title to a tract of land consisting of headrights of two hundred acres, situated on St. Diego swamp, at a place known by the name of Clarke's Rice Plantation, bounded on the north by lands of Francis Sanchez, deceased, and on the south by lands of Robert Andros, deceased, and on the east and west by vacant lands; which title your memorialists derive from a grant made to said Pedro R. de Cala by Governor White.   And your memorialists further show that the deceased, at the time of his death, was in actual possession of said lands; that he was a subject of Spain and resident of St. Augustine, November 10, 1823.

WILLIAM REYNOLDS, *for the heirs of P. R. de Cala.*

[Here follows the translation of a concession by Governor White of the land to Pedro R. de Cala, dated August 4, 1803.]

DECREE BY THE BOARD.

We find in this case that Governor White, on the memorial of Pedro R. de Cala, conceded to him the land formerly belonging to one Ellerbee; the concession bears date August 4, 1803.   We confirm the claim to the heirs of the aforesaid Cala.   April 13.

I hereby certify that it appears of record in my office that there was granted to John Ellerbee, on May 12, 1803, two hundred acres of land by Governor White, on the same conditions that the same land was previously granted to Thomas Ellerbee by Governor Quesada, October 20, 1791.

In testimony whereof, I have hereunto set my hand and seal of office, at the city of St. Augustine, [L. S.]   December 24, 1825.

WILLIAM REYNOLDS, *Keeper of the Public Archives.*

(Endorsed:)—"To be filed in the case of Cala, for 200 acres."

No. 13.—See REPORT No. 1.

Robert Hutchinson vs. *The United States.   For one hundred and fifty acres of land.*

MEMORIAL.

To the honorable the commissioners appointed to ascertain claims and titles to lands in East Florida:

The petition of Robert Hutchinson respectfully showeth: That your memorialist claims title to a tract of land consisting of one hundred and fifty acres, situated on the bank of Little St. Mary's river, at the first mount above the mouth of said river; which title your memorialist derives from a concession made to him September 11, 1811, by Governor Estrada, in virtue of—*a certified* copy of which concession is herewith presented, and dated as above.   And your memorialist further showeth that he is legally in possession of said lands; that he is a citizen of the United States and resident of Florida.   All of which is respectfully submitted, &c.

ROB'T HUTCHINSON.

[Here follows the translation of a certified copy of concession by Governor Estrada to claimant of the 150 acres of land, dated September 11, 1811.]

TERRITORY OF FLORIDA, *County of Duval:*

This day personally appeared before me Charles Hogans, and, being sworn, deposeth and saith that he is knowing to Mr. Robert Hutchinson improving a piece of land on St. Mary's river, about two miles above Little St. Mary's; and that he has cultivated the same, or that it has been done by his direction, for more than ten years past.

CHARLES HOGANS.

Sworn to and subscribed before me January 16, 1824.

WM. G. DAWSON, *J. P.*

DECREE BY THE BOARD.

The claimant submitted, as evidence of title, a certified copy of concession made to him by Governor Estrada, dated September 11, 1811, for the land claimed.   It was proven that he had cultivated the same for more than ten years.   We confirm the title.   April 13.

No. 14.—See Report No. 1.

E. Waterman's heirs vs. *The United States. For two hundred and sixty acres of land.*

MEMORIAL.

To the honorable the commissioners appointed to ascertain claims and titles to lands in East Florida:

The petition of Sarah Waterman, in behalf of herself and heirs of the estate of E. Waterman, showeth: That your memorialist claims title to a tract of land consisting of two hundred and sixty acres, on Bell's river, bounded on the northeast by Bell's river, on the south and west by lands of the said Waterman, and on the other side by lands vacant at the time of survey, as will appear by the plat thereof hereto annexed, and marked A; begins at a pine and runs thence south 39° west, 36 chains, to another pine; thence north 51° west, 75 chains, to another pine; thence 39° east, 36 chains, to an oak; thence in a direct line to the edge of Bell's river, and along the margin of said river to the first point; and which survey was made, February 5, 1816, by Geo. J. F. Clarke; which title your memorialist derives, in behalf as aforesaid, from a royal grant made to Joseph Howell by Governor Coppinger, in virtue of the royal order of October 29, 1790, who sold to the said E. Waterman in his lifetime; and that the said grant bears date February 22, 1816, and herewith filed, marked B. And your memorialist further showeth that she, in behalf of the heirs of said estate, is in actual possession of said lands; that she is a citizen of the United States and resident of Florida. All which is respectfully submitted.

ARCH'D CLARK, *Attorney for Ex. and heirs of E. Waterman.*

[Here follows the translation of the royal title made by Governor Coppinger to Joseph Howell, who afterwards sold his right to the 260 acres to Eleazer Waterman, as the said royal title sets forth, the title being dated February 22, 1816, and in virtue of the royal order of 1790.]

[Here follows the translation of the certificate and plat of survey of the 260 acres by Geo. J. F. Clarke, dated February 5, 1816.]

DECREE BY THE BOARD.

A royal title for the land claimed, made by Governor Coppinger to Eleazer Waterman, deceased, who obtained it from Joseph Howell, dated February 22, 1816; also a certificate and plat of survey of the same by G. J. F. Clarke, dated February 5, 1816, being produced by the heirs of the aforesaid Waterman, and being satisfactory, we confirm the title to claimants. April 14.

No. 15.—See Report No. 1.

John Addison vs. *The United States. For one thousand four hundred and fourteen acres of land.*

MEMORIAL.

To the honorable the commissioners appointed to ascertain claims and titles to lands in East Florida:

The petition of John Addison respectfully showeth: That your memorialist claims title to a tract of land consisting of one thousand four hundred and fourteen acres, situated on the river Tomoka, at a place called Carricfergus, to the southward of the city of St. Augustine, bounded on the north by lands of John Bunch, on the west by the public road, on the south by the lands of Gabl. William Perpall, and on the east by the river Tomoka; beginning at a pine marked A, thence north 25° east, 125 chains and 50 links, to a pine with the same mark; thence north 80° west, 85 chains, begins at a stake and ends at a pine with the same mark; thence north 75° east, 95 chains, to a pine with the same mark, as will be seen by a plat and certificate made in favor of memorialist by Robert McHardy, dated May 10, 1816, filed with the proceeding in the office of the public archives at St. Augustine; which title your memorialist derives from a royal title made to him June 8, 1816, by Governor Coppinger, in virtue of the royal order of October 29, 1790, as will be seen by a certified copy of said royal title herewith filed. And your memorialist further showeth that he is in actual possession of said lands, and was before the cession of this Territory to the United States; that he is a citizen of the United States and resident of East Florida. All of which is respectfully submitted, &c.

JOHN ADDISON.

[Here follows the translation of the royal title made by Governor Coppinger of the 1,414 acres of land, dated June 8, 1817, in virtue of the royal order of 1790.]

DECREE BY THE BOARD.

A royal title made to claimant for the land claimed by Governor Coppinger, June 8, 1817, being submitted as evidence of title, and being satisfactory, we confirm the claim. April 15.

TESTIMONY.

John Addison vs. *The United States. For one thousand four hundred and fourteen acres of land.*

Francis J. Fatio, being sworn, states that in the year 1820 he saw claimant on the land claimed; that there were buildings and other improvements on the land which was then in cultivation, and has ever understood that claimant occupied and cultivated said land.

F. J. FATIO.

Before the board April 15, 1825.

No. 16.—See Report No. 1.

Domingo Acosta vs The United States.   For six hundred and ninety-five acres of land.

MEMORIAL.

To the honorable the commissioners appointed to ascertain claims and titles to lands in East Florida:

The petition of Domingo Acosta respectfully showeth: That your memorialist claims title to a tract of land consisting of six hundred and ninety-five acres, situated in three surveys, as follows: 250 acres on the east side of St. John's river, at a place called Mount Tucker, 250 acres on the east side of Lake George, and 195 acres on the east side of St. John's river, at the first point above a place called Mount Royal, and are bounded as follows: 250 acres at Mount Tucker begins at a water oak near the river St. John's and runs east, 53 chains, to a pine; thence north, 48 chains, to another pine; thence west, 53 chains, to a pine on the banks of said river; thence along its meanders to the beginning, as will be seen by a plat and certificate dated June 1, 1821, and marked A; 250 acres on the east side of Lake George begins at an ash on the banks of said lake and runs north 60° east, 34 chains, to a pine; thence south 40° east, 74 chains, to another pine; thence south 60° west, 34 chains, to an ash on the banks of the said lake; thence along the margin of the said lake to the beginning, as will be seen by a plat and certificate dated April 10, 1821, and marked B; 195 acres at Mount Royal begins at an elm on the banks of the river St. John's and runs south 75° east, 56 chains, to a pine; thence north 50° east, 36 chains, to a pine; thence north 75° west, 55 chains, to an elm on the banks of said river; thence along the meanders of said river to the beginning, as will be seen by a plat and certificate dated May 30, 1820, and marked C, which several plats and certificates were made by George J. F. Clarke; which title your memorialist derives from a royal title made to him on March 20, 1817, by Governor Coppinger, in virtue of the royal order of March 29, 1815, as will be seen by a certified copy herewith presented, and marked E.   And your memorialist further showeth that he is legally in possession of said lands, and was so before the cession of this Territory to the United States; that he is a citizen of the United States, and a resident of Fernandina, in Amelia island, East Florida.   All of which is respectfully submitted, &c.

BERNARDO SEGUI, *Attorney in fact for Domingo Acosta.*

[Here follows the translation of a plat and certificate of survey of 250 acres, at Mount Tucker, by G. J. F. Clarke, dated June 1, 1821.]

[Here follows the translation of a plat and certificate of survey of 250 acres, at Lake George, by G. J. F. Clarke, dated April 10, 1821.]

[Here follows the translation of a plat and certificate of survey of 195 acres, at Mount Royal, by G. J. F. Clarke, dated May 30, 1820.]

[Here follows the translation of a royal title made by Governor Coppinger to Domingo Acosta for the 695 acres, dated March 20, 1817.]

DECREE BY THE BOARD.

The claimant in this case exhibited a royal title made to him by Governor Coppinger for the land described in his memorial, dated March 20, 1817, in virtue of the royal order of March 29, 1815; also three separate certificates and plats of survey of the same; all of which being satisfactory to the board, they confirmed the title to claimant.   April 15.

No 17.—See Report No. 1.

Antonio Andrew vs. The United States.   For one hundred and twenty acres of land.

MEMORIAL.

To the honorable the commissioners appointed to ascertain claims and titles to lands in East Florida:

The petition of the widow and heirs of Antonio Andrew respectfully showeth: That your memorialists claim title to a tract of land consisting of one hundred and twenty acres, situated on the North river, at a place known by the name of Sta. Catalina, about nine miles north of St. Augustine, bounded on the north by the lands of James R. Hanham, on the south by those of Juan Segui, on the east by Guana creek, and on the west by the North river; the first line runs north 44° east, 74 chains 50 links; the second runs south 44° west, 70 chains; which title your memorialists derive from a royal title made to Lorenzo Capella, April 10, 1804, by Governor White, in virtue of the royal order of October 20, 1790, who sold the same to Antonio Andrew, deceased, as appears by a conveyance dated February 16, 1805, herewith presented, and marked A.   And your memorialists further show that they are in actual possession of said lands, and were so before the cession of this Territory to the United States; that they are citizens of the United States and residents of Florida.   All of which is respectfully submitted, &c.

JUAN F. ANDREW,
For himself, and other heirs of Antonio Andrew.

[Here follows the translation of the royal title for the hundred and twenty acres by Governor White to Lorenzo Capella, dated April 10, 1804, in virtue of the royal order of 1790.]

[Here follows the translation of the conveyance from Capella to Antonio Andrew, dated February 17, 1805.]

DECREE BY THE BOARD.

In this case we find that the land claimed was granted in absolute property to Lorenzo Capella by Governor White, on April 10, 1804, in virtue of the royal order of 1790.   Capella, on February 17, 1805, by his deed, conveyed the same to claimant.   We confirm the claim.   April 15.

No. 18.—See Report No. 1.

Thomas Andrew vs. *The United States. For three hundred and seven acres of land.*

MEMORIAL.

To the honorable the commissioners appointed to ascertain claims and titles to lands in East Florida:

The memorial of Thomas Andrew, by his attorney, Farq'r Bethune, respectfully showeth: That your memorialist claims title, as guardian of the grandchildren of Margaret O'Neal, deceased, on their behalf, and of the legal heirs of said Margaret, to a tract of land consisting of three hundred and seven acres, situated on Langford creek, near Amelia island, having the following lines and boundaries: the first line runs north 40° east, beginning at a stake marked with a cross on the margin of Langford creek, and ending at an oak with the same mark, and is in length 40 chains; the second runs south 75° east, beginning at said oak and ending at another with the same mark, is in measure 11 chains; the third runs south 40° east, beginning at the last oak and ending at another with the same mark, is in length 8 chains; the fourth runs south 13° east, beginning at said oak and ending at another with the same mark, is in measure 40 chains; the fifth runs south 25° west, beginning at said oak and ends at another with the same mark, is in measure 40 chains; the sixth runs south 45° west, beginning at said oak and ending at a live-oak with the same mark, and measures 25 chains; the seventh runs west, beginning at the last-mentioned oak and ends at a water oak, marked with a cross, on the bank of Langford creek, and measures 15 chains; the front runs along the margin of said creek; which title your memorialist derives from a grant in fee simple made to the heirs of said Margaret O'Neal by Governor White, on March 12, 1807, in virtue of the royal order of October 29, 1790. Your memorialist further showeth that the heirs of said Margaret O'Neal are now in actual possession of said land, and were so at the time of the cession; that they are inhabitants of Florida and residents of Duval county, as is also your memorialist. The grant to the heirs of Margaret O'Neal, marked A, and the survey, marked B, are annexed. All of which is respectfully submitted, &c.

THOMAS ANDREW,
Per his attorney, FARQ'R BETHUNE.

[Here follows the translation of a royal title for the land made by Governor White to Donna Margaret O'Neal, dated March 12, 1807, in virtue of the royal order of 1790.]

DECREE BY THE BOARD

The claimant, as guardian of the heirs of Margaret O'Neal, deceased, produced a royal grant for the land claimed made by Governor White to the said Margaret O'Neal, and dated March 12, 1807, in virtue of the royal order of 1790. We confirm the claim. April 15.

No. 19.—See Report No. 1.

Samuel Meers' heirs vs. *The United States. For two hundred acres of land.*

MEMORIAL.

To the honorable the commissioners appointed to ascertain claims and titles to lands in East Florida:

The petition of Susannah Cashen, in behalf of the orphan children of Samuel Meers, deceased, respectfully showeth: That your memorialist claims title to a tract of land consisting of two hundred acres, situated on Tyger island, in East Florida; which title your memorialist derives from a royal title made to the orphans of S. Meers by Governor Estrada, in virtue of the royal order of October 29, 1790, as will be seen by a certified copy thereof, dated October 17, 1811, herewith presented, and marked M. And your memorialist further showeth that she is legally in actual possession of said lands for the aforesaid orphan children of Samuel Meers, deceased; that she is a native of the United States and resident of St. Augustine. All of which is respectfully submitted, &c.

SUSANNAH CASHEN,
In behalf of the orphans of S. Meers.

[Here follows the translation of the royal title for the 200 acres of land made by Governor Estrada to Samuel Meers, dated October 17, 1811, in virtue of the royal order of 1790.]

DECREE BY THE BOARD.

A royal grant made by Governor Estrada to Samuel Meers, deceased, for the 200 acres of land, dated October 17, 1811, being produced as evidence of title, we confirm the title. April 15.

No. 20.—See Report No. 1.

Andrew Atkinson vs. *The United States. For four hundred and fifty acres of land.*

MEMORIAL.

To the honorable the commissioners appointed to ascertain claims and titles to lands in East Florida:

The petition of Andrew Atkinson respectfully showeth: That your memorialist claims title to a tract of land consisting of four hundred and fifty acres, more or less, on the St. John's river, at the place known by the name of the King's Plantation, or the Ship Yard, joining on the north with the river St. John's; on the south with pine land; on the east with a creek, which divides said lands of Vincent Ferrer; and on the west with the swamp of the said river St. John's; which title your memorialist derives from a royal grant made in virtue of the royal order of October 29, 1790, which grant and title bear date April 5, 1815. And your petitioner further showeth that he has been informed and believes that the aforesaid tract of land has been trespassed on, and is now in the occupation of one John C. Houston, of St. John's county; that your petitioner was a subject of the King of Spain when the Floridas were ceded to the United States; and that his residence at this time is Philadelphia, in the State of Pennsylvania.

ARCHD. CLARK, Attorney for the Memorialist.

[Here follows the translation of the royal title for the land made by Governor Coppinger to Andrew Atkinson, dated April 5, 1816, in virtue of the royal order of 1815.]

DECREE BY THE BOARD.

A royal title for the land described in the memorial of the claimant, made by Governor Coppinger, and dated April 5, 1816, in virtue of the royal order of 1815, having been exhibited, and being satisfactory, we confirm the title. April 15.

No. 21.—See REPORT No. 1.

John Houston vs. The United States. For one hundred acres of land.

MEMORIAL.

To the honorable the commissioners appointed to ascertain claims and titles to lands in East Florida:

The petition of John Houston respectfully showeth: That your memorialist claims title to a tract of land consisting of one hundred acres, situated on the island of Talbot, bounded north by lands of your memorialist, south by Fort George bar, east by marshes surrounding the island of Little Talbot, and west by Talbot river; which title your memorialist derives from a royal grant made to Spicer Christopher, April 12, 1809, by Governor White, in virtue of the royal order of 1790, who, by his last will, conveyed the same to your memorialist. And your memorialist further showeth that he is in actual possession of said lands, and was so at the time of the cession; that he is a citizen of the United States and resident of the Territory of Florida.

A. BELLAMY, Memorialist's Attorney.

[Here follows the translation of the royal title for the land made by Governor White, dated April 12, 1809, in favor of Spicer Christopher, in virtue of the royal order of 1790.]

DECREE BY THE BOARD.

The royal title made by Governor White to Spicer Christopher for the hundred acres, dated April 12, 1809, being submitted as evidence of title, and being satisfactory, the board confirm the claim. April 15.

No. 22.—See REPORT No. 1.

Susannah Cashen vs. The United States. For seven hundred acres of land.

MEMORIAL.

To the honorable the commissioners appointed to ascertain claims and titles to lands in East Florida:

The petition of Susannah Cashen, widow of James Cashen, deceased, respectfully showeth: That your memorialist claims title to a tract of land consisting of seven hundred acres, situated on the west side of Amelia island at a place known by the name of Plum orchard, bounded on the north by the lands of John Bachelot, on the south by vacant lands, on the east by vacant lands, and on the west by the marsh and a creek known by the name of St. Patrick's creek; a copy of the plat and certificate is herewith presented, made by Andres Burgevin in favor of James Cashen, deceased, and dated July 12, 1820, and marked No. 1; which title your memorialist derives from a royal title made to James Cashen by Governor Kindelan, in virtue of the royal order of October 29, 1790, a certified copy of which is herewith presented, dated June 11, 1814, and marked C. And your memorialist further showeth that she is in possession of said lands, and that her deceased husband was so, long before the cession of this Territory to the United States; that she is a native of the United States and resident of St. Augustine. All of which is respectfully submitted, &c.

SUSANNAH CASHEN.

[Here follows the translation of the royal title for the seven hundred acres of land made by Governor Kindelan to James Cashen, dated July 11, 1814, in virtue of the royal order of 1790.]
[Here follows the certificate and plat of survey by Andres Burgevin of the seven hundred acres.]

DECREE BY THE BOARD.

The claimant in this case exhibited, as evidence of title, the royal title made to her deceased husband by Governor Kindelan, dated April 11, 1814, in virtue of the royal order of 1790; a certificate and plat of survey was also exhibited. We confirm the claim. April 15.

No. 23.—See REPORT No. 1.

Thomas Andrew vs. The United States. For three hundred acres of land.

MEMORIAL.

To the honorable the commissioners appointed to ascertain claims and titles to lands in East Florida:

The memorial of Thomas Andrew, by his attorney, Farquhar Bethune, respectfully showeth: That your memorialist, as guardian of the grandchildren of Margaret O'Neal, deceased, claims titles on their behalf, and of the legal heirs of the said Margaret, to a tract of land consisting of three hundred acres, situated on Langford creek, and bounded as follows: on the north by lands granted to said Margaret O'Neal on the east by marshes and the waters of St. Mary's, on the west by Langford creek, and on the south by William Carney's land; which title is derived from a grant in fee simple to the children and heirs of said Margaret O'Neal, made by Governor White June 15, 1810, in virtue of the royal order of —— 29, 1790. Your memorialist further showeth that, as guardian of the grandchildren of the said Margaret O'Neal, your memorialist is now in possession of said land, and was so at the time of the cession; that he is an inhabitant of Florida and a resident of Duval county, as are also the said grandchildren of Margaret O'Neal. The grant to the heirs of Margaret O'Neal is annexed, marked A, and the survey is in the public archives attached to the title in fee simple. All of which is respectfully submitted, &c.

THOMAS ANDREW,
By his attorney, FARQUHAR BETHUNE.

[Here follows the translation of the royal title for the three hundred acres of land made by Governor White to Margaret O'Neal, dated June 15, 1810.]

DECREE BY THE BOARD.

The claimant, as guardian of the heirs of Margaret O'Neal, produced a royal title for the land claimed made by Governor White to said Margaret O'Neal, and dated June 15, 1810, in virtue of the royal order of 1790. The claim is confirmed. April 15.

No. 24.—See REPORT No. 1.

Andrew Atkinson vs. *The United States.   For two hundred acres of land.*

MEMORIAL.

To the honorable the commissioners appointed to ascertain claims and titles to lands in East Florida:

The petition of Andrew Atkinson, per his attorney, George Gibbs, respectfully showeth: That your memorialist claims title to a tract of land consisting of two hundred acres, situated between Dunn's creek and Trout creek, on the west side of the river St. John's. No further description can be obtained at the office of the public archives of the particular spot where this land lies; but as a plantation was cleared and buildings and other improvements put upon, and the conditions of the original so fully complied with as to enable your memorialist to obtain a royal title, he is ready to produce satisfactory proofs; which title your memorialist derives from a royal title made to him by Governor Coppinger, in virtue of the royal order of October 29, 1790, who obtained a grant for the same September 1, 1802, as per exhibit A A, and the royal title is dated November 17, 1817. And your memorialist further showeth that he is legally in actual possession of said lands; that he is a subject of Spain and resident of Philadelphia.

ANDREW ATKINSON,
By GEORGE GIBBS, *Attorney in fact.*

[Here follows the translation of the royal title for the land made by Governor Coppinger to Andrew Atkinson, dated November 17, 1817.]

DECREE BY THE BOARD.

A royal title for the land claimed, made by Governor Coppinger, dated November 17, 1817, in virtue of the royal order of 1790, being exhibited, and being satisfactory, the claim is confirmed. April 16.

No. 25.—See REPORT No. 1.

Moses Bowden vs. *The United States.   For two hundred and fifty acres of land.*

MEMORIAL.

To the honorable the commissioners appointed to ascertain claims and titles to lands in East Florida:

The petition of Moses Bowden respectfully showeth: That your memorialist claims title to a tract of land consisting of two hundred and fifty acres, situated on the south side of the river St. John's; which title your memorialist derives from a decree made to your memorialist April 15, 1815, by Governor Kindelan, in virtue of the royal order of 1790. And your memorialist further showeth that he is in actual possession of said lands, and was at the time of the cession; that he is a citizen of the United States and resident of the Territory of Florida.

A. BELLAMY, *Memorialist's Attorney.*

[Here follows the translation of a certified copy of concession by Governor Kindelan, dated April 5, 1815, to Moses Bowden.]

DECREE BY THE BOARD.

We ascertain the foregoing to be a valid Spanish grant by a certified copy of concession made by Governor Kindelan to claimant, dated April 5, 1815; being submitted as evidence of title, the claim is confirmed. April 16.

No. 26.—See REPORT No. 1.

Thomas Andrew vs. *The United States.   For five hundred acres.*

MEMORIAL.

To the honorable the commissioners appointed to ascertain titles and claims to lands in East Florida:

The petition of Thomas Andrew, by his attorney, Farq. Bethune, respectfully showeth: That your memorialist claims title to a tract of land consisting of five hundred acres, situated at St. Diego, and known by the following lines: the first runs south 10° east, beginning at a cabbage tree marked with a cross, and ending at a pine tree, is on measure 89 chains; the second runs south 80° west, beginning at said pine, and finishing at another with the same mark, and is in length 70 chains; the third runs north 10° west, beginning at said pine, and ending at another with the same mark, is in length 85 chains; the fourth runs north 80° east, 70 chains, beginning at said pine, and ending at the forementioned cabbage tree; which title your memorialist derives from a grant made to his deceased father, Robert Andrew, by Governor Quesada, in virtue of the royal order of October 29, 1790, as appears from the certificate of Don Pedro Marrot, dated May 12, 1793, and the survey by Josiah Dupont annexed, marked A. After cultivating said land your memorialist's father obtained from Governor White a title in fee simple, dated April 6, 1809, also annexed, marked B. And your memorialist further showeth that himself and sisters, heirs of said Robert Andrew, are now in actual possession of said lands; that they are inhabitants of Florida and residents of Duval county. Which is respectfully submitted, &c.

THOMAS ANDREW,
Per his attorney, FARQ. BETHUNE.

[Here follows the translation of the certificate and plat of survey by Pedro Marrot of 15 caballerias, (equal to 500 acres,) dated May 12, 1793, surveyed for Robert Andrew.]

[Here follows the translation of a royal title for the 500 acres of land made by Governor White to Robert Andrew, dated April 6, 1809, in virtue of the royal order of 1790.]

DECREE BY THE BOARD.

The claimant, on behalf of himself and sisters, heirs of Robert Andrew, deceased, exhibited evidence of title, a certificate and plat of survey by Marrot for the land claimed, dated May 12, 1793; also a royal title for the same by Governor White, dated April 6, 1809. We confirm the claim to the heirs aforesaid. April 16.

No. 27.—See REPORT No. 1.

Moses Bowden vs. *The United States. For two hundred acres..*

MEMORIAL.

To the honorable the commissioners appointed to ascertain claims and titles to lands in East Florida :

The petition of Moses Bowden respectfully showeth: That your memorialist claims title to a tract of land consisting of two hundred acres, situate on the south side of St. John's, adjoining lands granted to Gilbert, and on a place called San Antonio, as will appear by the annexed grant which is herewith presented; which title your memorialist derives from a royal grant made to your memorialist's father, Uriah Bowden, April 15, 1815, by Governor Kindelan, in virtue of the royal order of 1790. And your memorialist further showeth that he is in actual possession of said lands, and was so at the time of the cession; that he is a citizen of the United States and resident of the Territory of Florida.

A. BELLAMY, *Memorialist's Attorney.*

[Here follows the translation of the royal title for the 200 acres made by Governor Kindelan to Uriah Bowden, dated April 17, 1815.]

TERRITORY OF FLORIDA, *St. John's County :*

Personally appeared before Samuel Fairbanks, esq., George Petty, who, being duly sworn, deposeth and saith that he is well acquainted with Moses Bowden, and that he has been acquainted with the said Moses Bowden for twenty years last past, and that he has lived at a place on the east side of St. John's river called St. Antonio Point, on a place granted to his father, Uriah Bowden, by the Spanish government in the year 1793, said survey calling for two hundred acres; and this deponent further saith that he is knowing that the Spanish government granted one other tract to the said Moses Bowden for headrights, situate on the east side of St. John's river, at the mouth of Lake George, at a place called East Grove, said grant calling for 225 acres. Said grant by the Spanish government, to the best of his knowledge, was in the year 1814. And this deponent further saith that Moses Bowden applied to D. S. H. Miller, and gave him the papers to survey the place called East Grove, said Miller then being surveyor; and that he kept the papers for one year at least, but dared not attempt to survey said tract for fear of the Indians.

                                   his
GEORGE × PETTY.
                                  mark.

Sworn and subscribed to before me this 30th day of December, A. D. 1823.

SAMUEL FAIRBANKS, *J. P.*

DECREE BY THE BOARD.

In this case the claimant exhibited as evidence of title a royal grant for the 200 acres made to his father by Governor Kindelan April 17, 1815, in virtue of the royal order of 1790. The title is confirmed to claimant. April 16.

No. 28.—See REPORT No. 1.

Bagley's heirs vs. *The United States. For one thousand acres.*

MEMORIAL.

To the honorable the commissioners appointed to ascertain claims and titles to lands in East Florida :

Timothy Hollingsworth, guardian of Francis, Carlota, Margaret, and Isabel Bagley: Your memorialist claims title to a tract of land consisting of one thousand acres, situated at a place called Brown Fort, west of St. John's river, bounded as follows: commencing at a stake marked with a cross; thence north 3° east, 193 chains, to a pine with the same mark; thence south 33° west, 31 chains and 50 links, to a pine with the same mark, in William Gaine's line; thence north 39° east, 46 chains, to a pine tree with the same mark; thence north 40° west, 12 chains, to a pine tree with a cross; thence south 40° west, 100 chains, to a pine with a cross; thence south 50° east, 70 chains, to a pine with the same mark; thence north 10° west, 45 chains, to a laurel tree with a cross; north 80° west, 45 chains, to the beginning; which title your memorialist derives from a document upon file in the office of the keeper of the public archives, a certified copy of which is filed herewith, marked A. And your memorialist further showeth that he has actual possession of said lands; that at the change of flags he was a Spanish subject, and resident in this Territory; that he is a citizen and resident of ————.

T. HOLLINGSWORTH, Guardian, &c.

[Here follows the translation of the certificate and plat of survey by Pedro Marrot of 30 caballerias, (equal to 1,000 acres of land,) surveyed and delivered to the heirs of Bagley, dated April 3, 1793.]

DECREE BY THE BOARD.

In this case we find that Pedro Marrot, under the authority of the Spanish government, surveyed and delivered to the heirs of Bagley, deceased, the land described in their memorial to this board. The certificate of survey is dated April 3, 1793. The claim is confirmed. April 19.

No. 29.—See Report No. 1.

Bagley's heirs vs. The United States. For two hundred and forty-eight acres.

MEMORIAL.

To the honorable the commissioners appointed to ascertain claims and titles to lands in East Florida:

The memorial of Timothy Hollingsworth, guardian of Francis, Charlotte, Margaretta, and Isabel Bagley: Your memorialist claims title to a tract of land consisting of two hundred and forty-eight acres, situated at a place called Bagley, on Goodman's lake, in St. John's river, bounded as follows: the first line runs north 35° west, begins at a pine marked with a cross, and ends at a pine with the same mark, and measures 63 chains; thence south 55° west, 31 chains, to a stake with the same mark; thence south 45° west, 13 chains, to a pine with a cross, in the line of Ricard's malpass, known by Flenos; thence south 38° east, 61 chains, to a pine tree with a cross; thence north 55° east, 40 chains, to the beginning; which title your memorialist derives from the document filed herewith, which is a certificate made by Don Marrot, duly authorized for that purpose by the Spanish government; that he has laid off and measured the said two hundred and forty acres of land for memorialist, as guardian of the above-named children, he having exhibited to the said Marrot British titles for the said land. And your memorialist further showeth that he has actual possession of said lands; and that he is a Spanish subject, and resided in East Florida at the change of flags.

T. HOLLINGSWORTH, Guardian, &c.

[Here follows the translation of the certificate and plat of survey by Pedro Marrot of 248 acres of land surveyed and delivered to the heirs of Bagley, dated April 7, 1793.]

DECREE BY THE BOARD.

In this case we find that Pedro Marrot, under the authority of the Spanish government, surveyed and delivered to the heirs of Bagley, deceased, the quantity of land described in their memorial to this board. The certificate and survey is dated April 7, 1793. The claim is confirmed. April 19.

No. 30.—See Report No. 1.

Francisco Barbé vs. The United States. For five hundred acres of land.

MEMORIAL.

To the honorable the commissioners appointed to ascertain claims and titles to lands in East Florida:

The petition of Francisco Barbé respectfully showeth: That your memorialist claims title to a tract of land consisting of five hundred acres, situated at the head of the river Nassau, on Cedar creek, at a place called Thomas' swamp, bounded on the north and south by vacant lands, on the east by the lands of José Alvarez, and on the west by the lands of Henry Groves; the first line begins at a pine and runs north, 95 chains, to another pine; the second line commences at the last-mentioned pine and runs east, 53 chains, to a pine; the third line begins at the last pine and runs south, 95 chains, to another pine; the fourth line commences at the last pine and runs west, 53 chains, to the beginning, as will be seen by a certified copy of plat and certificate herewith presented, made by George J. F. Clarke, and dated the 8th of February, and marked A; which title your memorialist derives from a royal title made to your memorialist March 27, 1819, by Governor Coppinger, in virtue of the royal order of March 29, 1815, which is herewith filed, and marked B; as also certified copy of concession to memorialist of said land, dated April 10, 1817, herewith presented, and marked C. And your memorialist further showeth that he is actually seized and possessed of said lands, and was so before the cession of this Territory to the United States; that he is a citizen of the United States and resident of East Florida. All of which is respectfully submitted, &c.

FRANCIS BARBÉ.

[Here follows the translation of a concession made by Governor Coppinger of the 500 acres of land, dated April 10, 1817.]
[Here follows the translation of the certificate and plat of survey by G. J. F. Clarke of the 500 acres, dated February 8, 1817.]

DECREE BY THE BOARD.

A concession without condition, in virtue of the royal order of 1815, made by Governor Coppinger to claimant April 10, 1817, for the land in question, and a certificate and plat of survey of the same being submitted as evidence of title, the claim is confirmed.   April 10.

No. 31.—See REPORT No. 1.

William Berrie vs. The United States.   For one hundred acres of land.

MEMORIAL.

To the honorable the commissioners appointed to ascertain claims and titles to lands in East Florida:

The petition of ——— respectfully showeth: That your memorialist claims title to a tract of land consisting of one hundred acres, situated north of a place called Loftin's, which said place is called Turkey island, which said tract of land has never been surveyed, and your memorialist cannot therefore bound the same; which title your memorialist derives from a concession made to Thomas Mann by Governor White, in virtue of the royal order of ———, who sold the same to your memorialist November 2, 1805, and transferred the improvements thereon to your memorialist for $100, which said tract of land memorialist went into possession of and planted the very year he purchased it, and has been in possession ever since, with the acquiescence and consent of the Spanish government.   And your memorialist further showeth that he is in actual possession of said lands; that he is a citizen of the United States and resident of Camden county, Georgia.

BELTON A. COPP,
For WILLIAM BERRIE.

[Here follows the translation of a concession made by Governor White to Thomas Mann of the 100 acres, dated July 3, 1799.]

[Here follows a bill of sale from Thomas Mann to William Berrie of the land, dated November 2, 1805.]

EAST FLORIDA, *Duval County:*

In the matter of William Borrie's claim to a certain tract of land in Duval county, called Turkey island, on the river Nassau, granted to Thos. Mann:

William Braddock, an inhabitant of this county, planter, aged about 46 years, being duly sworn, says that for the last 27 years he has lived in that section of country between the St. Mary's and the St. John's known as part of Duval county.   Deponent says that he well knows William Berrie, and well knows that tract of land on the river Nassau commonly called Turkey island; that he was present at the purchase of the said tract by the said William Berrie from the said Thomas Mann, the date of which purchase I do not recollect particularly, but I believe it was in one of the years 1804,—'5, or '6; that said William Berrie paid one hundred dollars for the same to the said Thomas; that the said William Berrie, a year or two after the purchase, cultivated about eight acres of the said land in cotton, but the dews in the neighborhood were so bad that they destroyed the crop.   Deponent does not know whether Berrie has ever cultivated it since that time; that William Berrie removed to Georgia in 1812 or '13, in consequence of the troubles then existing in Florida, and has since not returned.   Deponent *says he is interested* in the subject-matter.

WILLIAM BRADDOCK.   [L. S.]

Sworn to before me this 23d of January, 1824.

JAMES J. O'NEILL, *J. P.*

DECREE BY THE BOARD.

The claimant in this case exhibited as evidence of his title to the land a concession for the 100 acres made by Governor White to one Thomas Mann July 3, 1799, who sold the same to him.   It appears by the affidavit of William Braddock that claimant, after the purchase of the tract, cultivated a part of it. We confirm the claim.   April 19.

No. 32.—See REPORT No. 1.

Susannah Cashen vs. The United States.   For one hundred acres.

MEMORIAL.

To the honorable the commissioners appointed to ascertain claims and titles to lands in East Florida:

The petition of Susannah Cashen, widow of James Cashen, deceased, respectfully showeth: That your memorialist claims title to a tract of land consisting of one hundred acres, situated on Amelia island, at a place called Red Bay, at the head of Beach creek, between the sand hills and the pine barren, bounded on the east by the lands of John Bachelot; which title your memorialist derives from a concession made to Solomon Miller June 26, 1802, by Governor White, in virtue of the royal order of ———, who sold the same to James Cashen, deceased, as will be seen by a conveyance of Solomon A. Miller to said Cashen, dated February 24, 1804, and attached to concession herewith presented, and marked C.   And your memorialist further showeth that she is legally in possession of said lands, and that her deceased husband was so before the cession of this Territory to the United States; that she is a native of the United States and resident of St. Augustine.   All of which is respectfully submitted.

SUSANNAH CASHEN.

[Here follows the translation of a certified copy of concession of the one hundred acres by Governor White to Solomon Miller, dated June 26, 1802.]

[Here follows a conveyance from Miller to James Cashen, dated February 24, 1804.]

DECREE BY THE BOARD.

In this case we find that Governor White conceded the land claimed to Solomon Miller June 26, 1802, and that Miller sold the same to claimant. The claim is confirmed. April 19.

No. 33.—See Report No. 1.

John Bellamy vs. *The United States.   For three hundred acres.*

MEMORIAL.

To the honorable the commissioners appointed to ascertain claims and titles to lands in East Florida :

The petition of John Bellamy respectfully showeth: That your memorialist claims title to a tract of land consisting of three hundred acres, situated on the river of Little St. Mary's, about six miles from its junction, bounded on the east by lands of David Braddock, west by lands of Joseph Higginbottom, north by said river, and south by public lands; which title your memorialist derives from a royal grant made to Robert Huchinson July 31, 1816, by Governor Coppinger, in virtue of the royal order of 1790, who sold the same to James Filman, and the said James Filman has since sold and conveyed the same to your memorialist. And your memorialist further showeth that he is in actual possession of said lands, and was so at the time of the cession; that he is a citizen of the United States and resident of the Territory of Florida.

A. BELLAMY, Memorialist's Attorney.

[Here follows the translation of the royal title for the land made by Governor Coppinger to Robert Hutchinson, dated July 31, 1816, in virtue of the royal order of 1790.]
[Here follows a deed of conveyance from Robert Hutchinson to James Tilman, dated August 10, 1818.]
[Here follows a conveyance from Tilman to claimant.]

DECREE BY THE BOARD.

The board having ascertained that the foregoing claim was a valid one under the late Spanish government, they therefore confirm it to claimant. April 21.

No. 34.—See Report No. 1.

Charles Breward vs. *The United States.   For two hundred and fifty acres.*

MEMORIAL.

To the honorable the commissioners appointed to ascertain claims and titles to lands in East Florida :

The petition of Charles Breward respectfully showeth: That your memorialist claims title to a tract of land consisting of two hundred and fifty acres, situated on Cedar creek of St. John's river; the first line beginning at a pine and running north 10° east, 40 chains, to a pine; second, north 80° west, 63 chains, to a pine; third, south 10° west, 40 chains, to a cypress; fourth, south 80° east, 63 chains, to the pine at the beginning; bounded on the first line by William Eubanks; which title your memorialist derives from a grant made to him by Governor Coppinger, in virtue of the royal order of 1790. A certified copy of his grant, dated March 18, 1817, accompanies this memorial, and the plat and certificate of survey by George J. F. Clarke will be filed when required. And your memorialist further showeth that he is in actual possession of said lands; that he has long been an inhabitant and resident of this province. Your memorialist will, as in duty bound, pray, &c.

GEO. J. F. CLARKE,
For CHARLES BREWARD.

[Here follows the translation of a concession made by Governor Coppinger of the two hundred and fifty acres of land to claimant, dated March 18, 1817.]

DECREE BY THE BOARD.

The board ascertain the above to be a valid Spanish grant previous to January 24, 1818, and confirm the title to the claimant. April 21.

No. 35.—See Report No. 1.

Farquhar Bethune vs. *The United States.   For four hundred and twenty-five acres of land.*

MEMORIAL.

To the honorable the commissioners appointed to ascertain claims and titles to lands in East Florida :

The memorial of Farquhar Bethune respectfully showeth: That your memorialist claims title to a tract of land consisting of four hundred and twenty-five acres, situated on the river St. Mary's, at a place called Cabbage swamp, with the following lines and boundaries: the first line runs south 60° west, 81 chains, which divides the tract from the land granted to Charles Sibdald; the second line runs south 30° east, 45 chains; the third line is formed by a creek which divides it from Isabella Higginbottom's land; the front of the tract is on the river St. Mary's; which title your memorialist derives from a grant to him by Governor Coppinger April 22, 1817, in virtue of the royal order of March 29, 1815. Your memorialist further showeth that he is in possession of said land, and was so at the time of the cession; that he is an inhabitant of Florida and resident of Amelia island. Annexed to this memorial are the title above referred to, marked A, and the plat and survey by Geo. J. F. Clarke, surveyor general, marked B. All of which is respectfully submitted.

FARQ'R BETHUNE.

[Here follows the translation of the royal title for the four hundred and twenty-five acres of land made by Governor Coppinger, dated April 22, 1817.]

[Here follows the translation of the certificate and plat of survey by Geo. J. F. Clarke of the four hundred and twenty-five acres.]

DECREE BY THE BOARD.

The board ascertain this to be a valid Spanish grant made previous to January 24, 1818, and confirm the title of the claimant. April 21.

No. 36.—See REPORT No. 1.

Sarah Bowden vs. *The United States. For one hundred and forty-two and a half acres.*

MEMORIAL.

To the honorable the commissioners appointed to ascertain claims and titles to lands in East Florida:

The petition of Sarah Bowden respectfully showeth: That your memorialist claims title to a tract of land containing one hundred and forty-two and a half acres, situated on Julington creek, which empties into St. John's river; the first line runs south 74° west, 36 chains, begins at a stake marked with a cross on the bank of a small creek, and ends at another with the same mark; second runs south 26° east, 44 chains, begins at said stake, and ends at a laurel with a cross on the banks of Julington creek; its front runs along the bank of said creek, and part on a small creek, forming an irregular figure, as is seen by a plat and certificate made by Pedro Marrot February 25, 1793; which title your memorialist derives from a survey made by Pedro Marrot, by order of Governor Quesada, February 25, 1793, which will more fully appear by a reference thereto, and which your memorialist begs leave to file herewith. And your memorialist further showeth that she is a citizen of the United States and resident in Florida.
SARAH BOWDEN,
By her attorney, B. PUTNAM.

[Here follows the translation of the certificate and plat of survey by Pedro Marrot of the land, dated February 25, 1793.]

DECREE BY THE BOARD.

The claimant produced a certificate of a survey made by Pedro Marrot, commissioned judge for the distribution of land under the royal order of 1790, which is ascertained to be valid under the Spanish laws and ordinances, and therefore confirmed April 21.

No. 37.—See REPORT No. 1.

Samuel Harrison vs. *The United States. For six hundred acres of land.*

MEMORIAL.

To the honorable the commissioners appointed to ascertain claims and titles to lands in East Florida:

The memorial of Samuel Harrison respectfully showeth: That he claims *title* in *and to a* certain tract or parcel of land containing eighteen caballerias, or six hundred acres, situated and being in East Florida aforesaid; that the said tract of land was granted to the said Samuel Harrison in absolute property under the order of 1790, being the quantity of land to which he was entitled under that order for himself, his family, and slaves, October 1, 1791, by Governor Quesada, then the governor of East Florida, while it belonged to the crown of Spain; that your memorialist submits and files the certified copy of the said original grant, by which the foregoing allegations will be proved, the said document being marked exhibit A. Your memorialist further avers and shows that the said tract of land had been taken possession of and considerably improved by the said Samuel Harrison, deceased, before the said grant thereof to him as aforesaid; that it has continued from that time to the present in the actual possession and occupancy in the *possession* of the said original grantee and his descendants; that it was in the possession and actual occupancy and cultivation of the heirs of the said original grantee at the time of the cession of this Territory to the United States, and is so at this time. Your memorialist further shows that the said land was surveyed by Pedro Marrot, and the aforesaid quantity laid off to the said Samuel Harrison, deceased, by the said Marrot, who was duly authorized for that purpose, as the quantity to which he, the said Samuel Harrison, was entitled as aforesaid, on or before February 14, 1792, as appears by a certified copy of the plat and certificate of the survey of the said land herewith filed, and marked exhibit B; that the said tract of land has the following lines and boundaries, that is to say: the first line begins at a pine marked X on the margin of the Nassau river, and runs north 10° west, to another pine marked X, 95 chains, and was, at the time of survey, bounded by lands of one Francis Dias Teran; the second line runs south 82° east, 50 chains, to another pine marked X on the margin of the marsh of Harrison creek. The other sides and parts of the said tract of land form irregular lines, and are by the marshes of the said creek and of Nassau river, as will more distinctly appear by a reference to the copy of the plat filed herewith. Your memorialist avers that he is, and that the other heirs of the said Samuel Harrison, deceased, were, at the time of the cession of the Territory to the United States, in the actual occupancy and possession of the said land, and inhabitants and settlers of East Florida; that they have at this time the actual possession and occupancy of the said land, and are inhabitants and settlers of East Florida. Wherefore your memorialist prays confirmation of the title of the heirs of the said Samuel Harrison, deceased, to the said land.
SAMUEL HARRISON,
By his attorney, JNO. DRYSDALE.

[Here follows the translation of a concession by Governor Quesada to Samuel Harrison, dated October 1, 1791.]

[Here follows the translation of the certificate and plat of survey by Pedro Marrot of the 600 acres surveyed for Samuel Harrison, and dated February 14, 1792.]

TERRITORY OF FLORIDA, *Duval County:*

Personally appeared before me, John Harrison, one of the justices of the peace in and for the said county, Daniel Vaughan and Peter Suarez, both of the county aforesaid, who, being duly sworn, *deposeth and saith* that they have been personally acquainted with Samuel Harrison, senior, of the island of Amelia, planter, and that he has been in possession of and improved a certain tract of land commonly known by the name of Seymore's Point for upwards of twenty years; and deponents further say that they have never known any other person to have settled or improved the said tract of land but the family of the said Samuel Harrison.

PETER SUAREZ.
DANIEL VAUGHAN.

Sworn to before me, at Amelia island, January 9, 1824.

JOHN HARRISON, *J. P.*

DECREE BY THE BOARD.

The claimant produced a concession from Governor Quesada, dated in 1791; also a certificate of survey for the 600 acres by Pedro Marrot, commissioned judge for the distribution of land, dated in 1792; also an affidavit of Daniel Vaughan and Peter Suarez, dated January 9, 1824, proving the possession and cultivation. It is therefore confirmed to claimant by the board. April 21.

No. 38.—See REPORT No. 1.

Samuel Harrison vs. *The United States. For five hundred acres of land.*

MEMORIAL.

TERRITORY OF FLORIDA, *East Florida:*

To the commissioners appointed to ascertain claims and titles to lands in East Florida:

The memorial of Samuel Harrison respectfully showeth: That your memorialist claims title, in fee simple absolute, in and to a certain tract or parcel of land consisting of five hundred acres, situated and being in East Florida aforesaid; that the said tract of land was granted to your memorialist in absolute property November 12, 1807, by Don Henry White, then the governor of East Florida, under and in virtue of the royal order of the King of Spain of October 29, 1790, as will appear by a certified copy of the original grant herewith submitted, and marked exhibit A; that the said tract of land was surveyed by order of the said Governor White on or before April 15, 1807, as appears by a certified copy of the plat and certificate of the survey thereof of that date by John Purcell, then the surveyor general of said province, herewith submitted and filed, and marked exhibit B. Your memorialist further shows that the said land is situated on the island of Amelia, in Duval county, and is known by the name of Harrison's old fields, and has the following lines, dimensions, and boundaries, that is to say: the first line begins on the edge of a marsh, and runs north 80° east, 62 chains 50 links, to the sea beach, and is bounded on the west and southwest by a creek called Half-moon creek and the marshes thereof, and on the south partly by another creek; the residue of the southern line of the said land runs from the head of the said last-mentioned creek directly to the sea beach, as will more distinctly appear by a reference to the plat thereof herewith submitted. Your memorialist further shows that the said land is now, and has been ever since the grant thereof to him as aforesaid, in his actual possession, occupancy, and cultivation, and is now, and has since that time been, the place of residence of himself and his family; that he was, at the time of the grant thereof to him as aforesaid, and at the time of the cession of this Territory to the United States, an actual settler on the said land, and an inhabitant of East Florida; and that he is now, and ever since the said cession has been, an inhabitant and settler of East Florida. Wherefore he prays confirmation of his title to the said land and its appurtenances.

SAMUEL HARRISON,
By his attorney, JNO. DRYSDALE.

[Here follows the translation of the royal title for the five hundred acres of land by Governor White to claimant, dated November 12, 1807, in virtue of the royal order of 1790.] .

DECREE BY THE BOARD.

The board ascertain this to be a valid Spanish grant for five hundred acres of land dated previous to January 24, 1818, and therefore confirm the same to claimant. April 21.

No. 39.—See REPORT No. 1.

Samuel Harrison vs. *The United States. For two hundred acres.*

MEMORIAL.

To the honorable the commissioners appointed to ascertain claims and titles to lands in East Florida:

The memorial of Samuel Harrison respectfully showeth: That your memorialist claims title to a certain tract of land consisting of two hundred acres, situated and being in East Florida aforesaid; that the said land was granted to your memorialist May 16, 1799, by a grant or decree of that date made by Don Henry White, then the governor of East Florida, as appears by a certified copy thereof herewith submitted and filed, marked exhibit A; that the said land consists chiefly of sand hills and marshes, and has never been surveyed; that it is situated at the west point of Amelia island, and has been in the actual possession and occupancy of your memorialist ever since the grant thereof to him as aforesaid.

Your memorialist further avers that at the time of the said grant he was an inhabitant and settler in East Florida, and that from that time to the present time he has continued *uninterruptedly* to be such inhabitant and settler. Wherefore he prays confirmation of title to the said lands and its appurtenances.

SAMUEL HARRISON,
By his attorney, JOHN DRYSDALE.

[Here follows the translation of a certified copy of concession by Governor White of the land to Samuel Harrison, dated May 16, 1799.]

TERRITORY OF FLORIDA, *Duval County:*

Personally appeared before me, John Harrison, one of the justices of the peace in and for the said county, Robert Harrison and Samuel Harrison, jr., both of the said county, who, being duly sworn, depose that Samuel Harrison, sr., of the island of Amelia, planter, has been in possession of a certain tract of land situated on the south end of the said island of Amelia, and has used the same for the use of cattle stock; and the deponents further depose that the said Samuel Harrison, sr., has had a large stock of cattle on the said tract for fifteen years and upwards.

ROBERT HARRISON.
SAMUEL HARRISON, JR.

Sworn and subscribed to before me this 9th January, 1824.

JOHN HARRISON, *J. P.*

DECREE BY THE BOARD.

The board ascertain this to be a valid Spanish grant made to the said Samuel Harrison previous to January 24, 1818, and therefore confirm the same. April 21.

No. 40.—See REPORT No. 1.

E. Hudnell vs. *The United States.   For one hundred acres.*

MEMORIAL.

To the honorable the commissioners appointed to ascertain claims and titles to lands in East Florida:

The petition of the heirs of E. Hudnall respectfully showeth: That your memorialists claim title to a tract of land consisting of one hundred acres, situated on St. John's river, and east side thereof, at a place called Talek, bounded north by the lands of Mrs. Plummer, south by the lands of Tasset, west by St. John's river, and east by vacant lands: beginning on St. John's river at a cypress, thence running south 70° east, 20 chains, with Tasset's land; thence north 15° east, 50 chains, to a pine; thence north 70° west, 20 chains, with Plummer's land, to a pine on St. John's river; thence up the river to the beginning; a plat and certificate of survey of the same, made by George J. F. Clarke, and dated June 8, 1821, is herewith submitted; which title your memorialists derive from a royal title made to José Garcia, December 5, 1817, by Governor Coppinger, in virtue of the royal order of March 29, 1815, who sold the same to E. Hudnall, by deed dated November 27, 1821, which title and deed are exhibited; and the said E. Hudnall having since departed this life, his heirs set up title to the land; and your memorialists further show that they are legally in possession of said lands, and were so at the time of the cession of this country by Spain to the United States; that they are citizens of the United States and residents of East Florida. They pray confirmation of title, &c.

JOHN B. STRONG, *Attorney.*

[Here follows the translation of a royal title made by Governor Coppinger for the land in favor of José Garcia, dated December 5, 1817, in virtue of the royal order of 1815.]

[Here follows the translation of a certificate and plat of survey by G. J. F. Clarke of the one hundred acres, dated June 5, 1821.]

[Here follows a deed of conveyance from Joseph Garcia and Jane, his wife, to Ezekiel Hudnall, dated November 27, 1821.]

DECREE BY THE BOARD.

The board ascertain this to be a valid Spanish grant made previous to January 24, 1818, and therefore confirm the same to claimants. April 21.

No. 41.—See REPORT No. 1.

William Berrie vs. *The United States.   For one hundred acres of land.*

MEMORIAL.

To the honorable the commissioners appointed to ascertain claims and titles to lands in East Florida:

The petition of William Berrie showeth: That your memorialist claims title to a tract of land consisting of one hundred acres, situated in the county of Duval, north and west of the river St. John's, called Snelling's old field, bounded on the south by the marsh of the river St. John's, on the east by marsh, and on the west by vacant lands; a plat of the survey is herewith ————; which title your memorialist derives from a concession made to him by Governor White, in virtue of the royal order of 1790. And your memorialist further showeth that he is in actual possession of said lands; that he is a citizen of the United States and resident of Camden, Georgia.

BELTON A. COPP, *Agent.*

[Here follows the translation of a concession by Governor White of the hundred acres in favor of William Berrie, dated June 16, 1801.]

[Here follows the translation of a certificate and plat of survey by Juan Purcell of the one hundred acres, dated March 15, 1807.]

EAST FLORIDA, *Duval County:*

William Braddock, an inhabitant of this county, planter, aged about forty-six years, being duly sworn, says that for the last twenty-seven years he has lived in the section of country between the St. Mary's and the St. John's, now known as part of Duval county. Deponent says he well knows William Berrie, and knows well the land claimed by him at Snelling's old field; that in the year 1802, or thereabouts, deponent will not positively say whether the year before or after, he lived with William Berrie and helped him to clear the land called Snelling's old field; that Berrie continued to plant said land from four to six years, when he exchanged lands with Andrew Tinker, his father-in-law; that the said Andrew Tinker continued to plant said land till ten years, (1812 or 1813,) when he, as well as Berrie, left Florida in consequence of the troubles then existing in the country. Deponent says that he is not interested in the matter of the foregoing deposition; that he shall neither gain nor lose whether the said grant be confirmed or not; that he is connected with William Berrie by marriage, the said Berrie and himself having married sisters; that William Berrie lives in Georgia.

WILLIAM BRADDOCK.

Sworn to before me this 23d January, 1824.

J. T. O'NEILL, *J. P.*

DECREE BY THE BOARD.

The board ascertained this to be a valid Spanish grant made to the said William Berrie previous to January 24, 1818, and therefore confirm the same. April 21.

No. 42.—See REPORT No. 1.

William Hobkirk's heirs vs. *The United States. For three hundred and twenty-five acres of land.*

MEMORIAL.

To the honorable the commissioners appointed to ascertain claims and titles to lands in East Florida:

The petition of William Hobkirk's heirs respectfully showeth: That your memorialists claim title to a tract of land consisting of three hundred and twenty-five acres, situated on the river St. Mary's, in East Florida, bounded on the front on the margin of St. Mary's river; which title your memorialists derive from a royal title made to William Hobkirk by Governor Coppinger, in virtue of the royal order of March 29, 1815, a copy of which royal title is herewith exhibited, bearing date upon the 24th day of September, 1816. And your memorialists further show that they are in actual possession of said lands, and that the said Hobkirk has been for many years; that they are citizens of the United States and residents of East Florida. They pray confirmation of title, &c.

WILLIAM HOBKIRK'S HEIRS.

[Here follows the translation of a royal title for the land made by Governor Coppinger to William Hobkirk, dated September 24, 1816, in virtue of the royal order of 1815.]

DECREE.

The board ascertain this to be a valid Spanish grant made to William Hobkirk previous to January 24, 1818, and confirm the title to the heirs. April 21.

No. 43.—See REPORT No. 1.

William Hobkirk's heirs vs. *The United States. For three hundred and fifty acres of land.*

MEMORIAL.

To the honorable the commissioners appointed to ascertain claims and titles to lands in East Florida:

The petition of William Hobkirk's heirs respectfully showeth: That your memorialists claim title to a tract of land consisting of three hundred and fifty acres, situated on Bill's creek, by Waterman's lands; which title your memorialists derive from a royal title made to William Hobkirk, deceased, by Governor Coppinger, in virtue of the royal order of March 29, 1815, a copy of which is herewith exhibited, marked A, and dated September 24, 1816. And your memorialists further show that they are in actual possession of said lands; that they are citizens of the United States and residents of East Florida, and were so before and at the cession to the United States. They pray confirmation of title, &c.

WILLIAM HOBKIRK'S HEIRS.

[Here follows the translation of the royal title for three hundred and fifty acres made by Governor Coppinger to William Hobkirk, dated September 24, 1816, in virtue of the royal order of 1815.]

DECREE.

The board ascertain this to be a valid Spanish grant made to William Hobkirk previous to January 24, 1818, and confirm the title to his heirs. April 25.

No. 44.—See REPORT No. 1.

Zephaniah Kingsley vs. *The United States. For one thousand acres of land.*

MEMORIAL.

To the honorable the commissioners appointed to ascertain claims and titles to lands in East Florida:

The petition of Zephaniah Kingsley, by his attorney, George Gibbs, respectfully showeth: That your memorialist claims title to a tract of land consisting of one thousand acres, situated on the St. Mary's river, on the south side thereof; bounded on the north by the St. Mary's river, on the east and south by Little St. Mary's river, and on the west by the plantation of Higginbottom; the first line begins at a sassafras and runs south 22° west, to a pine, 36 chains; second line, thence south 15° east, 33 chains, to another pine; third line, thence west, 15 chains, to another pine; fourth line, south 32° west, 30 chains, as far as the swamp called White Oak, running also by lands of Higginbottom 50 chains, by the northwest, to a pine; thence to a pine, 40 chains; sixth line, thence north 65° west, 50 chains; seventh line, south 45° west, 30 chains; eighth line, south 5 chains; ninth, south 79° east, 30 chains; tenth, south 68° east, 72 chains; which title your memorialist derives from a royal title made to him by Governor Estrada, in virtue of the royal order of October 29, 1790, per royal title herewith submitted, dated December 22, 1815, marked I, and to the other documents filed in the office of the public ———. And your memorialist further showeth that he is in actual possession of said lands, granted by royal title to him December 22, 1815, per exhibit I; that he is now a citizen of the United States and resident of St. Augustine.

ZEPH. KINGSLEY,
By GEORGE GIBBS, Attorney in fact.

[Here follows the translation of the royal title for the land made by Governor Estrada to claimant, dated December 22, 1815, in virtue of the royal order of 1790.]

[Here follows the translation of the certificate and plat of survey by George J. F. Clarke, dated ———.]

DECREE.

The board ascertain this to be a valid Spanish grant made to Zephaniah Kingsley previous to January 24, 1818, and confirm the title to him and his heirs.   April 25.

No. 45.—See REPORT No. 1.

Zephaniah Kingsley vs. The United States.   For three hundred acres of land.

MEMORIAL.

To the honorable the commissioners appointed to ascertain claims and titles to lands in East Florida:

The petition of Zephaniah Kingsley, by his attorney, George Gibbs, showeth: That your memorialist claims title to a tract of land consisting of three hundred acres, situated at the head of Saw-mill creek, bounded as follows: on the east by a line running north 11° east, 160 chains; on the north by a line running west 11° south, 30 chains; on the west by a line running south 11° west, 160 chains; and on the south by a line running east 11° south, 38 chains, as per plat marked H; which title your memorialist derives from a grant made to your memorialist January 18, 1816, by Governor Coppinger, in virtue of the royal order of October 29, 1790.   And your memorialist further showeth that he was, at the exchange of flags, and is now, in legal possession of said lands; that he is a citizen of the Territory of Florida and resident of said Territory.   All of which is respectfully submitted.

ZEPH. KINGSLEY,
By GEORGE GIBBS.

[Here follows the translation of the royal title for the three hundred acres made by Governor Coppinger to claimant, dated January 18, 1816, in virtue of the royal order of 1790.]

DECREE.

The board ascertain this to be a valid Spanish grant made to Zephaniah Kingsley previous to January 24, 1818, and confirm the title to him and his heirs.   April 25.

No. 46.—See REPORT No. 1.

Anna M. Kingsley vs. The United States.   For three hundred and fifty acres of land.

MEMORIAL.

To the honorable the commissioners appointed to ascertain claims and titles to lands in East Florida:

The petition of Anna M. Kingsley respectfully showeth: That your memorialist claims title to a tract of land consisting of three hundred and fifty acres, situated, two hundred and twenty-five thereof, on Dunn's lake, on the easterly side; the first line south 20° east, 33 chains, from a pine to a palm; second south 78° east, 46 chains, to a pine; third, north 62° east, 18 chains, to a live-oak; fourth, north 4° west, 40 chains, to a stake; fifth, south 56° west, 34½ chains, to a stake; sixth, north 38° west, 35 chains, to a stake; seventh, south 56° west, 12 chains, to a pine at the beginning.   One hundred and twenty-five acres on St. John's river, east side; first line, from a cypress to a pine, south 88° east, 65 chains—this line bounded by John Faulk; second line, south 65° west, 80 chains, to an orange, bounded by John Creighton; third line formed and bounded by said river, 40 chains, from the orange to the cypress; which title your memorialist derives from a grant made to her by Governor Coppinger, in virtue of the royal order of 1790, a certified copy of which, dated January 12, 1816, accompanies this petition; and the plat and certificate of survey, by George J. F. Clarke, will be filed when required.   And your memorialist further showeth that she is in actual possession of said lands, and that she has long been a resident of East Florida. Your memorialist will, as in duty bound, ever pray, &c.

GEO. J. F. CLARKE,
For ANNA KINGSLEY.

[Here follows the translation of a concession for the land made by Governor Coppinger to claimant, dated January 12, 1816.]

DECREE.

The board ascertain this to be a valid Spanish grant made to Anna M. Kingsley previous to January 24, 1818, and confirm the title to her and her heirs.   April 25.

No. 47.—See Report No. 1.

Zeph. Kingsley vs. The United States. For one hundred and fifty acres.

MEMORIAL.

To the honorable the commissioners appointed to ascertain claims and titles to lands in East Florida:

The petition of Zeph. Kingsley, by his attorney in fact, Geo. Gibbs, respectfully showeth: That your memorialist claims title to a tract of land consisting of one hundred and fifty acres, situated on the west side of the river St. John's, opposite the mouth of Dunn's creek, known by the name of the Orange Grove, in the swamps, bounded and beginning at a laurel tree on the margin of the swamp; thence north 22° west, 13 chains, to an oak tree; thence west, 14 chains, to an oak; thence south 64° west, 12 chains, to an oak; thence north 28° west, 9 chains, to an oak; thence south 16° west, 7 chains; thence north 30° west, 18 chains, to a gum tree; thence west, 6 chains, to an oak on the margin of the swamp; thence along the edge of the swamp to the beginning corner, per survey and certificate dated April 10, 1818, marked C; which title your memorialist derives from a concession made to William Hartley by Governor Coppinger, in virtue of the royal order of ———, who sold the same to your memorialist per receipt dated August 30, 1821, which is marked A, and decree bearing date December 13, 1817, marked B, are herewith enclosed. And your memorialist further showeth that he is in actual possession of said lands; that he is now a citizen of the United States and resident of the Territory of Florida.

ZEPH. KINGSLEY,

By GEORGE GIBBS, *Attorney in fact.*

[Here follows the translation of a concession made by Governor Coppinger to William Hartley of two hundred and fifty acres of land, dated December 13, 1817.]

[Here follows the translation of the certificate and plat of survey of one hundred and fifty acres of land by An. Burgevin, dated April 10, 1818.]

[Here follows the conveyance from Hartley to claimant, dated August 30, 1821.]

DECREE.

The board ascertain this to be a valid Spanish grant made previous to January 24, 1818, and confirm the title to claimant. April 26.

No. 48.—See Report No. 1.

John Bachelot vs. The United States. For three hundred acres of land.

MEMORIAL.

To the honorable the commissioners appointed to ascertain claims and titles to lands in East Florida:

The petition of John Bachelot respectfully showeth: That your memorialist claims title to a tract of land consisting of three hundred acres, situated on the north point of Amelia island, bounded on the north by the lands of John McQueen, on the south by the lands of Mrs. Jordine, on the east by the said hills and the beach, and on the west by the marsh of Beach creek, as will be seen by a copy of survey thereof made by John Purcell, dated December 24, 1807, and copied and certified by George J. F. Clarke; which title your memorialist derives from a royal title made to him June 10, 1816, by Governor Coppinger, in virtue of the royal order of October 29, 1790, a certified copy whereof is herewith presented. And your memorialist further showeth that he is legally in possession of the said lands, and was so at the time of the cession of this Territory by Spain to the United States; that he is a citizen of the United States and resident of St. Mary's, in Georgia. He prays confirmation of title, &c.

JOHN BACHELOT.

[Here follows translation of a royal title by Governor Coppinger, dated June 10, 1816.]

[Here follows translation of a certificate of survey and plat by John Purcell, dated December 24, 1807.]

DECREE.

John Bachelot vs. The United States. For three hundred acres of land.

The board having ascertained the above to be a valid Spanish title made to claimant, do confirm the same accordingly. April 26, 1825.

No. 49.—See Report No. 1.

Heirs of Sebastian Espinosa vs. The United States. For five hundred acres of land.

MEMORIAL.

To the honorable the commissioners appointed to ascertain claims and titles to lands in East Florida:

The memorial of Raman Sanchez, for himself and the other heirs of Sebastian Espinosa, deceased, respectfully showeth: That he claims title to a certain tract or parcel of land (being the whole of a grant) containing five hundred acres, situated and being in Diego plains, at a place called Uleridge, in East Florida; that this memorialist is unable to set forth the lines or boundaries of the said tract of land, with the exception of the northern boundary, which is on the lands granted to one Francisco X. Sanchez, a survey of the same having never been made; that the said land was granted to the said Sebastian Espinosa September 5, 1801, by Governor White, under and in virtue of a royal order from the King of Spain of October 29, 1790, as will appear by a certified copy of the said original grant or decree, and herewith submitted and filed, marked exhibit A; that possession of the said lands was soon after the said grant thereof taken and held by the said Sebastian Espinosa until the time of his death, which took place some time in the year 1819; that he performed all the conditions upon which the said land was granted to him, and obtained a grant thereof in absolute property March 31, 1818, from Don José Coppinger, then the governor of East Florida, as will appear by a certified copy of the last-mentioned grant herewith submitted and filed, and marked exhibit B, reference being thereto had; and that the said Sebastian Espinosa died intestate, and without will, whereupon the estate descended to your memorialist, and those other persons on behalf of whom this memorial is presented, as his heirs-at-law. Your memorialist avers that the said Sebastian Espinosa was, at the time the said land was originally granted to him, at the time it was confirmed as aforesaid, and at the time of his death, a resident and settler in East Florida, and a subject of the King of Spain; and that your memorialist and the other heirs of the said Sebastian Espinosa were, at the time of his death, and at the time of the cession of this Territory to the United States, and are now, residents and settlers of East Florida. Wherefore your memorialist claims confirmation of the title to the said tract of land to the heirs-at-law of the said Espinosa. And they will, as in duty bound, &c.

RAMAN SANCHEZ,
By his attorney, JOHN DRYSDALE.

[Here follows translation of a concession by Governor White to Sebastian Espinosa, dated September 5, 1801.]

DECREE.

Heirs of Sebastian Espinosa vs. *The United States.   For five hundred acres of land.*

This being a claim founded on a regular and valid Spanish grant, without condition, made previous to January 24, 1818, it is therefore confirmed.   April 29, 1825.

TESTIMONY.

S. Espinosa's heirs vs. *The United States.   For five hundred acres of land.*

G. W. Perpall, being sworn and interrogated, on the part of the claimants' attorney, whether he was acquainted with S. Espinosa during his lifetime, answered that he *was.*
Question. Where did he usually reside?
Answer. At a small plantation on Diego plains.
Question. Do you recollect the name of this place?
Answer. I do not recollect, but it was somewhere on Diego plains.

G. W. PERPALL.

Before the board in session April 28, 1825.

No. 50 —See REPORT No. 1.

Geo. J. F. Clarke vs. *The United States.   For one hundred acres of land.*

MEMORIAL.

To the honorable the commissioners appointed to ascertain claims and titles to lands in East Florida:

The petition of Geo. J. F. Clarke respectfully showeth: That your memorialist claims title to a tract of land consisting of one hundred acres of land, situated on Amelia island, to the northeast of the town of Fernandina, and place known by the name of Willow Pond; the first line of the survey of which begins at a live-oak, and runs north 79° east, thirty-one chains, to a live-oak, and bounded by John Bashlot; second line, north 10° west, forty-nine chains, to a live-oak, and bounded by John Bashlot; third line, south 53° west, forty-five chains, to a live-oak; fourth line south 10° east, seventeen chains, to the live-oak at the beginning; the plot and certificate of which survey, made by Andre Burgevin, will be filed when required; which title your memorialist derives from a grant made to him by Governor Estrada, in virtue of the royal order of 1790, a certified copy of which grant accompanies this petition, bearing date December 15, 1815. And your memorialist further showeth that he is in actual possession of said lands; that he is a native of East Florida and resident of the same. Your memorialist will, as in duty bound, ever pray, &c.

GEO. J. F. CLARKE.

[Here follows translation of a concession made December 15, 1815, by Governor Estrada.]

DECREE.

Geo. J. F. Clarke vs. *The United States.   For one hundred acres of land.*

The board ascertained this to be a *bona fide* valid Spanish grant, made previous to January 24, 1818, without conditions. It is therefore confirmed.   April 29, 1825.

No. 51.—See REPORT No. 1.

Sarah Breward vs. *The United States.   For three hundred acres of land.*

MEMORIAL.

To the honorable the commissioners appointed to ascertain claims and titles to lands in East Florida:

The petition of Sarah Breward respectfully showeth: That your memorialist claims title to a tract of land consisting of three hundred acres, situated, one hundred and sixty-two thereof on the waters of Nassau river, at the place called Doctor's island, and the three small neighboring islands surrounded by marshes; thirty-eight acres situated near the head of Pumpkin Hill creek, bounded on the north by Gilbert

McGlone, on the west by vacant lands, south by William Fitzpatrick, and east by marshes; and one hundred acres at Pumpkin Hill swamp, bounded on the north by marsh, east by Gilbert McGlone, and south and west by vacant lands; which two last tracts lie distant from each other about one and a half mile, and on the waters of Nassau river; which title your memorialist derives from an absolute grant made to the heirs of Francis Bowden by Governor Coppinger, in virtue of the royal order of 1790, as per a certified copy of the said title dated February 15, 1816, and a memorial and decree of August 17, 1816, amending a deficiency in said title; both of those documents accompany this petition, and the plat and certificate of survey by John Purcell will be filed when required. And your memorialist further showeth that she is in actual possession of said lands; that she has long been an inhabitant and resident of Florida. Your memorialist will, as in duty bound, pray, &c.

GEO. J. F. CLARKE,
For SARAH BREWARD.

[Here follows translation of a royal title by Governor Coppinger, dated February 13, 1816.]
[Here follows translation of a memorial and decree of Governor Coppinger, dated August 16, 1816, amending a deficiency in the above title.]

DECREE.

Sarah Breward vs. *The United States. For three hundred acres of land.*

The board having ascertained this to be a valid and *bona fide* Spanish grant made previous to January 24, 1818, to wit, a royal title or absolute grant, dated February 13, 1816, it is therefore confirmed to grantee. April 29, 1825.

No. 52.—See REPORT No. 1.

John A. Cavedo vs. *The United States. For three hundred and fifty acres of land.*

MEMORIAL.

To the honorable the commissioners appointed to ascertain claims and titles to lands in East Florida:

The petition of John A. Cavedo respectfully showeth: That your memorialist claims title to a tract of land consisting of three hundred and fifty acres, situated on Black creek, bounded as follows: first line runs west, sixty chains, beginning at a maple tree marked ☰, to a pine tree marked +; thence south, sixty chains, to a live-oak tree, bounded on the other side by Black creek and Little Black creek; which title your memorialist derives from a grant made to him by Governor Estrada, in virtue of the royal order of 1815, a certified copy of which, dated December 14, 1815, is filed herewith. And your memorialist further showeth that he is in actual possession of said lands; that he is a citizen of East Florida and resident of the same.

JOHN A. CAVEDO.

[Here follows translation of a concession made by Governor Coppinger, dated January 4, 1816.]

DECREE.

John A. Cavedo vs. *The United States. For three hundred and fifty acres of land.*

This being a valid Spanish concession made previous to January 24, 1818, it is therefore confirmed. April 29, 1825.

No. 53.—See REPORT No. 1.

John Bachelot vs. *The United States. For three hundred acres of land.*

To the honorable the commissioners appointed to ascertain claims and titles to lands in East Florida:

The petition of John Bachelot respectfully showeth: That your memorialist claims title to a tract of land consisting of three hundred acres, situated on Amelia island, at a place called White Point, bounded on the north by the lands of Elizabeth Jordine, on the south by the land of James Cashen, on the east by vacant land, and on the west by the marshes and waters of the river St. Mary's; a plat and certificate whereof is herewith exhibited, made by John Purcell, and copied and certified by George J. F. Clarke, dated April 2, 1807; which title your memorialist derives from a royal title made to him June 10, 1816, by Governor Coppinger, in virtue of the royal order of October 29, 1790, as will be seen by a certified copy of said title herewith exhibited. And your memorialist further showeth that he is legally in possession of said lands, and was so at the time of the cession of the province to the United States; that he is a citizen of the United States and a resident of St. Mary's, in Georgia. He prays confirmation of title, &c.

JOHN BACHELOT.

[Here follows translation of a royal title by Governor Coppinger, dated June 10, 1816.]

DECREE.

John Bachelot vs. *The United States. For three hundred acres of land.*

The board having ascertained the above to be a valid Spanish title to claimant, do confirm the same accordingly. April 29, 1825.

No. 54.—See Report No. 1.

Charles Seton vs. The United States.   For seven hundred acres of land.

MEMORIAL.

To Alexander Hamilton, W. W. Blair, and Davis Floyd, land commissioners, now sitting in St. Augustine, East Florida:

Memorial of Charles Seton, merchant and planter, residing in Fernandina, stating his right to the following tracts of land granted by authority of his Catholic Majesty Ferdinand VII: grant number 4, royal title for a tract of seven hundred acres of land, situated on the river St. Mary's, joining the old township formerly belonging to Thomas Cryer; first line, south 60° east, 15 chains, commencing at a stake with a cross on it, at the edge of the river St. Mary's, to a pine tree joining the land of Thomas Cryer; second line from that pine, south 25° east, 23 chains, to another pine with the same mark; third line, south 30° west, 95 chains, to another pine with the same mark; fourth line running north 60° west, 84 chains, to another pine of the same mark; fifth line running north 30° east, 84 chains, from that pine to a stake marked with a cross, on the edge of the river St. Mary's, vacant land on the 3d, 4th, and 5th line, fronting on the river St. Mary's and the marsh; granted by Governor White April 14, 1792, as per certificate annexed to George Arons, left by him to his wife Elizabeth Arons, and by her to her son, William Carney, both dying intestate, and purchased by me from the said William Carney April 28, 1818, for two thousand dollars, as per bill of sale annexed, with the plat, &c.   It is now called George Plantation.

CHARLES SETON.

[Here follows the translation of a certificate of survey and plat by Captain Don Pedro Marrot to George Arons, dated April 14, 1792.]
[Here follows translation of a royal title by Governor Coppinger of the above to William Carney, a legal representative of George Arons, dated August 26, 1818.]
[Here follows a conveyance from William Carney to Charles Seton, dated April 28, 1818, and relinquishment of dower by his wife, dated April 10, 1819.]

DECREE.

Charles Seton vs. The United States.   For seven hundred acres of land.

The board having ascertained the above to be a valid Spanish concession, and the deraignment to claimant being regular, do confirm the same accordingly.   May 4, 1825.

No. 55.—See Report No. 1.

Zephaniah Kingsley vs. The United States.   For three hundred acres of land.

MEMORIAL.

To the honorable the commissioners appointed to ascertain claims and titles to lands in East Florida:

The petition of Zephaniah Kingsley, by his attorney, Geo. Gibbs, showeth: That your memorialist claims title to a tract of land consisting of three hundred acres of land, situated on Doctor's creek, on the river St. John's, called Fuente del Llamo; the first line runs north 20° west, 77½ chains; second line runs north 70° east, 38.72 chains; third line runs south 20° east, 35 chains; the fourth line bounded by the bank of Doctor's creek, as will appear by the plat marked E; which title your memorialist derives from a grant made to William Kane August 19, 1809, by Governor White, in virtue of the royal order of October 29, 1790, who dying, his heirs sold the same to your memorialist, as per deed marked F, dated September 1, 1809.   And your memorialist further showeth that he was, at the exchange of flags, and now is, in legal possession of said lands; that he is a citizen of the Territory of Florida and resident of the said Territory.   All of which is respectfully submitted.

ZEPH. KINGSLEY,
By his attorney in fact, GEO. GIBBS.

[Here follows translation of a certificate of survey by Captain Don Pedro Marrot to William Kane, dated November 30, 1791.]
[Here follows translation of a royal title made by Governor White, dated August 9, 1809, to the widow and heirs of William Kane.]
[Here follows translation of a conveyance from William Kane's widow unto Zephaniah Kingsley, dated September 1, 1809.]
[Here follows a power from Elizabeth Kane, Margaret Kane, and Ann Kane, authorizing their mother, Elizabeth Kane, widow of William Kane, to make the aforementioned conveyance to Zephaniah Kingsley, dated September 1, 1809.]

DECREE.

Zephaniah Kingsley vs. The United States.   For three hundred acres of land.

The board having ascertained the above to be a valid Spanish title, and the deraignment to the claimant being regular, the same is confirmed accordingly.   May 4, 1825.

No. 56.—See Report No. 1.

Heirs of C. Griffith vs. The United States.   For four hundred and fifty acres of land.

MEMORIAL.

To the honorable the commissioners appointed to ascertain claims and titles to lands in East Florida:

The petition of William Downs, David Turner, Zachariah Haddoch, and Benjamin Simmons, husbands of Winney, Elizabeth, Sarah, and Eliza, heirs of Cornelius Griffith, respectfully showeth: That your memorialists claim title to a tract of land consisting of four hundred and fifty acres, situated on the head of Nassau river, distant from it about half a mile, between two creeks, which form said river; which title your memorialists claim from a survey made by Don Pedro Marrot, dated April 8, 1792, and returned to the office of the keeper of the public archives of the province of East Florida, a certified copy of which survey is filed herewith, as by a reference thereto will more fully and at large appear. And your memorialists further show that they are in legal possession of the said lands; and that they are citizens of the United States, and, with the exception of William Downs, are residents of this Territory. And your memorialists will ever pray, &c. Certified copy of survey, marked A, filed herewith.

WILLIAM DOWNS.
DAVID TURNER.
ZACHARIAH HADDOCK.
ABRAHAM SIMMONS,
By his attorney, DAVID B. MACOMB.

[Here follows translation of a survey and certificate of delivery to Cornelius Griffith by Captain Don Pedro Marrot, judge commissioned for the distribution of lands in East Florida, dated April 8, 1792.]

Cornelius Griffith's heirs vs. *The United States.* *For four hundred and fifty acres of land.*

The board having ascertained this to be a valid Spanish concession to Cornelius Griffith, deceased, do therefore confirm it to his heirs. May 4, 1825.

No. 57.—See REPORT No. 1.

Magdalena Juaneda vs. *The United States.* *For three hundred and eighty-five acres of land.*

MEMORIAL.

To the honorable the commissioners appointed to ascertain claims and titles to lands in East Florida :

The memorial of Magdalena Juaneda, widow of Nicholas Sanchez, deceased, claims title in and to three hundred and eighty-five acres of land, situated, lying, and being in East Florida aforesaid; that the said land was granted in absolute property to the said Nicholas Sanchez April 24, 1816, under royal order of the King of Spain, March 29, 1815, by Governor Don José Coppinger; that the said land is situated in Diego's plain, and is bounded on the south by lands of Sebastian Espinosa; on the north by lands of Francis X. Sanchez; on the east by the sea beach; and, as will appear by exhibit A, herewith filed, the west by vacant pine barren; and that the said Nicholas Sanchez departed this life about the year 1817, leaving those in behalf of whom this memorial is presented, your memorialist, his widow, and his children, as his heirs. Your memorialist further avers that the said Nicholas Sanchez was, at the time the said land was granted to him as aforesaid, and at the time of his death, an inhabitant and settler of East Florida, and subject of the King of Spain. Wherefor your memorialist, in behalf as aforesaid, prays confirmation of the title of the heirs of said Nicholas Sanchez in and to the said tract of land, in conformity to the acts of cession in such case made and provided.

MAGDALENA JUANEDA,
By the attorney, JNO. DRYSDALE.

[Here follows the translation of a royal title from Governor Coppinger to Nicholas Sanchez, deceased, dated April 24, 1816.]

DECREE.

Magdalena Juaneda, widow of Nicholas Sanchez, deceased vs. *The United States.* *For three hundred and eighty-five acres of land.*

The board having ascertained the above to be a valid Spanish title to Nicholas Sanchez, deceased, do confirm it to his widow and heirs accordingly. May 4, 1825.

No. 58.—See REPORT No. 1.

Joseph Gaunt vs. *The United States.* *For three hundred and twenty-five acres of land.*

MEMORIAL.

To the honorable the commissioners appointed to ascertain claims and titles to lands in East Florida :

The petition of Joseph Gaunt respectfully showeth: That your memorialist claims title to a tract of land consisting of three hundred and twenty-five acres, situated in Turnbull's swamp, to the west of Hillsboro' river; first line runs north 75° east, 80 chains, from a pine to a palm; second line runs north 15° west, 40¾ chains, to a palm; third line runs south 75° west, 80 chains, to a pine; fourth line runs south 15° east, 40¾ chains, to the pine at the beginning; which title your memorialist derives from an absolute title made to him by Coppinger, in virtue of the royal order of 1815, a certified copy of which, dated October 12, 1816, is herewith presented, and the plat and certificate of survey by George J. F. Clarke will be filed when required. And your memorialist further showeth that he is in actual possession of said lands; that he has long been an inhabitant and resident of this province. Your petitioner will, as in duty bound, ever pray, &c.

GEORGE J. F. CLARKE,
For JOSEPH GAUNT.

[Here follows the translation of a cession made by Governor Coppinger, dated October 12, 1816.]

DECREE.

Joseph Gaunt vs. *The United States.* *For three hundred and twenty-five acres of land.*

The board having ascertained this to be a valid Spanish concession without conditions, do therefore confirm it. May 4, 1825.

TESTIMONY.

Joseph Gaunt vs. *The United States. For three hundred and twenty-five acres of land.*

Francis J. Fatio, being sworn and examined by the board:
Question. Were you acquainted with Governor Coppinger?
Answer. I was.
Question. Have you seen him write?
Answer. Very frequently.
Question. From your knowledge of Governor Coppinger's handwriting, do you believe this to be his signature? (Here the original concession was exhibited to witness, upon which this claim in founded.)
Answer. I believe it to be the genuine signature of Governor Coppinger.
                                                               F. J. FATIO.
Before the board in session May 4, 1825.

No. 59.—See REPORT No. 1.

Magdalena Juaneda vs. *The United States. For three hundred acres of land.*

MEMORIAL.

To the honorable the commissioners appointed to ascertain claims and titles to lands in East Florida:

The memorial of Magdalena Juaneda, for herself and the other heirs of Nicholas Sanchez, deceased, respectfully showeth: That your memorialist, for herself and in behalf of the other heirs of Nicholas Sanchez, deceased, claim title to a certain tract or parcel of land containing three hundred acres, situated and being in the Territory of East Florida aforesaid; that the said land was originally granted February 3, 1800, by a concession of that date, to the said Nicholas Sanchez, deceased, made by Governor White, then the governor of East Florida, in virtue of the royal order of the King of Spain of October 29, 1790, as will appear by reference to the certified copy of the said concession, herewith filed, and marked exhibit A; that the said land is situated in Diego plains, at a place called Qui Qui; that it is bounded on the north by lands of Francisco Sanchez, east by Guana creek, and west and south by vacant land; that the said land was surveyed by Juan Purcell on or before June 23, 1809, as will appear by a reference to the certified copy of the plat and certificate of survey of that date, herewith filed, and marked exhibit B; that it has the following lines, to wit: the first line runs south 35° west, 20 chains; and the second line runs south 55° east, 200 chains, as appears by the plat and the royal title to the said land; that the heirs of the said Nicholas Sanchez obtained a royal title in absolute property for the said land April 2, 1819, as will appear by the certified copy herewith filed, marked exhibit C. Your memorialist further shows that the said Nicholas Sanchez departed this life many years ago, leaving your memorialist and those other persons in behalf of whom this claim is made his heirs; and that upon his death the said tract of land and its appurtenances devolved upon them; that the said Nicholas Sanchez was, when the said land was granted to him as aforesaid, a Spanish subject and inhabitant of East Florida, and so continued until his death; and that your memorialist and the other heirs of the deceased are inhabitants and settlers of East Florida, and were at the time of his death Spanish subjects and settlers in East Florida. Wherefore they pray that your honorable board will confirm their title to the said land and its appurtenances.
                                                      MAGDALENA JUANEDA,
                                           By the attorney, JNO. DRYSDALE.

[Here follows translation of a concession made by Governor White to Nicholas Sanchez, dated February 3, 1800.]
[Here follows translation of a certificate of survey and plat made by John Purcell, dated June 23, 1809.]

DECREE.

Magdalena Juaneda and other heirs of Nicholas Sanchez, deceased, vs. *The United States. For three hundred acres of land.*

The board having ascertained this to be a valid Spanish concession made to Nicholas Sanchez, deceased, do confirm the same to his widow and heirs. May 4, 1825.

No. 60.—See REPORT No. 1.

John Low vs. *The United States. For seven hundred and fifty acres of land.*

MEMORIAL.

To the honorable the commissioners appointed to ascertain claims and titles to lands in East Florida:

The petition of John Low respectfully showeth: That your memorialist claims title to a tract of land consisting of seven hundred and fifty acres, situated at *Belli* old field, on *Belli* river, bounded on the north by Belli creek, on the east by *McGirth's* creek, on the south by vacant land, and on the west by William Carney; which title your memorialist derives from an absolute grant made to him by Governor Estrada, in virtue of the royal order of 1790, as per a copy of said grant herewith presented, bearing date January 30, 1812. And your memorialist further showeth that he is in actual possession of said lands; that he has long been an inhabitant and resident of this province. Your memorialist will, as in duty bound, pray, &c.
                                                      GEO. J. F. CLARKE,
                                                          For JOHN LOW.

[Here follows translation of a royal title by Governor Estrada, dated January 30, 1812.]

DECREE.

John Low vs. *The United States. For seven hundred and fifty acres of land.*

The board having ascertained the above to be a valid Spanish royal title to claimant, do therefore confirm it. May 4, 1825.

No. 61.—See REPORT No. 1.

Widow and heirs of John Andrea vs. *The United States. For one hundred and sixty-one and one-third acres of land.*

MEMORIAL.

To the honorable the commissioners appointed to ascertain claims and titles to lands in East Florida:

The petition of Maria Mabrity, widow of John Andrea, deceased, respectfully showeth: That your memorialist claims title to a tract of land consisting of four caballerias and twenty-eight acres, situated on the North river and Guana creek, at a place called White Oyster Bank, bounded and beginning at a stake marked with a cross, at the edge of a marsh, on the North river; thence north 50° east, 74 chains and 50 links, to an oak at the edge of a marsh on Guana creek—this line bounds the lands of José Peso de Burgo; thence along said marsh to a laurel with the same mark; thence south 87° west, 40 chains, to an oak with the same mark; thence south, 10 chains, to a stake with the same mark; thence north 70° west, 10 chains, to a stake with the same mark, on the edge of a marsh of the North river; thence along said marsh and river to the beginning; which title your memorialist derives from a royal title made to Juan Andrea, by Governor White, in virtue of the royal order of October 29, 1790, a certified copy of which royal title is herewith presented, and dated July 10, 1804; also a certificate of the notary of government of the division of the estate of the said Andrea. And your memorialist further showeth that she is in actual possession of said lands; that she is a native of Florida and resident of St. Augustine. All of which is respectfully submitted, &c.

                    MARIA MABRITY, *Widow of John Andrea, deceased.*

[Here follows translation of a royal title to John Andrea, by Governor White, dated July 10, 1804.]
[Here follows certificate of the notary of government of the division of the estate of John Andrea, dated September 15, 1818.]

DECREE.

Widow and heirs of John Andrea vs. *The United States. For one hundred and sixty-one and one-third acres of land.*

The board having ascertained that the above is a valid Spanish title to John Andrea, deceased, do confirm it to his widow and heirs accordingly. May 6, 1825.

No. 62.—See REPORT No. 1.

Christina Hill vs. *The United States. Claim for four hundred and five acres of land.*

TERRITORY OF FLORIDA, *East Florida:*

To the honorable the commissioners appointed to ascertain claims and titles to lands in East Florida:

The memorial of Christina Hill, widow of Joseph Sanchez, deceased, respectfully showet :That she claims, in behalf of herself and her children, by her deceased husband, the said Joseph Sanchez, title in and to a certain tract or parcel of land consisting of four hundred and five acres, situated and being in East Florida aforesaid; that the said Joseph Sanchez, the husband of your memorialist, was one of the inhabitants of the city of St. Augustine who, by reason of his services as a militiaman during the rebellion of 1812 and 1813 in East Florida, became entitled to a grant of land under the order of the King of Spain of March 29, 1815; that he departed this life some time in the year 1814; that on November 16, 1815, your memorialist, in behalf of herself and her children, the heirs of the said Joseph Sanchez, applied for and obtained from Don José Coppinger, then the governor of East Florida, a concession of four hundred and five acres of land, the quantity to which her husband, the said Joseph Sahchez, would have been entitled under the royal order aforesaid if he had been alive, as will appear by a certified copy of said concession, which bears date the 17th November, the year last aforesaid, now submitted and filed, and marked exhibit A. The title of the heirs of the said Joseph Sanchez to the said land was, on April 16, 1818, confirmed by a grant thereof in absolute property, made to them by the said Governor Coppinger, as will appear by a reference to a certified copy of the said grant, now submitted and filed, and marked exhibit B. Your memorialist shows that the said land has not been surveyed, but that fifty acres, parcel of the aforesaid four hundred and five acres, are situated at a place called "Casino Loco;" and the residue thereof, that is to say, three hundred and fifty-five acres, are situated in Diego plains, and are bounded on the north by lands granted to one Sebastian Espinosa, as appears by exhibit marked A. Your memorialist further shows that she and the other heirs of Joseph Sanchez were, at the time the said lands were originally conceded and granted to them as aforesaid, and that they have since been, inhabitants and settlers of East Florida. Wherefore they pray a confimation of their title to the said land and their appurtenances, &c.

                    CHRISTINA HILL,
            By her attorney, JOHN DRYSDALE.

[A. Here follows translation of a concession by Governor Coppinger, dated November 17, 1817, to Christina Hill.]

DECREE.

Christina Hill vs. *The United States.   For four hundred and five acres of land.*

The board having ascertained the above to be a valid Spanish concession to claimant, do confirm the same accordingly.   May 12, 1825.

No. 63.—See REPORT No. 1.

Thomas Napier vs. *The United States.   For eight hundred acres of land.*

MEMORIAL.

To the honorable the board of commissioners appointed to ascertain claims and titles to lands in the Territory of East Florida:

The memorial of Thomas Napier respectfully showeth: That your memorialist is a citizen of the United States, resident in South Carolina; that your memorialist lays claim to a tract of land consisting of eight hundred acres, in East Florida, lying and being in the territory of Mosquito, in the *pazage* called Pantano, of the west of Turnbull, about three miles to the west of New *Sneyrna;* the first line standing to the northward and westward, near the east of the said Pantano, ninety chains, butting on lands of the government; the second line forming a rectangle with the first, running to the southwestward, and crossing the said Pantano, eighty-nine chains, butting on lands of the government; the third line striking off to the southward and eastward, ninety chains, butting on lands of the government; the fourth and last line standing from the third line northwardly and eastwardly, eighty-nine chains, butting on lands of Ambrose Hull; the whole tract forming a rectangular parallelogram of eight hundred acres, and having such boundaries and landmarks as are set forth in the plat of said land made by George J. F. Clarke; that your memorialist lays claim to said land on the ground of purchase from Isaac Wicks, who has been a resident of this province for the last forty years; that the said Isaac Wicks did obtain his right by purchase from Juan de Entralgo, who was in respectable official situation in this province under the Spanish government, and that the said Juan de Entralgo obtained his right by special grant from said government; that in support of his claims your memorialist submits, or will in time submit, the original deed of conveyance from Isaac Wicks to your memorialist; an authenticated copy of the conveyance from Juan de Entralgo to Isaac Wicks; an authenticated copy of the grant from Governor Coppinger to Juan de Entralgo, together *with the memorial of the said governor;* an authenticated copy of the plat and certificate of survey made by George J. F. Clarke, dated February 20, 1810; the original documents comprehended under the foregoing last three heads being in the Spanish language in the office of the keeper of the public archives.   All which is respectfully submitted.

THOMAS NAPIER,
By his attorney, RICHARD B. FARMAND.

[Here follows translation of a royal title made by Governor Coppinger to Juan de Entralgo, dated November 15, 1817.]

[Here follows translation of the certificate of survey and plat by George J. F. Clarke, dated February 20, 1818.]

[Here follows translation of a memorial to the governor, and his decree, dated February 26, 1818, ordering the aforesaid plat to be placed in the archives.]

[Here follows translation of a conveyance from Juan de Entralgo to Isaac Wicks, dated August 20, 1818.]

[Here follows a conveyance from Isaac Wicks to Thomas Napier, dated April 22, 1822.]

DECREE.

Thomas Napier vs. *The United States.   For eight hundred acres of land.*

The board having ascertained the above to be a valid Spanish title, and the deraignment to claimant being regular, do confirm the same accordingly.   May 12, 1825.

No. 64.—See REPORT No. 1.

John Middleton vs. *The United States.   For two hundred acres of land.*

MEMORIAL.

To the honorable the commissioners appointed to ascertain claims and titles to lands in East Florida:

The memorial of John Middleton, by his attorney, Farquhar Bethune, respectfully showeth: That your memorialist claims title to a tract of land consisting of two hundred acres, situated on the west side of the river St. John's, on Cedar branch, within the following lines: the first runs east, measuring fifty-eight chains; the second line runs north, thirty-five chains; the third runs west, fifty-eight chains; the fourth runs south, and measures thirty-five chains; which title your memorialist derives from a grant made to William Garvin by Governor Coppinger, on March 29, 1817, in virtue of the royal order of March 29, 1815; which grant was made for a place called formerly Langley Bryan, but there being to that previous claims, said Garvin had surveyed in lieu thereof the same quantity at the place above described, as appears from the certificate of George Clarke, surveyor general; which tract was conveyed to your memorialist, who further showeth that he is in actual possession of the above-described lands, and was so at the time of the cession; that he is a citizen of the United States and resident of Amelia island.   Attached to this memorial are the title in fee simple, A; the conveyance from William Garvin, B; and the plat and survey by the surveyor general, C.   All of which is respectfully submitted.

JOHN MIDDLETON,
Per his attorney, FARQUHAR BETHUNE.

[Here follows translation of a royal title made by Governor Coppinger to William Garvin, dated March 29, 1817.]

[Here follows a conveyance from William Garvin to John Middleton, dated December 3, 1821.]

[Here follows translation of a certificate of survey and plat by George J. F. Clarke, dated April 6, 1817.]

DECREE.

John Middleton vs. *The United States.* *For two hundred acres of land.*

The board having ascertained the above to be a valid Spanish title, and the deraignment to claimant being regular, do confirm the same accordingly. May 12, 1825.

No. 65.—See Report No. 1.

William Hartley vs. *The United States.* *For two hundred and fifty acres of land.*

MEMORIAL.

To the honorable the commissioners appointed to ascertain claims and titles to lands in East Florida:

The petition of William Hartley respectfully showeth: That your memorialist claims title to a tract of land consisting of two hundred and fifty acres, situated at the headwaters of Goodby's lake, near Wills' swamp; which title your memorialist derives from a concession made to him by Governor Coppinger, a certified copy of which is herewith presented, and dated December 13, 1817. And your memorialist further showeth that he is legally in possession of said lands, and was so previous to the cession of this then province to the United States; that he is a citizen of the United States and resident of East Florida. All of which is respectfully submitted.

JOHN DRYSDALE, *Attorney for Claimant.*

[Here follows the translation of a concession for the two hundred and fifty acres of land by Governor Coppinger to claimant, dated December 13, 1817.]

DECREE.

The board ascertain this to be a valid Spanish grant made previous to January 24, 1818, and confirm the title to claimant. May 30.

No. 66.—See Report No. 1.

Frederick Hartley vs. *The United States.* *For four hundred and fifty acres of land.*

MEMORIAL.

To the honorable the commissioners appointed to ascertain claims and titles to lands in East Florida:

The petition of Frederick Hartley respectfully showeth: That your memorialist claims title to a tract of land consisting of four hundred and fifty acres of land, at a place called St. Nicholas, St. John's river; which title your memorialist derives from a decree of Governor White, May 17, 1803, under the royal order of 1790. And your memorialist further showeth that he is in actual possession, and was so at the time of the cession; that he is a citizen of the United States and a resident of the Territory of Florida.

A. BELLAMY, *Attorney.*

[Here follows translation of a concession for two hundred acres by Governor White, dated May 7, 1803.]

DECREE.

Frederick Hartley vs. *The United States.* *For four hundred and fifty acres of land.*

The board having ascertained that the concession was made for only two hundred acres of four hundred and fifty solicited, and that the said concession was a valid one under the Spanish government, do confirm two hundred acres to claimant accordingly. May 30, 1825.

No. 67.—See Report No. 1.

Hannah Nobles vs. *The United States.* *For two hundred and eight acres of land.*

MEMORIAL.

To the honorable the commissioners appointed to ascertain claims and titles to lands in East Florida:

The petition of Hannah Nobles respectfully showeth: That your memorialist claims title to a tract of land consisting of about two hundred and eight acres, situated on the St. John's river, bounded on two sides by the said river, and the land of Isaac Bowden on the other two sides; the first line begins at a laurel tree on the margin of the river St. John's; runs thence north 45° east, 64 chains, to a pine; thence north 45°, 15 chains, to a cypress on the margin of the river St. John's; thence following the course of the said river to the first said comm'r tree, per certificate of survey, memorial, and decree, dated December 20, 1791, marked P; which title your memorialist derives from a royal title made to Susannah Cowan, and confirmed to Robert Cowan by Governor Kindelan, in virtue of the royal order of October 28, 1790, per royal title herewith submitted, dated April 24, 1815, marked L. And the said Robert Cowan, by his last will and testament filed in the office of the clerk of the county court for the county of St. John's, devised and bequeathed the same, all his real and personal property and effects, to your memorialist, as by reference to the said will and testament will fully appear. And your memorialist further showeth that she is in actual possession of said lands; that she is a citizen of the United States and resident of the Territory of Florida.

her
HANNAH ⋈ NOBLES.
mark.

Witness to the mark of Hannah Nobles:
        GEORGE GIBBS.

[Here follows translation of a royal title made by Governor Kindelan to Robert Cowan, dated April 24, 1815.]

[Here follows translation of a plat and certificate by Don Pedro Marrot, dated December 20, 1791.]

DECREE.

Hannah Nobles vs. *The United States. For two hundred and eight acres of land.*

The board having ascertained the above to be a valid Spanish royal title, and by will of grantee bequeathed to claimant, the same is confirmed accordingly. May 30, 1825.

No. 68.—See REPORT No. 1.

James R. Hanham vs. *The United States. For one hundred and seventy and two-thirds acres of land.*

MEMORIAL.

To the honorable the commissioners appointed to ascertain claims and titles to lands in East Florida:

The petition of James R. Hanham respectfully showeth: That your memorialist claims title to one hundred and seventy and two-thirds acres, situated between the North river and the river Guana, called El Burgos, bounded as follows: beginning at a stake marked with a cross, on the edge of a marsh on North river, and running north 50° east, to an oak similarly marked, on the Guana, its length being 74 chains and 50 links; thence down the Guana to an oak marked with a cross; thence south 44° west, 74 chains and 50 links, to a stake on the marsh of the North river; thence with the river and marsh to the beginning; which title your memorialist derives from a grant made to José Peso de Burgo by Governor Quesada, in virtue of the royal order of 1790, who sold the same *to Jane* Triay and Francisco Triay, who sold the same by their attorney, Andres Pacetty, to your memorialist, as will appear by the documents filed with this memorial. And your memorialist further showeth that he is in actual possession of said lands; that he now cultivates and improves them; that he was in Pensacola July 10, 1821; and that he now resides in St. Augustine. All of which is respectfully submitted.
        JAMES R. HANHAM.

[Here follows translation of a certificate of survey and delivery, with a plat by Don Pedro Marrot, to José Peso de Burgo, dated May 26, 1793. At foot is a note by the secretary of government, certifying that a decree was made September 11, 1798 authorizing the exchange of the above with Francisco and Juan Triay.]

[Here follows a conveyance to James R. Hanham, dated May 20, 1822.]

DECREE.

James R. Hanham vs. *The United States. For one hundred and seventy and two-thirds acres of land.*

The board having ascertained the above to be a valid Spanish survey and delivery, and the deraignment to claimant being regular, do confirm it to him accordingly. May 30, 1825.

No. 69.—See REPORT No. 1.

Abraham Hanian vs. *The United States. For fifty acres of land.*

MEMORIAL.

To the honorable the commissioners appointed to ascertain claims and titles to lands in East Florida:

The petition of Abraham Hanian respectfully showeth: That your memorialist claims title to a tract of land consisting of fifty acres, situated at Little Grove, on the east side of St. John's river, and north of the military station of Buena Vista, which has not been surveyed to him, but is bounded by the said river and vacant lands; which title your memorialist derives from a grant made to him by Governor Coppinger, in virtue of the royal order of 1815, a certified copy of which, dated September 18, 1816, accompanies this petition. And your memorialist further showeth that he is in actual possession of said lands; that he has long been an inhabitant and resident of East Florida. Your petitioner will, as in duty bound, pray, &c.
        GEORGE J. F. CLARKE,
        For ABRAHAM HANIAN.

[Here follows translation of a concession by Governor Coppinger, dated September 18, 1816.]

DECREE.

Abraham Hanian vs. *The United States. For fifty acres of land.*

This being a valid Spanish concession made to claimant previous to January 24, 1818, it is therefore confirmed. May 30, 1825.

No. 70.—See Report No. 1.

John M. Hanson, guardian of Francis Miles, an infant, vs. The United States.   For two hundred acres of land.

MEMORIAL.

To the honorable the commissioners appointed to ascertain claims and titles to lands in East Florida:

The petition of John M. Hanson, guardian of Francis Miles, an infant, respectfully showeth: That your memorialist claims title to a tract of land consisting of two hundred acres, situated on the North river, bounded on the north by land of Manuel Marshal, southeast by lands of John Salome, and east and west by royal lands.   Your memorialist further shows that Barbara Hainsman, who had a title from the British government for said lands, remained here after the year 1784, and had the title to the said lands confirmed to her by the Spanish government, as will appear by the documents A and B filed herewith, and others in the office of the keeper of the public archives.   And your memorialist further showeth that he is in actual possession of said lands; that he (and his ward) resided in St. Augustine in 1821, and does so now.

GEORGE MURRAY, for Petitioner.

[Here follows translation of certificate of survey and delivery, with a plat by Don Pedro Marrot, commissioned judge for the distribution of lands in East Florida, dated June 2, 1793, to Barbara Hainsman.]

[Here follows translation of a conveyance from Barbara Hainsman to Francisco X. Sanchez, dated September 11, 1797.]

DECREE.

John M. Hanson, guardian of Francis Miles, an infant.   For two hundred acres of land.

The board having ascertained the above to be a valid Spanish survey and delivery of the above land to Barbara Hainsman, and that she had conveyed it to Francisco X. Sanchez, from whom claimant derives as one of his heirs, the same is confirmed to him accordingly.   May 30, 1825.

No. 71.—See Report No. 1.

Francis Miles, a minor, by John M. Hanson, his guardian, vs. The United States.   For three hundred acres of land.

MEMORIAL

To the honorable the commissioners appointed to ascertain claims and titles to lands in East Florida:

The petition of Francis Miles, a minor, by John M. Hanson, as guardian, respectfully showeth: That your memorialist claims title to a tract of land consisting of three hundred acres, situated on the river St. John's, at a place called Terios, bounded as follows: beginning at a laurel marked with a cross, at the edge of said river, running north 45° east, 67 chains and 44-100 of a chain; thence south 45° east, 38 chains and 72-100 of a chain, to a pine with the same mark; thence south 45° west, 77 chains 44-100, to a gum tree on the bank of said river; which title your memorialist derives from an absolute grant made to the heirs of Francisco Xavier Sanchez by Governor White, in virtue of the royal order of 1790; and your memorialist claims title to said lands, as guardian to the said F. Miles, as one of the heirs of Francisco X. Sanchez, it having been allotted to him in the division of the estate of the said Sanchez.   And your memorialist further showeth that he is in actual possession of the said lands; a certified copy of the grant made February 4, 1811, is herewith filed; that he is a citizen of the United States and resident of St. Augustine.

JOHN M. HANSON,
For FRANCIS MILES.

[Here follows translation of a royal title made by Governor White to Francisco X. Sanchez, dated February 4, 1811.]

DECREE.

Francis Miles, a minor, by John M. Hanson, his guardian, vs. The United States.   For three hundred acres of land.

The board having ascertained the above to be a valid Spanish royal title to Francisco X. Sanchez, from whom claimant derives as one of his heirs, the same is confirmed to him accordingly.   May 30, 1825.

No. 72.—See Report No. 1.

Heirs of Ezekiel Hudnall vs. The United States.   For two hundred and fifty-five acres of land.

MEMORIAL.

To the honorable the commissioners appointed to ascertain claims and titles to lands in East Florida:

The petition of S. Streeter, administrator of the estate of E. Hudnall, deceased: Your memorialist claims title to a tract of land consisting of two hundred and forty-five acres, situated on the north bank of the river St. John's, nearly opposite the Fort of St. Nicholas, and on the east of a creek called Hogan's creek; which title your memorialist derives from a concession made to Daniel Hogans by Governor Coppinger, in virtue of the royal order of 1790, who sold the same to E. Hudnall; a certified copy of said concession is herewith presented, dated March 18, 1817.   And your memorialist further showeth that he is legally in possession of said lands; that he is a citizen of the United States and resident of St. Augustine.   All of which is respectfully submitted.

J. B. STRONG, Attorney

[Here follows translation of a concession by Governor Coppinger to Daniel Hogans, dated March 18, 1817, and a conveyance to E. Hudnall, dated November 11, 1818.]

[Here follows translation of a survey, and a plat by George J. F. Clarke, dated May 9, 1817, to the same.]

DECREE.

Ezekiel Hudnall's heirs vs. *The United States.   For two hundred and twenty-five acres of land.*

The board having ascertained the above to be a valid Spanish concession, and the deraignment being regular to Ezekiel Hudnall, the same is confirmed to his heirs.   May 30, 1825.

No. 13.—See REPORT No. 1.

[*Ezekiel Hudnall's heirs* vs. *The United States.   For five hundred acres of land.*

MEMORIAL.

To the honorable the commissioners appointed to ascertain claims and titles to lands in East Florida:

The petition of Squire Streeter, administrator of the estate of E. Hudnall, showeth: That your memorialist claims title to a tract of land consisting of five hundred acres, situated in the place known as the Barranco de las Calabazas, to the south and near the mouth of the river Nassau; which title your memorialist derives from a title made to Ezekiel Hudnall by Governor White, in virtue of the royal order of 1790. And your memorialist further showeth that said Hudnall was, at the time of his death, in actual possession of said lands, as will appear by the document lodged in the office of the secretary of the commissioners; that he was a citizen of the United States and resident of St. Augustine.

J. B. STRONG, *Attorney.*

[Here follows translation of a concession by Governor White, dated January 29, 1802.]

DECREE.

Ezekiel Hudnall's heirs vs. *The United States.   For five hundred acres of land.*

The board having ascertained that the above is a valid Spanish concession made to E. Hudnall, deceased, do confirm it to his heirs accordingly.   May 30, 1825.

No. 14.—See REPORT No. 1.

William Eubanks vs. *The United States.   For two hundred acres of land.*

MEMORIAL.

To the honorable the commissioners appointed to ascertain claims and titles to lands in East Florida:

The petition of William Eubanks respectfully showeth: That your memorialist claims title to a tract of land consisting of two hundred acres; one hundred and seventy acres of land thereof on *Big Cedar* creek, St. John's river; 1st line, east, fifty chains, from a pine to a pine; 2d, north 35° east, thirty-five chains, to a pine; 3d line, west, fifty chains, to a pine; 4th, south 10° west, thirty-five chains, to the pine at the beginning, and thirty acres, taking in the whole of Burton island, on the Nassau river; which title your memorialist derives from a grant made to him by Governor Coppinger, in virtue of the royal order of 1790; a copy of said grant, under date of March 18, 1817, is presented herewith, and the above documents of survey by George J. F. Clarke will be filed when required. And your memorialist further showeth that he is in actual possession of said lands; that he has long been a resident of this province. Your memorialist will ever, as in duty bound, pray, &c.

GEO. J. F. CLARKE, *for the Petitioner.*

[Here follows translation of a concession by Governor Coppinger, dated March 18, 1817, for one hundred and fifty acres of land.]

William Eubanks vs. *The United States,   For one hundred and fifty acres of land.*

The board having ascertained the above to be a valid Spanish concession for only one hundred and fifty acres of land, and not for two hundred, as set forth in the memorial, do confirm the same to the claimant accordingly.   June 6, 1825.

No. 15.—See REPORT No. 1.

Robert Harrison vs. *The United States   For seven hundred and sixty-five acres of land.*

MEMORIAL.

To the honorable the commissioners appointed to ascertain claims and titles to lands in East Florida:

The memorial of Robert Harrison respectfully showeth: That he claims title to a certain tract or parcel of land situated and being in East Florida, consisting of seven hundred and sixty-five acres; that the said land was granted to your memorialist April 1, 1816, by Don José Coppinger, then the governor of East Florida, under the royal order of the King of Spain of October 29, 1790, as will appear by a certified copy of the original grant or concession of the said land herewith submitted and filed, and marked exhibit A; that the said land is situated at an island not having hitherto been named, near the place called Roundabout, on the river Nassau, at the distance of about twenty-five miles north of the bar; and your memorialist further avers and shows that he was, before and at the time of the cession of this Territory to the United States, and has continued until this time, a settler and inhabitant of East Florida, having the said land in his actual possession and occupancy. Wherefore, he prays a confirmation of his title to the said land and its appurtenances.

ROBERT HARRISON,
By his attorney, JOHN DRYSDALE.

[Here follows translation of a concession by Governor Coppinger, dated May 10, 1816.]

DECREE.

Robert Harrison vs. *The United States.   For seven hundred and sixty-five acres of land.*

The board having ascertained this to be a valid Spanish concession made to claimant, do confirm it to him accordingly.   June 6, 1825.

No. 76.—See Report No. 1.

John Silcock vs. *The United States.   For three hundred acres of land.*

MEMORIAL.

To the honorable the commissioners appointed to ascertain claims and titles to lands in East Florida:

The petition of John Silcock respectfully showeth: That your memorialist claims title to a tract of land consisting of three hundred acres, situated three miles from the head of the river Nassau, in the county of Duval, beginning at a stake marked with a cross; thence south, 55 chains, to a pine with the same mark; thence east, 55 chains, to a pine with the same mark; thence north, 55 chains, to a stake with the same mark; thence west, 55 chains, to the beginning, as will be seen by a plat and certificate made by Pedro Marrot, by order of the Spanish government, in favor of memorialist, and dated March 18, 1792; which title your memorialist derives from a grant made to him by Governor Quesada, in virtue of the royal order of October 29, 1790.   And your memorialist further showeth that he is legally, and was in actual possession, and cultivated said lands until he was obliged to abandon them on account of the revolution of the year 1812; that he is a citizen of the United States and resident of East Florida.   All of which is respectfully submitted, &c.

JOHN SILCOCK.

[Here follows translation of a certificate of survey and a plat by Pedro Marrot, dated March 18, 1792.]

DECREE.

John Silcock vs. *The United States.   For three hundred acres of land.*

The board having ascertained the above to be a valid Spanish title made by Don Pedro Marrot, judge commissioned for the survey and distribution of lands in East Florida, do confirm the same accordingly. June 6, 1825.

No. 77.—See Report No. 1.

Lewis Guibert vs. *The United States.   For four hundred acres of land.*

MEMORIAL.

To the honorable the commissioners appointed to ascertain claims and titles to lands in East Florida:

The petition of Lewis Guibert respectfully showeth: That your memorialist claims title to a tract of land consisting of four hundred acres, situated to the east of the river St. John's; the first line runs north 10° east, 24 chains, to a pine; the second, north 65° west, 76 chains, to another pine; the third, south 55° west, 48 chains, to another pine; the fourth, south 65° east, 76 chains, to another pine; the fifth, south 10° west, 24 chains, to another pine; and the sixth, north 57° east, 48 chains, to another pine; which title your memorialist derives from a grant made to Edward M. Wanton by Governor White, in virtue of the royal order of 1790, who sold the same to your memorialist; which said tract of four hundred acres is in part of a grant of seven hundred and fifty acres made to the said Edward M. Wanton on December 23, 1801.   And your memorialist further showeth that he is in actual possession of said lands; that he is a citizen of the United States and resident of Florida.   In confirmation of the title of your memorialist, he begs leave to refer this honorable board to the memorial of the said Edward M. Wanton, and the decree thereon, dated November 23, 1801; the royal title of April 26, 1820, attached to which will be found the certificate of survey of George J. F. Clarke, public surveyor, for the said four hundred acres, and from which the within description is taken; and also to the bill of sale from Wanton to your memorialist, dated May 18, 1820—all on file in the office of the public archives of this city.

THOMAS F. CORNELL,
Attorney for LEWIS GUIBERT.

[Here follows translation of a concession by Governor White, dated November 23, 1801, to Edward M. Wanton.]
[Here follows translation of a royal title by Governor Coppinger, dated April 26, 1820, to the same.]
[Here follows translation of a certificate of survey and a plat by George J. F. Clarke, dated November 17, 1819.]
[Here follows translation of a conveyance from Edward M. Wanton to Lewis Guibert, dated May 18, 1820.]

DECREE.

Lewis Guibert vs. *The United States.   For four hundred acres of land.*

The board having ascertained the above to be a valid Spanish concession, and the deraignment being regular to claimant, do confirm the same accordingly.   June 6, 1825.

No. 78.—See Report No. 1.

Stephen Eubanks vs. The United States. For three hundred and twenty-five acres of land.

MEMORIAL.

To the honorable the commissioners appointed to ascertain claims and titles to lands in East Florida:

The petition of Stephen Eubanks, jr., respectfully showeth: That your memorialist claims title to a tract of land consisting of three hundred and twenty-five acres of land, situated on Trout creek, St. John's river, which title your memorialist derives from a grant made to him by Governor Coppinger in virtue of the royal order of 1790. A copy of his said grant, bearing date March 18, 1817, your memorialist herewith presents, and will file his documents of survey when required. And your memorialist further showeth that he is in actual possession of said lands; that he has long been an inhabitant and resident of this country. And he will, as in duty bound, pray, &c.

GEO. J. F. CLARKE,
For STEPHEN EUBANKS.

[Here follows translation of a concession made March 18, 1817, by Governor Coppinger.]

DECREE.

Stephen Eubanks, jr., vs. The United States. For three hundred and twenty-five acres of land.

The board having ascertained the above to be a valid Spanish concession, do confirm the same accordingly. June 6, 1825.

No. 79.—See Report No. 1.

Ezekiel Hudnall's heirs vs. The United States. For two hundred acres of land.

MEMORIAL.

To the honorable the commissioners appointed to ascertain claims and titles to lands in East Florida:

The petition of the heirs of Ezekiel Hudnall, deceased, respectfully showeth: That your memorialists *claim* title to a tract of land consisting of two hundred acres, situated at the south head of St. Pablo creek, and beginning *at laurel*, running thence south 7° west, 50 chains, to a pine; thence south 83° west, 4 chains, with Solomon Miller's land, to a pine; thence north 7° east, 50 chains, *to pine;* thence north 83° east, 40 chains, with Francisco Richard's lands, to the beginning, as will be seen by a plat and certificate of George J. F. Clarke, dated June 7, 1821, herewith submitted; which title your memorialists derive from a concession made to Selvey Taylor April 14, 1817, by Governor Coppinger, in virtue of the royal order of ————, who sold the same to E. Hudnall, as per deed herewith submitted, dated November 28, 1821, who, since that time, departed this life, resident in East Florida; and your *memorialists* further show that they are legally in the possession of said lands, and were so by *original* ———— *granted* at the time of the cession of this Territory by Spain to the United States; that they are citizens of the United States and residents of East Florida. They pray concession of title, &c.

JOHN B. STRONG, *Attorney.*

[Here follows translation of a concession to Selvey Taylor by Governor Coppinger, dated April 14, 1817.]
[Here follows translation of a certificate of survey and plat by George J. F. Clarke, dated June 7, 1821.]
[Here follows a conveyance from Selvey Taylor to Ezekiel Hudnall, dated November 28, 1821.]

DECREE.

Ezekiel Hudnall's heirs vs. The United States. For two hundred acres of land.

The board having ascertained the above to be a valid Spanish concession, and the deraignment to claimants being regular, the same is confirmed accordingly. June 6, 1825.

[No. 80 was not sent to the General Land Office by the commissioners.]

No. 81.—See Report No. 1.

José Alvarez vs. The United States. For three hundred and fifty-five acres of land.

MEMORIAL.

To the honorable the commissioners appointed to ascertain claims and titles to lands in East Florida:

The petition of José Alvarez respectfully showeth: That your memorialist claims title to a tract of land consisting of three hundred and fifty-five acres, situated at a place known by the name of Thomas' swamp, near the river Nassau, bounded on the north, south, and west, by vacant lands, and on the east by the lands of Henry Grover; the first line commences at a pine and runs south 80° east, 71 chains, to a another pine; thence south 10° west, 50 chains, to another pine; thence north 80° west, 71 chains; thence north 10° east, 50 chains, to the beginning, as will be seen by a plat and certificate herewith presented, made by George J. F. Clarke, dated February 2, 1817, and marked A; which title your memorialist derives from a royal title made to José Alvarez September 9, 1816, by Governor Coppinger, in virtue of the royal order of March 29, 1815, which is herewith presented and marked B, as also a certified copy of the concession of said lands to memorialist, and dated September 9, 1816, and marked C. And your memorialist further showeth that he is legally seized and possessed of said lands, and was so before the cession of this Territory to the United States; that he is a citizen of the United States and resident of East Florida. All of which is respectfully submitted.

JOSÉ ALVAREZ.

[Here follows translation of a royal title by Governor Coppinger, dated September 9, 1816.]
[Here follows translation of a certificate of survey and plat by George J. F. Clarke, dated February 2, 1817.]

DECREE.

José Alvarez vs. *The United States. For three hundred and fifty-five acres of land.*

This being a valid Spanish title made previous to January 24, 1818, it is therefore confirmed. June 13, 1825.

No. 82.—See REPORT No. 1.

Zephaniah C. Gibbs vs. *The United States. For one hundred and twenty-one acres of land.*

MEMORIAL.

To the honorable the commissioners appointed to ascertain claims and titles to lands in East Florida:

The petition of Zephaniah C. Gibbs respectfully showeth: That your memorialist claims title to a tract of land consisting of one hundred and twenty-one acres, more or less, situated on the head of the Guana river to the west, *on St. Diego plains, by St. Diego plains,* on the west, on lands belonging to Francis P. Sanchez *on the north, on the banks of the sea, those to the east,* and on lands belonging to Philip Downs to the south; the first line begins at a laurel tree, running north 10° west, 42 chains, to a stake; the second line runs north 8° east, 29 chains, to a palma real tree; the third line runs east 10°, 42 chains, to a stake; the fourth line runs south 72° west, 29 chains, to the laurel tree, the beginning; conceded per royal title herewith submitted, with reference for further information to the office of the archives of the Territory, marked Z; which title your memorialist derives from a royal title made to the late Francis X. Sanchez, by Governor White, in virtue of the royal order of October 29, 1790; and on a division of the estate of the said Francis X. Sanchez amongst his heirs, this said tract of land fell to John M. Sanchez, his son, which, by reference to the archives of the Territory, will fully appear; and the said John M. Sanchez sold the same to your memorialist, per deed now in possession of Samuel Fairbanks, esq., for the purpose of taking the acknowledgment of the wife of the said Sanchez to the same. And your memorialist further showeth that he is in actual possession of the said lands; that he is a citizen of the United States and resident of St. Augustine. November 17, 1823.

ZEPH. C. GIBBS,
By GEORGE GIBBS.

[Here follows translation of a royal title made by Governor White, dated February 12, 1811, to Francisco Xavier Sanchez.]
[Here follows a deed of conveyance from John M. Sanchez and Margaretta, his wife, heirs of F. X. Sanchez, dated May 8, 1823, to Zephaniah C. Gibbs.]

DECREE.

Zephaniah C. Gibbs vs. *The United States. For one hundred and twenty-one acres of land.*

The board having ascertained the above to be a valid Spanish title made previous to January 24, 1818, and the deraignment being regular to claimant, it is therefore confirmed to him. June 13, 1825.

No. 83.—See REPORT No. 1.

Zephaniah Kingsley vs. *The United States. For fifty acres of land.*

MEMORIAL.

To the honorable the commissioners appointed to ascertain the claims and titles to lands in East Florida:

The petition of Zephaniah Kingsley, by George Gibbs, attorney in fact, respectfully showeth: That your memorialist claims title to a tract of land consisting of fifty acres, situated on St. John's bluff, on the south side of the said river, bounded by St. John's river on the north, on lands now or late belonging to Dr. Bartolo de Castro, and on the east by a creek and marsh; the first line appears to begin at a stake on the margin of the said St. John's river, the boundary *between it and the aforesaid lands of Manuel Rou. Tunering, nearly south to a stake, as per plat of* survey by George Clarke, and dated April 15, 1817, submitted, marked M; which title your memorialist derives from a royal title made to Francisco Estacholy by Governor Coppinger, in virtue of the royal order of October 29, 1790, who sold the same to your memorialist per deed dated March 27, 1817, marked N, and a royal title for the same, dated March 15, 1817, also submitted, marked O. And your memorialist further showeth that he is in actual possession of said lands; that he is a citizen of the United States and resident of ———.

ZEPHANIAH KINGSLEY,
By GEORGE GIBBS, *Attorney in fact.*

[Here follows translation of a royal title by Governor Coppinger, dated March 15, 1817, to Francisco Estacholy.]
[Here follows a conveyance from Francisco Estacholy to Zephaniah Kingsley, dated March 27, 1817.]
[Here follows a plat by George J. F. Clarke, dated April 15, 1817.]

DECREE.

Zephaniah Kingsley vs. *The United States.   For fifty acres of land.*

The above being a valid Spanish title made previous to January 24, 1818, and the deraignment regular to claimant, it is therefore confirmed to him.   June 13, 1825.

No. 84.—See REPORT No. 1.

John G. Rushing vs. *The United States.   For two hundred and five acres of land.*

MEMORIAL.

To the honorable the commissioners appointed to ascertain claims and titles to lands in East Florida:

The petition of John G. Rushing, by G. Gibbs, his attorney in fact, respectfully showeth: That your memorialist claims title to a tract of land consisting of two hundred and five acres, situated on the north side of the river St. John's, and beginning on Little Dunn's creek at a poplar tree; the first line running north 23° east, 54 chains, to a pine; the second line running south 67° east, 26 chains, to a pine; third line running south 23° west, 119 chains, to a pine; the fourth running south 45° west, 13 chains, to a pine on Big Dunn's creek; thence up the same to the fork of Little Dunn's creek; thence up the same to the beginning of the first line, as per concession dated November 27, 1815, marked A, and survey of the same by George Clarke, dated February 1, 1818, marked B, herewith *enclosed;* which title your memorialist derives from a decree in concession made to John G. Rushing by Governor Estrada, in virtue of the royal order ——, agreeably to a certified copy of a decree signed by Thomas de Aguilar, dated November 17, 1815, and further reference to the office of the archives.   And your memorialist further showeth that he is in actual possession, having built on and improved the said lands; that he is a citizen of the United States and resident of the said Territory.

JOHN G. RUSHING,
By GEORGE GIBBS, Attorney in fact.

[Here follows the translation of a concession by Governor Estrada, dated November 27, 1815.]
[Here follows the translation of a certificate of survey and plat by George J. F. Clarke, dated February 1, 1818.]

DECREE.

John G. Rushing vs. *The United States.   For two hundred and five acres of land.*

The board having ascertained the above to be a valid Spanish concession, do confirm the same accordingly.   June 13, 1825.

No. 85.—See REPORT No. 1.

John Christopher vs. *The United States.   For fifty acres of land.*

MEMORIAL.

To the honorable the commissioners appointed to ascertain claims and titles to lands in East Florida:

The memorial of John Christopher, by his attorney in fact, Farquhar Bethune respectfully showeth: That your memorialist claims title to a tract of land consisting of fifty acres, situated on the river Nassau, and bounded on the west by other land belonging to your memorialist; which title your memorialist derives from a grant originally made to John Tucker on May 24, 1804, by Governor White, in virtue of the royal order of October 29, 1790, a certified copy of which is annexed, marked A; which tract was exchanged by said Tucker with Gilbert Mann for another, as appears by a paper marked B, and was by said Mann conveyed to your memorialist, as appears by a paper marked C.   And your memorialist further shows that he is now in actual possession of said lands, and has been since the year 1807; that he is a citizen of the United States and resident of Duval county.   All of which is respectfully submitted.

JOHN CHRISTOPHER,
By his attorney FARQUHAR BETHUNE.

[Here follows translation of a concession to John Tucker by Governor White, dated May 24, 1804.]
[Here follows a transfer from John Tucker to Gilbert Mann, dated January 22, 1807.]
[Here follows a transfer from Gilbert Mann to John Christopher, dated October 31, 1807.]

DECREE.

John Christopher vs. *The United States.   For fifty acres of land.*

The board having ascertained the above to be a valid Spanish concession, and the deraignment to claimant being regular, it is therefore confirmed to him.   June 14, 1825.

TESTIMONY.

John Christopher vs. *The United States.   For fifty acres of land.*

Isaac Carter sworn:
Question. Do you know the tract claimed by Mr. Christopher?
Answer. I do.   Mr. Tucker sold the said land to the present claimant, who has had possession of the

same and made several crops thereon. Witness had in his possession a note of hand given by the said Christopher to Tucker for the said tract.

ISAAC CARTER.

Before the board in session May 18, 1825.

No. 86.—See Report No. 1.

Zephaniah Kingsley vs. *The United States.   For one hundred acres of land.*

MEMORIAL.

To the honorable the commissioners appointed to ascertain claims and titles to lands in East Florida:

The petition of Zephaniah Kingsley, by his attorney, George Gibbs, showeth: That your memorialist claims title to a tract of land consisting of one hundred acres, situated on the south side of St. John's river, commonly called St. John's Bluff; on the north by St. John's river, on the east by lands formerly of Francisco Stacholy, on the south by vacant land, on the west by a ship yard creek, as will more fully appear by *the marked* A, and other documents herewith submitted; which title your memorialist derives from a grant made to Manuel Romero March 17, 1817, by Governor Coppinger, in virtue of the royal order of October 29, 1790, who sold the same to your memorialist, as per deed marked B, and dated March 27, 1817.   And your memorialist further showeth that he was, at the exchange of flags, and now is, in actual possession of said lands; that he is a citizen of the Territory of Florida and resident of said Territory.   All of which is respectfully submitted.

ZEPH. KINGSLEY,
By his attorney in fact, GEORGE GIBBS.

[Here follows translation of a royal title made by Governor Coppinger to Don Manuel Romero, dated March 17, 1817.]

[Here follows translation of a certificate of survey and plat by George J. F. Clarke, dated April 15, 1817.]

[Here follows translation of a conveyance from Don Manuel Romero to Don Zephaniah Kingsley, dated March 27, 1817.]

DECREE.

Zephaniah Kingsley vs. *The United States.   For one hundred acres of land.*

The board having ascertained the above to be a valid Spanish title, and the deraignment to claimant being regular, it is therefore confirmed.   June 16, 1825.

No. 87.—See Report No. 1.

Hannah Nobles vs. *The United States.   For one hundred acres of land.*

MEMORIAL.

To the honorable the commissioners appointed to ascertain claims and titles to lands in East Florida:

The petition of Hannah Nobles respectfully showeth: That your memorialist claims title to a tract of land consisting of one hundred acres, situated on Wills' swamp, on the south side of the river St. John's, bounded on all sides by government lands; the first line runs north 75° east, 25 chains; the second line running east 40 chains; the third running west 75°, 25 chains; the fourth running north 15° west, 40 chains, as by reference to the archives of the Territory will more fully appear; which title your memorialist derives from a royal title made to your memorialist by Governor Coppinger, in virtue of the royal order of October 29, 1790, as per the said royal title herewith submitted, and dated March 26, 1819; which land was granted her April 23, 1816, by the said Governor Coppinger, as therein set forth, marked G.   And your memorialist further showeth that she is in actual possession of said lands; that she is now a citizen of the United States and resident of the Territory of Florida.

her
HANNAH X NOBLES.
mark.

Witness to the mark of Hannah Nobles: GEORGE GIBBS.

[Here follows translation of a concession by Governor Coppinger, dated April 23, 1816.]

[Here follows translation of a certificate of survey and plat by George J. F. Clarke, dated May 13, 1817.]

DECREE.

Hannah Nobles' heirs vs. *The United States.   For one hundred acres of land.*

The board having ascertained the above to be a valid Spanish concession to claimant, do confirm it accordingly.   June 16, 1825.

No. 88.—See Report No. 1.

Lorenzo Capo's heirs vs. *The United States.   For one hundred and seventy-five acres of land.*

MEMORIAL.

To the honorable the commissioners appointed to ascertain claims and titles to lands in East Florida:

The heirs of Lorenzo Capo, deceased, respectfully show: That your memorialists claim title to a tract of land consisting of one hundred and seventy-five acres, situated in the Twelve-mile swamp adjoining the lands of Lewis Scholfield, but has never been surveyed.   In 1819 Governor Coppinger made an order for the survey of said tract by Andrew Burgevin, but the said Burgevin never complied with the said order, which is herewith presented; which title your memorialists derive from a grant made to the said Lorenzo Capo by Governor White, in virtue of the royal order of 1790, as appears by the *secretary's* certificate *herewith* presented, dated February 24, 1808. And your memorialists further show that the said Lorenzo Capo was in actual possession of said lands from the grant till 1812, when one of his sons was taken prisoner by the revolutionists and detained about six months, and the plantation broken up, and has not been resumed, owing to the poverty of the claimants; that they are citizens of the United States and residents of East Florida. St. Augustine, October 10, 1823.

JOHN B. STRONG, *Attorney for Claimants.*

[Here follows translation of a concession by Governor White, dated February 24, 1808.]
[Here follows the affidavit of Anthony Hindsman before the presiding judge of the county court, dated April 21, 1825, proving compliance with the conditions.]

DECREE.

Lorenzo Capo's heirs vs. *The United States. For one hundred and seventy-five acres of land.*

The above being a valid Spanish concession, with conditions which were complied with, dated previous to January 24, 1818, it is therefore confirmed June 16, 1825.

No. 83.—See REPORT No. 1.

John Frazer's executors vs. *The United States. For five hundred acres of land.*

MEMORIAL.

To the honorable the commissioners appointed to ascertain claims and titles to lands in East Florida:

The petition of Philip R. Yonge and Zephaniah Kingsley, as executors of John Frazer, respectfully showeth: That your memorialists claim title to a tract of land consisting of five hundred acres, situated on the St. Mary's river, about twelve —— from the island of Amelia, by the same on all sides, being an island, and called the Roundabout, or Cut-off which title your memorialists derive from a concession, dated May 2, 1810, to said John Frazer, deceased, by Governor White, in virtue of the royal order of ——, as by reference to the documents in the office of the public archives will more fully appear, copies not being procurable in time, and the originals mislaid. And your memorialists further show that said executors of the said John (the same having been by virtue of said concession taken possession of, improved, and cultivated) died a subject of Spain; that one of the said executors is a resident of ——; that said Frazer is a citizen of Great Britain; the other a resident of the Territory of Florida.

PHILIP R. YONGE,
ZEPH. KINGSLEY,
Executors of John Frazer, deceased,
By GEORGE GIBBS, *Attorney in fact.*

[Here follows the translation of a concession by Governor White, dated May 2, 1810, to John Frazer, deceased.]

DECREE.

Executors of John Frazer, deceased, vs. *The United States. For five hundred acres of land.*

This being a valid Spanish concession without conditions, made previous to January 24, 1818, it is therefore confirmed. June 22, 1825.

No. 90.—See REPORT No. 1.

John Bellamy vs. *The United States. For fifty acres of land.*

MEMORIAL.

To the honorable the commissioners appointed to ascertain claims and titles to lands in East Florida:

The petition of John Bellamy showeth: That your memorialist claims title to a tract of land consisting of fifty acres, situated at Jacksonville, on the St. John's river, south by the river St. John's, east and north by a creek making out of said river, and west by land granted to Z. Hogans; which title your memorialist derives from a royal grant made to John Mestre December 3, 1816, by Governor Coppinger, in virtue of the royal order of 1815, who sold the same to John Brady, and the said John Brady has since sold and conveyed the said lands to your memorialist. And your memorialist further showeth that he is in actual possession of said lands, and was so at the time of the cession; that he is a citizen of the United States and resident of the Territory of Florida.

A. BELLAMY, *Memorialist's Attorney.*

[Here follows the translation of a concession by Governor Coppinger, dated November 18, 1816, to John Mestre, and a plat by G. J. F. Clarke, dated February 21, 1817.]
[Here follows a conveyance from John Mestre to John Brady, dated June 1, 1822.]
[Here follows a conveyance from John Brady to John Bellamy, dated January 29, 1823.]

DECREE.

John Bellamy vs. *The United States. For fifty acres of land.*

This being a valid Spanish concession made to John Mestre previous to January 24, 1818, and being regularly conveyed to claimant, it is therefore confirmed to him. July 12, 1825.

No. 91.—See Report No. 1.

Heirs of Matthias Pons vs. The United States.   For four hundred acres of land.

MEMORIAL.

To the honorable the commissioners appointed to ascertain claims and titles to lands in East Florida:

The petition of the heirs of Matthias Pons, deceased, by Francis Marin, administrator, respectfully showeth: That your memorialists claim title to a tract of land consisting of four hundred acres, situated on the river Matanzas, known by the name of Casapula, to the south of St. Augustine, bounded on the north by lands of Fernando Falany, on the east by Matanzas river, on the south by lands of Pedro Chovet, and on the west by vacant lands, as will be seen by a plat and certificate of survey made by John Purcell, which is attached to the proceedings relating to this grant in the archives office; which title your memorialists derive from a royal title made to Matthias Pons September 17, 1814, by Governor Kindelan, in virtue of the royal order of October 29, 1790, a copy of which royal title is herewith presented; and the said Matthias Pons since that time departed this life, leaving Antonia Pons, wife of Francis Marin, Agathy Pons, Francis Pons, and Peter Pons, his children and heirs. And your memorialists further show that they are in actual possession of the said lands, and that they and their ancestors for many years have been; that they are citizens of the United States and residents of East Florida. They pray confirmation of title, &c.

FRANCIS MARIN, *Administrator of said deceased.*

[Here follows translation of a royal title made by Governor Kindelan, dated September 17, 1814.]

DECREE.

Matthias Pons' heirs vs. The United States.   For four hundred acres of land.

The board having ascertained the above to be a valid Spanish title, do confirm the same accordingly. August 9, 1825.

No. 92.—See Report No. 1.

Susannah Cashen vs. The United States.   For two hundred and fifty acres of land.

MEMORIAL.

To the honorable the commissioners appointed to ascertain claims and titles to lands in East Florida:

The petition of Susannah Cashen, widow of James Cashen, respectfully showeth: That your memorialist claims title to a tract of land consisting of two hundred and fifty acres, situated on Amelia island, near those formerly granted to him by the Spanish government, bounded on the north and east by lands belonging to Mr. Jordine, and on the south and west by vacant lands, as will be seen by a plat and certificate made by Juan Purcell in favor of James Cashen, deceased, dated November 30, 1807, and marked No. 2; which title your memorialist derives from a concession made to James Cashen by Governor White, in virtue of the royal order of 1790, as will appear by the same herewith presented, dated October 7, 1805, and marked No. 2. And your memorialist further showeth that she is legally in possession of said lands, and was so before the cession of this Territory to the United States; that she is a native of the United States and resident of St. Augustine. All of which is respectfully submitted, &c.

SUSANNAH CASHEN.

[Here follows a translation of a memorial to Governor White, dated September 27, 1805, soliciting a concession of the above, and a decree of the governor dated October 7, 1805.] .

[Here follows translation of a survey and plat by John Purcell, dated November 30, 1807.]

[Here follows translation of a resurvey of the said land by George J. F. Clarke, dated February 2, 1816.]

Susannah Cashen vs. The United States.   For two hundred and fifty acres of land.

The board having ascertained the above to be a valid Spanish concession, do confirm the same accordingly.   August 9, 1825.

No. 93.—See Report No. 1.

Pedro Pons vs. The United States.   For eight hundred and seventy-five acres of land.

MEMORIAL.

To the honorable the commissioners appointed to ascertain claims and titles to lands in East Florida:

Your memorialist claims title to a tract of land consisting of eight hundred and seventy-five acres, situated in Mills' swamp, on the river Nassau: the first of survey beginning at a pine and running south 25° east, ninety-seven chains, to a pine; second line, south 70° west, ninety chains, to a pine; third line, north 25° west, ninety-seven chains, to a pine; fourth line, north 70° east, ninety chains, to the pine at the beginning; which title your memorialist derives from an absolute title made to him by Governor Coppinger, in virtue of the royal order of 1815, and bearing date July 4, 1817, a certified copy of which accompanies this petition; and the plat and certificate of survey by George J. F. Clarke will be filed when required. And your memorialist further showeth that he is a native of East Florida and resident of the same. Your memorialist will, as in duty bound, pray, &c.

GEORGE J. F. CLARKE,
For PEDRO PONS.

[Here follows the translation of a royal title made by Governor Coppinger, dated June 4, 1817.]

DECREE.

Pedro Pons vs. The United States. For eight hundred and seventy-five acres of land.

. The board having ascertained the above to be a valid Spanish title, do confirm the same accordingly. August 9, 1825.

No. 94.—See REPORT No. 1.

Thomas Suarez vs. The United States. For five hundred acres of land.

MEMORIAL.

To the honorable the commissioners appointed to ascertain claims and titles to lands in East Florida:

The petition of Thomas Suarez, administrator of Antonio Suarez, deceased, respectfully showeth: That your memorialist claims title to a tract of land consisting of five hundred acres, situated on the island of Amelia, at a place called Black Point, bounded as will be seen by the royal grant made to Antonio Suarez, which is herewith presented; which title your memorialist derives from a royal grant made to Antonio Suarez, July 17, 1809, by Governor White, in virtue of the royal order of 1790. And your memorialist further showeth that he is in actual possession of said lands, and was so at the cession; that he is a citizen of the Territory and a resident of Duval county.

A. BELLAMY, *Claimant's Attorney.*

[Here follows the translation of a royal grant from Governor White to Antonio Suarez, dated July 27, 1809.]

DECREE.

Thomas Suarez, administrator of Antonio Suarez, vs. The United States. For five hundred acres of land.

The board having ascertained the above to be a valid Spanish title, do confirm the same accordingly. August 9, 1825.

No. 95.—See REPORT No. 1.

Domingo Fernandez vs. The United States. For three hundred acres of land.

MEMORIAL.

To the honorable the commissioners appointed to ascertain claims and titles to lands in East Florida:

The memorial of Domingo Fernandez, by his attorney, Farquhar Bethune, respectfully showeth: That your memorialist claims title to a tract of land consisting of three hundred acres, situated on Amelia island, and contained within the following lines and boundaries: the first line runs north 80° east, is in measure 37 chains, and is bounded by lands of said Fernandez; the second line runs south 11° east, measures 49 chains, and is bounded by lands of said Fernandez; the third line runs north 80° east, measures 30 chains; the fourth line runs south 11° east, is in measure 26 chains, bounded by the sand hills of the sea-beach; the fifth line runs west, measures 76 chains, bounded by vacant land; the sixth line runs north 11° west, is in length 64 chains, bounded by lands of John Bashlott; which title your memorialist derives from a grant made to James Adamson by Governor White, June 1, 1802, in virtue of the royal order of 1790, which tract was purchased from said Adamson *from* your memorialist. Your memorialist further showeth that he obtained from Governor Coppinger the full or royal title, dated April 11, 1817; that he is now and has been in actual possession of the said land for the last eighteen years; that he is an inhabitant of Florida and resident of Amelia island. The grant above alluded to is annexed. All of which is respectfully submitted, &c.

DOMINGO FERNANDEZ,
Per his attorney, FARQUHAR BETHUNE.

[Here follows the translation of a royal title made by Governor Coppinger, dated April 11, 1817.]

DECREE.

Domingo Fernandez vs. The United States. For three hundred acres of land.

The board having ascertained the above to be a valid Spanish grant, do confirm the same accordingly. August 16, 1825.

No. 91.—See REPORT No. 1.

Heirs of Cornelius Griffith vs. The United States. For three hundred acres of land.

MEMORIAL.

To the honorable the commissioners appointed to ascertain claims and titles to lands in East Florida:

The petition of William Downs, David Turner, Zachariah Haddock, and Abraham Simmons, husbands of Winney, Elizabeth, Sarah, and Eliza, heirs of Cornelius Griffith, respectfully showeth: That your memorialists claim title to a tract of land consisting of three hundred acres, situated on the banks of the river St. Mary's; bounded on the east by a creek known by the name of Mill creek, distant about a mile from said creek, and bounded on all other sides by vacant lands; which title your memorialists claim from a concession made to Cornelius Griffith on December 4, 1802, by Governor White, by virtue of a royal order of 1790, as by a more particular reference to the archives of the province of East Florida, and by a certified copy of said concession, filed herewith, will more fully and at large appear. And your memorialists further show that they are in legal possession of the said lands, and that they are citizens of the United States, and are, with the exception of said Downs, residents of this Territory. And your memorialists will ever pray, &c.

WM. DOWNS,
DAVID TURNER,
ZACH. HADDOCK, and
ABRAM. SIMMONS,
By their attorney, DAVID B. MACOMB.

Certified copy of concession filed herewith, marked B.

[Here follows translation of a concession made to Cornelius Griffith by Governor White, dated December 9, 1802.]

DECREE.

Heirs of Cornelius Griffith vs. The United States. For three hundred acres of land.

The board having ascertained the above to be a valid Spanish concession, and that the claimants are lawful heirs to the grantee, do confirm the same accordingly. August 16, 1825.

TESTIMONY.

C. Griffith's heirs vs. The United States. For three hundred acres of land.

Joseph Summerall sworn:
Question. How long was the claimant in possession of the land on Nassau?
Answer. About five years.
Question. How long since claimant obtained possession of this land?
Answer. Many years since; the land was surveyed by Pedro Marrot and Samuel Eastlake. The claimant was ordered off the land by the Spanish governor during the revolution of the year 1794, and is since dead; has three legal heirs in this Territory, and one out of it.

JOSEPH SUMMERALL.

Daniel Hogans sworn in the claim of 100 acres:
Question. When did claimant settle the land now claimed by him on Trout creek?
Answer. In the year 1808.
Question. How long did he remain there?
Answer. From 1808 to 1813, when he died. The land has since been occupied by his son-in-law.
Question. Has he any heirs within the Territory?
Answer. He has three heirs living within the Territory, and one without.

DANIEL HOGANS.

Before the board in session May 16, 1825.

No. 97.—See REPORT No. 1.

George J. F. Clarke vs. The United States. For one thousand acres of land.

MEMORIAL.

To the honorable the commissioners appointed to ascertain claims and titles to lands in East Florida:

The petition of George J. F. Clarke respectfully showeth: That your memorialist claims title to a tract of land consisting of one thousand acres, situated, five hundred acres thereof on the head of the north branch of Durbin's swamp, to the west of the part of said swamp called the Big Bend; the first line of the survey of the same beginning at a pine, and running south 40° east, 60 chains, to a pine; second line runs north 50° east, 83½ chains, to a pine; third line runs north 40° west, 60 chains, *west* to a pine; fourth line, south 50° west, 83½ chains, to the pine at the beginning; and five hundred acres in Picolata swamp, on the west side of St. John's river: the first line beginning at a cypress, and running north 67° west, 69 chains, to a pine; *fourth line*, east 45 chains, to a cypress; and the fifth, north 45° east, to the cypress at the beginning; and this last bounded by St. John's river; which title your memorialist derives from a grant made to him for headrights by Governor Kindelan, in virtue of the royal order of 1790; a certified copy thereof is hereunto annexed, and which grant was made to him on May 9, 1815. The two aforesaid surveys were made by Andres Burgevin, and the plats and certificates of them will be filed whenever required. And your memorialist further showeth that he is in actual possession of said lands; that he is a native of East Florida and resident of the same. Your memorialist will, as in duty bound, pray, &c.

GEO. J. F. CLARKE.

[Here follows translation of a concession made by Governor Kindelan, dated May 9, 1815.]

George J. F. Clarke vs. The United States. For one thousand acres of land.

The board having ascertained the above to be a valid Spanish concession, do confirm the same accordingly. August 17, 1825.

No. 98 —See Report No. 1.

Domingo Fernandez vs. *The United States. For one hundred and fifty acres of land.*

MEMORIAL.

To the honorable the commissioners appointed to ascertain claims and titles to lands in East Florida :

The memorial of Domingo Fernandez, by his attorney, Farquhar Bethune, respectfully showeth: That your memorialist claims title to a tract of and consisting of one hundred and fifty acres, situated on Amelia island, bounded on the north by a creek which forms the point of said tract, on the south by other lands of your memorialist, on the east by lands granted to Andrew Atkinson, and on the west by the harbor of Fernandina; which title your memorialist derives from a grant made to him by Governor White, in virtue of the royal order of October 29, 1790. After cultivating said tract more than ten years, your memorialist obtained from Governor White a title in fee simple for the same, dated August 19, 1807; which title accompanies this memorial, marked A. The survey of this tract will be produced when required. Your memorialist further showeth that he is now in actual possession of said land, and was so at the time of the cession; that he is an inhabitant of Florida and a resident of Amelia island. All of which is respectfully submitted.

DOMINGO FERNANDEZ,
By his attorney, FARQUEAR BETHUNE.

[Here follows the translation of a royal title by Governor White, dated August 19, 1807.]

DECREE.

Domingo Fernandez vs. *The United States. For one hundred and fifty acres of land.*

The board having ascertained the above to be a valid Spanish title, do confirm the same accordingly August 17, 1825.

No. 99 —See Report No. 1.

Susannah Cashen vs. *The United States. For two hundred and thirty acres of land.*

MEMORIAL.

To the honorable the commissioners appointed to ascertain claims and titles to lands in East Florida :

The petition of Susannah Cashen respectfully showeth: That your memorialist claims title to a tract of land consisting of two hundred and thirty acres, situated on the banks of the river St. Mary's, at a place known by the name of Old Township, bounded on the north by the lands of Spicer Christopher, and on the south with Brant's lands; which title your memorialist derives from a concession made to Joseph Ried July 13, 1804, by Governor White, in virtue of the royal order of October 29, 1790, who sold the same to Moses Harrell by deed of conveyance dated February 8, 1811, and signed by Joseph Ried and Nancy Ried, and herewith presented, and marked A; also a memorandum of agreement between Harrell for said lands and improvements thereon, dated November 12, 1811, and signed by James Cashen and Moses Harrell, and marked B. And your memorialist further showeth that she is legally in possession of said lands, and that her said husband was so before the cession of this Territory to the United States; that she is a native of the United States and a resident of St. Augustine. All of which is respectfully submitted.

SUSANNAH CASHEN.

[Here follows the translation of a concession made by Governor White, dated July 13, 1804.]
[Here follows a transfer from Joseph Ried and Nancy Ried to Moses Harrell, dated February 5, 1811.]
[Here follows a transfer from Moses Harrell to James Cashen, dated November 12, 1811.]
[Here follows the deposition of William Braddock, before Charles Seaton, justice of the peace, proving occupation and possession of the above, dated June 10, 1825.]

DECREE.

Susannah Cashen vs. *The United States. For two hundred and thirty acres of land.*

The board having ascertained the above to be a valid Spanish concession, and that it was occupied and possessed according to the terms thereof, and also that the deraignment is clear to the claimant, do confirm it accordingly. August 17, 1825.

No. 100.—See Report No. 1.

Francis Richard vs. *The United States. For four hundred and sixty-six acres of land.*

MEMORIAL.

To the honorable the commissioners appointed to ascertain claims and titles to lands in East Florida :

The petition of Francis Richard respectfully showeth: That your memorialist claims title to a tract of land consisting of four hundred and sixty-six acres, situated at a place called Branchester, St. John's river; the first line beginning at a bay, north 70° east, 70 chains, to a pine; third line, south 70° west, to a gum; fourth line formed and bounded by said river; which title your memorialist —— from an absolute title made to him by Kindelan, in virtue of the royal order of 1790, a certified copy of which accompanies this petition, bearing date March 20, 1815, the plat of which, by Samuel Eastlake, will be filed when required. And your memorialist further showeth that he is in actual possession of said lands; that he has long been a resident of this province. Your memorialist will, as in duty bound, pray, &c.

GEO. J. F. CLARKE,
For FRANCIS RICHARD.

[Here follows the translation of a royal title from Governor Kindelan, dated March 20, 1815.]

DECREE.

Francis-Richard vs. *The United States. For four hundred and sixty-six acres of land.*

The board having ascertained the above to be a valid Spanish grant, do confirm it accordingly. August 17, 1825.

No. 101.—See REPORT No. 1.

Francis Richard vs. *The United States. Claim for two hundred and thirty acres of land.*

MEMORIAL.

To the honorable the commissioners appointed to ascertain claims and titles to lands in East Florida:

The petition of Francis Richard respectfully showeth: That your memorialist claims title to a tract of land consisting of two hundred and thirty acres, situated at a place called Parque, on St. John's river; the first line beginning at a gum, north 70° east, 23 chains, and to a pine; second, south 100 chains, to a pine; third, west 25 chains, to a cherry tree; fourth line formed and bounded by the said river; which title your memorialist derives from an absolute grant made to him by Governor Kindelan, in virtue of the royal order of 1790, a certified copy of which, dated March 20, 1815, accompanies this petition. The plat and certificate of survey by Samuel Eastlake will be filed when required. And your memorialist further showeth that he is in actual possession of said lands; that he has long been an inhabitant and resident of this country. Your memorialist will, as in duty bound, pray, &c.

GEO. J. F. CLARKE,
For FRANCIS RICHARD.

[Here follows the translation of a royal title by Governor Kindelan, dated March 20, 1815.]

DECREE.

Francis Richard vs. *The United States. For two hundred and thirty acres of land.*

The board having ascertained the above to be a valid Spanish title, do confirm the same accordingly. August 17, 1825.

No. 102.—See REPORT No. 1.

Domingo Fernandez vs. *The United States. For one hundred acres of land.*

MEMORIAL.

To the honorable the commissioners appointed to ascertain claims and titles to lands in East Florida:

The memorial of Domingo Fernandez, by his attorney, Farquhar Bethune, respectfully showeth: That your memorialist claims title to a tract of land containing one hundred acres, situated on Amelia island, bounded on the north by other lands of your memorialist, on the east by John McClure's land, on the south by Isabella Jardine's land, and on the west by Amelia river; which title your memorialist derives from a grant made to him by Governor White August 21, 1803, in virtue of the royal order of October 29, 1790; for which tract, after cultivating it more than ten years, your memorialist obtained a title in fee simple from Governor Kindelan, dated September 1, 1813, which title is hereunto annexed, marked A. The plat and survey of this tract is in the archives. Your memorialist further showeth that he is now in actual possession of said land, and was so at the time of the cession, and for many years previous; that he is an inhabitant and resident of East Florida. All of which is respectfully submitted, &c.

DOMINGO FERNANDEZ,
By his attorney, FARQUHAR BETHUNE.

[Here follows translation of the royal title by Governor Kindelan, dated September 1, 1813.]

DECREE.

Domingo Fernandez vs. *The United States. For one hundred acres of land.*

The board having ascertained the above to be a valid Spanish title, do confirm the same accordingly. August 17, 1825.

No. 103.—See REPORT No. 1.

Jane Murray vs. *The United States. For six hundred acres of land.*

MEMORIAL.

To the honorable the commissioners appointed to ascertain claims and titles to lands in East Florida:

The memorial of Jane Murray respectfully showeth: That your memorialist claims title to a tract of land containing six hundred acres, situate, lying, and being at Mosquito, at the place known as the plantation of McDougal, about eight miles from the wharf of Turnbull, and fronting on the river Hillsborough; which title your memorialist derives from a grant made by Governor White July 28, 1803, as will appear by the decree on file in the office of the archives, and a certificate by Don Juan Pierra, herewith filed.

JANE MURRAY,
By her attorney, B. A. PUTNAM.

[Here follows translation of the certificate of concession made by Governor White July 28, 1803.]

[Here follows a letter from John Addison to George Murray, dated New Smyrna, February 9, 1807, stating his being about to plant the land of the latter.]

[Here follows the deposition of Dr. James Hall, proving the occupation and cultivation of the above by George Murray, before Elias B. Gould, J. P., July 18, 1825.]

DECREE.

Jane Murray vs. *The United States.   For six hundred acres of land.*

The board having ascertained the above to be a valid Spanish concession, the conditions of which have been complied with, and that the claimant is legal representative of the grantee, do confirm the same accordingly.   August 23, 1825.

TESTIMONY.

Jane Murray vs. *The United States.   For six hundred acres of land.*

Farquhar Bethune, being sworn, states that he was acquainted with George Murray, the original claimant; that witness went on the tract claimed the latter end of the year 1803, or beginning of 1804, and found claimant in possession; claimant had a house built on said land, and planted and improved the land.

FARQUHAR BETHUNE.

Before the board in session June 13, 1825.

No. 104.—See Report No. 1.

John Christopher vs. *The United States.   For five hundred acres of land.*

MEMORIAL.

To the honorable the commissioners appointed to ascertain claims and titles to lands in East Florida:

The petition of John Christopher respectfully showeth: That your memorialist claims title to a tract of land consisting of five hundred acres, situated on and near the mouth of the river Nassau, at a place called St. Maria, bounded as will be seen by the royal grant herewith presented; which title your memorialist derives from a royal grant made to Spicer Christopher April 8, 1809, by Governor White, in virtue of the royal order of 1790; the same fell to your memorialist by the will of the said Spicer Christopher, deceased.   And your memorialist further showeth that he is in actual possession of said lands, and was so at the cession; that he is a citizen of the United States and resident of East Florida.

BELLAMY, *Memorialist's Attorney.*

[Here follows translation of a royal title made to Spicer Christopher, dated April 8, 1809, by Governor White.]

DECREE.

John Christopher vs. *The United States.   For five hundred acres of land.*

The board having ascertained the above to be a valid Spanish title, and that it was by the will of the grantee left to claimant, do confirm the same accordingly.   August 23, 1825.

No. 105.—See Report No. 1.

Domingo Fernandez vs. *The United States.   For two hundred acres of land.*

MEMORIAL.

To the honorable the commissioners appointed to ascertain claims and titles to lands in East Florida:

The memorial of Domingo Fernandez, by his attorney, Farquhar Bethune, respectfully showeth: That he claims title to a tract of land consisting of six caballerias, or about two hundred acres, situated on the main land opposite Amelia island, and known by the name of the Orange Grove, contained within the following lines: the first line runs south 10° east, beginning at the bank of the creek and terminating at a water oak marked with a cross on the margin of a marsh, and is in length 80 chains; the second line runs south 80° west, beginning at said crossed tree and terminates with a stake with the same mark, and is in length 20 chains; the third line runs north 20° west, beginning at said stake and terminating with a pine tree marked with a cross, on the margin of a marsh, and is in length 80 chains; its front runs on the bank of a creek which comes from the river St. Mary's, and forms an irregular figure; which title your memorialist derives from a grant made to Maria Mattair by Governor Quesada February 20, 1792, in virtue of the royal order of October 29, 1790; the said Maria Mattair dying, said tract descended to her children and heirs, Lewis Mattair and his sister, wife of your memorialist—one-half to each; which heirs obtained from Governor White a title in fee simple for said tract, dated April 25, 1807; one-half of said tract in right of his wife, one of the co-heirs of said Maria Mattair, deceased; the other half in virtue of a purchase made from Lewis Mattair of his half, as will appear from his deed of conveyance, dated April 11, 1820.   The title in fee simple to the heirs of Maria Mattair, marked A, and the deed from Lewis Mattair, marked B, are annexed to this memorial.   Your memorialist further showeth that he is now, and was in actual possession of said land at the cession; that he is an inhabitant of East Florida and a resident of Amelia island.   All of which is respectfully submitted, &c.

DOMINGO FERNANDEZ,
By his attorney, FARQUHAR BETHUNE.

[Here follows a translation of a royal title from Governor White, dated April 25, 1807.]

[Here follows a translation of a conveyance from Lewis Mattair to Domingo Fernandez of one-half of the above, dated April 11, 1820.]

DECREE.

Domingo Fernandez vs. The United States.   For two hundred acres of land.

The board having ascertained the above to be a valid Spanish title, and the deraignment being clear, do confirm it accordingly to claimant.   August 23, 1825.

No. 106.—See REPORT No. 1.

John Houston vs. The United States.   For six hundred acres of land.

MEMORIAL.

To the honorable the commissioners appointed to ascertain claims and titles to lands in East Florida:

The petition of John Houston respectfully showeth: That your memorialist claims title to a tract of land consisting of six hundred acres, situated at the north end of the island of Talbot, bounded north by Nassau sound, south by lands of your memorialist, east and west by marshes, which will be seen by reference to the decree in the keeper of the archives' office; which title your memorialist derives from a decree made to Spicer Christopher December 4, 1795, in virtue of the royal order of 1790; the same fell to Lewis Christopher at the distribution, according to the will of the late Spicer Christopher, who sold the same to your memorialist; and your memorialist further showeth that he is in actual possession of said lands, and was so at the time of the cession; that he is a citizen of the United States and resident of the Territory of Florida.

                                      A. BELLAMY, *Memorialist's Attorney.*

[Here follows translation of the concession to Spicer Christopher, dated December 2, 1795, made by Governor Quesada.]

[Here follows translation of a royal title for the same, dated November 6, 1819, by Governor Coppinger, in favor of the heirs of grantee.]

DECREE.

John Houston vs. The United States.   For six hundred acres of land.

The board having ascertained this to be a valid Spanish grant, made to Spicer Christopher, deceased, by Governor Quesada, and it also appearing of record that said John Houston is one of the heirs of said Christopher, the same is therefore confirmed to claimant.   August 25, 1825.

TESTIMONY.

John Houston vs. The United States.   For six hundred acres of land.

Francis J. Fatio, being sworn, says that he knows that Spicer Christopher resided for a number of years on Talbot island, in the Territory of Florida, and that the land above claimed is a part of the land on which he resided.

                                      F. J. FATIO.

Before the board in session August 24, 1825.

No. 107.—See REPORT No. 1.

Domingo Fernandez vs. The United States.   For two hundred and twenty-eight acres of land.

MEMORIAL.

To the honorable the commissioners appointed to ascertain claims and titles to lands in East Florida:

The memorial of Domingo Fernandez, by his attorney, Farquhar Bethune, respectfully showeth: That he claims title to a tract of land consisting of two hundred and twenty-eight acres, situated on the west side of Amelia river, with the following lines and boundaries: the first line runs west, and measures forty-eight chains, bounded by Andrew Tucker's land; the second line runs north 36° east, is in length sixty-four chains, and bounded by William Berry's land; the fourth line runs south 73° west, is in length sixty-six chains, and bounded by the lands of Lewis Mattair; which title your memorialist derives from a grant made to him by Governor Coppinger April 10, 1817, in virtue of the royal order of March 29, 1815, which grant is hereunto annexed, marked A.   The survey by the surveyor general is in the archives and will be furnished when required.   Your memorialist further shows that he is now in actual possession of said land, and was so at the time of the cession; that he is an inhabitant of Florida and a resident of Amelia island.   All of which is respectfully submitted.

                                      DOMINGO FERNANDEZ,
                              By his attorney, FARQUHAR BETHUNE.

[Here follows translation of a royal title made by Governor Coppinger, dated April 10, 1817.]

DECREE.

Domingo Fernandez vs. The United States.   For two hundred and twenty-eight acres of land.

The board having ascertained the above to be a valid Spanish title, do confirm the same accordingly. August 27, 1825.

No 108.—See REPORT No. 1.

Henry Yonge vs. *The United States.   For one hundred and ninety acres of land.*

MEMORIAL.

To the honorable the commissioners appointed to ascertain claims and titles to lands in East Florida:

The memorial of Henry Yonge showeth: That your memorialist claims title to one hundred and ninety acres of land, situated in Lofton's swamp, and that the same is bounded as set forth in the original survey and plat thereof, made by George J. F. Clarke, surveyor, dated June 8, 1817, and herewith filed, and marked exhibit A.   That the said tract of land was surveyed and set off to your memorialist in virtue of a grant made by Governor Coppinger March 15, 1817, to your memorialist; and that the said grant is on file amongst the public archives of the Territory.

HENRY YONGE,
By his agent, PETER MITCHEL.

[Here follows the translation of a concession made by Governor Coppinger, dated March 15, 1817.]
[Here follows translation of a certificate of survey and a plat by George J. F. Clarke, dated June 8, 1817.]

DECREE.

Henry Yonge vs. *The United States.   For one hundred and ninety acres of land.*

The board having ascertained the above to be a valid Spanish concession, do confirm the same accordingly.   August 27, 1825.

No. 109.—See REPORT No. 1.

Henry Yonge vs. *The United States.   For four hundred and eighty acres of land.*

MEMORIAL.

To the honorable the commissioners appointed to ascertain claims and titles to lands in East Florida:

The memorial of Henry Yonge showeth: That your memorialist claims title to four hundred and eighty acres of land on St. Mary's river, and that the same is bounded as set forth in the original survey and plat hereof, made by George J. F. Clarke surveyor, and dated April 1, 1816, and herewith filed, and marked exhibit A.   That the said land was granted to Henry Yonge, and is part of a grant of nine hundred and eighty acres made by Governor Estrada December 22, 1815, in virtue of a royal order of 1815; and that the said grant is of record amongst the public archives.

[Here follows translation of a royal title by Governor Estrada, dated December 22, 1815, for nine hundred and eighty acres of land.]
[Here follows translation of a certificate of survey and a plat by George J. F. Clarke, dated April 1, 1816.]

DECREE.

Henry Yonge vs. *The United States.   For four hundred and eighty acres of land.*

The board having ascertained the above to be a valid Spanish royal title for nine hundred and eighty acres of land, in two tracts, the one of five hundred and the other of four hundred and eighty acres, and this claim being one of them, the same is confirmed accordingly.   August 27, 1825.

No. 110.—See REPORT No. 1.

[*Henry Yonge* vs. *The United States.   For five hundred acres of land.*

MEMORIAL.

To the honorable the commissioners appointed to ascertain claims and titles to lands in East Florida:

The memorial of Henry Yonge showeth: That your memorialist claims title to five hundred acres of land, situated on St. Mary's and Little St. Mary's river, and that the same is bounded as set forth in the original survey and plat thereof, made by George J. F. Clarke, surveyor, and dated April 3, 1816, and herewith filed, and marked exhibit B.

That the said land was granted to Henry Yonge, and is part of a grant of nine hundred and eighty acres made by Governor Estrada December 22, 1815, in virtue of a royal order of 1815; and that the said grant is of record among the public archives.

HENRY YONGE.

[Here follows translation of a royal title by Governor Estrada, dated December 22, 1815, for 980 acres of land.]
[Here follows translation of a certificate of survey and a plat by George J. F. Clarke, dated April 3, 1816.]

DECREE.

Henry Yonge vs. *The United States.   For five hundred acres of land.*

The board having ascertained the above to be a valid Spanish royal title for 980 acres of land, divided into two tracts, one of 500 acres and the other of 480 acres, and this claim being one of them, the same is confirmed accordingly.   August 27, 1825.

No. 111.—See Report No. 1.

Francis Richard vs. The United States.   For one hundred and ten acres of land.

MEMORIAL.

To the honorable the commissioners appointed to ascertain claims and titles to lands in East Florida:

The petition of Francis Richard respectfully showeth: That your memorialist claims title to a tract of land consisting of one hundred and ten acres, situated on St. John's river, at Point Santa Isabella; the first line runs north 85° west, 58 chains, and bounding on George Atkinson's land; the second, south 40° east, 52 chains, and bounded by lands of Philip F. Fatio; which title your memorialist derives from an absolute title made to him by Governor Coppinger, in virtue of the royal order of 1790, a certified copy of which your memorialist presents herewith, dated, first grant, January 8, 1801, surveyed by George J. F. Clarke March 1, 1812, carried into absolute title January 27, 1818.   The plat and certificate of survey will be filed when required.   And your memorialist further showeth that he is in actual possession of said lands; that he has long been an inhabitant and resident of East Florida.   Your memorialist will, as in duty bound, pray, &c.

GEO. J. F. CLARKE,
For FRANCIS RICHARD.

[Here follows the translation of a concession made by Governor White, dated January 9, 1801.]
[Here follows translation of a royal title by Governor Coppinger, dated January 27, 1818, in confirmation of the above concession.]
[Here follows translation of a certificate of survey and a plat by George J. F. Clarke, dated March 1, 1812.]

DECREE.

Francis Richard vs. The United States.   For one hundred and ten acres of land.

The board having ascertained this to be a valid Spanish concession, do confirm it accordingly. September 2, 1825.

No. 112.—See Report No. 1.

Joseph Simeon Sanchez vs. The United States.   For one thousand acres of land.

MEMORIAL.

TERRITORY OF FLORIDA, *East Florida:*

To the honorable the commissioners appointed to ascertain claims and titles to lands in East Florida:

The memorial of Joseph Simeon Sanchez, for himself and the other heirs of Francisco Xavier Sanchez, deceased, respectfully showeth: That your memorialist, for himself and the other heirs of the said Francisco Xavier Sanchez, deceased, claims title to a certain tract of land situated and being in East Florida aforesaid; that the said tract of land was originally granted to the said Francisco X. Sanchez by the British government while East Florida was a province and dependency of the crown of Great Britain; that after the acquisition of said province by the Spanish government, to wit: March 4, 1793, the said tract of land was conceded and confirmed to the said Francisco X. Sanchez by the Spanish government, as will fully appear by a reference to the original decree, of record in the office of the keeper of the public archives of East Florida, confirming the said land to the said Francisco X. Sanchez; that the said Francisco X. Sanchez departed this life some time about the year 1808, leaving your memorialist and those for whose benefit this claim is made; that he died in the actual occupancy and possession of the said land; was surveyed by one Robert McHardy, as surveyor appointed by the government for that purpose, about April 26, 1819, as will appear by a reference to the certified copy of the plat and certificate of survey of that date herewith filed, and marked exhibit A; that the said one thousand acres were surveyed in four different tracts of unequal quantities near each other, and are situated in Diego plains, at a place in the said plains called "Montes de San Diego" in the Spanish language.   Your memorialist begs leave to refer to the plat of the said survey as setting forth the lines of the said different tracts.   Your memorialist further shows that the heirs of the said Francisco X. Sanchez obtained a royal title or grant in absolute property for the said tract of land, June 5, 1821, from Don José Coppinger, then the governor of East Florida, as will appear by a certified copy of the said grant herewith filed, marked exhibit B.   Your memorialist further represents and shows that the said Francisco X. Sanchez became and was a Spanish subject when the Spanish decree herein first mentioned was made to him for the said land, and also an inhabitant and settler of East Florida, and so continued to the time of his death; that the heirs of the said Francisco X. Sanchez were all, at the time of the death of the said Francisco X. Sanchez, inhabitants and settlers of East Florida and Spanish subjects, and have ever since continued to be, and are now, inhabitants and settlers thereof.   Wherefore they pray a confirmation of this title to the said tract of land and its appurtenances.

JOSEPH S. SANCHEZ,
By his attorney, JOHN DRYSDALE.

[Here follows the translation of a memorial of Francisco X. Sanchez, dated March 3, 1793, and a decree ordering the survey to be made by Don Pedro Marrot, dated March 4, 1793.]
[Here follows the translation of a memorial requesting that the above survey should be made by Robert McHardy, in consequence of the certificate of the former having been mislaid, dated October 30, 1818, and a decree granting the same, dated October 31, 1818.]
[Here follows plat and survey by Robert McHardy, dated April 26, 1819.]
[Here follows the translation of a royal title by Governor Coppinger to the children and heirs of Don Francisco X. Sanchez, dated June 5, 1821.]

DECREE.

José Simeon Sanchez and other heirs of Francisco X. Sanchez, deceased, vs. The United States.   For one thousand acres of land.

The board having ascertained that the title of claimant is a valid Spanish title, do confirm the same accordingly.   September 14, 1825.

No. 113.—See Report No. 1.

Joseph Simeon Sanchez, for himself and the other heirs of Frances X. Sanchiz, deceased, vs. The United States. For one hundred acres of land.

MEMORIAL.

TERRITORY OF FLORIDA, *East Florida:*

To the honorable the commissioners appointed to ascertain claims and titles to lands in East Florida:

The memorial of José Simeon Sanchez respectfully showeth: That in behalf of himself and the other heirs of the said Francisco X. Sanchez, deceased, he claims title to a certain tract of land containing one hundred acres, situated and being in the county of St. John's, in East Florida aforesaid; that the said tract of land was conceded originally to the said Francisco X. Sanchez August 4, 1801, by Governor White, then the governor of East Florida, and while it was a dependency of the Spanish crown, under and in virtue of the royal order of the King of Spain of October 29, 1790, as will appear by a certified copy of the said concession herewith filed, marked exhibit A; that the said tract of land was surveyed, by authority, by Andres Burgevin, as appears by the certified copy of the original plat and certificate of survey herewith filed, marked exhibit B; that the said land is situated at a place called in the Spanish language "Montes de Puercos," in Diego plains; that it has the following lines and dimensions, that is to say: the first line begins at a palmetto tree marked with a ×, and runs south 75° east, 50 chains, to a pine marked with a ×; the second line runs north 15° east, 20 chains, to a pine marked ×; the third line runs north 75° west, 50 chains, to a palmetto marked ×; and the fourth line runs thence to the place of beginning, as will distinctly appear by a reference to the copy of the said plat herewith filed. Your memorialist further shows that the said Franc sco X. Sanchez departed this life some time about the year 1808, upon which the said land devolved upon your memorialist and those for whose benefit this claim is made; that the heirs of the said Francisco X. Sanchez obtained a title in absolute property to the said tract of land, June 5, 1821, from Don José Coppinger, then the governor of East Florida, as will appear by a certified copy of a royal title of that date herewith submitted and filed, and marked exhibit C. And your memorialist avers that the said Francisco X. Sanchez was, at the time of the original concession as aforesaid and at the time of his death, an inhabitant and settler of East Florida and a subject of the King of Spain; that your memorialist and the other heirs of the said Francisco X. Sanchez were, at the time of the death of the said Francisco X. Sanchez, and at the time of the cession of this Territory to the United States, Spanish subjects and inhabitants and settlers of East Florida, and have ever since been and now are settlers of the same. Wherefore your memorialist prays confirmation of the title of the heirs of the said Francisco X. Sanchez to the said land and appurtenances.

                                        JOSEPH SIMEON SANCHEZ,
                                By his attorney, JOHN DRYSDALE.

[Here follows a translation of a concession by Governor White, dated August 4, 1801.]
[Here follows the plat and translation of the certificate of survey by Andres Burgevin, dated March 30, 1819.]
[Here follows the translation of a royal title by Governor Coppinger, dated June 5, 1821.]

DECREE.

Heirs of Francis X. Sanchez vs. The United States. For one hundred acres of land.

The board having ascertained the above to be a valid Spanish concession, complied with, do confirm the same accordingly. September 14, 1825.

No. 114.—See Report No. 1.

Daniel Hulbert vs. The United States. For two hundred acres of land.

MEMORIAL.

To the honorable the commissioners appointed to ascertain claims and titles to lands in East Florida:

The petition of Daniel Hulbert respectfully showeth: That your memorialist claims title to a tract of land consisting of two hundred acres, situated four miles north of the city of St. Augustine, bounded north by lands of memorialist, south by the ford called Navaro and plantation called Chebre, on the east by vacant lands, and on the west by vacant pine barren; which title your memorialist derives from a grant made to John Tatton by Governor Quesada, in virtue of the judicial sale made December 15, 1792, who sold to José Antonio Iguinez, by his agent, Michael O'Reilley, December 3, 1794, and, as the property of said Iguinez, the said tract was sold at public sale, under execution, at the suit of John Baptiste Collins, issued March 28, 1814, when the said tract was afterwards sold, June 8, 1818, and memorialist became the purchaser; all of which will be seen by documents made by Governor Coppinger, dated July 23, 1818, a certified copy of which is herewith presented. And your memorialist further showeth that he is in actual possession of the said lands, and was so at the time of the cession of this province to the United States; that he is a citizen of the United States and resident of East Florida. He prays confirmation of his title, &c.

                                        DANIEL HULBERT.

[Here follows a judicial sale made to John Tatton by Governor Quesada, dated December 15, 1792.]
[Here follows a power of attorney from John Tatton to the Rev. Michael O'Reilley, dated Havana, January 28, 1793.]
[Here follows a conveyance from the Rev. Michael O'Reilley to Thomas Travers, dated St. Augustine, August 18, 1794.]
[Here follows a conveyance from Thomas Travers to José de Antonio Iguinez, dated St. Augustine, December 3, 1794.]

[Here follows a judicial sale made of the aforesaid two hundred of acres land by Governor Coppinger to Daniel Hulbert, dated St. Augustine, July 23, 1818.]

DECREE.

Daniel Hulbert vs. The United States. For two hundred acres of land.

The board having ascertained this to be a valid Spanish grant made previous to January 24, 1818, to John Tatton, and afterwards sold by order of the Spanish tribunal to the claimant, they therefore confirm the same. September 14, 1825.

No. 115.—See REPORT No. 1.

Heirs of Jesse Fish vs. The United States. For five hundred acres of land.

MEMORIAL.

To the honorable the commissioners appointed to ascertain claims and titles to lands in East Florida:

The memorial of the heirs of Jesse Fish respectfully showeth: That your memorialists claim title to a tract or parcel of land containing five hundred acres, situated at the head of Matanzas river, at a place known, during the time the British held this province, by the name of Tod's fields; which tract of land was granted by the Spanish government to the deceased Don Jesse Fish, April 1, 1791, for headrights, as will more fully appear by a memorial and decree exhibited, and marked A. And your memorialists further show that the said tract of land has continued in the possession and has been cultivated by the deceased Jesse Fish and his heirs since April 1, 1791, to the present day. Your memorialists further show that they are at present residents of the Territory of Florida, &c.

G. W. PERPALL, *for the heirs of Jesse Fish*

[Here follows translation of a concession made by Governor Quesada to Jesse Fish, dated April 1, 1791.]
[Here follows translation of a royal title for the same, dated April 24, 1819, by Governor Coppinger to the heirs of Jesse Fish.]

DECREE.

Heirs of Jesse Fish vs. The United States. For five hundred acres of land.

The board having ascertained the above to be a valid Spanish concession, do confirm the same accordingly.

TESTIMONY.

Sarah Fish vs. The United States. For five hundred acres of land.

G. W. Perpall, being sworn, states that he came to East Florida in 1803, and that Mr. Fish was then in possession of said tract and cultivated it ever since to his death, and that his heirs have also cultivated it, except in the year 1812. It was surveyed by Charles W. Clarke, who has lands to the south of said tract; and as Mr. Clark took into his tract the lands which Mr. Fish asked for, for which reason witness believes that the plat was laid aside.

Heirs of Jesse Fish vs. The United States. For five hundred acres of land.

G. W. Perpall, being sworn, states that Jesse Fish cultivated the said tract of land in the year 1803, and continued to do so until his death, when his heirs have done so up to the present period.

G. W. PERPALL.

Before the board in session September 14, 1825.

No. 116.—See REPORT No. 1.

Heirs of Andrew Dewees vs. The United States. For two thousand two hundred and ninety acres of land.

MEMORIAL.

To the honorable the commissioners appointed to ascertain claims and titles to lands in East Florida:

The petition of the heirs of Andrew Dewees, by their attorney, George Gibbs, respectfully showeth: That your memorialists claim title to a tract of land consisting of two thousand two hundred and ninety acres, or sixty-nine caballerias, situated on the south side of St. John's river, and on the east side by Pablo creek, and bounded by the same as follows: the first line runs south on the edge of a marsh of the river St. John, to a stake on the beach marked with a cross, one hundred and ninety-five chains; the second line runs west from the said stake to a pine marked with a cross at the edge of a marsh on Pablo creek, adjoining the land of John McQueen, one hundred and thirty chains; and the third line runs to the north of Pablo creek; and the fourth line runs to the marsh on St. John's river, according to a certificate given by Don Pedro Marrot, dated February 8, 1792—reference to which in the office of archives; which title your memorialists derive from a royal grant made to Andrew Dewees, the father of your memorialists, by Governor White, in virtue of the royal order of October 29, 1790, as by reference to the royal title herewith exhibited, dated May 4, 1804, marked D, will more fully appear. And your memorialists further show that they are in actual possession of said lands; and that they are citizens of the United States, and part of them residents of the said plantation, in the Territory of Florida.

MARY DEWEES,
By GEORGE GIBBS, &c.

[Here follows the translation of a royal title by Governor White, dated May 4, 1804.]

DECREE.

Heirs of Andrew Dewees vs. *The United States. For two thousand two hundred and ninety acres of land.*

The board having ascertained the above to be a valid Spanish grant, and that the heirs of Andrew Dewees are now, and have been previous to the cession of this province, in the actual occupancy and cultivation of the same, do confirm it accordingly.   September 26, 1825.

TESTIMONY.

The heirs of Andrew Dewees vs. *The United States. For two thousand two hundred and ninety acres of land.*

George Gibbs, being sworn, says that some of the heirs are actually in possession of the whole or some part of the said tract, and do now cultivate the same.

GEORGE GIBBS.

Before the board in session September 26, 1825.

No. 117.—See REPORT No. 1.

Seymour Pickett vs. *The United States. Claim for two hundred and fifty acres.*

MEMORIAL.

To the honorable the commissioners appointed to ascertain claims and titles to lands in East Florida :

The petition of Seymour Pickett respectfully showeth: That your memorialist claims title to a tract of land consisting of two hundred and fifty acres, situated at a place called Hodguin's Plantation; first line runs south 55° east, 55 chains, to a stake second line runs north 35° east, 55 chains, to a pine; third line runs north 55° west 55 chains; the fourth line runs south 35° west, 55 chains, to a gum, as appears by the royal title hereunto annexed, dated May 26, 1815; which title your memorialist derives from a grant made to Reuben Hogan by Governor Kindelan, in virtue of the royal order of 1790, who sold the same to your memorialist, as appears by the instrument herewith presented, annexed to the royal title. And your memorialist further showeth that he is in actual possession of said lands, and has been since the cession; that he is a citizen of the United States and resident of Florida.   St. Augustine, November 23, 1823.

JOHN B. STRONG, *Attorney for Claimant.*

[Here follows the translation of a royal title made to Reuben Hogan by Governor Kindelan, dated May 25, 1815.]
[Here follows a conveyance from Reuben Hogan to Seymour Pickett, in presence of D. S. H. Miller, acting judge of St. John's district, without a date.]

DECREE.

Seymour Pickett vs. *The United States. For four hundred and fifty acres of land.*

The board having ascertained that the above is a valid Spanish grant, and that the deraignment to the claimant is proved, do confirm the same accordingly.   September 26, 1825.

No. 118.—See REPORT No. 1.

Heirs of Constance McFee vs. *The United States. For four hundred and forty-six acres of land.*

MEMORIAL.

To the honorable the commissioners appointed to ascertain claims and titles to lands in East Florida :

The memorial of the heirs of Constance McFee respectfully showeth: That your memorialists claim title to a tract of land consisting of four hundred and forty-six acres, situated on the river St. John's, on Julington and Cunningham creeks, and beginning with an oak tree marked X, and concludes with a pine tree marked X, joining the plantation of Hannah Moore; which title your memorialists derive from a grant in 1791 made to their ancestor, Angus Clark, by Governor Quesada, in virtue of the royal order of 1790, who inherited the same December 12, 1804.   And your memorialists further show that they are, and have been, by their agent, in actual possession of said lands; that they are natives of Georgia and residents of the West Indies.   St. Augustine, December 1, 1823.

GABRIEL G. PERPALL,
Attorney for heirs of Constance McFee.

[Here follows translation of a concession from Governor Quesada to Angus Clark, dated December 10, 1791.]
[Here follows translation of a judicial decree by Governor White, with the assistance of his assessor general, declaring the validity of Angus Clark's testamentary settlement in favor of his only daughter, Constance McFee, dated December 12, 1804.]

DECREE.

Heirs of Constance McFee vs. *The United States. For four hundred and forty-six acres.*

The board having ascertained the above to be a valid Spanish concession, and the inheritance of claimants established, do confirm the same accordingly.   September 30, 1825.

TESTIMONY.

The heirs of Constance McFee vs. The United States. For four hundred and forty-six acres of land.

G. W. Perpall, being sworn on the part of claimants, states that he has heretofore been acting as attorney in fact for Mrs. Constance McFee, and that he has been in possession of the above-named tract of land for more than twelve years, and has kept possession of and cultivated said tract for her use and benefit.

G. W. PERPALL.

Before the board in session September 30, 1825.

No. 119.—See Report No. 1.

Archibald Clarke and Elihu Atwater vs. The United States.   Claim for two hundred acres.

MEMORIAL.

To the honorable the commissioners appointed to ascertain claims and titles to lands in East Florida:

That your memorialists claim title to a tract of land consisting of two hundred acres, situated on the St. John's river, at or near a place called Jolly's old field, and also near the place called Cowford; which title your memorialists derive from a concession made to William Lee by Governor Quesada, in virtue of the royal order of October 29, 1790, who sold the same to Samuel Betts, by deed dated September 5, 1803, who subsequently, on the 20th day of June, 1806, conveyed the said land to James Hall, esq., of St. John's county, who, on the eleventh of September instant, conveyed the same to your memorialists. And your memorialists further show that the said William Lee, the original grantee, was in actual possession of said land, and improved the same for years, as they have been informed and believe; that they are citizens of the United States and residents of Georgia.

ARCHIBALD CLARKE, for self and
ELIHU ATWATER.

[Here follows a translation of a concession made to James William Lee by Governor Quesada, dated November 11, 1794.]

[Here follows a conveyance from James W. Lee to Samuel Betts, dated September 5, 1803.]

[Here follows a conveyance from Samuel Betts to James Hall, dated June 20, 1806.]

[Here follows a conveyance from James Hall to Archibald Clarke and Elihu Atwater, dated September 11, 1823.]

[Here follows the deposition of Joseph Summerall, taken before Samuel Fairbanks, justice of the peace, May 11, 1824, proving occupation and cultivation of the above land by James W. Lee.]

[Here follows the deposition of Eleanor Hall to the same effect as the foregoing, dated May 12, 1824.]

DECREE.

Archibald Clarke and Elihu Atwater vs. The United States.   For two hundred acres of land.

The board having ascertained the above to be a valid Spanish concession, and the occupation and cultivation by the grantee, with the deraignment to the claimants, being duly proved, they confirm the same accordingly.   September 30, 1825.

No. 120.—See Report No. 1.

Elihu Woodruff and others vs. The United States.   For three hundred and fifty acres of land.

MEMORIAL.

To the honorable the commissioners appointed to ascertain claims and titles to lands in East Florida:

The petition of the subscribers respectfully showeth: That your memorialists claim title to a tract of land consisting of three hundred and fifty acres, situated on the river St. John's, in the vicinity of a place called Rollestown, about six miles southward of the post of Buena Vista, bounded on the west by lands granted to a certain Clarkworthy; which title your memorialists derive from a title made to John Moore, a free colored man, by Governor White, in virtue of the royal order of October 29, 1790, who sold the same to your memorialists. They would state that the title to Moore bears date November 9, 1805, as appears by a certified copy thereof, herewith filed, marked A, and that he conveyed the same to your memorialists by his certain deed dated upon the third day of May, 1823; which said deed is herewith exhibited, marked B. And your memorialists further show that they are in actual possession of the said lands; that they are citizens of the United States and residents of East Florida. All of which is respectfully submitted, &c.

ELIHU WOODRUFF.
SIDNEY P. HARRIS.
JAMES MAVER.

[Here follows the translation of a royal title from Governor White to John Moore, dated November 9, 1805.

[Here follows a conveyance from John Moore to claimants, dated May 3, 1823.]

DECREE.

Elihu Woodruff and others vs. The United States.   For three hundred and fifty acres of land.

The board having ascertained the above to be a valid Spanish title, and the deraignment to claimants being regular, do confirm the same accordingly.   October 26, 1825.

No. 121 —See Report No. 1.

Philip and Mary Dewees vs. The United States.   Claim for one hundred acres of land.

MEMORIAL.

To the honorable the commissioners appointed to ascertain claims and titles to lands in East Florida :

The petition of Philip Dewees and Mary Dewees, his wife, respectfully showeth: That your memorialists claim title to a tract of land consisting of one hundred acres, situated on Guana river, bounded by St. Diego plains to the west, the lands late the property of John M. Sanchez to the north, the Guana marsh to the east, and the lands of the late Nicholas Sanchez to the south; the first line running north 5° west, 44 chains, to a stake; the second line, south 72° west, 29 chains, to a laurel; the third line, south 5° east, to a laurel, 35 chains; the fourth line running east 29 chains to the first corner; which title your memorialists derive from a royal title made to the late Francis X. Sanchez by Governor White, in virtue of the royal order of October 29, 1790, from whose estate Mary Sanchez, the wife of Philip Dewees, inherited the same as one of the heirs of the said Francis X. Sanchez, deceased, upon a division of the same, as per royal title marked A, dated February 6, 1811. And your memorialists further show that they are in actual possession of said lands; that they are now citizens of the United States and residents of the Territory of Florida.

PHILIP DEWEES.
MARY DEWEES.

[Here follows the translation of a royal title for the above one hundred acres of land in favor of the children and heirs of Francisco Xavier Sanchez, deceased, made by Governor White February 6, 1811.]

DECREE.

Philip and Mary Dewees vs. The United States.   For one hundred acres of land.

The board having ascertained that the above is a valid Spanish grant, and that the claimants are heirs to the grantee, do confirm it accordingly.   October 7, 1825.

No. 122.—See Report No. 1.

Thomas Moy vs. The United States.   For three hundred and fifty acres of land.

MEMORIAL.

To the honorable the commissioners appointed to ascertain claims and titles to lands in East Florida :

The petition of Thomas Moy respectfully showeth: That your memorialist claims title to a tract of land consisting of three hundred and fifty acres, situated at Row's Bluff, on Bell's river; first line, north 39° east, 107 chains, from a stake to a pine; second line, 50° west, 42 chains, to a gum; third, north 39° east, 83 chains, to a pine; fourth line formed and bounded by Bell's river; the first line bounded by James Smith, the second by Josiah Smith; which title your memorialist derives from a grant made to him by Governor Coppinger, in virtue of the royal order of 1790; the plat and certificate of which, signed by G. J. F. Clarke, are herewith presented. And your memorialist further showeth that he is in actual possession of said lands; that he has been a long time a resident of Florida. Your memorialist will, as in duty bound, ever pray, &c.

G. J. F. CLARKE,
For THOMAS MOY.

[Here follows translation of a certificate of survey and plat, dated September 21, 1819, by George J. F. Clarke.]

DECREE.

Thomas Moy vs. The United States.   For three hundred and fifty acres of land.

The board having ascertained by the evidence adduced that the claimant occupied and cultivated the above tract, and that the surveyor general surveyed to claimant said tract by the order of Governor Coppinger made in the year 1817, do confirm the same to claimant.   November 4, 1825.

TESTIMONY.

Thomas Moy vs. The United States.   For three hundred and fifty acres of land.

Charles W. Clarke, being duly sworn, doth depose and say that, at the time the survey in this case bears date, the claimant was actually residing on the land embraced by the survey; had been for many years before, but does not know whether he resides there at present or not.

CHARLES W. CLARKE.

Before me September 21, 1825.

D. FLOYD.

No. 123.—See Report No. 1.

John Wingate vs. The United States.   For two hundred acres of land.

MEMORIAL.

To the honorable the commissioners appointed to ascertain claims and titles to lands in East Florida :

The petition of John Wingate respectfully showeth: That your memorialist claims title to a tract of land consisting of two hundred acres, situated on Lofton's swamp, Nassau river; the first line south 65°

east, 40 chains, from a pine to a pine; second, north 25° east, 50 chains, to a pine; third, north 65° west, 40 chains, to a pine; fourth, south 25° west, 50 chains, to the pine tree at the beginning—the first line bounded by Eleazer Waterman, and the fourth by the same; which title your memorialist derives from a grant made to him by Governor Coppinger, in virtue of the royal order of 1790, as —— by the accompanying plat and certificate by George J. F. Clarke. And your memorialist further showeth that he is in actual possession of said lands; that he has long been a resident of East Florida. Your memorialist will, as in duty bound, ever pray, &c.

GEO. J. F. CLARKE,
For JOHN WINGATE.

[Here follows the certificate of survey and plat by George J. F. Clarke, dated October 4, 1818.]

DECREE.

John Wingate vs. *The United States. For two hundred acres of land.*

The board having ascertained by the evidence adduced that the claimant occupied and cultivated the above tract, and that the surveyor general surveyed to claimant said tract by order of Governor Coppinger made in the year 1817, do confirm the same to claimant. November 4, 1825.

TESTIMONY.

John Wingate vs. *The United States. For two hundred acres of land.*

Charles W. Clarke, being duly sworn, doth depose and say that at the time this survey bears date the claimant was residing on the land embraced by this survey; that is, he had a house on the place, and a small piece of ground cleared, that is, three or four acres. And further this deponent saith not.

CHARLES W. CLARKE.

Before me September 21, 1825.

D. FLOYD.

No. 124.—See REPORT No. 1.

Thomas Prevatt vs. *The United States. For five hundred and fifty acres of land.*

MEMORIAL.

To the honorable the commissioners appointed to ascertain claims and titles to lands in East Florida:

The petition of Thomas Prevatt respectfully showeth: That your memorialist claims title to a tract of land consisting of five hundred and fifty acres, situated on St. Mary's river; first line south 30° east, 114 chains, from a stake to a pine; second line south 60° west, 60 chains, to a pine; third line north 30° west, to a pine, 30 chains; fourth line north 60° east, 15 chains, to a pine; fifth line north 30° west, 84 chains, to a pine; sixth line north 60° east, 45 chains, to a stake, at the beginning; which title your memorialist derives from a grant made to him by Governor Coppinger, in virtue of the royal order of 1790, as appears by the accompanying document signed by George J. F. Clarke. And your memorialist further showeth that he is in actual possession of said lands, and that he has long been an inhabitant and resident of East Florida. He will, as in duty bound, ever pray, &c.

GEO. J. F. CLARKE,
For THOMAS PREVATT.

[Here follows translation of a certificate of survey and a plat by George J. F. Clarke, dated May 14, 1818.]

DECREE.

Thomas Prevatt vs. *The United States. For five hundred and fifty acres of land.*

The board having ascertained by the evidence adduced that the claimant occupied and cultivated the above tract, and that the surveyor general surveyed it to him by the order of Governor Coppinger made in the year 1817, do confirm the same accordingly.

TESTIMONY.

Thomas Prevatt vs. *The United States. For five hundred and fifty acres of land.*

E. Stafford, being sworn, says he is acquainted with Thomas Prevatt; that the said Prevatt was living where he now resides ever since about the year 1810, on St. Mary's river.

E. STAFFORD.

No. 125.—See REPORT No. 1.

Frederick Hartley vs. *The United States. For six hundred acres of land.*

MEMORIAL.

To the honorable the commissioners appointed to ascertain claims and titles to lands in East Florida:

The petition of Frederick Hartley respectfully showeth: That your memorialist claims title to a tract of land consisting of six hundred acres, situated on Old Field branch, Julington creek, St. John's river;

first line, north 34° west, 80 chains, from a pine to a pine; second, north 40° east, 75 chains, to a pine; third, south 34° east, 80 chains, to a pine; fourth, south 40° west, 75 chains, to a pine at the beginning—the first line bounded by George Hartley; which title your memorialist derives from a grant made to him by Governor Coppinger, in virtue of the royal order of 1790, as by the plat and certificate of George J. F. Clarke presented herewith. And your memorialist further showeth that he is in actual possession of said lands; that he has long been a resident of East Florida. Your memorialist will, as in duty bound, ever pray, &c.

GEORGE J. F. CLARKE,
For F. HARTLEY.

[Here follows the translation of certificate of survey and plat by George J. F. Clarke, dated July 3, 1819.]

DECREE.

Frederick Hartley vs. *The United States.   For six hundred acres of land.*

The board having ascertained by the evidence adduced that the claimant occupied and cultivated the above tract, and the surveyor general surveyed it to claimant by order of Governor Coppinger made in the year 1817, do confirm the same to claimant.   November 4, 1825.

Frederick Hartley vs. *The United States.   For six hundred acres of land.*

Charles W. Clarke, being duly sworn, doth depose and say that, at the time the survey in this case bears date, Frederick Hartley, the claimant, lived on the land embraced by the survey, and had done so several years before, and still continues to reside there, or did so last year.

CHARLES W. CLARKE.

Before me September 21, 1825.

D. FLOYD.

No. 126.—See Report No. 1.

Peter Sevilly vs. *The United States.   For six hundred acres of land.*

MEMORIAL.

To the honorable the commissioners appointed to ascertain claims and titles to lands in East Florida:

The petition of Peter Sevilly respectfully showeth: That your memorialist claims title to a tract of land consisting of two hundred and fifty acres, situated on Long bay, about seven miles to the northwest of St. Augustine; first line, north 30° west, 32 chains, from a pine to a pine; second, north 75° west, 32 chains, to a pine; third, south 15° west, 25 chains, to a pine; fourth, south 75° east, 25 chains, to a pine; fifth, south 30° east, 18 chains, to a pine; sixth, north 80° east, 25 chains, to a pine at the beginning; which title your memorialist derives from a grant made to him by Governor Coppinger, in virtue of the royal order of 1790, as per the copy and certificate of survey by G. J. F. Clarke, herewith presented. And your memorialist further showeth that he is in actual possession of said lands; that he is a native of East Florida and resident of the same.   Your memorialist will, as in duty bound, ever pray, &c.

GEORGE J. F. CLARKE,
For PETER SEVILLY.

[Here follows translation of a certificate of survey and plat by George J. F. Clarke, dated July 8, 1819.]

DECREE.

Peter Sevilly vs. *The United States.   For one hundred and fifty acres of land.*

The board having ascertained by the evidence adduced that the claimant occupied and cultivated the above tract, and that the surveyor general surveyed to claimant said tract by order of Governor Coppinger made in the year 1817, do confirm the same to claimant.   November 4, 1825.

TESTIMONY.

Peter Sevilly vs. *The United States.   For one hundred and fifty acres of land.*

Charles W. Clarke, being duly sworn, doth depose and say that, at the time this survey bears date, and for two years or more before, the claimant had a cultivated improvement on the land embraced by the survey, and still has to this time.

CHARLES W. CLARKE.

Before me September 21, 1825.

D. FLOYD.

No. 127.—See Report No. 1.

George Henning vs. *The United States.   For two hundred acres of land.*

MEMORIAL.

To the honorable the commissioners appointed to ascertain claims and titles to lands in East Florida:

The petition of George Henning respectfully showeth: That your memorialist claims title to a tract of land consisting of two hundred acres, situated on Bell's river near Row's bluff; the first line of survey beginning at a stake, south 39° west, 40 chains, to a pine; second, south 50° east, to a pine, 50 chains; third, north 39° east, 40 chains, to a live-oak; fourth, formed and bounded by Bell's river; which title your memorialist derives from a grant made to him by Governor White, in virtue of the royal order of 1790, as will appear by the accompanying certificate of said grant, dated October 2, 1805. The certificate and plat of survey will be filed when required. And your memorialist further showeth that he is in actual possession of the said lands; that he has long been an inhabitant and resident of East Florida. Your memorialist, as in duty bound, will pray, &c.

GEO. J. F. CLARKE,
For GEORGE HENNING.

[Here follows translation of a certified copy of a decree made by Governor White, dated October 2, 1805.]

DECREE.

George Henning vs. *The United States. For two hundred acres of land.*

The board having ascertained the above to be a valid Spanish concession, and the cultivation and occupation thereof being proved, the board do confirm the same accordingly. November 4, 1825.

TESTIMONY.

George Henning vs. *The United States. For two hundred acres of land.*

Charles W. Clarke, being duly sworn, doth depose and say that he has known this place to be occupied by claimant for twenty years or upwards, and was still occupied in the year 1823 to the knowledge of this deponent.

CHARLES W. CLARKE.

Before me September 21, 1825.

D. FLOYD.

No. 128.—See REPORT No. 1.

George Hartley vs. *The United States. For four hundred acres of land.*

MEMORIAL.

To the honorable the commissioners appointed to ascertain claims and titles to lands in East Florida:

The petition of George Hartley respectfully showeth: That your memorialist claims title to a tract of land consisting of four hundred acres, situated on Old Field branch, Julington creek, St. John's river; first line, north 34° west, 80 chains, from a pine to a pine; second, south 75° west, 50 chains, to a cypress; third, south 34° east, 80 chains, to a pine; fourth, north 75° east, 50 chains, to the pine at the beginning; bounded on the first line by Frederick Hartley, and on the fourth by Joseph Summerall; which title your memorialist derives from a grant made to him by Governor Coppinger, in virtue of the royal order of 1790, as per the accompanying plat and certificate by George J. F. Clarke. And your memorialist further showeth that he is in actual possession of said lands; that he has long been a resident of this province. Your memorialist will, as in duty bound, ever pray, &c.

GEO. J. F. CLARKE,
For GEORGE HARTLEY.

[Here follows the translation of a certificate of survey and plat by George J. F. Clarke, dated July 4, 1819.]

DECREE.

George Hartley vs. *The United States. For four hundred acres of land.*

The board having ascertained by the evidence adduced that the claimant occupied and cultivated the above tract, and that the surveyor general surveyed it to him by the order of Governor Coppinger made in the year 1817, do confirm the same accordingly. November 4, 1825.

TESTIMONY.

George Hartley vs. *The United States. For four hundred acres of land.*

Charles W. Clarke, being duly sworn, doth depose and say that, at the time the survey bears date in this case, the claimant, George Hartley, was residing on the land contained in said survey, and, from appearances, had raised a crop there the year before. He still resides there, or did last year.

CHARLES W. CLARKE.

Before me September 21, 1825.

D. FLOYD.

No. 129.—See REPORT No. 1.

Martha Dell vs. *The United States. For four hundred and fifty acres of land.*

MEMORIAL.

To the honorable the commissioners appointed to ascertain claims and titles to lands in East Florida:

The petition of Martha Dell respectfully showeth: That your memorialist claims title to a tract of land consisting of four hundred and fifty acres, situated on St. Mary's river; the first line of which runs south 32° west, 50 chains, from a poplar to a pine; second line formed and bounded by St. Mary's river; fourth line formed and bounded by the swamp of Brushy creek; which title your memorialist derives from a grant made to her by Governor Coppinger, in virtue of the royal order of 1790, according to the plat and certificate by George J. F. Clarke, presented with this petition. And your memorialist further showeth that she is in actual possession of said lands; that she has long been a resident of East Florida. Your memorialist will ever, as in duty bound, pray, &c.

G. J. F. CLARKE,
For MARTHA DELL.

[Here follows a translation of a certificate of survey and a plat by George J. F. Clarke, dated May 26, 1818.]

DECREE.

Martha Dell vs. The United States. For four hundred and fifty acres of land.

The board having ascertained by the evidence adduced that the claimant occupied and cultivated the above tract, and that the surveyor general surveyed to claimant said tract by order of Governor Coppinger made in the year 1817, do confirm the same to claimant. November 4, 1825.

TESTIMONY.

Martha Dell vs. The United States. For four hundred and fifty acres of land.

Ellis Stafford, being sworn, says that he is acquainted with Martha Dell; that she settled on St. Mary's river in the year 1814 or 1815, and resided there until the year 1817 or 1818, when the place was taken possession of by Maxey Dell, and held under her until now.

E. STAFFORD.

No. 130.—See REPORT No. 1.

William McCulley vs. The United States. For three hundred acres of land.

MEMORIAL.

To the honorable the commissioners appointed to ascertain claims and titles to lands in East Florida:

The petition of William McCulley respectfully showeth: That your memorialist claims title to a tract of land consisting of three hundred acres, situated on St. Mary's river, high up; the first line, south 74° east, 50 chains, from a pine to a pine; second line, south 16° west, 60 chains, to a pine; third line, north 74° west, 50 chains, to a pine; fourth line, north 16° east, 60 chains, to the pine at the beginning; which title your memorialist derives from a grant made to him by Governor Coppinger, in virtue of the royal order of 1790, as will appear by the accompanying documents, signed by George J. F. Clarke. And your memorialist further showeth that he is in actual possession of said lands; that he has long been a resident of East Florida. Your memorialist will, as in duty bound, every pray, &c.

GEORGE J. F. CLARKE,
For WILLIAM McCULLEY.

[Here follows translation of a certificate of survey and plat by George J. F. Clarke, dated September 8, 1818.]

DECREE.

William McCulley vs. The United States. For three hundred acres of land.

The board having ascertained by the evidence adduced that the claimant occupied and cultivated the above tract, and that the surveyor general surveyed it to him by the order of Governor Coppinger made in the year 1817, do confirm the same accordingly. November 4, 1825.

TESTIMONY.

William McCulley vs. The United States. For three hundred acres of land.

E. Stafford, being sworn, says that he knows William McCulley; says he settled on St. Mary's river, high up the river, in the year 1807, and continued to reside there until the insurrection, when he was broke up; afterwards he went back and stayed one year, and made a crop in 1813; since that time a person has *held* possession and cultivated under him up to the present time.

ELLIS STAFFORD.

No 131.—See REPORT No. 1.

Edward Dixon vs. The United States. For one hundred acres of land.

MEMORIAL.

To the honorable the commissioners appointed to ascertain claims and titles to lands in East Florida:

The petition of Edward Dixon respectfully showeth: That your memorialist claims title to a tract of land consisting of one hundred acres situated on Pigeon creek, St. Mary's river; first line, south 71° east, 35 chains, from a stake to a pine; second, south 19° west, 29 chains, to a pine; third, north 71° west, 35 chains, to a pine; fourth line, formed and bounded by Pigeon creek; which title your memorialist derives from a grant made to him by Governor Coppinger, in virtue of the royal order of 1790, as per accompanying plat and certificate by George J. F. Clarke. And your memorialist further showeth that he is in actual possession of said lands; that he has long been a resident of East Florida. Your memorialist will, as in duty bound, pray, &c.

GEO. J. F. CLARKE,
For EDWARD DIXON.

[Here follows the translation of a certificate of survey and a plat by George J. F. Clarke, dated May 14, 1818.]

Edward Dixon vs. *The United States.   For one hundred acres of land.*

The board having ascertained by the evidence adduced that the claimant occupied and cultivated the above tract, and the surveyor general surveyed it to him by order of Governor Coppinger made in the year 1817, do confirm the same accordingly.

Edward Dixon vs. *The United States.   For one hundred acres of land.*

E. Stafford, being sworn, says that he is acquainted with Edward Dixon; that the said Dixon settled on Pigeon creek, St. Mary's river, about the year 1814, and has resided there ever since the last year; since which time he has a man residing there.

ELLIS STAFFORD.

No. 132.—See Report No. 1.

William and John Lofton vs. *The United States.   For three hundred acres of land.*

To the honorable the commissioners appointed to ascertain claims and titles to lands in East Florida:

The petition of William and John Lofton respectfully showeth: That your memorialists claim title to a tract of land consisting of three hundred acres, situated on north of Julington creek, St. John's river; first line, north 25° west, 62 chains, from a cypress to a pine; second, south 65° west, 50 chains, to a pine; third, south 45° degrees east, 84 chains, to a cypress; fourth line formed and bounded by Julington creek; which title your memorialists derived from a grant made *to him* by Governor Coppinger, in virtue of the royal order of 1790, as will appear by the accompanying document, signed by George J. F. Clarke. And your memorialists further show that they have long been in actual possession of said lands; that they are natives of this province, and residents of the same. Your memorialists will, as in duty bound, ever pray, &c.

GEO. J. F. CLARKE, *for the Petitioners.*

[Here follows the translation of a certificate of survey and plat by George J. F. Clarke, dated July 6, 1819.]

William and John Lofton vs. *The United States.   For three hundred acres of land.*

The board having ascertained by the evidence adduced that the claimant occupied and cultivated the above tract, and that the surveyor general surveyed to claimant said tract by order of Governor Coppinger made in the year 1817, do confirm the same to claimant. November 4, 1825.

No. 133.—See Report No. 1.

Joseph Prevatt vs. *The United States.   For four hundred acres of land.*

To the honorable the commissioners appointed to ascertain claims and titles to lands in East Florida:

The petition of Joseph Prevatt respectfully showeth: That your memorialist claims title to a tract of land consisting of four hundred acres, situated on Turner's swamp, St. Mary's river; first line, north 27° west, 47 chains, from a pine to a pine; second line, north 63° east, 75 chains, to a pine; third, south 27° east, 54 chains, to a stake; fourth, south 63° west, 65 chains, to a stake; fifth, north 30° west, 10 chains, to a stake; sixth, south 60° west, 29 chains, to the pine at the beginning; which title your memorialist derives from a grant made to him by Governor Coppinger, in virtue of the royal order of 1790, as will appear by the annexed documents signed by George J. F. Clarke. And your memorialist further showeth that he is, and for many years has been, in actual possession of said lands; that he has long been a resident of East Florida. Your petitioner will, as in duty bound, pray, &c.

GEORGE J. F. CLARKE,
For JOSEPH PREVATT.

[Here follows translation of a certificate of conveyance and plat made by George J. F. Clarke, dated October 10, 1818.]

Joseph Prevatt vs. *The United States.   For four hundred acres of land.*

The board having ascertained by the evidence adduced that the claimant occupied and cultivated the above tract, and that the surveyor general surveyed it to him by the order of Governor Coppinger made in the year 1817, do confirm the same accordingly. November 4, 1825.

Joseph Prevatt vs. *The United States.   For four hundred acres of land.*

E. Stafford, being sworn, says he is acquainted with Joseph Prevatt; that said Prevatt settled where he now resides about nine years ago, and has continued to reside there ever since. His place is on St. Mary's river.

E. STAFFORD.

No. 134.—See REPORT No. 1.

James Plummer vs. The United States.   For three hundred acres of land.

MEMORIAL.

To the honorable the commissioners appointed to ascertain claims and titles to lands in East Florida :

The petition of James Plummer respectfully showeth: That your memorialist claims title to a tract of land consisting of three hundred acres of land, situated on the north of Julington creek, St. John's river; first line, north 15° west, 40 chains, from a live-oak to a pine; second, north 75° east, 77 chains, to a pine; third, south 15° east, 40 chains, to a gum; fourth line formed and bounded by Julington creek; bounded on the second and third sides by Robert Pritchard; which title your memorialist derives from a grant made to him by Governor Coppinger, in virtue of the royal order of 1790, as per document of survey by George J. F. Clarke herewith presented. And your memorialist further showeth that he is in actual possession of said lands; that he has long been a resident of East Florida. Your petitioner will, as in duty bound, ever pray, &c.

GEO. J. F. CLARKE,
For JAMES PLUMMER.

[Here follows the translation of a certificate of survey and plat by George J. F. Clarke, dated July 18, 1819.]

DECREE.

James Plummer vs. The United States.   For three hundred acres of land.

The board having ascertained by the evidence adduced that the claimant occupied and cultivated the above tract, and that the surveyor general surveyed to claimant said tract by order of Governor Coppinger made in the year 1817, do confirm the same to claimant. November 4, 1825.

TESTIMONY.

James Plummer vs. The United States.   For three hundred acres of land.

Charles W. Clarke, being duly sworn, doth depose and say that at the time of the survey, and for two years before, the claimant in this case was residing on the land embraced by his survey, but whether he still resides there this deponent cannot say.

CHARLES W. CLARKE.

Before me September 21, 1825.

D. FLOYD.

[Nos. 135 to 173, inclusive, were not returned to the General Land Office by the commissioners.]

No. 1.—See REPORT No.2.

Charles Seton vs. The United States.   For one thousand four hundred acres.

To Messrs. Alex. Hamilton, W. W. Blair, and D. Floyd, commissioners now sitting in St. Augustine, East Florida:

Memorial of Charles Seton, merchant and planter, residing in the town of Fernandina, stating his right to the following land, granted by authority of his Catholic Majesty Ferdinand VII.

GRANT NO. 1.

A grant for 1,400 acres of land on the river Nassau, as per plat annexed; the first line commencing at the river Nassau, below the juncture with Thomas' creek, running due south, 100 chains, to a pine tree; second line running due west, 118 chains, to a pine tree; third line, due north, 95 chains, to a pine tree, and through the marsh to Thomas' creek, down Thomas' creek to the river Nassau, up the river Nassau until it joins plat No. 2; vacant land on the south and west line granted by Governor Kindelan March 1, 1815, being a full tract for my headright, which has been settled, and buildings are now on it; 1,251 acres in one plot, and 149 acres in the plot of 520   Terms complied with in full. Fernandina, October 15, 1823.

CHARLES SETON.

[Translation.]

Don Charles Seton, inhabitant and merchant of Fernandina, in the island of Amelia, with due respect, states to your excellency that he is one of the first who established themselves on that island, from the prosecution of whose commerce and usefulness much advantage has accrued to the royal treasury; he has complied with all the obligations of a good citizen subject, and is grateful for the benefits which this government bestows through the hands of your excellency on those individuals who have the honor and satisfaction of being subject to it. Through all which, and having a family, and having some slaves, subsistence for whom is at present precarious from the change of circumstances in the commerce of said island, and for the purpose of employing them in agriculture, thereby to insure their subsistence and that of his family: Wherefore he prays your excellency that, taking into consideration the proofs which he has offered of his good faith and true allegiance, and also his said family, consisting, with your memorialist, of five white persons and twenty slaves, property in which he will prove, if required, your excellency will have the goodness to grant 1,400 acres of land in full property, or by concession, under the circumstances with which this government has formerly made such, appointing said concession to be made on the river Nassau, in the vacant places which he shall point out, and give an account of for its confirmation. Which favor he hopes to obtain from the justice of your excellency.

CHARLES SETON.

Señor GOVERNOR.

DECREE.

St. AUGUSTINE, *March* 1, 1815.

Taking into consideration what Don Carlos Seton sets forth in this memorial, let there be granted to him the 1,400 acres of land which he solicits, without injury to a third person, and in a vacant place, with the understanding that as soon as he expressly points out those which suit him, and presents the survey and plat, with the proof of his having improved them in a suitable manner, there shall be delivered to him a title in absolute property without occasion for passing more time. This decree serving in the meantime to prove the grant which is made him of said lands, which, authenticated in a copy with the preceding memorial, shall be granted him by the present notary, in whose office the proceedings will be deposited.

KINDELAN.

Before me—

JUAN DE ENTRALGO, *Notary of Government pro tem.*

I certify the foregoing to be a true and correct translation from a document in the Spanish language.

F. J. FATIO, *S. B. L. C.*

[Translation.]

Don George Clarke, lieutenant of the local militia of St. Augustine, Florida, and surveyor, appointed by the government of the said place and province: I certify that, by concession of the government in favor of Carlos Seton, I have surveyed and laid off twelve hundred and fifty-one acres of land on the river Nassau, at a place known by the name of Houston's swamp, which in locality, class, and survey, agrees with the following plat and its copy kept in the book of surveys in my charge. Fernandina, May 16, 1816.

G. J. F. CLARKE.

[Here follows the plat.]

I certify the foregoing to be a true and correct translation from a document in the Spanish language.

F. J. FATIO, *S. B. L. C.*

[Translation.]

Don George Clarke, lieutenant of the local militia of St. Augustine, Florida, and surveyor general, appointed by the government of said place and province: I certify that this government having granted to Don Carlos Seton a portion of lands on the river Nassau, I have measured and laid off, in a part, five hundred and twenty acres on the said river, and at a place named Roundabout, which is equal in its situation and survey to the following plat, and agreeable to its copy preserved in the book of surveys in my charge. Amelia Island, May 16, 1816.

G. J. F. CLARKE.

[Here follows the plat.]

I certify the foregoing to be a true and correct translation from a document in the Spanish language.

F. J. FATIO, *S. B. L. C.*

DECREE BY THE BOARD.

The board having ascertained that this was a valid grant under the late Spanish government, they therefore recommend it to Congress for confirmation. April 12.

No. 2.—See REPORT No. 2.

James A. Hutchinson's heirs vs. The United States. For two thousand acres of land.

MEMORIAL.

To the honorable the commissioners appointed to ascertain claims and titles to lands in East Florida:

The petition of James A. Hutchinson, for himself and the other heirs of James Hutchinson, late a Spanish subject, residing in East Florida, deceased, respectfully showeth: That your memorialist, for himself and the said heirs, claims title to a tract of land consisting of two thousand acres, situated on an island in the lagoon, which runs south from the mouth of Indian river to Jupiter inlet; which title your memorialists derive from a grant or concession made to the said James Hutchinson, deceased, by Henry White, governor of the province of East Florida, in virtue of the royal order of October 29, 1790, as well as in consideration that the said James Hutchinson had abandoned two thousand acres of land that had been previously granted to him on the first hammock south of Indian river, all of which will appear in the accompanying document marked A, bearing date April 17, 1807. Your memorialist further shows that the said James Hutchinson took actual possession of the said island and made improvements thereon; and that at the time of his death, which happened in August, 1808, before he could have the lands surveyed, his family, twelve in number, (see documents marked C and B,) resided on the tract of two thousand acres. In consequence of the death of the said James Hutchinson, and the helpless condition of his family, they were compelled to leave the island and return to their friends in the United States. This they did with the approbation of Governor White. The situation of the lands claimed being so remote from the inhabited part of the province, and surrounded by Indians, your memorialists have not been able to reoccupy the said lands. They therefore pray that their title to the said two thousand acres, as granted to the said James Hutchinson, may be confirmed; and, as in duty bound, they will ever pray.

GEORGE MURRAY, *Attorney for Petitioners.*

The petitioners are residing now in the State of Mississippi.

A.

[Translation.]

St. Augustine, *East Florida*, April 13, 1807.

To the governor:

Don James Hutchinson, the only inhabitant in the vicinity of the river Ys, (Indian river,) respectfully showeth: That your excellency was pleased to grant him two thousand acres of land in the first hammock to the south of said river; but finding that said hammock, on the main, was very much exposed to the incursions of the Indians, and with little hopes of being protected by other immediate settlements, he has therefore established himself on an island extending from said river to the entrance of Jove, and is formed by the creek named Santa Lucia on the west and the ocean on the east, consisting of a narrow strip of land, the greatest part sand hills, with only a piece of hammock, where your memorialist has established himself, and contains about three hundred and fifty acres, there being no other spot that admits of cultivation, as the rest consists of said sand hills, mangroves, and palmettos, and some spots of low land which experience has taught your memorialist are suitable for raising swine, to which he intends particularly to dedicate himself. Agreeable, therefore, to the reasons above stated, he begs your excellency will be pleased to grant him the said island in place of the former grant of the two thousand acres of land, where he considers himself rather more protected from the Indians, who commit acts of depredation and violence when they find a single family, and he can, without being molested, attend to the raising of cattle.

J. HUTCHINSON.

St. Augustine, *April* 14, 1807.

Admit from the memorialist the return he makes of the two thousand acres of land granted him on the river Ys, and, in place thereof, he is permitted to reside on the island where he has established himself, for the reasons he sets forth, until the land be measured according to the number of his family and working hands he may have.

WHITE.

A certificate was given.

PIERRA.

Note.—The certificate of the two thousand acres of land granted him on the river Ys, he said, was lost with the rest of his papers in the gale which took place in September of the preceding year.

PIERRA.

I certify the foregoing to be a true and correct translation from a document in the Spanish language on file in the office of the public archives of St. Augustine.

F. J. FATIO, *S. B. L. C.*

C.

STATEMENT.

In the summer of the year 1808 I saw my brother (now deceased) James Hutchinson, who was then settled on an island at the mouth of Indian river, in East Florida, then and since called "Hutchinson's island." I then understood from him that, in consequence of his relinquishing a settlement he had made previously, he was to receive the whole of the island where he then was located; that the number of his family, and others with him, would entitle him thereto, and that Governor White had been pleased so to decree. He had lived in Florida a number of years, but how long I do not now recollect. In the month of September, 1808, and not many weeks after I had the above-mentioned interview, I received an account of his death, which happened about the last of August preceding. I immediately wrote on and made arrangements to bring his wife and young children to this State, first making application to Governor White to obtain leave for them to *visit* the United States *during pleasure.* This I had always believed, and do still believe, was granted by Governor White to answer the purpose intended by *him,* as well as the friends of the widow and her family, *that such absence should not operate as an abandonment of their lands;* and, under this express understanding, the family came to Georgia, leaving, however, a young man, who had for some time composed one of the household, in charge of the settlement, to look after it for them or in their behalf. The widow and children arrived in Savannah some time in the month of November, 1808. Some time after this, (the particular time I do not recollect,) the eldest son of my deceased brother was, by his mother and myself, fitted out to go and look after and take charge of the said island property. I heard of him in Florida, but have not heard from him for several years, and he is now believed to be dead. In all this lapse of time it never was, as I believe, the intention of the widow or her children to give up or abandon their just and equitable claim to the property, for the attainment and safe-keeping of which my brother lost his life, leaving a large and helpless family.

JOSEPH HUTCHINSON.

State of Georgia, } *Notary Public's Office.*
  City of Augusta, }

I, John G. Cowling, notary public for the city of Augusta aforesaid, duly admitted, lawfully appointed and sworn, do hereby certify that, on the date of the day hereof, personally came and appeared before me Colonel Joseph Hutchinson, who, being duly sworn, deposeth and saith that the facts set forth in the above statement, within his own knowledge, are true, and such as relate to the knowledge of others he believes to be true; and he further swears that he is no ways interested in the above-mentioned claim, nor will be gainer or loser by the issue or event.

Given under my hand and seal of office, at Augusta aforesaid, April 24, 1823.

JOHN G. COWLING, *N. P.* [L. S.]

B.

ADDITIONAL STATEMENT.

Colonel Joseph Hutchinson, of the city of Augusta, in the State of Georgia, further states, on oath, and in addition to the statement made by him of this date, viz: That the number of his late brother's family, when he brought them from Florida, as mentioned in his other statement, were twelve, consisting of the widow and seven children, and four negroes; besides which, the deponent understood, and so believes, that one child died on the island, and that a number of negroes had been stolen or carried off by pirates or wreckers. The deponent further states that the reasons which induced him to cause the said family to be brought away were, that the husband and father being dead, they had no protector, and were exposed to the marandings of wreckers and Indians, and that it was always the intention of the family to return when they could do so with safety. The deponent further saith that he was possessed of a large parcel of paper and written documents belonging to said family, which they brought with them from Florida, among which he thinks it very probable there were some which would have been material in the final adjustment of their claim to said land, but that the whole of them were consumed by the fire which destroyed this deponent's property in Augusta in the year 1817.

JOSEPH HUTCHINSON.

Subscribed and sworn to before me April 24, 1823.

JOHN G. COWLING, Notary Public.

B.

[Translation.]

St. Augustine, August 22, 1803.

Señor Governor: Don James Hutchinson, a new settler admitted under the protection of his Catholic Majesty, with due respect, presents himself to your excellency, and states that it is his intention to establish himself in this province, applying himself to agriculture, with his slaves, twenty in number, and his family, consisting of his wife and seven children; and he also intends to procure more slaves with the value of the lands he possesses in Georgia; and in order to carry his intentions into effect, he prays your excellency to be pleased to grant him two thousand acres of planting land in the territory of Indian river, on the south side of the bar, on the bank of the said bar to the south, said lands beginning at the first hammock on said bank; which land he promises to cultivate within the term which the government grants to the other inhabitants, and possibly in less.

J. HUTCHINSON.

St. Augustine, August 23, 1803.

Let there be granted to this party the land which he solicits, without injury to a third person, and until, according to the number of workers he may have for its cultivation, the corresponding quantity shall be assigned him, it being well understood that he shall take possession of said land within the term of six months, counted from the date.

WHITE.

A certificate issued.

PIERRA.

I certify the foregoing to be a true and correct translation from a document in the Spanish language.
F. J. FATIO, S. B. L. C.

Territory of Florida, County of Mosquito:

Personally appeared before me, Horatio S. Dexter, a justice of the peace for said county, Andreas Roach, and, being duly sworn, deposeth and saith that about the year 1807 he was employed by James Hutchinson to assist in forming a settlement on Hillsborough island, near Jupiter inlet; that while in the employ of said Hutchinson, the deponent, with several slaves, the property of said Hutchinson, erected three buildings, and cleared and planted on said island about thirty-five acres of land; that the deponent was employed about eight months the first time, and six months the second, and five months the third time; the two latter periods the employment of the deponent was principally in that of fishing and wrecking. And deponent further says that the family of the said Hutchinson consisted of nine white persons and five slaves; and the said Hutchinson continued to occupy and plant the land of said island about six years, when said Hutchinson was drowned on his passage from St. Augustine to Indian river. And the deponent further saith that the family of said Hutchinson removed to the State of Georgia after his said decease.

his
ANDREAS ⋈ ROACH.
mark.

Sworn to before me August 4, 1825.

HORATIO S. DEXTER, J. P.

DECREE.

Heirs of James Hutchinson vs. The United States. For two thousand acres of land.

The board having ascertained the above to be a valid Spanish concession, the conditions of which were complied with, do recommend the same to Congress for confirmation. September 20, 1825.

No. 3.—See Report No. 2.

Catalina de Tesus Hijuelos vs. The United States. For two thousand acres of land.

MEMORIAL.

To the honorable the commissioners appointed to ascertain claims and titles to lands in East Florida:

The petition of Catalina de Tesus Hijuelos respectfully showeth: That your memorialist claims title to a tract of land consisting of two thousand acres, situated about forty miles west from Buena Vista, in the part called the Big Grove, bounded as follows: beginning at a stake and running south fifty-five degrees west, one hundred chains, to a stake; thence north thirty-five degrees west, two hundred chains, to a stake; thence north fifty-five degrees east, one hundred chains, to a stake; thence south thirty-five degrees east, two hundred chains, to the beginning, (see plat by Burgevin, marked B;) which title your memorialist derives from a grant made to her by Governor Coppinger, in virtue of the royal order of 1815, as the legal representative of her son, Francisco de Entralgo, of the third battalion of Cuba, and who died in consequence of wounds received in the service of his country in 1812, (see document marked I.)   And your memorialist further showeth that she has legal possession of said lands; that she is a Spanish subject now in Cuba, and that on July 10, 182_, she was an inhabitant of St. Augustine.   She prays that her title to the said two thousand acres of land may be confirmed; and, as in duty bound, &c.

CATALINA T. HIJUELOS,
By GEORGE MURRAY.

[Translation.]

Don José Coppinger, colonel of the royal armies, political and military governor *pro tem.*, and chief of the royal domain of this city of St. Augustine, Florida, and its province, for his Majesty:

Whereas, by a royal order of March 29, 1815, his Majesty has deigned to approve the favor and rewards proposed by my predecessor, Brigadier Don Sebastian Kindelan, for the officers and soldiers, both regulars and militia, who assisted in its defence at the time of the rebellion, one of the said favors being the distribution of lands in proportion to the number of the family each one may have; that on the 30th May of the present year, Donna Catalina de Tesus Hijuelos, widow, and the mother of Don Francisco de Entralgo, formerly a volunteer in the third battalion of Cuba, presented herself, making mention of the merit and services of her said son, who died in consequence of wounds received from individuals of the said rebellion, soliciting the concession of two thousand acres of land; they were granted to her at a place known by the name of the Big Hammock, distant forty miles, a little more or less, from the port of Buena Vista, or the west side of the river St. John's, its survey beginning on the north side of said place, and following the boundaries of those granted to Don Antonio Alvarez and Don Tomas de Aguilar, as my decree of the same date accredits, made to the proceedings moved for by the said Donna Catalina, which exist in the archives of the notary of government: Wherefore, I have granted, as in the name of his Majesty I do grant, to the said Donna Catalina de Tesus Hijuelos the said two thousand acres of land at the place expressed, for herself, her heirs and successors, in absolute property, and to expedite to her, as by these presents I do, the correspondent title, by which I separate the royal domain from the right and dominion it had to said lands; and I cede and transfer it to the said Donna Catalina de Tesus Hijuelos, her heirs and successors, that, in consequence, they may possess it as their own, use and enjoy it, without any encumbrance, with all its entrances, outlets, uses, customs, rights, and services, which it has had, and in fact can belong and appertain to it; and, at their will, sell, cede, transfer, and alienate it as may best suit them.   To all which I interpose my authority, as I can and of right ought, in virtue of the sovereign will.

Given under my hand, and countersigned by the undersigned secretary of this government, brevet lieutenant of the army, Don Tomas de Aguilar, and by the officer of the secretary's office, Don Antonio Alvarez, whom I have named for assistant witnesses for the purpose, on account of the interested being mother to the said notary of government and royal domain.   St. Augustine, Florida, December 7, 1817.

JOSÉ COPPINGER.

By command of his excellency:
TOMAS DE AGUILAR.
ANTONIO ALVAREZ.

This is conformable to the original which exists in the archives of the notary of government and the royal domain; and at the desire of the party, I sign and seal these presents, with the assistant witnesses, on common paper, the stamped not being in use.   St. Augustine, Florida, December 7, 1817.

JOSÉ COPPINGER.

TOMAS DE AGUILAR.
ANTONIO ALVAREZ.

I certify the foregoing to be a true and correct translation from a document in the Spanish language on file in the office of the public archives of St. Augustine.

F. J. FATIO, *S. B. L. C.*

[Translation.]

Don Andres Burgevin, as surveyor, named by a decree of this government on the 11th June of this present year, in favor of the interested: I certify that I have measured and laid off for Donna Catalina de Tesus Hijuelos a piece of land which contains two thousand acres, situated on the great hammock which goes from the river Oke Coka, and runs towards the Indian villages named Alachua; said land is distant five miles from said river of Oke Coka, and bounded on the south by lands of Don Tomas de Aguilar, and on the north side by lands of Don Gabriel G. Perpall, and being in its other circumstances conformable to the accompanying plat; for the confirmation of which I give these presents, and sign in St. Augustine, Florida, September 9, 1819.

ANDRES BURGEVIN.
ANDRES BURGEVIN.

This copy is taken from the original.
[The plat is annexed.]

I certify the foregoing to be a true and correct translation from a document in the Spanish language.

F. J. FATIO, *S. B. L. C.*

DECREE.

The board having ascertained the foregoing to be a valid Spanish grant for the two thousand acres made previous to January 24, 1818, do therefore recommend it to Congress for confirmation.   December 14, 1825.

No. 4.—See REPORT No. 2.

Zephaniah Kingsley vs. *The United States. For two thousand six hundred and eleven acres of land.*

MEMORIAL.

To the honorable the commissioners appointed to ascertain certain claims and titles to lands in East Florida:

The petition of Zephaniah Kingsley, by George Gibbs, showeth: That your memorialist claims title to a tract of land consisting of two thousand six hundred and eleven acres, more or less, situated on the west side of St. John's river, and on the south by Doctor's lake or creek, called Laurel Grove, on the south by Doctor's lake, on the east by the river St. John's, on the north by land now or late the property of John Arnold, and on the west by a marked line; which line commences on the west line of the said Arnold, beginning on the river St. John's, running west 35 chains, thence north 18 chains, thence west 30 chains, thence south 35 chains; another line, beginning on the St. John's river, running south 80° west, 95 chains; thence south 10° east, 46 chains; thence south 80° west, 55 chains; thence south 10° east, 80 chains; thence south 65° east, 28 chains, to the aforesaid; thence, from the last corner, south 60° west, 105 chains; thence south 20° west, 63½ chains, to crook; thence south 3° west, 26 chains, to the Doctor's lake; thence north 33 chains, thence west 33 chains, thence south 33 chains, to the Doctor's lake; which title your memorialist derives from a grant made to William Pengree by Governor Estrada, in virtue of the royal order of October 29, 1790, whose widow, Rebecca Pengree, duly authorized by the Spanish tribunal for that purpose, as reference to the documents in the office of the archives will more fully appear, to sell the said lands and plantation, and did accordingly sell the same to your memorialist November 26, 1803, as per deed of sale herewith exhibited, marked Z. K. And your memorialist further showeth that he is in actual legal possession of said lands; that he is a citizen of the United States and resident of the Territory of Florida.

ZEPHANIAH KINGSLEY,
By GEORGE GIBBS, *Attorney in fact.*

[Translation.]

Don Pedro Marrot, captain of the third battalion of the infantry regiment of Cuba, and judge commissioned by his excellency the governor and commander-in-chief of this province of East Florida for the survey and laying off of lands ordered to be distributed by command of his Majesty: I certify that at the plantation called Laurel Grove there have been measured for the inhabitant Don William Pengree, whose family consists, under the oath which he has taken, of fifty-one persons, in the following form: husband, wife, and one son, with forty-eight negro slaves; for which family there have been delivered to him fifty-two caballerias and twenty acres of land, which is part of what corresponds to him. The first line runs south 80° west; begins by a red oak, on the bank of the river, with a cross and ends with a pine tree of the same mark; it measures 95 chains. The second line runs south 10° east; begins by said pine tree and ends by another with the same mark; it measures 46 chains. The third runs south 80° west; begins by said pine tree and ends with another; it measures 55 chains. The fourth, south 10° east; begins by said pine tree and ends with a stake marked with a cross; it measures 80 chains. The fifth runs south 65° east; begins by said stake and ends with an ash on the bank of Doctor's creek; it measures 28 chains: its front runs part on the bank of said creek and part on the bank of the river St. John—all according to the orders which I have. The interested signed it with the surveyor, Don Samuel Eastlake. In proof of which, and that it may serve for the information of the secretary of this government, to whom the interested have to apply for their respective titles, I give the present copy of the original, which remains in my possession. River St. John's, December 7, 1791.

PEDRO MARROT.
SAMUEL EASTLAKE.

[Here follows the plat.]

I certify the foregoing to be a true and correct translation from a document in the Spanish language on file in the office of the public archives.

F. J. FATIO, *S. B. L. C.*

[Translation.]

Don Pedro Marrot, captain of the third battalion of the infantry regiment of Cuba, and judge commissioned by the government and commander-in-chief of this province of East Florida for the survey of lands commanded to be distributed by order of his Majesty: I certify that at the plantation called Cook there have been measured and delivered three caballerias of land to the inhabitant Don William Pengree, on account of what corresponds to him. The first line runs north; begins by a pine tree marked with a cross and ends with a stake with the same mark; it measures 33 chains. The second runs west; begins by said stake and ends with another with the same mark; it measures 33 chains. The third runs south; begins by said stake and ends with a pine tree with the same mark; it measures 33 chains: this line bounds the land of the said Pengree, known as Pengree. The fourth runs east; begins by the said pine tree and ends by another marked with the same mark of a cross; it measures 33 chains—all according to the orders which I have. The interested signed jointly with me and the surveyor, Don Josiah Dupont. In proof whereof, and that it may serve for information at the office of the secretary of this government, to whom the parties have to apply for their respective titles, I give these presents in book. River St. John's, February 18, 1793.

PEDRO MARROT.
JOSIAH DUPONT.

[Here follows the plat.]

I certify the foregoing to be a true and correct translation from a document in the Spanish language on file in the office of public archives.

F. J. FATIO, *S. B. L. C.*

[Translation.]

Don Pedro Marrot, captain of the third battalion of the infantry regiment, &c., &c.: I certify that at the plantation called Laurel Spring there have been surveyed and delivered eighteen caballeras, and twenty-six acres of land (on account of what corresponds to him) to the inhabitant Don William Pengree. The first line runs south 75° east; begins with an ash marked with a cross on the bank of Doctor's creek, and ends with a stake of the same mark; this line bounds the lands of said Pengree known as Laurel Grove; it measures 28 chains. The second runs south 60° west; begins by said stake and ends with a pine tree with the same mark; it measures 105 chains. The third runs south 20° west; begins by the said pine tree and ends by a stake with the same mark; it measures 63 chains and 50 links. The fourth runs north 87° west; begins by said stake and ends with another marked with the same mark of a cross, on the bank of the said Doctor's creek; it measures 26 chains; its front runs on the bank of the said creek—all according to the orders I have. The interested signed this jointly with me and the surveyor, Don Josiah Dupont. In proof whereof, and that it may serve for information at the office of the secretary of this government, to whom the parties have to apply for their respective titles, I give these presents at Laurel Spring, river St. John's, and Doctor's creek, February 16, 1793.

PEDRO MARROT.

[Here follows the plat.]

I certify the foregoing to be a true and correct translation from a document in the Spanish language on file in the office of the public archives.

F. J. FATIO, S. B. L. C.

[Translation.]

Don Pedro Marrot, &c., &c.: I certify that in the plantation called Good-fortune there have been measured and delivered three caballerias and twenty-one acres of land (which completes what he is entitled to) to the inhabitant William Pengree. The first line runs west; begins by a maple marked with a cross on the bank of the river St. John's and ends by a pine tree with the same mark, bounding the lands by Jona. Arnold; it measures 35 chains. The second runs north; begins by said pine and ends by another with the same mark, bounding also the lands of the said Arnold; it measures 18 chains. The third line runs west; begins by said pine tree and ends by another with the same mark; it measures 30 chains. The fourth runs south; begins by said pine tree and ends with a live-oak of the same mark; it measures 35 chains. The fifth runs south 80° west; begins by said live-oak and ends with a red oak marked with the same mark of a cross, on the bank of the river St. John's; it measures 65 chains; this line bounds the lands of the said Pengree known as Laurel Grove; its front runs on the bank of the said river—all according to the orders which I have. The interested signed this jointly with me and the surveyor, Don Josiah Dupont. In proof whereof, and that it may serve for information at the office of the secretary of government, where the parties are to apply for their respective titles, I give these presents at Good-fortune, river St. John's, February 19, 1793.

PEDRO MARROT

[Here follows the plat.]

JOSIAH DUPONT.

I certify the foregoing to be a true and correct translation from a document in the Spanish language on file in the public archives.

F. J. FATIO, S. B. L. C.

[Here follows the translation of a conveyance from the widow of William Pengree to claimant, dated November 26, 1803.]

DECREE.

The board having ascertained the above to be a valid Spanish grant made to William Pengree, whose widow sold and conveyed it to claimant, do therefore recommend it to Congress for confirmation. December 15.

No. 5.—See Report No. 2.

Zephaniah Kingsley vs. The United States. For two thousand acres of land.

MEMORIAL.

To the honorable the commissioners appointed to ascertain claims and titles to lands in East Florida:

The petition of Z. Kingsley, by his attorney, George Gibbs, showeth: That your memorialist claims title to a tract of land consisting of two thousand acres, situated in Twelve-mile swamp; bounded on the south by lands of George Clarke, on the north by lands of Philip R. Yonge, on the east by a line running north 22° west, 199 chains, and on the west by a line running south 22° east, 199 chains, as per plat marked 6; which title your memorialist derives from a grant made to your memorialist January 18, 1816, by Governor Coppinger, in virtue of the royal order of October 29, 1790, herewith submitted; and further reference is made to the documents in the office of the public archives of the Territory. And your memorialist further showeth that he was, at the exchange of flags, and is now, in legal possession of said lands; that he is a citizen of the Territory of Florida and resident of said Territory. All of which is respectfully submitted.

ZEPH. KINGSLEY,
By GEORGE GIBBS, Attorney in fact.

[Translation.]

Title of property.

Don José Coppinger, lieutenant colonel, &c., &c., &c.:

Whereas, in a royal order communicated to this government October 29, 1790, by the captain general of the Island of Cuba and the two Floridas, it is provided, amongst other things, that lands should be surveyed gratis to those foreigners who, of their own free will, present themselves to swear allegiance to our sovereign, in proportion to the workers which each family have; that Don Zeph. Kingsley having presented himself as one of them, he solicited from the government, and there were granted to him, two thousand acres of land, situated at a place known by the name of Twelve-mile swamp, which land is known and distinguished under the following dimensions and boundaries: the first line runs east; its measurement consists of 110 chains; its measurement begins by an oak marked with a cross, on the western edge of a swamp, which ends with a pine tree marked with a cross on the opposite side. The second line runs north 22½° west; its measurement consists of 199 chains; begins with said pine tree and ends with another of the same kind marked with a cross. The third line runs west; its measurement consists of 110 chains; begins by said pine tree and ends with another marked with a cross. The fourth line runs south 22½° east; its measurement consists of 199 chains; begins by said pine tree and ends with the oak aforesaid, where the first line began, as results from the certificate given by the surveyor general appointed by this government, Don George Clarke, dated October 20, 1815, with the corresponding plat, which he has attested in continuation of it; and as no title has been issued for the security and proof of his dominion to the said lands, that he has made buildings on them, cultivated them, and finally complied with all the other conditions which the government has established for grants and concessions of this nature, existing in the titles delivered to other settlers, as is set forth in the proceedings moved by the interested, soliciting that the corresponding title should be issued to him for the land which he has already measured and laid off, and of which he is in possession: Wherefore, and in consideration of everything, I have granted, as in the name of his Majesty I do grant, unto the said Don Zeph. Kingsley the said two thousand acres of land in absolute property, for himself, his heirs and successors, and despatch to him, as by these presents I do, the corresponding title by which I separate the royal domain from the right and dominion it had to said land; and I cede and transfer it unto the said Kingsley, his heirs and successors, that, in consequence, they may possess it as their own, use and enjoy it, without any encumbrance whatsoever, with all its entrances, outlets, uses, customs, rights, and services, which it has had, has, and of custom and by law belong or may appertain unto it; and, at their will, sell, cede, transfer, and alienate it as may best suit them. To all which I give the sanction of my authority, as I can and of right ought to do, in virtue of the sovereign will.

Given under my hand, and countersigned by the undersigned notary *pro tem.* of government and the royal domain, in this city of St. Augustine, Florida, January 18, 1816.

JOSÉ COPPINGER.

By command of his excellency:
JUAN DE ENTRALGO, *Notary of Government and the Royal Domain pro tem.*

I certify the foregoing to be a true and correct translation from a document in the Spanish language on file in the office of the public archives.

F. J. FATIO, *S. B. L. C.*

DECREE.

The board having ascertained that the above is a valid Spanish grant for the two thousand acres made to the claimant, do therefore recommend it to Congress for confirmation. December 15.

No. 6.—See REPORT No. 2.

Zephaniah Kingsley vs. The United States. For two thousand acres of land.

MEMORIAL.

To the honorable the commissioners appointed to ascertain claims and titles to lands in East Florida:

The petition of Zephaniah Kingsley, by his attorney George Gibbs, respectfully showeth: That your memorialist claims title to a tract of land consisting of two thousand acres, more or less, situated on the island called Drayton island, at the entrance of Lake George, bounded on all sides by the river St. John's and Lake George, it being an island, as per royal title certified by Juan de Entralgo, government notary, dated July 27, 1821, per exhibit K; to which and to other documents in the office of the archives of the Territory, will more fully appear by reference to the same; which title your memorialist derives from a royal title made to George Sibbald for part by Governor Kindelan, in virtue of the royal order of October 29, 1790, who sold your memorialist fifteen hundred acres of the said island, being all his interest and right in the same; and the rest and residue of the said island was granted to your memorialist by the same Governor Kindelan, as per the aforementioned title, reference to the documents in the office of the public archives, will more fully appear. And your memorialist further showeth that he is in actual possession of said lands; that he is now a citizen of the United States and resident of St. Augustine.

ZEPHANIAH KINGSLEY,
By GEORGE GIBBS, *Attorney in fact.*

[Translation.]

Title of property in favor of Don Zephaniah Kingsley, of Drayton island.

Don Sebastian Kindelan and O'Regan, knight of the order of St. James, brigadier of the royal armies, political and military governor of this city of St. Augustine, Florida, and its province:

Whereas, in a royal order communicated to this government October 29, 1790, by the captain general of the Island of Cuba and the two Floridas, it is provided, amongst other things, that lands should be granted and surveyed gratis to those foreigners who, of their own free will, offer themselves to swear allegiance to our sovereign, in proportion to the number of workers each family may have; that Don George Sibbald having presented himself as one of them, he solicited from the government, and had granted unto him, fifteen hundred acres of land on October 6, 1804, in the island called Drayton, at the entrance of Lake George, in the river St. John's, which he ceded to Don Zeph. Kingsley, with all its improvements, to whom it was adjudged in *solutum*, in virtue of the agreement of the parties authorized by a decree of this said government of July 18, 1811; and afterwards, by a decree of the 4th of September of the same year, there was granted to the aforesaid Kingsley five hundred acres more, which were vacant in the said island, which, in all, might contain about two thousand acres, more or less, as appears more at length from the documents and certificates which are annexed to the proceeding moved by the said Kingsley, soliciting that there should be issued in his favor the corresponding title for the lands which the said island of Drayton contains: Wherefore, and considering that he has already passed more than ten years of an uninterrupted possession to obtain the useful and directed dominion to the said island of Drayton, made buildings on it, cultivated it, and finally complied with all the other conditions established by the government for grants and concessions of this nature, existing in the titles delivered to other settlers, as is set forth and proved in the said proceeding, I have granted, as in the name of his Majesty I do grant, unto the aforesaid Don Zephaniah Kingsley the said Drayton island, for himself, his heirs and successors, in absolute property; and in despatching to him, as by these presents I do, the corresponding title by which I separate the royal domain from the right and dominion it had to said land; and I cede and transfer it unto the said Kingsley, his heirs and successors, that, in consequence, they may possess it as their own, use and enjoy it, without any encumbrance whatsoever, with all its entrances, outlets, uses, customs, rights, and services, which it has had, has, and of custom and by law belong and may appertain unto it; and, at their will, sell, cede, transfer, and alienate it as may best suit them. To all which I give the sanction of my authority as I can, and of right ought to do, in virtue of the sovereign will.

Given under my hand, and countersigned by the undersigned notary of government and the royal domain, in this said city of St. Augustine, Florida, January 7, 1815.

SEBASTIAN KINDELAN.

By command of his excellency:
JUAN DE ENTRALGO, *Notary of Government pro tem.*

I certify the foregoing to be a true and correct translation from a document in the Spanish language on file in the office of the public archives.

FRANCIS J. FATIO, *S. B. L. C.*

DECREE.

The board having ascertained that this claim is covered by a British grant, they therefore order that it be reported to Congress for their determination. December 15.

No. 7.—See REPORT No. 2.

Domingo Fernandez vs. *The United States.   For one thousand one hundred and fifty acres of land.*

MEMORIAL.

To the honorable the commissioners appointed to ascertain claims and titles to lands in East Florida:

The memorial of Domingo Fernandez, by his attorney, Farquhar Bethune, respectfully showeth: That your memorialist claims title to a tract of land consisting of one thousand one hundred and fifty acres, situated on Big Dun's creek, St. John's river, and contained within the following lines: the first line runs north 20° east, is in length 130 chains, bounded by vacant land; the second line runs south 70° east, is in length 70 chains, and also bounded by vacant land; the third line runs south 25° east, is in length 29 chains, bounded by Lewis Christopher's land; the fourth line runs south 20° west, and measures 110 chains, bounded by John Houston's land; which title your memorialist derives from a grant made to him by Governor Coppinger April 10, 1817, in virtue of the royal order of March 29, 1815. Your memorialist further showeth that he is now in actual possession of said land, and was so at the time of the cession; that he is an inhabitant of Florida and resident of Amelia island. The title, marked A, is annexed; the survey will be produced when required. All of which is respectfully submitted.

DOMINGO FERNANDEZ,
By his attorney, FARQUHAR BETHUNE.

[Translation.]

Title of property of one thousand one hundred and fifty acres of land on Big Dun's creek, in favor of Don Domingo Fernandez.

Don José Coppinger, colonel of the royal armies, political and military governor *pro tem.*, and chief of the royal domain in this city of St. Augustine, Florida, and its province:

Whereas, in a royal order of March 29, 1815, his Majesty has deigned to approve of the favor and rewards proposed by my predecessor, Brigadier Don Sebastian Kindelan, for the officers and soldiers, both regulars and militia, of this province, who assisted in its defence in the time of the rebellion, one of the said favors being the distribution of lands in proportion to the number of family each individual may have; that Don Domingo Fernandez, an inhabitant of Amelia island, of this province, having presented himself, showing the concession of one thousand seven hundred acres of land made him by this government by decree of August 19, 1814, in consideration of his tried services performed in said defence in person, by his slaves and in implements, as appears more at length from the certificate of the proceedings given by the secretary of said government, and soliciting that, according to the royal order, there should be issued a title of property of one thousand one hundred and fifty acres on account of the said one thousand seven hundred, on the creek called Big Dun's creek, on the south side of the river St. John's, which land is known and distinguished under the following dimensions and boundaries: the first line runs north twenty degrees east, measures one hundred and thirty chains, bounding public lands; the second runs south seventy degrees east, measures seventy chains, bounding also public lands; the third line runs south twenty-five degrees east, measures twenty-nine chains, bounding the lands of Lewis Christopher; the fourth line runs south twenty-nine degrees west, measures one hundred and ten chains, bounding the land of John Houston, as appears from the certificate of the surveyor, Don George Clarke, dated November 28, 1816, which, with the corresponding authenticated plat, is annexed to the proceedings on the matter which exist in the archives of the present notary, with my decree of this date, in which I have thought proper to grant said petition: Wherefore, I have granted, as in the name of his Majesty I do grant, unto the said Don Domingo Fernandez the said one thousand one hundred and fifty acres of land at the place already pointed out, without injury to a third person, for himself, his heirs and successors, in absolute property; and in despatching to him, as by these presents I do, the corresponding title by which I separate the royal domain from the right and dominion it had to said land; and I cede and transfer it unto the aforesaid Don Domingo Fernandez, his heirs and successors, that, in consequence, they may possess it as their own, use and enjoy it, without any encumbrance whatsoever, with all its entrances, outlets, uses, customs, rights, and services, which it has had, has, and of custom and by law belong and may appertain unto it; and, at their will, sell, cede, transfer, and alienate it as may best suit them. To all which I give the sanction of my authority, as I can and of right ought to do, in virtue of the sovereign will.

Given under my hand, and countersigned by the undersigned notary of Government and the royal domain, in this city of St. Augustine, April 10, 1817.

JOSÉ COPPINGER.

By command of his excellency:
JUAN DE ENTRALGO, *Notary of Government, &c.*

I certify the foregoing to be a true and correct translation from a document in the Spanish language on file in the office of the public archives.

THOMAS MURPHY, *Ad. Clerk B. L. C.*

DECREE.

The board having ascertained the above to be a valid Spanish grant for the one thousand one hundred and fifty acres made to claimant, do therefore recommend it to Congress for confirmation. December 16.

[Nos. 8, 9, and 10, were not returned by the commissioners to the General Land Office.]

No. 1.—See REPORT No. 3.

Juan Blas Entralgo vs. The United States. For four thousand acres of land.

MEMORIAL.

To the honorable the commissioners appointed to ascertain claims and titles to lands in East Florida:

The petition of Juan Blas Entralgo respectfully showeth: That your memorialist claims title to a tract of land consisting of four thousand acres, situated about five miles east of Spring Garden, and bounded as follows: beginning at the head of a mountain, and running south 60° west, 100 chains, to a stake; thence south 30° east, 105 chains, to a stake; thence north 60° east, 235 chains 20 links, to a pine marked ═; thence north 30° west, 220 chains, to a pine marked ╋ ╋; thence south 60° west, 135 chains 20 links, to a stake; thence south 30° east, 115 chains, to the beginning; which title your memorialist derives from a grant made to F. M. Arredondo by Governor Coppinger, in virtue of the royal order of 1815, who sold the same to your memorialist, as will appear by document A, which, together with the grant to Arredondo, marked B, is herewith filed. And your memorialist further showeth that he has legal possession of said lands, and that he was a Spanish subject, living in St. Augustine, at the change of government in 1821, and that he now resides in Havana. In consideration of what is herein set forth, he prays his title to the said 4,000 acres may be confirmed.

J. B. ENTRALGO,
By GEORGE MURRAY. *Attorney for Memorialist.*

[Translation.]

SEÑOR GOVERNOR: Don Fernando de la Maza Arredondo, jr., an inhabitant of this city, with due respect, states to your excellency that, from the beginning of the insurrection of the year 1812, he took up arms and acted as commandant of a party of cavalry to reconnoitre the enemy, one of whom he took prisoner afterwards when they presented themselves in sight of this city; and afterwards the memorialist continued performing service in the militia, and patrolling at night, when necessary, for the guard and defence of this city, without pay, rations, or any emolument; at which time he performed other important services for the Government, among others, provision of meat and victuals for the support of the garrison; all of which is known to your excellency. And as his Majesty, in his royal order of March 29, 1815, has deigned to reward with a distribution of lands the faithful inhabitants who contributed to the defence of this province, the memorialist being one of them, and, as is more fully expressed, one of those whom the laws and royal dispositions regard with attention, distinguishing the merit and quality of the services; as, besides all the other circumstances which concur, it is also a very powerful one that he is a native of the country, established in it with more than eighty negroes of his property: Wherefore, he prays your excellency to be pleased to grant him, in absolute property, ten thousand acres of land situated, to wit: five thousand acres of them on a hammock, which is about five or six miles to the east of Spring Garden, and the other five thousand to the west of the river St John's, in the neighborhood of a creek known as Black creek, near Flemings' island, and the lake near Doctor's lake; titles of dominion to which to be made out and delivered as soon as the surveyor accomplishes the survey and laying off of both tracts of land, and that the corresponding plats are formed, which shall designate and mark out perfectly the situation and boundaries. A favor which he hopes for from the justice of your excellency. St. Augustine, Florida, March 18, 1817.

FERNANDO DE LA MAZA ARREDONDO.

 St Augustine, *March* 20, 1817.

In virtue of the services which Don Fernardo de la Maza Arredondo has performed and alleges, which are certain and notorious, and using the authority which I exercise agreeably to the intentions and desires of his Majesty to reward his faithful subjects, which the laws recommend in similar cases, and considering the large number of slaves he possesses, I have granted, as in the name of his Majesty and his royal justice which I administer, I do grant, in absolute property, and with a title of dominion from this day and henceforward, to the said Don Fernando de la Maza Arredondo, the ten thousand acres of land in the places he solicits, without injury to a third person, for which the corresponding titles of property shall be issued as soon as the survey and laying off are performed by the surveyor. This decree, in the meanwhile, serving for an equivalent with which the proceedings shall be filed in the notary's office, giving to the interested an authenticated copy for his security.

COPPINGER.

Before me—

JUAN DE ENTRALGO, Notary of Government.

I certify the foregoing to be a true and correct translation from a document in the Spanish language on file in the office of the public archives of St. Augustine.

F. J. FATIO, S. B. L. C.

[Translation.]

CONVEYANCE.

Be it known that I, Don Fernando de la Maza Arredondo, jr., an inhabitant of this province, declare that I really sell to Don Juan de Entralgo, notary of government and the royal domain in this city, four thousand acres of land, which I hold as my property in this province, situated about five miles to the east of Spring Gardens, known under the following dimensions: the first line begins at the head of a hammock and runs south 60° west, measures 100 chains, and ends with a stake; the second runs south 30° east, contains 105 chains, and ends also with a stake; the third line runs north 60° east, measures 235 chains 20 links, and ends with a pine marked =; the fourth line runs north 30° west, measures 220 chains, and ends with a pine marked × ×; the fifth line runs south 60° west, measures 135 chains 20 links, and ends with a stake; the sixth line runs south 30° east, measures 115 chains, and ends at the head of the said hammock; which 4,000 acres of land, with a portion more, this Government granted me, in absolute property and dominion, as a reward for services, March 20, 1817, and the corresponding title was issued to me on the 9th of August of the year last, as all appears in the archives of the said notary. And I sell the said 4,000 acres of land under the dimensions and other things, which are explained, with all its entrances, outlets, uses, customs, rights, and services, which it has had, has, and belong, or may appertain to it, free of all encumbrance, at the price of $4,000, which the purchaser has paid me in cash; which sum I acknowledge as delivered to my will. I renounce proof, laws of delivery, exception to money not counted, fraud, and everything else in the case, for which I grant a receipt in form; in virtue of which I separate myself from the right of property, possession, use, seigniory, and other rights, real and personal, which I had or held to said lands; and I cede, renounce, and transfer them to the purchaser, and whoever shall represent his right, that they may possess, sell, and alienate them at their will, in virtue of this deed which I deliver in his favor as a mark of real delivery; from which it is seen that he has acquired the possession without occasion for other proof, from which I release him. And I oblige myself to the eviction and guarantee of this sale in sufficient form, and as may best suit, in favor of the purchaser, with my goods, present and future, power and submission to the tribunals of his Majesty, that they may force me to compliance as by sentence consented to and passed in authority of an adjudged case, on which I renounce all the laws, customs, rights and privileges in my favor, and formal exceptions which prohibit it. And I, the said Juan de Entralgo, being present, accept in my favor this deed, and by it receive as purchased the aforesaid 4,000 acres of land at the price and agreement upon which they were sold to me, and I acknowledge them as delivered to my will. I renounce proof, laws of delivery, those of a thing not seen or received, fraud, and everything else in the case; for which I grant a receipt in form. In testimony of which, this is dated in the city of St. Augustine, Florida, January 5, 1821.

FERNANDO M. ARREDONDO.
JUAN DE ENTRALGO.

I, Don José Coppinger, colonel of the royal armies, military governor, political chief, and sub-delegate of ultramarine possessions for this said city and province, certify that I know the parties who have granted, delivered, and signed in my presence, and in that of the assistant witnesses, whom I have chosen for this act, Don Tomas de Aguilar and Don Antonio Alvarez, there being no other notary in the entire province. There being witnesses to this deed, Don José Mariano Hernandez, Don Bernardo Sequi, and Don José Bernardo Reyes, residents present.

COPPINGER.

Tomas de Aguilar.
Antonio Alvarez.

This is conformable to the original which exists in the archives of the said government notary, to which I refer; and at the desire of the parties, sign the present copy, with the assistant witnesses, on two leaves of common paper, the stamped not being in use. St. Augustine, Florida, January 5, 1821.

JOSÉ COPPINGER.

Antonio Alvarez.
Tomas de Aguilar.

I certify the foregoing to be a true and correct translation from a document in the Spanish language on file in the office of the public archives of St. Augustine.

F. J. FATIO, S. B. L. C.

[Translation.]

Don Andres Burgevin, of this place, and private surveyor: I certify that, by an order of this governor, made August 20, 1819, I have measured, in favor of Don Fernando de la Maza Arredondo, jr., a piece of land which contains 4,000 acres of land, which is five miles to the east of Spring Gardens, being part of a greater quantity which was granted to him March 20, 1817. In proof of which I give these presents, which I sign at St. Augustine, Florida, July 25, 1820.

ANDRES BURGEVIN.

[Here follows the plat.]

I certify the foregoing to be a true and correct translation from a document in the Spanish language on file in the office of the public archives of St. Augustine.

F. J. FATIO, *S. B. L. C.*

DECREE.

Juan B. Entralgo vs. *The United States. For four thousand acres of land.*

The board having ascertained the above to be a valid Spanish concession made to F. M. Arredondo previous to January 24, 1818, who conveyed the above 4,000 acres to claimant, do therefore recommend it to Congress for confirmation. July 12, 1824.

No. 2.—See REPORT No. 3.

Juan B. Entralgo vs. *The United States. For ten thousand four hundred acres of land.*

MEMORIAL.

To the honorable the commissioners appointed to ascertain claims and titles to lands in East Florida:

The petition of Juan B. Entralgo respectfully showeth: That your memorialist claims title to a tract of land consisting of ten thousand and four hundred acres, situated on the St. John's river to the west, and about twelve miles south of Lake George, bounded as follows: commencing at a pine marked thus ═, running south 20° east, 322 chains, to a pine tree marked as the first; thence north 70° west, 323 chains, to a pine, same mark; thence north 20° east, 322 chains, to a pine with same mark; thence south 70° east, 323 chains, to the beginning; this tract is nearly equally divided by a stream running from the west into St. John's river; which title your memorialist derives from a grant made to Antonio Huertas by Governor Coppinger, in virtue of the royal order of March 29, 1815, who sold the same to your memorialist December 4, 1821. The concession was made September 15, 1817, (see a certified copy of the document filed herewith, as is also a plat of the land.) And your memorialist further showeth that he is in possession of said lands; that he resides in Cuba, but at the change of flags was in St. Augustine.

JUAN B. ENTRALGO,
By GEORGE MURRAY.

[Translation.]

ST. AUGUSTINE, *Florida, September* 15, 1817.

SEÑOR GOVERNOR: Don Antonio Huertas, an inhabitant of this city, with due respect, states to your excellency that, although he has obtained a concession of ten thousand acres of land on March 27, 1813, for the pasture of cattle, in the rearing of which this party has employed himself for many years; as the said land is almost all composed of pine land and very little arable, and the memorialist being one of the individuals who, by his well known and constant good services in defence of this province, and by his having been one of the first settlers of it, is entitled by every claim to be rewarded with a greater number of acres, as the laws so provide which treat in the matter, as from the character of his services, which he omits stating, as they are well known to your excellency, not only those which he has performed in the service of his Majesty, in which he has been employed since the age of 18 years, but the extraordinary ones of succoring the garrison of this city in calamitous times, and in the insurrection, making a sacrifice of his interests, and encountering perils, by the help of which he can say he has preserved the said garrison: Wherefore, he prays your excellency to be pleased to grant him 15,000 acres of land more, in absolute property and dominion, on a creek which comes from the west, and joins the river St. John's about 12 miles to the south of Lake St. George; its survey to commence about four or five miles to the west of the river St. John's, and dividing the said lands in two parts by said creek, reserving the delivery of the title in form until the memorialist finds it convenient to proceed to the survey and demarcation of said land, by an intelligent person, during the difficulties which exist at this day, and from the absence of the surveyor, Don George Clarke, who is named by the Governor. A favor which he hopes for from the justice of your excellency.

ANTONIO HUERTAS.

ST. AUGUSTINE, *September* 15, 1817.

In attention to what this party represents, and the services which he sets forth being certain, I grant him, in the name of his Majesty, and of his royal justice, which I administer, the fifteen thousand acres of land which he solicits, that he may possess and enjoy it in absolute property and dominion; and, in order to make this grant secure, let a certified copy be furnished him of this proceeding, which shall be lodged in the archives of the notary, where titles in form shall be issued when the survey and plats are accomplished, as is expressed by the interested.

COPPINGER.

I certify the foregoing to be a true and correct translation from a document in the Spanish language on file in the office of the public archives of St. Augustine.

F. J. FATIO, *S. B. L. C.*

[Translation.]

St. Augustine, *Florida, April* 5, 1821.

Don Andres Burgevin, of this city, and private surveyor: I certify that, in virtue of authority conferred on me by a decree of December 13, 1820, made at the instance of Don Antonio Huertas, I have surveyed for this individual several pieces of land, which, to the number of fifteen thousand acres, were granted him as a reward for services, on a creek which comes from the west and joins the river St. John's about twelve miles to the south of said Lake St. George—the land divided by said creek—one of said tracts being ten thousand four hundred acres, which are bounded on the east by another of six hundred, and on the other sides by vacant lands, whose figure and demarcation the foregoing plat points out; and for its confirmation, and the purposes convenient to the interested, I sign these presents.

ANDRES BURGEVIN.

[The plat follows.]

I certify the foregoing to be a true and correct translation from a document in the Spanish language on file in the office of the public archives of St. Augustine.

F. J. FATIO, *S. B. L. C.*

[Translation.]

St. Augustine, *Florida, December* 4, 1821.

I cede and renounce in favor of Don Juan Blas de Entralgo, all the right, title, and dominion which I have to the ten thousand four hundred acres of land contained in this document of property, on account of having sold him the same for the sum of *five thousand* ————, for which I deliver him a formal receipt.

ANTONIO HUERTAS.

Witness: Domingo Reyes.

I certify the foregoing to be a true and correct translation from a document in the Spanish language.

F. J. FATIO, *S. B. L. C.*

DECREE

The board having ascertained the above to be a valid Spanish concession made previous to January 24, 1818, do therefore recommend it to Congress for confirmation.   June 30, 1824.

[Translation.]

John B. de Entralgo vs. The United States.   For ten thousand four hundred acres of land.

B. Segui, being duly sworn, states that he has seen Antonio Huertas write, and believes the name attached to the conveyance from said Huertas to Entralgo to be his own handwriting, but is not positive.   Witness states that, after the cession of this Territory, and the archives taken away from the Spanish notary, it was customary for some person to have conveyances drawn out in the manner of the one presented in the above case.

B. SEGUI.

Before the board in session June 29, 1824.

José B. Reyes, being duly sworn, states that the signature of Antonio Huertas in the deed to John B. Entralgo is the genuine one of said party.

JOSÉ B. REYES.

Before the board in session June 30, 1824..

No. 3.—See Report No. 3.

Wm. Travers vs. The United States.   For eight thousand acres of land.

MEMORIAL.

To the honorable the commissioners appointed to ascertain claims and titles to lands in East Florida:

The petition of William Travers respectfully showeth: That your memorialist claims title to a tract of land consisting of eight thousand acres, situated on the west side of Long lake, on the west side of St. John's river, about forty miles south of Lake George, bounded as follows: first line runs south, and is bounded by lands of Felipe R. Yonge; thence west one hundred and forty chains; thence south eight chains; thence west two hundred and fifteen chains, and terminates at a pine tree; thence north, two hundred and forty chains, to a cypress tree which title your memorialist derives from an absolute grant made to Felipe Robert Yonge by Governor Coppinger, in virtue of the royal order of March 29, 1815, who sold the same to your memorialist; a certified copy of the grant, which was made February 22, 1817 is filed herewith.   And your memorialist further showeth that he has possession of said lands; that he resided in St. Augustine at the change of flags, and still does so; that he is a citizen of the United States and resident of St. Augustine.

WM. TRAVERS.

[Translation of a royal title to P. R. Yonge for 25,000 acres is filed in claim of William Travers for 12,000 acres, recommended for confirmation July 12, 1824.]
[Power of attorney from Philip R. Yonge to Juan B. Entralgo is filed in the aforesaid claim.]

[Translation.]

CONVEYANCE.

Be it known that I, Don Juan B. Entralgo, notary of government and of the public domain in this city, as attorney of Don Philip Robert Yonge, citizen of this province, now absent, which power he has conferred on me in this office, May 29, 1819, before Señor Don José Coppinger, colonel of the national armies, military governor and political chief of this province, and before witnesses, assisting for the want of another notary in the province, which power is not revoked, and is ample for what shall be said; in virtue of which I also have an order or instruction in writing from the said principal, and of the same date for the purpose. I declare that I really sell to Don William Travers, an inhabitant and merchant of this city, eight thousand acres of land, the property of my said principal, situated on the west side of the Long lake, distant about forty-five miles to the south of Lake George, to the west of the river St. John's, which are a part of 13,000 acres which, under date of February 11, 1817, were granted by this government to the said Don Philip Robert Yonge, in absolute property and dominion, as a reward for his services, and for which a corresponding title was issued on the 22d of the same month, the plat and survey of which, made by the private surveyor, Don Andrew Burgevin, August 2, 1819, with the other documents referred to, and which form the proceedings existing in my archives; the said dimensions being known under the following form: the first line runs south, bounding the 5,000 acres remaining to the person who empowers me; the second line, west, measures 140 chains; the third line, south, eight chains; the fourth line, west, 215 chains, and terminates with a pine tree; the fifth line north, 240 chains, beginning with said pine and terminating with a cypress, as appears by another plat made by said surveyor on the 20th of May last in consequence of superior order; all which is added to the said proceeding. And I sell him the said 8,000 acres of land at the place, under the dimensions, and on the terms set forth, with all its entrances, outlets, uses, customs, rights, and services, which it has and belong to it, free of all encumbrance, (as I, the seller, certify, as appears from the book of mortgages in my charge, which I have searched for the purpose,) at the price of eight thousand dollars, which the purchaser has paid me in cash, which sum I acknowledge as delivered to my will. I renounce proof, laws of delivery, exception to money not counted, fraud, and everything else in the case, for which I grant a formal receipt, in virtue of which I separate the said Don Philip R. Yonge from the right of property, possession, use, seigniory, and other rights, real or personal, which he had or held to the said 8,000 acres of land, and that I cede, renounce, and transfer them to the said Don William Travers, and whoever represents his rights, that they may, as their own, possess, sell, and alienate them at their will, in virtue of this writing, which I deliver in his favor as a mark of real delivery, by which it may be seen that he has acquired the possession, without occasion for further proof, from which I relieve him. And I oblige the said Don Philip R. Yonge to the eviction and guarantee of this sale in sufficient form, and as may best suit, in favor of the purchaser, with all his property, present and future, power and submission to the tribunals of his Majesty, that they may compel me to compliance with it, as by sentence consented to and passed in authority of an adjuged case; moreover, I renounce all the laws, customs, rights, and privileges in his favor, and everything in form which prohibits it. And I, the aforesaid Don William Travers, being present, accept in my favor this writing, and by it receive as purchased the said 8,000 acres at the price and terms they were sold to me on, and I acknowledge them as delivered to my will. I renounce proof, laws of delivery, those of a thing not seen or received, fraud, and all other things in the case, for which I deliver a formal receipt. In testimony of which, this is dated in the city of St. Augustine, Florida, December 22, 1820. I, the notary, as the only one in this city, and as the seller, sign this writing for myself, and before me, with the purchaser and the witnesses, who are Don Pedro Miranda, Don Jose Mariano Hernandez, and Don Fernando M. Arredondo, jr., inhabitants present. By me and for myself.

JUAN B. ENTRALGO.
WIL'M TRAVERS.

This is conformable to the original which exists in the archives in my charge, to which I refer; and, at the desire of the party, sign and seal these presents, in St. Augustine, Florida, the day of the date.

JUAN DE ENTRALGO, *Notary of Government.*

I certify the foregoing to be a true and correct translation from a document in the Spanish language on file in the office of the public archives of St. Augustine.

F. J. FATIO, *S. B. L. C.*

DECREE.

William Travers vs. *The United States.   For eight thousand acres of land.*

The board having ascertained the above to be a valid title made previous to January 24, 1818, and this claim being part thereof, regularly conveyed to claimant, it is therefore recommended to Congress for confirmation.   June 29, 1824.

No. 4.—See REPORT No. 3.

William Travers vs. *The United States.   For twelve thousand acres of land.*

MEMORIAL.

To the honorable the commissioners appointed to ascertain claims and titles to lands in East Florida:

The petition of William Travers respectfully showeth: That your memorialist claims title to a tract of land consisting of twelve thousand acres, situated at the lagoon called south of Lake George, in St. John's river, bounded as follows: first line, south 65° west, 320 chains, beginning at a palmetto tree *marked*   *to a pine tree* with the same mark; thence north 25° west, 400 chains, to a stake; thence north 65° east, 320 chains, to a stake on the bank of said lagoon; which title your memorialist derives from an absolute grant to Felipe Roberto Yonge by Governor Coppinger, in virtue of the royal order of March 29, 1815, who sold the same to your memorialist; a certified copy of the grant, which was made February 22,

1817, is herewith filed. And your memorialist further showeth that he has possession of said lands; that he resided in St. Augustine at the change of flags, and still does so; that he is a citizen of the United States and resident of St. Augustine.

WILLIAM TRAVERS.

Title of property for twenty-five thousand acres of land in favor of Don Felipe R. Yonge.

Don José Coppinger, lieutenant colonel of the royal armies, &c., &c.:

Whereas, by a royal order of March 29, 1815, his Majesty has deigned to approve the gifts and favors proposed by my predecessor, Don Sebastian Kindelan, for the officers and soldiers, both regular and militia, of this province, who assisted in its defence at the time of the rebellion, one of the said favors being the distribution of royal lands; and considering that Don P. Robt. Yonge has made evident to me the distinguished and extraordinary services by which he has contributed personally and with his money to the defence of this said province at different times, and principally during the insurrection which took place in the year 1812, with the sacrifice of his property, and saving to the royal treasury, as the memorial which he has presented me of the date of the 5th December of the last year more fully shows; in consideration of which, and in virtue of the authority which I exercise, I have judged fit, by my decree of the 11th instant, to accede to his solicitations as set forth, and that, in remuneration, there shall be granted him twenty-five thousand acres of land, with a title in absolute property, to the south of the place known as Spring Garden, in this form: twelve thousand acres of them in the neighborhood of the lake or lagoon called and known as Valdes', and the thirteen thousand remaining at the lake higher up, known as Long lake, all on the west of the river St. John's, with the reserve of establishing the boundaries and dimensions when he proceeds to the survey of both tracts of land, as is shown by the said memorial and decree, which exist in the archives of the notary: Wherefore, and in consideration of the said commendable services, agreeably with the will of the sovereign, and with what the laws recommend for distinguished rewards to those who are deserving, attending to the quality of said services, and of the persons who have performed them, I have granted, and in the name of his Majesty, whose royal justice I administer, I do grant, unto the said Don Philip R. Yonge the said twenty-five thousand acres of land in the places pointed out, without prejudice to a third person, for himself, his heirs and successors, in absolute property; and, in expediting to him, as by these presents I do, the corresponding title of property by which I separate from the royal domain in the right of dominion it had to said lands; and I cede and transfer it to the said Don Philip R. Yonge, and his heirs and successors, that, in consequence, they may possess it as their own, use and enjoy it, without any encumbrance whatsoever, with all its entrances, outlets, uses, customs, rights, and services, which it has had, has, and in fact and law belong or appertain to it; and, at their will, sell, cede, transfer, and alienate it as may best suit them. In all which I interpose my judicial authority as I can, and of right ought, in virtue of the sovereign will and what has been set forth.

Given under my hand, and countersigned by the notary of government and the royal domain, in this said city of St. Augustine, Florida, February 22, 1816.

JOSÉ COPPINGER.

By order of his excellency:
JUAN DE ENTRALGO, *Notary of Government and Royal Domain.*

I certify the foregoing to be a true and correct translation from a document in the Spanish language on file in the office of the public archives of St. Augustine.

F. J. FATIO, *S. B. L. C.*

[Translation.]

POWER.

Be it known that I, Don Philip R. Yonge, an inhabitant and merchant of this province, resident in this city, declare that I give all my full, ample, and sufficient power, which is required, and may be necessary in law, unto Don Juan de Entralgo, notary of government and the royal domain in this said city, especially that he may in my name, and representing my proper person, rights, and actions, administer, and do administer, all and every my property, both landed and movable and immovable, sell some and purchase for me others, rent or mortgage them for the prices and terms which he shall adjust and agree to, delivering the deeds, receipts, and letters of payment which may be necessary, which from now I approve and ratify, as if I were present at their delivery; for which sale of lands, houses, or any my property whatsoever which I may have in this said province, he shall govern himself precisely by the instructions which I have given and shall give him on the subject, since with them I confer on him sufficient power, without any other limitation, free, open, and general administration, incidences and dependencies, power to prepare causes for judgment, to swear and substitute, revoke substitutes, and name others with substitution in form; and for the fulfilment of what he shall perform in virtue of this power, I bind myself, with my property, present and future power, and submission to the tribunals of his Majesty, that they may compel me to its performance, as by sentence consented to and passed in authority of an adjudged case, on which I renounce all laws, customs, rights, and privileges, in my favor, and the general in form which prohibits it. In testimony of which this is dated in the city of St. Augustine, Florida, May 29, 1819.

PH. R. YONGE.

I, Don José Coppinger, colonel of the royal armies, political and military governor of this city and its province, for his Majesty, certify, for the want of another notary, that I know the grantor, who acknowledged the same, and signed with me, and the assistant witnesses I have chosen for this act, Don Tomas de Aguilar and Don Antonio Alvarez, there being also witnesses to this power present Domingo Reyes, Don Manuel Fuertes, and Don Nicholas Garrido.

COPPINGER.

ANTONIO ALVAREZ.
TOMAS DE AGUILAR.

I certify the foregoing to be a true and correct translation from a document in the Spanish language on file in the office of the public archives of St. Augustine.

F. J. FATIO, *S. B. L. C.*

CONVEYANCE.

Be it known that I, Don Juan de Entralgo, notary of government and the public domain in this city, as attorney for Don Philip Robert Yonge, citizen of this province, now absent, which power he has conferred on me in this office, May 29, 1819, before Señor Don José Coppinger, colonel of the national armies, military governor and political chief of this said city and its province, and before witnesses assisting for want of another notary in the province, which power is not revoked, and will be sufficient for what shall be said; in virtue of which I also have written orders and instructions of the same principal and of the same date for the purpose. I declare that I really sell to Don William Travers, inhabitant of this city, twelve thousand acres of land of the property of my said principal, situated on the lake named "Second," on the west side of said lake, which were granted him by this government as a reward for services February 11, 1817; and on the 22d of the same a complete title of absolute property and dominion was issued to him, the dimensions of which are distinguished under the following form: the first line runs south 65° west, measures three hundred and twenty chains, beginning with a palmetto marked ☰, and finishing with a pine of the same mark; the second line begins with said pine, running north 25° west, measures four hundred chains, and ends with a stake; the third line begins with said stake, north 75° east, measures three hundred and twenty chains, and terminates with another stake in the neighborhood of Second lake, as appears from the plat formed by the surveyor, Don Andrew Burgevin, August 2, 1819, agreeable to superior order, which, with the other documents I refer to, are added to the proceedings in the business, which are in the archives in my charge; and I sell him the said twelve thousand acres of land at the place, and under the dimensions and terms expressed, with all its entrances, outlets, uses, customs, rights, and services, which they have and belong to them, free of all encumbrance, (as I, the seller, certify, from the result of the book of mortgages, which I have searched for the purpose,) at the price of twelve thousand dollars, which the purchaser has paid me in cash, which sum I acknowledge as delivered to my will. I renounce proof, laws of delivery, exception to money not counted, fraud, and everything besides in the case, for which I deliver a formal receipt; in virtue of which I separate from him who empowered me the right of property, possession, use, seigniory, and other actions, real and personal, which he had or held to the said twelve thousand acres of land, which I cede, renounce, and transfer to the purchaser, and whoever shall represent his right, that they may possess, sell, and alienate them at their will, in virtue of this writing which I deliver in his favor as a mark of real delivery, with which it is seen that he has acquired its possession, without occasion for any other proof, from which I deliver him. And I oblige myself to the eviction and guarantee of this sale in due form, and as may be most favorable to the purchaser, with the property of my principal, present and future power, and submission to the tribunal of his Majesty, that they may compel him to its compliance, as by sentence consented to and passed in authority as a thing adjudged, on which I renounce all laws, customs, rights, and privileges in his favor, and everything in form which prohibits it. And being present, I, the said purchaser, accept in my favor this writing, and by it receive as purchased the said twelve thousand acres of land at the price and agreement which they were sold to me; and I acknowledge them as delivered to my disposal, with a renunciation of proof, laws of delivery, those of a thing not seen or received, fraud, and everything else in the case, for which I deliver a formal receipt. In testimony of which, this is dated in the city of St. Augustine, Florida, December 22, 1820. I, the notary, as the only one in this city, and as the seller, sign this writing for myself, and before me, with the purchaser and the witnesses, who are Don Pedro Miranda, Don José Mariano Hernandez, and Don Fernando de la Maza Arredondo, jr., witnesses present for me and before me.

JUAN DE ENTRALGO.
WILLIAM TRAVERS.

I certify the foregoing to be a true and correct translation from a document in the Spanish language on file in the office of the public archives of St. Augustine.

F. J. FATIO, S. B. L. C.

DECREE.

The board having ascertained that the foregoing is a valid Spanish grant made previous to January 24, 1818, do therefore recommend it to Congress for confirmation. July 12, 1824.

No. 5.—See REPORT No. 3.

John B. Entralgo vs. The United States. For four thousand acres of land.

MEMORIAL.

To the honorable the commissioners appointed to ascertain claims and titles to lands in East Florida:

The petition of Juan B. Entralgo respectfully showeth: That your memorialist claims title to a tract of land consisting of four thousand acres, situated at a place called Big Spring, on the river St. John's, and about twenty-five miles south of Lake George, on the west bank, bounded as follows: on the east by St. John's river, on the north by lands of Pedro Miranda, on the south by vacant lands, on the west by lands also belonging to Pedro Miranda, (see description in the grant filed herewith;) which title your memorialist derives from a grant made to Pedro Miranda by Governor Coppinger, in virtue of the royal order of March 29, 1815, who sold the same to your memorialist, (see document A,) the said four thousand acres being part of a grant made, as above stated, to Pedro Miranda for ten thousand acres, dated April 11; and this title is founded upon a memorial and concession made September 16, 1817, by Governor Coppinger. And your memorialist further showeth that he has possession of said lands, and was, at the exchange of flags, living in St. Augustine; at present he resides in Cuba.

JUAN B. ENTRALGO,
By GEORGE MURRAY.

[Translation.]

St. Augustine, *Florida, September* 16, 1817.

Señor Gobernador : Don Pedro Miranda, first pilot of the bar, and captain of the port, with due respect, states to your excellency that the government is well aware of the services which the memorialist has performed, from the insurrection in this province in the year 1812, contributing with his person and property to its defence, besides there having been, and now being in his charge, several extraordinary commissions, for which he has never had any recompense. It is also certain and well known that, in the insurrection of the year 1794, he was likewise engaged in an extraordinary manner, and employed in other commissions for the royal service, having contributed, on all occasions, with his greatest exertions, to the economy of the royal treasury. For these considerations, and that of having served his Majesty from his youth, and being of the first families that came on the occupation of this province, which circumstance of being a settler makes him entitled to the favor of a grant of lands, as has been given to others, since those which your excellency has been pleased to grant him do not equal your liberality to those: Wherefore, he prays your excellency to be pleased to grant him, in absolute property and dominion, ten thousand acres of land on a creek which runs from the west, and joins the river St. John's, called in English Big spring, about twenty-miles to the south of Lake St. George; the said land to be divided in two parts by said creek, and to have one of its fronts on the river St. John's, leaving free the concession of two thousand acres which were made to him on the first of July last, reserving the titles of property until he can complete the survey and plat, it being out of his power at present to pay the expenses. A favor he hopes from the justice of your excellency.

PEDRO MIRANDA.

St. Augustine, *Florida, September* 16, 1817.

In attention to what Don Pedro Miranda represents in the foregoing memorial, and as the services he mentions are certain, agreeing at the same time with what the laws and royal orders direct for the encouragement of population, I grant him, in the name of his Majesty, and of his royal justice, which I administer, the ten thousand acres of land in the places which he points out, that he may enjoy them in absolute property and dominion; for which end, and that he may prove this grant, let a certified copy of the *proceeding* be furnished him, which shall be lodged in the notary's archives, from whence titles in form shall be given him speedily, or whenever required by the interested.

COPPINGER.

I certify the foregoing to be a true and correct translation from a document in the Spanish language on file in the office of the public archives of St. Augustine.

F. J. FATIO, *S. B. L. C.*

[Translation.]

Don Andres Burgevin, inhabitant of this city and private surveyor: I certify that, in consequence of power conferred upon me by a decree of December 12, 1820, made at the instance of Don Pedro Miranda, I have surveyed for this individual *various pieces of land, to the number of ten thousand acres were granted* him as a reward for services, on a creek which comes from the west and joins the river St. John's, called in English Big spring, about twenty-five miles to the south of Lake St. George; the land divided in two parts by said creek, having one of its fronts on said river St. John's; one of the said pieces being the following four thousand acres, which are bounded on the east by said river St. John's, on the north by lands of the interested, on the south by lands *also* vacant, and on the west by another piece of three thousand four hundred acres of the said interested; and, for its confirmation, I sign these presents at St. Augustine, Florida, April 5, 1821.

ANDRES BURGEVIN.

[Plat is annexed.]

Royal title to P. Miranda for 4,000 acres, part of a concession of 10,000 acres to him, is not translated. The following translation is at foot of it.

[Translation.]

St. Augustine, *Florida, December* 5, 1821.

I cede and renounce in favor of Don Juan Blas de Entralgo all the right, title, and dominion which I have to the four thousand acres of land which this document of property contains, for having sold them at the rate of one thousand five hundred dollars, for which I deliver a formal receipt.

PEDRO MIRANDA.

Witnesses present:
    Francs. J. Fatio.
    Ruperto Saavedra.

I certify the foregoing to be a true and correct translation from a document in the Spanish language.

FRANCS. J. FATIO, *S. B. L. C.*

DECREE.

J. B. Entralgo vs. *The United States.   For four thousand acres of land.*

The board having ascertained the above to be a valid Spanish concession made previous to January 24, 1818, and this claim being part thereof, and conveyed to claimant, it is therefore recommended to Congress for confirmation. June 29, 1824.

No. 6.—See Report No. 3.

Antonio Huertas vs. *The United States.   For ten thousand acres of land.*

MEMORIAL.

To the honorable the commissioners appointed to ascertain claims and titles to lands in East Florida:

The memorial of Antonio Huertas, late of St. Augustine, in East Florida aforesaid, now residing at Havana, in the Island of Cuba, respectfully showeth: That your memorialist claims title to ten thousand acres of land, situated on Six-mile creek, bounded westward by the said creek, eastward by the large mount, southward by the road of Picolata, running northward to its termination, being the same land formerly granted to Panton, Leslie & Co., and afterwards relinquished by them. The grant to your memorialist of the said land was made March 27, 1813, in virtue of the royal order of October 29, 1790, and an absolute title granted to your memorialist by Governor Coppinger July 20, 1816. The original grant, absolute title, and survey, are in the office of public records in the city of St. Augustine, kept by Wm. Reynolds, esq. And your memorialist further showeth that he was a resident inhabitant of East Florida at the time of its cession to the United States, and in possession of the said land; that he had for about thirty-six years previous to said cession resided in the city of St. Augustine, whence he removed to the Havana in the year 1822. All of which is respectfully submitted. St. Augustine, February 25, 1823.

                                                                        ANTONIO HUERTAS.
                                      By his attorney, JOHN RODMAN.

                                        [Translation.]

Title of property in favor of Don Antonio Huertas for ten thousand acres of land in the place known as Six-mile creek.

Don José Coppinger, lieutenant colonel of the royal armies, civil and military governor *pro tem.*, and chief of the royal finance of this city of St. Augustine, of Florida, and its province:

Whereas, by a royal order communicated to this government October 29, 1790, by the captain general of the Island of Cuba and two Floridas, it is provided, among other things, that to those foreigners who, of their free will, present themselves to swear allegiance to our sovereign, lands should be measured them gratis in proportion to the laborers each family may have; that Don Antonio Huertas, of this place, having presented himself, he solicited of the government, and there were granted him, March 27, 1813, ten thousand acres of land for the raising of stock, in consideration of his faithful and constant services to the country, and for the injuries which he suffered by the insurrection of this province; which lands are known by the name of the Six-mile creek, and are distinguished under the following boundaries: commencing on the west by said creek, on the east by the Big wood, on the south by the Picolata road, and following north to where it corresponds; and *the said lands being the same which the house of Panton, Leslie & Co. ——————, to whom they were granted;* and as the said Don Antonio Huertas has solicited, there should be expedited to him the title of absolute property, as he has established a cowpen on said lands where he rears stock, as he has made appear by evidence; in virtue of which, and in attention to his said good services, I have granted him by my decree of the 17th of the present month, placed on the proceedings moved by the aforesaid Don Antonio Huertas, where all appears more in detail, and is filed in the office of the present notary: Wherefore, and in consideration of all, I have thought proper to grant, as in the name of his Majesty I do grant, to the said Don Antonio Huertas the said ten thousand acres of land, for himself, his heirs and successors, in absolute property, and in granting to him, as by these presents I do, the corresponding title by which I separate the royal domain from the right and dominion which it had in said land; and I cede and transfer it to the aforesaid Don Antonio Huertas, his heirs and successors, that, in consequence thereof, they may possess it as their own, use and enjoy without any encumbrance whatever, with all its entrances, outlets, uses, customs, rights, and services, which it has had, has, or by fact and law may belong or appertain to it; and, being their will, they may sell, cede, transfer, and alienate it as may best suit them. To all of which I interpose my authority as far as I can, and by right ought, in virtue of what has been set forth and of the sovereign will.

Given under my hand, and countersigned by the undersigned notary *pro tem.* of government and royal finance, in this city of St. Augustine, Florida, July 20, 1816.

                                                                        JOSÉ COPPINGER.
        By order of his excellency:
            JUAN DE ENTRALGO, *Notary of Government and Royal Finance.*

I certify the foregoing to be a true and correct translation from a document in the Spanish language on file in the office of the public archives of St. Augustine.

                                      FRANCO. J. FATIO, *S. B. L. C.*

                                        DECREE.

Antonio Huertas vs. The United States.   For ten thousand acres of land.

The board having ascertained this to be a valid Spanish title made previous to January 24, 1818, it is therefore recommended to Congress for confirmation. September 1, 1824.

                            No. 7.—See REPORT No. 3.

Juan B. Entralgo vs. The United States.   For twenty thousand acres of land.

                                        MEMORIAL.

To the honorable the commissioners appointed to ascertain claims and titles to lands in East Florida:

The petition of Juan B. Entralgo respectfully showeth: That your memorialist claims title to a tract of land consisting of 20,000 acres, situated at Chacala, in the district of Alachua, and 45 miles west of St. John's river, embracing the residence of the late Indian chief Payne, and bounded as follows: beginning at a pine tree and running east, 625 chains, to a pine; thence north, 320 chains, to a stake; thence west, 625 chains, to a stake; thence south, 320 chains, to the beginning, (see survey and plat made by Burgevin and filed herewith, marked C;) which title your memorialist derives from a grant made to George J. F. Clarke by Governor Coppinger, in virtue of the royal order of March 29, 1815, who sold to your memorialist the said 20,000 acres, being part of a grant of 22,000 acres made December 17, 1817, which is filed herewith, marked A, as is also the deed from Clarke to your memorialist, marked B. And your memorialist further showeth that he has legal possession of said lands, and that he is a Spanish subject residing in Cuba, but at the cession in 1821 was an inhabitant of St. Augustine. He prays his title to the said 20,000 acres may be confirmed.

JUAN B. ENTRALGO,
By GEORGE MURRAY.

A.

CONVEYANCE.

Title of property of 22,000 acres of land in favor of Don Jorge Clarke, in the hammocks of Cuscowillo and Chacala.

Don José Coppinger, colonel of the royal armies, governor, political and military, *pro tem.*, and chief of the royal domain of this city of St. Augustine, Florida, and its province, for his Majesty:

Whereas, in a royal order of March 29, 1815, his Majesty has deigned to approve of the favors and rewards proposed by my predecessor, Brigadier Don Sebastian Kindelan, for the officers and soldiers, both veterans and militia, of this province, who assisted in its defence at the time of the rebellion, one of the said favors being the distribution of public lands; and as Don Jorge Clarke, lieutenant of local militia has represented to me the distinguished services which he has rendered, both personally and in a pecuniary manner, in the defence of this said province at several periods of invasion, with the sacrifice and abandonment of his interest and property, like a faithful subject as he has been, worthy of every recompense for his zeal, love, and fidelity to the sovereign; which extraordinary services, which are well known to me, are set forth by his memorial of the 13th instant: in virtue of which I have thought proper, by my decree of this day, to accede to his request relative to the grant of twenty-two thousand acres of land, with a title in absolute property, in the hammocks known by the name of Cuscowillo and Chacala, situated on the west of the part of the river St. John's where there was a store of the house of Panton, Leslie & Company, and about 45 miles distant from it; all of which appears more at large from the said memorial and decree which exist in the archives of the present notary: Wherefore, and in attention to the said recommendable services, agreeaby to the sovereign will, and what the laws enjoin for the rewarding, with distinction to those who may be entitled, attending to the quality of the services and that of the persons who may perform them, I have granted, as in the name of his Majesty and of his royal justice, which I administer, I do grant, unto the aforesaid Don Jorge Clarke the said twenty-two thousand acres of land in the place pointed out, without injury to a third person, for himself, his heirs and successors, in absolute property, and despatch to him, as by these presents I do, the corresponding title by which I separate the royal domain from the right and dominion it had to said land; and I cede and transfer it to the aforesaid Don Jorge Clarke, his heirs and successors, that, in consequence, they may possess it as their own, use and enjoy it, without any encumbrance whatsoever, with all its entrances, outlets, uses, customs, rights, and services, which it has had, and of custom and by law belong and may appertain to it; and, at their will, sell, cede, transfer, and alienate it as may best suit them. To all which I give the sanction of my authority, as I can and of right ought to do, in virtue of the sovereign will.

Given under my hand, and countersigned by the undersigned notary of government and the royal domain, in this city of St. Augustine, Florida, December 17, 1817.

JOSÉ COPPINGER.

By command of his excellency:
	JUAN DE ENTRALGO, *Notary of Government and the Royal Domain.*

I certify the foregoing to be a true and correct translation of a document in the Spanish language on file in the office of the public archives.

F. J. FATIO, *S. B. L. C.*

[Translation.]

B.

CONVEYANCE.

Be it known that I, Don George Clarke, an inhabitant of this province, residing in the town of Fernandina, but at present in this city, covenant that I really sell unto Don Juan de Entralgo, notary of government and the royal domain, in it twenty thousand acres of land, which I hold as my property, in the territory of Alachua, and a place named Chacala hammock, on the west side of the river St. John's, where there was a store of the house of Panton, Leslie & Company, and distant from it about 45 miles: the first line, east, measures 625 chains; the second line, north, measures 320 chains; the third line, west, measures 625 chains; and the fourth line, south, measures 320 chains; which twenty thousand acres of land belong to the twenty-two thousand granted me by this government, as a reward for services, December 17, 1817, and for which the corresponding title of property was made me on the same day, having proceeded to the survey by the private surveyor, Don Andrew Burgevin, who made the necessary plat August 2, 1819, which is added to the original proceeding of said concession, and is in the archives of the said notary; and I sell the said twenty thousand acres of land in the place and under the dimensions marked out, and with all their entrances, outlets, uses, customs, rights, and services, which it has, or of right belong to it, free of all encumbrance, (as appears from the book of mortgages which is in charge of the said notary,) at the price of $20,000, which the purchaser has paid to my entire satisfaction, which I acknowledge as delivered to my will. I renounce proof, laws of delivery, exception to money not counted, fraud, and every other thing in the case, for which I deliver a formal receipt; in virtue of which I separate myself from the right of property, possession, use, seigniory, and other rights, real and personal, which belong or appertain to the twenty thousand acres of land above mentioned, as I cede, renounce, and transfer it to the purchaser, and whoever shall represent his right, that he may possess, sell, and alienate it at his will, in virtue of this deed which I grant in his favor as a mark of real delivery, by which it is seen that he has acquired possession of it without occasion for other proof, from which I release him as I remain released from the eviction and guarantee of this sale to which I do not bind myself. And I, the said Don Juan de Entralgo, being present, do accept in my favor this deed, and by it receive as purchased the said twenty thousand acres of land at the price and agreement at which they have been sold to me, and I acknowledge them as delivered to my will. I renounce proof, laws of delivery, those of a thing not seen or received, fraud, and everything else in the case, for which I deliver a formal receipt in form. In testimony of which, this is dated in the city of St. Augustine, Florida, February 7, 1820.

GEORGE J. F. CLARKE.
JUAN DE ENTRALGO.

I, Don José Coppinger, colonel of the royal armies, political and military governor of this city and province, certify that I know the parties, who also have delivered and signed it in my presence, and that of the assistant witnesses, whom I have chosen for the purpose, Don Tomas de Aguilar and Don Antonio Alvarez, for want of another notary in all the province. There being witnesses to this deed Don Domingo Reyes, Don Pedro Miranda, and Don Fernando Arredondo, jr., inhabitants present.

JOSÉ COPPINGER.

Tomas de Aguilar.
Antonio Alvarez.

This is conformable to the original which exists in the archives of the said notary of government, to which I refer; and at the request of the party, sign this present copy, with the assistant witnesses, on two leaves of common paper, the stamped not being in use. St. Augustine, Florida, February 7, 1820.

JOSÉ COPPINGER.

Tomas de Aguilar.
Antonio Alvarez.

I certify the foregoing to be a true and correct translation from a document in the Spanish language on file in the office of the public archives of St. Augustine.

F. J. FATIO, S. B. L. C.

[Translation.]

SURVEY.

Don Andres Burgevin, an inhabitant of this city, and surveyor, appointed by Don George Clarke and authorized by the government, under date of April 20, 1819, for the survey of his land: I certify that I have measured and laid off for the said Don George Clarke twenty thousand acres of land in the territory of Alachua, and a place named Chachala, on the west of the river St. John's, and distant from it about forty-five miles, in part of a greater quantity which were granted him by a title of property December 17, 1817, and appears in its circumstances, conformable to the following plat and its original delivered into the archives of the notary of this government. In proof of which I give these presents, which I sign at St. Augustine, Florida, August 2, 1819.

ANDRES BURGEVIN.

[Here follows the plat.]

I certify the foregoing to be a true and correct translation from a document in the Spanish language on file in the office of the public archives of St. Augustine.

F. J. FATIO, S. B. L. C.

DECREE.

Juan B. Entralgo vs. The United States. For twenty thousand acres of land.

The board having ascertained the above to be a valid Spanish title made to G. J. F. Clarke previous to January 24, 1818, and this claim for twenty thousand acres thereof being regularly conveyed to claimant, it is therefore recommended to Congress for confirmation. June 29, 1824.

No. 8.—See REPORT No. 3.

Francis J. Avice vs. The United States. For six thousand acres of land.

MEMORIAL.

To the honorable the commissioners appointed to ascertain claims and titles to lands in East Florida :

The memorial of Francis J. Avice respectfully showeth: That your memorialist claims title to a tract of land consisting of six thousand acres, situated on the river St. John's, bounded north by lands granted to Juan Huertas, and south by land of John Moore, east by vacant lands, and west by the river St. John's, which were granted to John Huertas by the Spanish government August 26, 1814, in virtue of the royal order of October 29, 1790, and for which lands the said Huertas received a title from Governor Coppinger, by virtue of authority in the said Coppinger for that purpose reposed by the Spanish government, December 24, 1817; which title and a plat of the survey of said tract of land are herewith filed, and marked C and D. And your memorialist further showeth that he became the proprietor of said tract of land by virtue of a bill of sale from the said John Huertas to your memorialist, dated September 12, 1821, which is also herewith exhibited, and marked L; your memorialist further showeth that he is actually legally seized and possessed of said land; that he is a citizen of the United States and resident of the city of St. Augustine. All of which is respectfully submitted, &c.

FRANCIS J. AVICE.

[Translation.]

Title of property in favor of Don Juan Huertas of fifteen thousand acres of land.

Don José Coppinger, colonel of the royal armies, civil and military governor *pro tem.*, and chief of the royal finance of this city and province, by his Majesty:

Whereas, by royal order communicated to this government October 29, 1790, by the captain general of the Island of Cuba and the two Floridas, among other things, it was provided that to strangers who, of their own free will, shall present themselves to swear allegiance to our sovereign, lands shall be laid out for them free of expense, in proportion to the number of laborers each family may have; that Don Juan Huertas having presented himself, he solicited of this government the concession of fifteen thousand acres of land as a compensation for his well-known services, and for the purpose of establishing a cowpen and the raising of black cattle, which was granted him August 26, 1814, in consideration of the truth of his petition, according to the following boundaries: five thousand acres at a place called Tocoy, five miles above Picolata, bounded on the north by the lands of Don Manuel Solana, on the southwest by vacant lands, and on the west by the river St. John's; and the remaining ten thousand acres on the banks of the river, about twelve miles above a place called the Ferry, below John B. Rayant, bounded on the south by *the —— of John Mure;* and from thence east to the head of Deep creek, taking in the east and west banks of said creek, and bounded on the north by the southwest line of Tocoy, and on the west by the river St. John's, as results from a certificate given by the secretary of this said government, with the said date of August 26, 1814, which is found attached to the proceedings instituted by the above-mentioned Don Juan Huertas, praying that the corresponding title of the said lands be given him: Therefore, and in consideration that the above-mentioned Don Juan Huertas has fully proved his having established said cowpen, and that he employs himself with the object of said concession, as is seen by the said proceedings filed in the archives of the present notary, and according to my decree of the 22d of the present month, I have granted, and by these presents do grant, in the name of his Majesty, to the said Don Juan Huertas, his heirs and successors, the said fifteen thousand acres of land in absolute property; and I hereby, and by these presents, deliver him the corresponding title by which I separate it from the royal domain, from the right and dominion it held in said land; and I cede and transfer it to the aforesaid Don Juan Huertas, his heirs and successors, that, in consequence thereof, they may possess it as their own, make use of and enjoy it, free from any claim whatever, with all its entrances, outlets, uses, customs, rights, appurtenances, and all and in general which hath, doth, or may belong or pertain thereto; and, it being their wish, they may sell, cede, transfer, barter, and alienate it at their will and pleasure. To all which I interpose my authority, as far as possible, and according to law, in virtue of the sovereign will.

Given under my hand, and countersigned by the undersigned notary of government and royal finance, in the city of St. Augustine, Florida, December 24, 1817.

JOSÉ COPPINGER.

By order of his excellency:
JUAN DE ENTRALGO, &c., &c.

Conformable to the original on file in the archives under my charge, to which I refer; and at the request of the party, do seal and sign the present copy in St. Augustine, September 18, 1821.

JUAN DE ENTRALGO. [L.S.]

Don Andres Burgevin, of this city, and private surveyor: I certify that I have measured and laid off for Don Juan Huertas a tract of land containing six thousand acres, being part of one of ten thousand acres, situated at Buena Vista, which I measured by order of this government for the said Don Juan Huertas; and, being conformable in all its parts to the following plat, I sign in St. Augustine, Florida May 30, 1820.

ANDRES BURGEVIN.

A copy.

A. BURGEVIN.

[Here follows the plat.]

I certify the foregoing to be a correct translation from two documents in the Spanish language.

F. J. FATIO, *S. B. L. C.*

[Translation.]

Know ye that I, Don Juan Huertas, resident of this city, do really sell to Don Francisco Julian Avice 6,000 acres of land, situated between the old fort of Buena Vista and a place where the military post is stationed or properly known by the name of Moore; which 6,000 acres of land are part of 15,000 conceded to me by this government, giving me for the same a title of absolute property December 24, 1817, which are known and distinguished under the following dimensions and boundaries: bounded on the north by the lands of Don Pedro Cocifaco, near the old fort of Buena Vista; on the east by vacant lands; on the south by those of Moore; and on the west by the river St. John's; and I sell him the boundaries and dimensions already explained in the place pointed out, with all its entrances, outlets, uses, customs, rights, and appurtenances, which it has, or may belong to it, free from any claim whatever, in the sum of $3,075, which the purchaser has paid me in cash. In virtue of all which I separate myself from the right of property and possession I had to said land, which I cede, renounce, and transfer in favor of the purchaser, and in whomsoever may represent his right, that he may, as his own, dispose of it at his will, binding myself to the *eviction* and goodness of this sale in favor of the purchaser with my present and future property, with power to the tribunals that they may compel me to the compliance thereof. And I, the said Don Francisco J. Avice, being present, do accept in my favor this deed, and by it received as purchased the said 6,000 acres of land in the price and manner they are sold me. Both parties signing these presents in the presence of the witnesses, who also signed, in St. Augustine, September 12, 1821.

JUAN HUERTAS.
F. J. AVICE.

Witnesses: FRANCO. J. FATIO.
          CHARLES VIGNOLES.

I certify the foregoing to be a true and correct translation from a document in the Spanish language.

F. J. FATIO, *S. B. L. C.*

DECREE.

The board having ascertained the above to be a valid Spanish grant made previous to January 24, 1818, do therefore recommend it to Congress for confirmation. April 14, 1824.

No. 9.—See Report No. 3.

Joseph M. Arredondo vs. The United States. For twenty thousand acres of land.

MEMORIAL.

To the honorable the commissioners appointed to ascertain claims and titles to lands in East Florida:

The petition of Joseph M. Arredondo respectfully showeth: That your memorialist claims title to a tract of land consisting of twenty thousand acres, situated at a place called the Big Hammock, about twenty miles from the river Suwanee; which title your memorialist derives from a royal title made to him by Governor Coppinger, in virtue of the royal order of March 29, 1815; a certified copy of the said title is herewith filed, and is dated March 20, 1817. And your memorialist further showeth that he is legally in possession of said lands, and was so before the cession in 1821; that he is a Spanish subject, native of East Florida, and at present a resident of the Island of Cuba.

JOSÉ. M. ARREDONDO.

[Translation.]

Title of property in favor of Don José de la Maza Arredondo for twenty thousand acres of land.

Don José Coppinger, lieutenant colonel of the royal armies, political and military governor *pro tem.*, and chief of the royal domain of the city of St. Augustine, Florida, and its province:

Whereas, by royal order of March 29, 1815, his Majesty has been pleased to approve the favors and rewards proposed by my predecessor, Brigadier General Don Sebastian Kindelan, for the officers and soldiers, both of the regulars and of the militia, of this province, who contributed to the defence thereof during the rebellion, one of the said favors being the concession of vacant lands; and whereas Don José de la Maza Arredondo, captain of the local militia of the Spanish company in the town of Fernandina, has made known to me the distinguished and extraordinary services rendered by him, in a personal and pecuniary manner, in the defence of this said province during the insurrection therein, with economy to the royal revenue as a faithful subject, as is fully stated in his memorial, dated the 18th of the present month, according to which, by my decree of this day, I have thought proper to accede to his prayer relative to the granting of him twenty thousand acres of land, with a title of absolute property, in the lands known by the name of Alachua, about eighty miles distant from this city, at a place called Big Hammock, about twenty miles from the river Suwanee, and sixty miles west of St. John's river, not preventing, as soon as there is an opportunity, and the tranquillity of the province is entirely re-established, that a survey of the lands be made, that the limits and boundaries may be made known by the corresponding plat, as will be fully seen by the said proceedings filed in the office of archives of the present notary: Wherefore, and in consideration of said commendable services, agreeably to the will of the sovereign, and what is set forth in the laws to recompense with distinction those who may be worthy, according to the nature of said services, and the individuals who have rendered them, I have thought proper to grant, and by these presents do grant, in the name of his Majesty and his royal justice, which I administer, to the said Don José de la Maza Arredondo the said twenty thousand acres of land in the place pointed out, without injury to a third person, for himself, his heirs, and successors, in absolute property; and in granting, as I do by these presents, the corresponding title by which I separate the royal domain from the right and domain it had to said land; and I cede and transfer the same to the above-mentioned Don José de la Maza Arredondo, his heirs and successors, that they may, in consequence thereof, possess the same as their own, make use of and enjoy it, free from any encumbrance whatever, with all its entrances, outlets, uses, customs, rights, and services, which it has had, has, and of custom and by law belong or may appertain thereto; and, being their will, they may sell, cede, transfer, and alienate it as may best suit them. To all which I give the sanction of my authority, as I can, and of right ought to do, in virtue of the sovereign will.

Given under my hand, and countersigned by the undersigned notary of government and royal domain, in this said city of St. Augustine, Florida, March 20, 1817.

JOSÉ COPPINGER.

By order of his excellency:
JUAN DE ENTRALGO, *Notary of Government and the Royal Domain.*

I certify the foregoing to be a true and correct translation from a document in the Spanish language filed in the office of the public archives.

F. J. FATIO, *S. B. L. C.*

DECREE.

Joseph M. Arredondo vs. The United States. For twenty thousand acres of land.

The board having ascertained the above to be a valid Spanish title made previous to January 24, 1818, do therefore recommend it to Congress for confirmation. April 16, 1824.

No. 10.—See Report No. 3.

Charles W. Bulow's executors vs. The United States. For four thousand acres of land in two tracts.

MEMORIAL.

To the honorable the commissioners appointed to ascertain claims and titles to lands in East Florida:

The memorial of John Geddes, Duke Goodman, and William Lance, executors of the last will and testament of Charles W. Bulow, deceased, on behalf of the heirs of the said Bulow, respectfully showeth:

That the heirs of said Bulow claim title to four thousand acres of land comprised in two separate tracts, as follows: the first tract is situated between the rivers Tomoca and Matanzas, in the place called Graham's swamp, containing three thousand four hundred and eighty-six acres, bounded on the west by the public road from Mosquito to St. Augustine, on the north and northeast by a marsh and the Haul-over creek, and on the south by the lands of Mr. Ormond. The second tract contains five hundred and fourteen acres, is situated on the west side of the river Halifax, bounded on the south by John Russell's land, on the north by Farquhar Bethune's land, and on all other sides by vacant lands; which two tracts above mentioned, making four thousand acres, were granted to John Russell by the Spanish government under Governor Estrada, July 28, 1812, in exchange for a vessel called the schooner Barbarita, which will fully appear by a reference to a volume of original documents on the subject, stitched together, and remaining in the office of public archives kept by W. Reynolds, esq., in this city, to which are annexed the order of survey, certificates of survey, and plats. And your memorialists further show that, immediately on receiving said grant, the said John Russell took possession of the said land, but a few years afterward died, and the title to the same was confirmed by the Spanish government to his heirs, as appears by the above documents; that the said Charles W. Bulow purchased from the heirs of Russell, for a valuable consideration, August 1, 1821, the two tracts of land aforesaid, the deed of conveyance for which is recorded in the public office of records in the city of St. Augustine, kept by Mr. Tingle; that, in virtue of said purchase, the said Charles W. Bulow immediately took possession of the said tracts of land, and planted and improved a part of one of the tracts, and erected buildings; that your memorialists still keep a great number of slaves on the said land employed in the cultivation of the *cane;* that the said Charles W. Bulow died in the city of St. Augustine a few months ago, a citizen of the United States. All of which is respectfully submitted by

JOHN RODMAN, Attorney for Claimants.

St. Augustine, *November* 29, 1823.

Charles W. Bulow's executors vs. The United States. For six hundred and seventy-five acres of land.

MEMORIAL.

To the honorable the commissioners appointed to ascertain claims and titles to lands in East Florida:

The memorial of John Geddes, Duke Goodman, and William Lance, executors of the last will and testament of Charles W. Bulow, deceased, on behalf of the heirs of said Bulow, claim title to six hundred and seventy-five acres of land, situated on the west side of the Halifax river, bounded on the north by lands of John Russell, on the south by lands of Fulano Dean, on the east by lands of John Russell, and on the west by vacant land; which said tract of six hundred and seventy-five acres are granted to the said John Russell by the Spanish government under Governor Estrada, July 12, 1828, on what is called *headrights,* in virtue of the royal order of October 29, 1790; the original grant for which, with the survey and plat, is annexed to and forms a part of a volume of original documents relating to two tracts, comprising four thousand acres of land, which were granted to John Russell at the same time, in exchange for a vessel called the Barbarita; which said volume of original documents are stitched together, and remaining in the office of public archives kept by W. Reynolds, esq., in this city. And your memorialists further show that, immediately on receiving said grant, the said John Russell took possession of the said land, but a few years afterwards died, and the title to the same was confirmed by the Spanish government to his heirs, as appears by the above-mentioned document; that the said Charles W. Bulow purchased from the heirs of Russell, for a valuable consideration, August 1, 1821, the said tract of six hundred and seventy-five acres, together with the two tracts making four thousand acres aforesaid, the deed of conveyance for which is recorded in the public office of records in the city of St. Augustine kept by Mr. Tingle; that in virtue of the said purchase the said Charles W. Bulow immediately took possession of the said tracts of land, and planted and improved a part of one of the tracts of land, and erected buildings; that your memorialists still keep a great number of slaves on the said land employed in the cultivation of the cane; that the said Charles W. Bulow died in the city of St. Augustine a few months ago, a citizen of the United States. All of which is respectfully submitted by

JOHN RODMAN, Attorney for Claimants.

St. Augustine, *November* 29, 1823.

[Translation.]

PETITION.

To his excellency the governor:

I, Mr. John Russell, a new settler in this province, do appear before your excellency, and, with due respect say that when I took the oath of fidelity and allegiance to his Catholic Majesty his excellency Don Juan José de Estrada, governor *pro tempore* of this province, insinuated to me that the government was in want of a vessel, the size of which should be calculated to go in and out over the bar of this harbor; and that as the funds of the royal treasury were exhausted, and such vessel could not be paid for in specie, they would be glad to buy it and pay for it with a grant of land proportioned to its value. In consequence of that insinuation, I ordered the building of the schooner in which I have just arrived to this port with my family and some of my slaves, called the Perseverance, of fifty-eight tons burden, drawing only six feet when loaded. The capacity of the vessel is equal to three hundred flour barrels and more; her timbers and materials are of the best quality, which can be ascertained by a survey of experienced men; on account of all which, besides being a fast sailing vessel, she is well calculated for this port, and I offer the same to the government, contenting myself to receive in payment for it the title of absolute domain and property to four thousand acres of land situated in some part of this province, as I may fix my choice; also, the absolute title of such lands which I have petitioned for, and which I am entitled to in virtue of my headrights, according to the number of persons composing my family and that of my slaves. Therefore, I beg your excellency to consider my preceding proposal as being actually made, and to accept it should your excellency deem it just and reasonable. St. Augustine of Florida, July 3, 1812.

JOHN RUSSELL.

DECREE.

Let the governor *pro tem.*, my predecessor, Don Juan José de Estrada, give such information as may be in his power.

KINDELAN.

INFORMATION.

When I admitted as a vassal of his Catholic Majesty our lord Don Ferdinand VII, the petitioner, which took place in the preceding year as it appears by the oath he took, which is registered in the office of the secretary of the government, he represented to me that in Providence, of which place he was an inhabitant, he had left on the stocks a schooner in which he intended to bring to this place his family and property, and he believed that vessel was very well calculated for the service of this port, and he would offer it for sale to the administrator of the royal domain in case it would suit. Having received this information, and knowing the general scarcity of specie in the royal treasury, I gave him to understand, through the organ of Mr. John Forbes, that if he thought proper to make a gracious present of the same to the King, in that case, as soon as he would take possession of the lands which he was to have as a new settler, the royal title to them would be immediately granted to him, which otherwise he was not entitled to until after having cultivated them for ten years without intermission. The said Forbes insinuated to me that the proposal had not been disagreeable to the petitioner, who answered that when, in due time, the vessel with other circumstances relating to it would be examined, he would then enter into a treaty about it. This is what took place with respect to that business, and this is all the information I have to give your excellency, in conformity to the superior decree which precedes. St. Augustine, July 8, 1812.

JUAN JOSÉ DE ESTRADA.

DECREE.

St. Augustine, *Florida, July* 8, 1812.

Let the officers of the royal domain give their information.

KINDELAN.

St. Augustine, *Florida, July* 9, 1812.

The officers of the royal domain observe a notable difference between the exposition of Don Juan José de Estrada—having offered to Mr. John Russell the title of property to the lands which would be awarded to him in proportion to the number of persons comprising his family, provided he would convey to the royal domain the property of the schooner said to be building, from which title it would follow that he would immediately acquire the faculty of disposing of said lands as he would think fit, which otherwise he could not do, as the royal title to them would not be granted until after having cultivated them for ten years together and proving the same to the satisfaction of the government, and the exposition of Russell, saying that four thousand acres more were offered to him, with the faculty of locating them where he chose; but for all that, considering that Russell has every appearance of being a settler of good faith; that to all such lands are granted gratuitously; that a great number of acres are still left unceded, and of course without utility to anybody; considering, also, the situation in which we find ourselves, and the want of such a vessel as the proposed schooner is said to be for the service of this port; our opinion is that, after somewhat reducing the number of acres, or in case of a refusal on the part of Russell to accede to put a reduction, his proposal ought to be accepted in its full extent, with the reserve, however, of what his Majesty may determine, after taking cognizance of the subjects, and with the reserve of what may follow from the survey and her appraisement, made by proper judges, of the said vessel.

MANUEL LOPEZ.

DECREE.

Let this be communicated to the interested party, who, in his answer, will make known where he wishes to locate the lands he petitions for.

KINDELAN.

PETITION.

To his excellency the governor :

I, Mr. John Russell, a new settler of this province, with due respect appear before your excellency, and, being informed of the decrees and informations which have taken place relative to my annexed petition, say that, as I am not sufficiently acquainted with lands in this province, it is not in my power to designate precisely the site of the four thousand acres alluded to in my first petition, but I do promise, without hesitation, to take them out of the vacant lands situated between the head of the river Matanzas and the river Tomoca, in which territory the surveyor whom the governor may appoint will survey them in such place or places which I may select, and in which are also located the lands which, as a new settler, I solicited, which may be seen in my petition recorded in the secretary's office; as to the notable difference which the officers of the royal domain observe between my exposition and the information given by Don Juan José de Estrada, it would not have appeared to them so notable if they had read my first petition with more attention. In no part of it do I say that four thousand acres of land were offered to me, as said officers have it; my proposal is clear, plain, and just. Besides, as the value of my schooner is greater than that of the lands I solicit in payment of it, for this reason, as I do not accede to the reserve mentioned by the treasury department, of submitting ultimately to the decision of a superior authority, I expect to receive the lands at the moment I deliver up my vessel in the manner expressed in my petition, and the business will be then concluded. I therefore pray that your excellency will be pleased to determine what you may think proper on the subject.

JOHN RUSSELL.

St. Augustine, *Florida, July* 10, 1812.

DECREE.

St. Augustine, *Florida, July* 10, 1812.

Let the above proceedings be carried back to the treasury department, in order that the officers of the same may make their remarks.

KINDELAN.

INFORMATION.

St. Augustine, *Florida, July* 11, 1812.

Any one, without much meditation being required on his part, will perceive that Russell wishes to have the title of property to two tracts of land—one in payment for his schooner, and the other on his quality of a new settler, according to the number of his family; and that Don Juan José de Estrada spoke only of granting immediately the title of property to the tract which the petitioner had obtained for his headrights as a compensation for the schooner; but the treasury department waives all this, although at the same time the officers of the same are surprised at the expressions in which it is attempted to make void their first information; and they are now of opinion that the vessel may be surveyed and appraised by the King's master ship-carpenter and caulker, he being the only judge of such matters in this place, and by the captain of the schooner St. Augustine, Don Miguel Acosta, as soon as he arrives, and who it is expected will arrive in a very short time. However, your excellency will determine for the best.

MANUEL LOPEZ.

DECREE.

St. Augustine, *July* 11, 1812.

Be it as it seems proper to the officers of the royal treasury, who will appoint on their part a person to superintend the proposed operations.

KINDELAN.

SURVEY.

In conformity to the preceding decree, we went on board of the vessel which is the subject of this transaction. We examined it minutely, also everything respecting the masts and rigging thereof, and, after a consultation as to its value, we believe, according to our knowledge and conscience, that it is worth two thousand six hundred dollars, this being the sum resulting from the inventory which was taken. The whole proceeding took place in the presence of Don Tadeo de Arribas, commissioned by the treasurer to superintend the survey and the appraisement. In proof of which, we sign the document in St. Augustine, Florida, July 13, 1812.

RAFAEL DEAZ, *for Don Miguel Acosta, who cannot sign.*
FERNANDO DE LA MAZA ARREDONDO.

Under my inspection:
TADEO DE ARRIBAS.

DECREE.

St. Augustine, *July* 15, 1812.

Let these proceedings be returned to the treasury department for such purposes as may be convenient. Annex to them the appraisement which has been made in detail of the vessel and its appurtenances, the hull, the sails, &c., as without such document it is impossible to judge of the appraisement.

KINDELAN.

INFORMATION.

St. Augustine, *Florida, July* 15, 1812.

According to the report of good judges, the vessel is found with every necessary requisite, is in good state for service, and well calculated to go in and out over the bar of this harbor, which is very bad. The schooner which is at this time in the service of the governor was formerly the launch of the pilot of the bar, and for a long time was employed in piloting vessels in and out; it was afterwards rigged as a schooner, is now very old, and is not worth the expense of putting to it a new set of sails, which is much wanted; and would have been sold in the Havana last year if a vessel could have been procured fit for the same service. From these circumstances, from the difficulty of meeting another opportunity as good as this, and from the scarcity of specie in the royal treasury, it appears that we are justified and authorized to take advantage of this opportunity, without waiting for the decision of his Majesty, who, it is believed, will approve it as soon as he is well informed of the whole. But your excellency will determine what you may deem most proper. The officers of the department of the royal treasury abstain from speaking about lands, as the royal orders which regulate these matters have never been communicated to them, as they are not acquainted with the locality of those which Russell petitions for, as they do not know whether the same are or are not claimed by some other persons, as they are ignorant of their value, although this cannot be great, where there is still so much land unoccupied and distributing gratis.

MANUEL LOPEZ.

APPRAISEMENT.

St. Augustine, *July* 15, 1812.

In conformity to the decree of his excellency the governor of this place, dated this day, relative to the transactions with John Russell, a new settler of this province, the following appraisement has been formed by the master ship-carpenter, Don Rafael Deaz, and Don Miguel Acosta, captain of the King's schooner the St. Augustine, under the inspection of Don Tadeo de Arribas, commissioned by the treasurer, Don Manuel Lopez, comptroller of the royal treasury, of the schooner called Perseverance, commanded by Don Thomas Forrest, owned by the children of the said Russell, to wit: for the hull of the schooner, which measures from head to stern 54 feet 2½ inches, 16 feet and ½ inch beam; her hold 5 feet 10 inches deep, and 58½ tons burden, with her two masts, yards, bowsprit, topmast, &c., $1,938.

[Here follows the appraisement of the apparel and furniture of the schooner, which, with $1,938, the sum which the vessel, masts, yards, &c., is valued at, makes the amount of the appraisement at $2,600.]

RAFAEL DEAZ, *for Don Miguel Acosta, who cannot write.*
SQUIRE ARREDONDO.

Under my inspection:
TADEO DE ARRIBAS.

DECREE.

St. Augustine, *July* 17, 1812.

I approve the opinion of the officers of the treasury department; and, in conformity thereto, let the bargain relative to the said schooner be concluded with every requisite formality, and let the title of property be given to John Russell to four thousand acres in that part of the country he indicates in his last petition.

KINDELAN.

PETITION.

To his excellency the governor:

I, John Russell, a new settler of this province, with due respect, appear before your excellency and say that, knowing the purport of your excellency's decree which follows the proceedings concerning my said schooner Perseverance, to which I gave my assent, and expect at the same time to receive the titles of property to the land which have been granted to me as a new settler, of which I make mention in my first petition; in consequence of which I beg your excellency to order that the title of property to the four thousand acres which I am to receive as a consideration for my schooner, and the title of property to the lands granted to me as a new settler, be given to me at the same time.

JOHN RUSSELL.

St. Augustine, *July* 17, 1812.

DECREE.

Let the treasury department inform on the subject.

KINDELAN.

INFORMATION.

St. Augustine, *Florida, July* 17, 1812.

In the first petition which Russell presented on the 8th instant he offered his schooner on the condition that he would receive for it the title of 4,000 acres, and also the title of property to the lands which, as a new settler, he had petitioned for, proportioned to the number of his family; and the decree of your excellency of yesterday refers only to the 4,000 acres, the price of said schooner. The officers of the treasury are ignorant of the import of John Russell's petition, as they have already said, and say again, that they are as yet unacquainted with the royal orders by which such matters are regulated; but it appears to them that if the title of property be given to the petitioner to 4,000 acres in consideration of his schooner, the same may be given, also, for his other lands as a new settler, particularly as we understand that, without that condition, the proportion to the number of his family and the slaves he has imported. Your excellency will, nevertheless, determine what you will deem best.

MANUEL LOPEZ.

DECREE.

St. Augustine, *July* 20, 1812.

Let the above be communicated to the interested party.

KINDELAN.

PETITION.

To his excellency the governor:

I, John Russell, a new settler in this province, with due respect, appear before your excellency, and having received notification of the information of the treasury department, and of the decree of your excellency annexed to it, say that, as all the timbers of my schooner are mahogany, it is worth at least $5,000, although the surveyors appointed to survey and appraise her have limited its value to two thousand six hundred dollars. This difference is owing to their not having considered the intrinsic value of mahogany, and that of pine and other inferior timber, which do not cost half the labor which the mahogany does. Therefore, the genuine value of said schooner ought to be considered equivalent to $5,000, and I would not take less for her if I was to be paid in cash. At the same time I have to observe to your excellency that, during the war between Great Britain and the United States, it will be impossible for me to import in this province the rest of my slaves, and, considering the difficulty of exporting negroes from Bahama islands, I shall want at least twelve months from the time the said war is concluded to take away my slaves; and, as I wish to invest the greater part of my property in negroes, I have to beg your excellency to delay giving me the title to the lands which I petitioned for on the 22d of June last year, until the conclusion of the term mentioned; and as soon as this is granted to me, together with the title of property to the 4,000 acres of land already decreed by your excellency on the 16th instant, and that in case said lands could not be found in the place mentioned, when the surveyor shall have to survey them, they may be located in the part known under the name of Twelve-mile swamp. I am ready to deliver faithfully my vessel to the government; therefore beg your excellency to accede to this my petition, and order a certificate of the document, which will be drawn to that effect, be given to me to serve me as a guarantee.

JOHN RUSSELL.

St. Augustine, *Florida, July* 22, 1812.

DECREE.

St. Augustine, *July* 22, 1812.

Let this be communicated to the comptroller of the treasury, together with the document showing the oath of fidelity and allegiance which John Russell took before my predecessor, with everything relating to business.

KINDELAN.

Sт. Augustine, *Florida, July* 25, 1812.

Mr. John Russell declared on June 10, 1811, that he had in Providence a schooner, 62 tons burden, worth $6,000, with all her apparel, and one hundred negroes, and that he wished to import the whole to this province; that, in the same place, he had landed property to the amount of $15,000, nineteen horses, four hundred sheep, and sixty head of cattle. He has now brought property to the amount of $7,004 87 in effects, household furniture, sheep and horses, including his schooner, valued, as he says, at $5,000. He has also brought his wife and children, and eighteen slaves. What he petitions for now appears to be reasonable, and the officers of the treasury department, and that the title of the property may be given to him now according to the number of his family he presents, together with the title to four thousand acres already granted him for his schooner, and keep in reserve for him for the space of ten or twelve months after the conclusion of the war between Great Britain and the United States, the land contiguous to the first grant, in order to enlarge it in proportion to the number of hands he will import, and not grant the said lands reserved for John Russell to anybody else, although petitioned for, until the expiration of the stipulated period, and then only the government will be at liberty to grant the said reserved lands to anybody they please, in case John Russell should not have completed the importation of what he has mentioned in his declaration. If your excellency agree that, in conformity to this opinion, the said titles of property may be granted to the petitioner, you will be pleased also to order the delivery of the said schooner to Captain Miguel Acosta, with all the articles mentioned in the inventory, and whatever may belong to the said vessel, and might not have been included in said inventory, and would be necessary for the navigation of the same; and also the delivery of a certified copy of all these proceedings to the petitioner according to his wish.

MANUEL LOPEZ.

I, Don Tomas de Aguilar, secretary *pro tem.* of this government, certify that, in the book No. 10, in which are registered the oaths of fidelity which the non-settler takes, the oath taken by John Russell is registered in the second folio, the tenor of which is as follows: " In the city of St. Augustine, Florida, on June 10, 1811, before his excellency the governor *pro tem.* of this place and province, the lieutenant colonel of the army, Don Juan José de Estrada, appeared Mr. John Russell, born in South Carolina at the time it was a possession of the British crown, married and having five children, three of whom between sixteen and twenty-five years old, and the other two above eight years old, ship-carpenter by trade, but now dedicates himself to agriculture and of the Protestant persuasion; under which, and with every form required by law, took the oath of allegiance in the presence of the secretary, deceased, and promised to keep fidelity and remain a faithful vassal to our sovereign the Lord Don Ferdinand the Seventh, and to be faithful to the authorities constituted in his name, to bear arms in defence of the province against any enemy that would intend to invade it, and submit entirely to the laws of the kingdom. After having taken said oath, he took another relating to his property, and said that, in the harbor of Providence, he has a schooner of 60 tons which he values at $5,000, and a parcel of sails and rigging worth about $1,000; one hundred negroes in Nassau, eighty of whom are above sixteen years old, and the remaining from eight to sixteen years old; also, landed property to the value of $1,500 situated in said place of Nassau; nineteen horses, four hundred sheep, and sixty head of cattle; the whole of which or the value thereof, he intends to import to this province, and dedicate himself to the agriculture; and he signed the same with his excellency the governor, and the above-mentioned office, and which I affirm."

ESTRADA.
JOHN RUSSELL.
TOMAS DE AGUILAR.

Before me—

JOSÉ DE ZUBIZARETA, *Notary of Government.*

And in conformity of the preceding decree, I deliver the present copy in St. Augustine, July 28, 1812.

TOMAS DE AGUILAR.

To his excellency the governor:

Mr. John Russell, a new settler of this province, with due respect, appears before your excellency, and says that he has taken the oath of fidelity and allegiance to his Majesty, with the sincere intention to dedicate himself and the slaves he has, manifested in the solemn act of his oath, to the agriculture, and all the slaves whom he may acquire, with the proceeds of the land and other property which he has declared he owned on Bahama islands; and in order to realize the said project in its due time, he humbly begs your excellency to be pleased to grant to him 1,200 acres of uncleared lands, situated west of the river Halifax, bounded north by lands granted to Mr. Farquhar Bethune, and south by lands also granted to Mr. Patrick Dean; and three thousand acres, or the complement of what he is to have according to the number of his family and slaves, north of the mouth of the river Tomoca, or where it is limited by the said river Halifax, bounded south by lands granted to Mrs. Russell Ormond, widow of James Ormond, running north, and concluding both sides of the Smith's road, until the point which will terminate the lands petitioned for; and says he conforms himself to what his Majesty may please to determine, as to the quantity allotted, and the conditions of the grant. The whole of which is a favor which he expects to receive from the known justice of your excellency.

JOHN RUSSELL.

Sт. Augustine, *Florida, June* 19, 1811.

Reserving to act on the petition of John Russell at the time he shall have imported the property he has sworn to, let the officers of the secretary's office, where the said petition will be kept in reserve until said period, inform the petitioner of the method adopted, and the conditions prescribed by this government in grants of a similar nature; and to the whole of which due attention will be paid with respect to the grants now in question.

ESTRADA.
QUINTANO.

I, Tomas de Aguilar, secretary *pro tem.* of this government, do certify that the preceding copy is faithfully drawn from the original, which remains in the secretary's office under my charge; and in conformity to the decree of his excellency, I deliver the present in St. Augustine, Florida, July 18, 1812.

TOMAS DE AGUILAR.

DECREE.

St. Augustine, *July* 28, 1812.

In consequence of these proceedings, and of the information of the comptroller of the treasury relating to the acquisition of the schooner proposed by John Russell to the government in exchange for vacant lands, it is hereby declared that the said Russell is lawfully and absolutely proprietor of 675 acres of land, to be in the vacant lands west of the river Halifax, bounded north by lands granted to Mr. Farquhar Bethune, and south by others also granted to Mr. Patrick Dean, according to the said number of 675 acres to the family which Russell now presents, at the rate of 50 acres to himself, and the same number to his wife, both being head of family, and 25 acres for every one of his five children and 18 slaves, according to the customary rule observed in granting lands, and a reserve will be made; but no grant will be given of 2,050 acres, which will be the complement for the one hundred slaves which he said he would import, which reserved lands will be granted in proportion to the number of hands he will import; said reserve will have the full force for the space of ten months after the conclusion of the present war between Great Britain and the United States of America, and in the case John Russell, in the specified time, had not imported more hands, then the government will be at liberty to dispose of said lands as they please. It is also hereby declared that John Russell is equally absolute proprietor of the 4,000 acres of land mentioned in my decree of the 16th instant, situated between the Matanzas and Tomoca rivers; and in case that, at the time the surveyor will go and survey them, the said number of acres will not be found, let it be completed in that uncleared tract called *Twelve-miles* swamp; and after ascertaining the measurements and boundaries, which cannot be known now, the title of property will be granted to John Russell, and, in the interim, the certificates he solicits will be to him as an equivalent of the titles in form. And he will receive said certificate from the witness and assistant, Don Juan de Entralgo and Don Bernardo José Segui, as the only notary of the government and province is very sick. Let this determination be made known to John Russell, in order that, in virtue thereof, he deliver the schooner to the officers of the royal domain, and with her, all her appurtenances, of which the treasury department will receive due notice; let it be understood that said schooner will henceforward be called the Barbarita, and will be manned by a captain, a pilot, a boatswain, and five sailors; let a consultation take place to determine the precise salary of every one of them; and let this be communicated to the officers of the royal treasury that they may carry it into effect.

KINDELAN.

[Here this part of the record contains irrelevant matter.]

PETITION.

To his excellency the governor:

Mr. John Russell, a new settler of this province, respectfully represents to your excellency that, as he is entitled to 4,000 acres of land, situated between the rivers Matanzas and Tomoca, which the government thought fit to grant him in exchange for a schooner to him belonging; and also to 675 acres of land west of the river Halifax, corresponding with the number of persons composing his family, and which he manifested in his oath when he was admitted as a new settler, with the reserve that said grant would be increased after completing the introduction of his slaves; and as he wishes to have the two tracts surveyed, and as there is no surveyor general in this place to do it, he begs your excellency may be pleased to authorize to that effect Mr. William Lawrence, who is acquainted with that possession, and has performed the duties of it in the case of other persons. And the petitioner doubts not that he will receive this favor from the well-known justice of your excellency.

JOHN RUSSELL.

St. Augustine, *Florida, February* 29, 1813.

DECREE.

St. Augustine, *March* 1, 1813.

Let the comptroller's office inform on the subject.

KINDELAN.

INFORMATION.

St. Augustine, *March* 10, 1813.

In the decree of your excellency, dated July 28, 1812, it was ordered to give to John Russell a copy of the whole proceedings relating to the mentioned lands, in order that the said copy should serve him as an equivalent of the titles of property which would be given to him in due form as soon as the said lands could be surveyed, the measurement and boundaries being unknown at the said date. In the same decree it was ordered to keep in reserve, for the use of John Russell, until ten months after the conclusion of the present war between Great Britain and the United States of America, as much land as corresponded to the complement of 100 negroes, whom he declared he would import, after which period the government was to be at liberty to dispose of said lands in case that the petitioner should not then have brought a greater number of hands. Considering the above circumstance, and considering also that every time Russell would bring in more hands the survey should be repeated, it appears that, as the copy he has obtained is equivalent to the title itself, the want of which cannot be prejudicial to him, as in such a case the government should interfere in his behalf, it is proper to wait until the said epoch of ten months after the conclusion of the war between the mentioned powers, and then at once survey and assign the boundaries of such lands as the petitioner will be then entitled to; and let a copy of this and of the decree which will follow, be given to him, if he requires it, in order that he may at all times prove his desire to obtain the titles. But your excellency will determine, as you think proper, whether the survey ought to take place now or be delayed, so that the interested party be best satisfied, as the treasury department is deficient in the knowledge of these particulars.

MANUEL LOPEZ.

DECREE.

St. Augustine, *March* 10, 1813.

Let it be done in conformity to the opinion of the comptroller. Therefore let the copy called for by the officer be drawn by Don Juan Entralgo and Don José Bernardo Segui, who, after having accepted the commission, and sworn to the fulfilment of it, will serve as witnesses and assistants in lieu of the notary; and all this being done, let it be annexed to the former proceedings, and delivered to the interested party.

KINDELAN.

PETITION.

To his excellency the governor:

Don José Mariano Hernandez, a planter of this province, with due respect to your excellency, represents that, for reasons which may be important to him, it is necessary to him that the annexed document in the English language should be translated into the Spanish *idiom;* and to that effect he begs your excellency to be pleased to order the translation to be made by a capable person; after which, that the original be returned to him, and he will promptly defray the expenses attending it. This favor he expects from the justice of your excellency.

JOSEPH M. HERNANDEZ.

St. Augustine, *Florida, January* 31, 1820.

DECREE.

St. Augustine, *February* 1, 1820.

The presentation of the annexed document is acknowledged, and, as there is no public interpreter, let it be translated by Don Bernardo Segui, who is capable to do it; let his acceptation and oath be previously received before the present notary, and, after it is done, let the information of it be given.

COPPINGER.

Before me—

JUAN DE ENTRALGO, *Notary of Government.*

St. Augustine, on the same day, month and year, I notified the preceding decree to Don José Mariano Hernandez; to which I certify.

ENTRALGO.

NOTIFICATION AND OATH OF THE INTERPRETER.

On the same day I notified to Don Bernardo Segui the appointment of interpreter, given to him in the said decree, who, after having taken cognizance of it, said he accepted, and did accept it, promising under his oath, legally taken, to exercise well and faithfully the functions of this charge to the utmost of his understanding and knowledge, and signed the same; to which I certify.

BERNARDO SEGUI.

Before me—

JUAN DE ENTRALGO.

[Translation.]

POWER OF ATTORNEY.

Georgia, *Glynn County:*

Be it known that I, Mary Russell, of the State and county aforesaid, administratrix of John Russell, formerly an inhabitant of the province of East Florida, in virtue of various causes and considerations which move me thereunto, have appointed ordained, authorized, and elected, and by this do appoint, ordain, authorize, and elect, Mr. José M. Hernandez, of the province of East Florida, my true and legal attorney, in order that for me, and in my name, and for my personal use and benefit, he may ask, demand, present himself to collect and receive all such sums of money, debts, and other claims that might be due to the estate of my husband, deceased, and to make use, in my name, of all the means the law requires to obtain the recovery of the same, to attach if necessary, or to compromise and liquidate with the corresponding and sufficient discharge; and in order that he may proceed for me in all my affairs and legal acts with the necessary latitude, in the same manner as if I was personally present, appoint attorneys under him, and revoke them as he thinks fit, and give to the said, my attorney, the most ample faculties which in right belongs to him as such

In testimony thereof, I sign and seal the present power December 16, 1819, and in the forty-fourth year of the independence of the United States of America.

MARY RUSSELL. [L. S.]

Acknowledged, signed, and sealed in our presence.

George Marsh, *Justice of the Peace.*
T. Abrahams *Notary Public of Glynn county.*

The preceding translation is well and faithfully made, according to the best of my knowledge and understanding, and I refer to the original thereof; and, in conformity to the superior mandate, I drew and sign it in St. Augustine, Florida, February 3, 1820.

BERNARDO SEGUI.

DECREE.

St. Augustine, *February* 3, 1820.

I have seen the preceding translation, and let the same be communicated to the petitioner for his legal purposes.

COPPINGER.

Before me—

JUAN DE ENTRALGO.

NOTIFICATION.

St. Augustine, on the same day, month and year, I notified the present decree to Don José Mariano Hernandez; which I certify.

ENTRALGO.

PETITION.

St. Augustine, *February* 3, 1820.

Don José Mariano Hernandez, a planter of this province, respectfully represents to your excellency that the documents, and the translation thereof annexed, prove that he is fully authorized by Mrs. Maria Russell, widow and administratrix of Mr. John Russell, formerly an inhabitant of this province, to attend to all the business which he left undecided in it; and as he must always have before him said instrument for the legal uses of his commission, and in order that the same may not be mislaid, the petitioner begs your excellency may be pleased to order the present secretary to give him a certified copy of the power aforesaid, and to record the original thereof in the public archives, there to remain safe against any accident. Therefore, may it please your excellency to provide in conformity to this petition; which favor is expected from the known justice of your excellency.

JOSEPH M. HERNANDEZ.

DECREE.

St. Augustine, *February* 4, 1820.

Granted.

COPPINGER.

Before me—

JUAN DE ENTRALGO.

NOTIFICATION.

St. Augustine, on the same day, month and year, I notified the preceding decree to Don José Mariano Hernandez; which I certify.

ENTRALGO.

It is conformable to the originals, which remain in the archives under my charge; and, in obedience to superior orders, I seal and sign the present certified copy in St. Augustine, Flórida, February 5, 1820.

JUAN DE ENTRALGO.

PETITION.

To his excellency the governor:

Don José Mariano Hernandez, a planter of this province, in his capacity of attorney of Mrs. Maria Russell, widow and administratrix of Mr. John Russell, as it is proved by the power duly annexed, with due respect represents to your excellency that in the year 1812 the government admitted as a new settler of this province the said Russell, deceased. He brought to this place from the island of New Providence, as part of his property a schooner, which he proposed to convey to the treasury department in exchange for four thousand acres of land, and the title of property to such as were granted to him in proportion to the number of his family and slaves, in his quality of a new settler; and the government having acceded to the said proposition, as it is proved by the documents recorded in the secretary's office, he petitioned that the four thousand acres of land granted for the consideration of said schooner might be located and surveyed between the rivers Matanzas and Tomoca, which so essential a requisite did not take place for reasons detailed in said proceedings, in which the government offers to interfere in his behalf against any other claimant, in order that, in case a sufficient number of acres could not be found unlocated in the place aforesaid, he may be entitled to complete the same in the swamp called the Twelve-mile swamp. The said John Russell having taken sick and died in Fernandina, his widow met with many difficulties to import the remainder of the slaves whom she owned in New Providence, and lost by that the hope of obtaining more lands than those which were granted to them at the time of their emigration to this province, and, by the same reasons, was prevented from petitioning again for the location and survey of said lands; which location and survey are indispensable circumstances, although she considers herself as the absolute proprietor of said land, in virtue of the proceedings aforesaid. Therefore, she now petitions that the said location and survey may be carried into effect in the place designated by the surveyor, Don George Clarke, who is now in this city, and she begs your excellency to order in conformity to her petition, which act of justice she expects from the correct administration of your excellency. St. Augustine, February 8, 1820.

JOSEPH M. HERNANDEZ.

DECREE.

Let the power of attorney which has been presented be annexed to the proceedings referred to, and let the whole be presented again.

COPPINGER.

Before me—

JUAN DE ENTRALGO, *Notary of Government.*

NOTIFICATION.

In St. Augustine, in the same month and year, I notified the preceding decree to Don José Mariano Hernandez; which I certify.

ENTRALGO.

DECREE.

St. Augustine, *February* 11, 1820.

Having seen, let the survey, as solicited, be made by the surveyor, George Clarke.

COPPINGER.

Before me—

JUAN DE ENTRALGO, *Notary of Government.*

NOTIFICATION.

In St. Augustine, on the same day, month and year, I notified the preceding decree to Don José Mariano Hernandez; to which I certify.

ENTRALGO.

PETITION.

To his excellency the governor:

Don Santiago Russell, an inhabitant of this province, with due respect, represents to your excellency that, for the purposes which may be convenient to him, he finds it necessary that, by the interpreter whom your excellency may authorize to that effect, the annexed English document may be translated in the Spanish language. Therefore, he begs your excellency will be pleased to order the same to be done, and he will pay the expenses thereof. Florida, June 13, 1821.

JAMES RUSSELL.

DECREE.

St. Augustine, *June* 13, 1821.

The annexed document is presented, and, as there is no public interpreter, let the translation be made by Don Bernardo Segui, after his having accepted and sworn to his commission; and when done, let it be brought forward.

COPPINGER.

Before me—

JUAN DE ENTRALGO, *Notary of Government.*

NOTIFICATION.

In St. Augustine, on the same day, month and year, I notified the preceding decree to Mr. James Russell; to which I certify.

ENTRALGO.

NOTIFICATION, ACCEPTATION, AND OATH.

On the same day I notified to Don Bernardo Segui the appointment of interpreter given to him; and he said that he accepted it, and did accept it, promising, under his legal oath, to exercise well and faithfully the functions of his commission according to his best knowledge and understanding, and signed; to which I certify.

BERNARDO SEGUI.

Before me—

JUAN DE ENTRALGO.

[Translation.]

Island of Bahama, *New Providence:*

In the name of God, amen. I, John Russell, of the island of St. Salvador, do give, make known, and declare this to be my last will and testament: I give, bequeath, and leave all the property, real and personal, I may possess in these islands, in the State of Georgia, and anywhere else, to my consort, Maria Russell, and to my children, Isabel Russell, James Russell, James Hunter Russell, William Edward Russell, Richard Henry Russell, Maria Amelia Anna Russell, and to any other child my consort aforesaid may have by me in future, for them or their survivors; to have and to hold said property in equal parts or proportions, subject to the directions, limitations, and restrictions which will be detailed, to wit: It is my will that all my property be united and managed, under the directions of my executor or executors who will be named, in the most advantageous manner for the benefit of all my legatees aforesaid, until the youngest surviving child be twenty-one years old, if it is a male child, and eighteen years old if it is a female child, and then an equal division of my property will take place among the survivors; and should any of my children during the minority of the youngest marry, or should any other circumstance occur which would make it necessary to appraise said property, I charge and authorize my executors, in behalf of my children, to pay the most prudent attention, so that every one may have their due proportion and to that effect to appraise the property according to the circumstances of the times, and leave undivided the remainder of the property belonging to the other legatees; and I declare that it is also my wish that, should any of my children die and leave after them lawful heirs, the said heirs shall have the portion due to the deceased; otherwise, said portion will be added to the common stock and belong to the surviving legatees. I do elect and appoint as my executor and executors of this my last will and testament my consort aforesaid, my son, James Hunter Russell, and Robert Leach, of the State of Georgia; and I do hereby revoke and annul whatever other disposition I may have made before this moment. In testimony of which, I, John Russell, testator aforesaid, do sign and seal this instrument on the 18th January, of the year of our Lord 1811.

JOHN RUSSELL. [L.S.]

Signed, sealed, made known, and declared by John Russell, testator aforesaid, to be his last will and testament, in our presence; and at his request, and in the presence of all of us, we have subscribed our names. Fernandina, August 1, 1814.
Witnesses: JOHN ARMSTRONG.
DAVID BETHELL.
J. F. THOMPSON.

The preceding will has been opened in our presence.

FILIPE R. YONGE.
FARQUHAR BETHUNE.

SECRETARY'S OFFICE, *Glynn County:*
Registered in the book D, folio 16, this 31st day of May, 1815.

T. ABRAHAMS.

GEORGIA, *Glynn County:*
Before me, P. Gibson, magistrate in said county, personally appeared Mr. John Armstrong, of the island of Bahama, now a resident in the State of Georgia, who, being duly sworn, declared that the said John Russell signed, sealed, and made known, and declared the preceding instrument to be his last will and testament, and that witness, together with David Bethell and F. J. Thompson, subscribed their names thereto, having been called to witness the same. Witness also declares that when the testator aforesaid executed said will he was in a good state of health, and enjoying the mental faculties unimpaired.

JOHN ARMSTRONG.
Sworn to before me this 4th day of May, 1815.

P. GIBSON, *Justice of the Peace.*

The preceding translation is well and faithfully made according to my best knowledge and understanding, for which I refer to the original; and, in conformity to superior orders, I sign the present in St. Augustine, of Florida, June 14, 1821.

BERNARDO SEGUI.

DECREE.

ST. AUGUSTINE, *June* 14, 1821.
Let the preceding be delivered to the petitioner, who will use it according to right.

COPPINGER.
Before me—

JUAN DE ENTRALGO.

NOTIFICATION.

In St. Augustine, on the same day, month, and year, I notified the preceding decree to Mr. James Russell; which I certify.

ENTRALGO.

PETITION.

Mrs. Maria Russell, a new settler of this province, in the proceedings that have occurred before the tribunal of your excellency relating to 4,000 acres of land, granted as an equivalent of the vessel which my husband, deceased, sold to his Majesty for the public service of this place, which vessel was then called the Perseverance, and afterwards the Barbarita, and to 675 acres which are granted agreeably to the number of our family, and of the slaves whom we imported in this province, in the most proper form my right may require, which right was acknowledged by the act of this government, dated July 28, 1812, which comprehends the two grants aforesaid, appears before your excellency, in the person of my attorney, and say that, in consequence of my petition having been acceded to, as appears by said act, dated February 11, 1820, I took the necessary measures to ascertain the survey of the wooded lands to be found in the territory situated west of the river Halifax, bounded north by lands belonging to Mr. Farquhar Bethune, and south by lands belonging to Mr. Patrick Dean, where the 675 acres belonging to my family are to.be located, and the 4,000 acres to be located from the head of the river Matanzas to the river Tomoca is more minutely explained in said act, dated July 28, 1812; but it appears that after the surveyor, Mr. George Clarke, had taken the points my deceased husband fixed upon, in conformity to the grants, that all times they may serve as the basis of the survey, which the superior decrees declare in the most ample manner ought to be favorably made in behalf of the grantee, I find that within the limits of the points alluded, to the government has granted four tracts, to wit: one of 800 acres to Mr. Isaac Wicks; one of 1,100 acres to Mr. P. Lynch; one of 500 acres to Mr. James Darley; and another of a smaller size to Mrs. Mariano Wicks. Therefore, in addition that these new grantees in no case whatever can or ought to prejudice my right, as their grants are subsequent to the conclusion of my contract with the government, and as my singular, extraordinary, and privileged requisition cannot have any relation, or meet with any competition with any of them, except that they ought to be ejected from their assumed points, I will offer to your excellency other short reflections, by which your excellency will see that in the case that I should wish to occupy the vacant lands they have left, my acquisition would be illusory, as said lands are of no value whatever, as it appears that these new grantees have located their grants on the only spots that would give a value to mine, which, without —— or equivocation, is to consist of wooded lands, for which very reason the government, in case I should not find the complement of my lands in the wooded parts of it for the cultivation between the two rivers aforesaid, gave me the right of completing my said grant in the wood known by the name of Twelve-mile swamp, in order that my contract with the government might be fulfilled in all its parts. Neither the series of vicissitudes which have prevented to carry into effect the survey and fixing the boundaries, as it is indicated in various parts of the proceedings, can, it appears to me, intercept my rights to said wooded lands, and this is proved sufficiently, without adducing others, by the two particulars already exposed, which I consider as decisive, as they cannot be contested by the four new grantees; neither do I consider that against both exceptions the right sense of justice which distinguishes, your excellency can oppose a determination which may be contrary to the acts of your worthy predecessors: Therefore, with due reverence, I beg your excellency be pleased to acknowledge this my presentation, together with a draught, simple, but conformable to the original, which shows that the boundaries which correspond with my grant comprehend within them the possessions aforesaid, in order that, on consideration thereof, and of all that has been exposed, your excellency be pleased to order that the grantees aforesaid yield to my right; and in order to obtain this end, I hope that your excellency will have the goodness to order, with a view that the interested parties may have the shortest notice of it, that the secretary of this government do notify a certification of the royal order obtained in approbation of my said contracts, the whole of which appears to me agreeable to justice in general, and in particular to which distinguishes your administration; and I swear that I do not proceed from malice, &c. Moreover, in order to legalize my lawful representation as it ought to be, I beg your excellency be pleased to order the notary in this cause, who is the only one employed in this government, to annex to the proceedings a certificate of the substitution of power granted by Don José Mariano Hernandez, and also to acknowledge the presentation of the certificate of the will, which is duly annexed to it. I claim justice *ut supra*

JAMES H. RUSSELL.

DECREE.

St. Augustine, *June* 14, 1821.

Let it be communicated to the auditor of war.

COPPINGER.

Before me—

JUAN DE ENTRALGO.

NOTIFICATION.

In St. Augustine, on the same day, month and year, I notified the preceding decree to Mr. James Russell; which I certify.

ENTRALGO.

PETITION.

St. Augustine, *June* 16, 1821.

Mr. James Russel, an inhabitant of this province, in his capacity of a lawful heir and executor of Mr. John Russell, deceased, in continuation of the proceedings, the object of which is to claim certain lands allotted to his father aforesaid, and in order to proceed in other particulars in the best legal form, appears before your excellency, and says that in order to produce a greater proof of what is asserted in the proceedings, although the survey of said lands have been prevented by a variety of circumstances which have been mentioned, still I can do it now with propriety, in observing, when I take possession, to draw a line north and south on the road which, west of this place, leads to the territory of Mosquito, stopping on the N. NW. to the S. SE., and remarking a pine tree north on the boundary line of Mr. Francis Pellicer, and another south on the boundary line of Mr. Ormond's land, from which two points, both marked B R, the lines had to run east in order to embrace Mr. John Russell's property: Therefore, I hope your excellency will be pleased to order the admission of such witnesses as I am ready to produce, who, under their legal oaths, will declare whether or no whatever I have related is certain, from which the spoliation of the grantee has suffered in his absence, will evidently appear, and in consideration of all which your excellency will be pleased —— the restitution to be made in *toto*. Therefore, I supplicate your excellency to provide, in conformity to my petition, the issuing the titles of property which are wanting as a matter of form. I claim justice. Moreover, as some witnesses are to be examined who are not acquainted with the Spanish language, I pray your excellency to be pleased to appoint an interpreter to make the necessary translations. I claim justice, &c.

JAMES RUSSELL.

DECREE.

St. Augustine, *June* 16, 1821.

As to the first and principal point of the petition, let the information offered be admitted according to law, and let the witnesses appear and make their declaration before the auditor of war, and according to the merits of the case I will dispose what is most convenient; and as to the second point, as there is no public interpreter, let Don Bernardo Segui be appointed, he having previously accepted the oath of office.

COPPINGER.
ARREDONDO.

Before me—

JUAN DE ENTRALGO.

NOTIFICATION.

In St. Augustine, on the same day, month, and year, I notified to Don Bernardo Segui the appointment of interpreter given to him, on which he said that he accepted, and he did accept it, promising, on his oath, legally taken, to exercise well and faithfully the functions of his commission, according to the best of his knowledge and understanding, and signed; which I certify.

BERNARDO SEGUI.

Before me—

JUAN DE ENTRALGO.

DECLARATION.

In the city of St. Augustine, of Florida, June 16, 1821, before Don Juan de Arredondo y Santelices, auditor of war, of this place and province appeared Mr. Robert McHardy, an inhabitant and planter of the same, married, who, in the hands of the auditor, before me, notary, and through the organ of the interpreter, Don Bernardo Segui, made oath in a legal form, and promised to tell the truth in all he might know relating to the questions that will be put to him respecting the case, and the meaning of the representation which precedes, and said that, in the year 1813, he accompanied Mr. James Russell when he went with some of his slaves to take possession of the lands which this government had given him in consideration of the schooner Barbarita, and in his capacity of new settler, between the rivers Tomoca and Matanzas, in which place Russell himself designated the limits by marking some trees with letters which still exist, and affirmed that what he has said is the truth; that he is forty-five years old; that the law exceptions which have been made known to him do not affect him. And his declaration having been read to him, he affirmed and signed it, together with the auditor and the interpreter; which I certify.

ROBERT McHARDY.
BERNARDO SEGUI

Before me—

JUAN DE ENTRALGO.

DECLARATION.

In continuation appeared Don Francisco Pellicer, an inhabitant of this place, married, who, in the hands of the auditor, before me, the secretary, took his legal oath, promising to tell the truth in all what he might know relating to what he may be interrogated upon relating to the same business; said that he has seen the marks of letters which are found on two trees, one on the east and the other on the west; which two points embrace the wooded land, which is situated between the rivers Matanzas and Tomoca, where this government granted lands to the deceased, Mr. John Russell; which marks, as witness has been informed by his own children, were made by Mr. John Russell himself, as a mark of the limits and boundaries which were to enclose said granted lands; that this act of John Russell is of public notoriety, as well as his going personally with his slaves to do it. Witness says that what he has deposed is the truth; that he is 67 years of age; that the law exceptions do not affect him; and he signed his deposition. The auditor affixed his flourish; which I certify.

(A flourish.)
FRANCISCO PELLICER.

Before me—

JUAN DE ENTRALGO.

DECLARATION.

In continuation appeared Don José Mariano Hernandez, one of the members of the constitutional council of this place, who, before me, the secretary, took his legal oath, promising to tell the truth in all he might know, upon which he might be interrogated, relating to the representation of Mr. James Russell, and said that, on the wooded lands situated between the rivers Matanzas and Tomoca, he has seen some trees marked with initials, which operation he knows, from public notoriety, was made by the deceased Mr. John Russell at the same time he went with his slaves to mark the limits and take possession of the lands which he obtained from this government in exchange for a schooner which he sold to the revenue department, and of those lands which were awarded to him as a new settler. And witness has no doubt that the deceased John Russell aforesaid went on the mentioned lands with said intent, and that this happened immediately after he was declared the owner of said lands. And witness says, under his oath, that all this is the truth; that he is thirty-three years of age, and signed his deposition; and the auditor put his flourish; which I certify.

(One flourish.)
JOS. M. HERNANDEZ.

Before me—

JUAN DE ENTRALGO.

ACT.

St. Augustine, June 18, 1821.

Seeing the preceding, and Mr. James Russell having proved that he is a lawful son and heir of the deceased Mr. John Russell, and of the age of twenty-five years, he is hereby considered as a party in this, and as such can represent what he will think convenient on all and whatsoever rights belonging to his deceased father; the remuneration of Don José M. Hernandez as accepted, and the mentioned James Russell having sufficiently proved the spoliation of the land which the Treasury Department sold to the deceased in consideration for the schooner which was bought of him for the service of this place, and of the lands which were granted to him as a new settler, as appears in the proceedings entered into to that effect, and by which this process begins, as appears also in the documents he has presented, and the declarations taken of witnesses; first of all, let the possession which he claims be restored to him, with the reserve of the respective right which the actual possessors may consider themselves to hold in order that they make use of it should they think proper so to do; in virtue of which, in order that the restitution may be carried into effect, let Don Francisco José Fatio be commissioned for that special act, with all the faculties the law requires in consideration of the physical impossibility in which the auditor and the only notary of this province are of going personally to execute said act of restitution; which impossibility is occasioned not only by the great distance of said lands, but also because said officers cannot for a moment leave this capital in this critical epoch of the delivery thereof to the government of the United States: this most important event claiming all their attention, let the necessary orders be given to the said commissioner, in order that he may be assisted by witnesses; discharge the duties of said commission; of the result of which he will make his report.

COPPINGER.
ARREDONDO.

Before me—

JUAN DE ENTRALGO.

NOTIFICATION.

In St. Augustine, on the same month and year, I notified the preceding act to Mr. James Russell; which I attest.

ENTRALGO.

NOTE.—On the same day the order aforesaid was issued and delivered to Mr. Francisco José Fatio; which I certify.

ENTRALGO.

PETITION.

I, James Russell, an inhabitant of this province, in continuation of the proceedings relating to the claim of lands belonging to the estate of my deceased father, and in consequence of the decree issued this day, in which it is ordered that I be put in possession of said land in the most legal form, I expose to your excellency that, as the alderman Don Francisco Fatio has been appointed by your excellency as a commissioner to carry said decree into execution, I beg your excellency be pleased, in order to made the survey and fix the boundaries of said lands in conformity to the tenor of the decree dated February 11, 1820, and agreeably to the grant and restitution which is made, to order that Don George Clarke, the surveyor general, go on the spot to execute the said survey. I therefore beg your excellency be pleased to order in conformity to my petition. I claim justice.

JAMES H. RUSSELL.

DECREE.

ST. AUGUSTINE, June 19, 1821.

Granted. Assessor's fees $3. Let the costs accrued be regulated and paid.

COPPINGER.
ARREDONDO.

Before me—

JUAN DE ENTRALGO.

NOTIFICATION.

In St. Augustine, on the same day, month and year, I notified the preceding decree to Mr. James Russell; which I certify.

ENTRALGO.

Another. On the same day I notified the same to Don George Clarke; which I certify.

ENTRALGO.

ORDER.

Don José Coppinger, colonel of the national armies, military governor, political chief, and ultramarine sub-delegate of this place and province, &c., by these presents:

I confer unto Don Francisco José Fatio all the faculties required by law, to the effect that, with two assistant witnesses, whom he will appoint in due form to assist him in this commission, he transport himself on the lands which were by this government sold to the deceased, John Russell, and on those lands which were granted to the same as a new settler; said lands, situated between the Matanzas and Tomoca, and there put Mr. James Russell, a lawful son and heir of said John Russell, deceased, in possession of said lands, which are hereby restored to him in consequence of what has been represented and proved on the proceedings relating thereto, with the reserve of the respective rights which the actual occupiers may consider to possess in the lands aforesaid, in order that they may make use of said right if they think proper; and after putting down, in writing, the result, said commissioner will make his report, as it is already ordered in my decree of this day, which I issued in conformity to the petition of Mr. James Russell aforesaid, with the consultation of the auditor of war. St. Augustine, of Florida, June 18, 1128.

JOSÉ COPPINGER.

By order of his excellency:
JUAN DE ENTRALGO, <i>Notary of Government.</i>

APPOINTMENT OF WITNESSES.

I, Francis José Fatio, an inhabitant of St. Augustine, of East Florida, having repaired to the plantation called the Good Retreat, in order to carry the preceding order into execution, did appoint as assistant witnesses Don José Simeon Sanchez and Don Francisco Pellicer, who accepted the office, and promised, under their legal oath, well and faithfully to the discharge of their duty, and signed.

FRANC. PELLICER.
JOSÉ SIMEON SANCHEZ.
FRANC. J. FATIO.

REPORT.

In Tomoca, June 21, 1821, in conformity to the tenor of the preceding order, I, Francisco José Fatio, accompanied by the witnesses, assistants, who subscribe this, and by Mr. James Russell, we went to the place aforesaid, riding about on horseback; and, taking said James Russell by the hand, I put him in possession of the lands referred to in my commission. There he called aloud, pulling up the grass, threw up sand in the air, broke branches of trees, and did other things indicating possession, which he took quietly and peacefully, and without contradiction. And in proof thereof, I make this report, which I sign, together with the witnesses and the interested party.

FRANCO. PELLICER.
FRANCO. JOSÉ FATIO.
JOSÉ SIMEON SANCHEZ.
JAS. H. RUSSELL.

DECREE.—ACTS.

Before me—

(Two flourishes.)
JUAN DE ENRTALGO.

NOTIFICATION.

In St. Augustine, on the same day, month and year, I notified the preceding decree to Mr. James Russell; which I certify.

ENTRALGO.

ACT.

St. Augustine, *June* 26, 1821.

Seen the above. I approve all that the law admits—the proceedings of the constitutional alderman, Don Francisco José Fatio; and, in consequence thereof, I declare Mr. James Russell to be in possession of the lands, the restitution of which he has claimed, and in which he will be protected. Let the costs latterly incurred be regulated, and let the mentioned Russell pay the same.

COPPINGER.
ARREDONDO.

NOTIFICATION.

St. Augustine, on the same day, month and year, I notified the preceding act to Mr. James Russell; which I certify.

ENTRALGO.

PETITION.

To his excellency the governor:

I, James Russell, an inhabitant of this province, with due respect represent to your excellency that the survey being concluded, and the boundaries fixed of the 4,675 acres of land which I have claimed from this tribunal as being of right the property of my deceased father, whom I, as his heir and executor, represent according to the tenor of the proceedings relating to that affair, and as said survey is proved by the two draughts certified and annexed to the act, and on register in the archives of this government, and that the present notary delivered me the certificates of the whole proceedings; I therefore beg your excellency to order, in conformity to my petition; which favor I expect to receive. Florida, June 28, 1821.

JAS. H. RUSSELL.

DECREE.—ACTS.

St. Augustine, *June* 28, 1821.

Before me—

(Two flourishes.)
JUAN DE ENTRALGO.

NOTIFICATION.

In St. Augustine, on the same day, month and year, I notified the preceding decree to Mr. James Russell; which I certify.

ENTRALGO.

DECREE.

St. Augustine, *June* 30, 1821.

Seen. Granted in every particular.

COPPINGER.
ARREDONDO.

Before me—

JUAN DE ENTRALGO.

NOTIFICATION.

In St. Augustine, on the same day, month and year, I notified the preceding decree to Mr. James Russell; which I certify.

ENTRALGO.

This copy is conformable to the originals which remain on the archives under my charge, to which I refer; and in obedience to the superior order issued at the request of the interested party, I seal and sign the present certificate contained in forty-seven leaves of common paper, as stamped paper is not used here. St. Augustine, Florida, July 6, 1821.

JUAN DE ENTRALGO, *Notary of Government, &c.*

Don Gabriel W. Perpall, Don José M. Hernandez, and Don William Travers, mayor and aldermen, constitutional members of the council of this city, certify that Don Juan de Entralgo, by whom the preceding certificate appears to be sealed and signed, is the notary of government and of the treasury department, as he states himself; that he is the only one in that capacity in this place and province; that he is faithful, legal, and trusty; and that full faith and credit has always been given to those who have filled the said two offices. And in proof thereof, and at the request of the interested party, we sign the present in St. Augustine, Florida, July 6, 1821.

GABRIEL W. PERPALL.
JOSEPH M. HERNANDEZ.
WILLIAM TRAVERS.

Don George Clarke, lieutenant of the militia of the city of St. Augustine, of Florida, and surveyor general, by the appointment of the government of said place and province: I certify that, in consequence of the superior order issued June 19, 1821, relating to the proceedings made at the request of Mr. James

Russell, claiming four thousand acres of land, bargained for with the government by his deceased father, I have made the survey and marked the boundaries of three thousand four hundred and eighty-six acres of land, as a part of the said four thousand, in the place called Graham's swamp, situated between the rivers Matanzas and Tomoca, the particulars of which are *conform* to the following draught, and to the original, which remains in my possession. St. Augustine, June 25, 1821.

GEO. J. F. CLARKE.

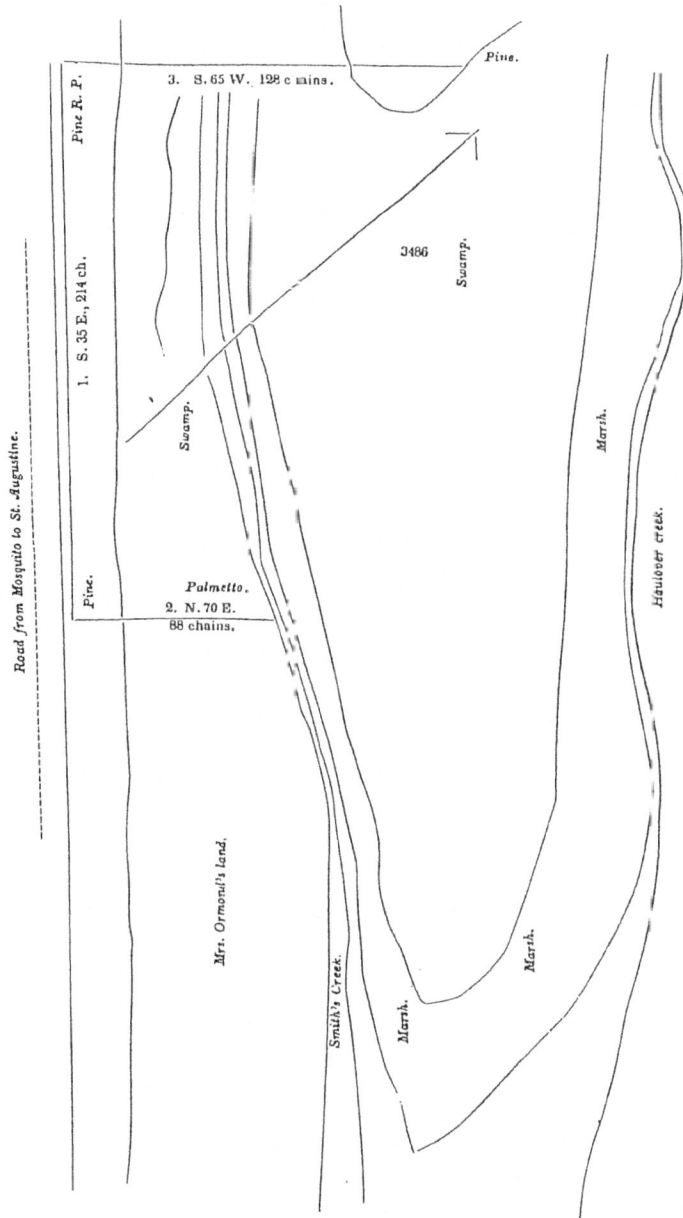

Don George Clarke, lieutenant of the militia of St. Augustine, Florida, and surveyor general, appointed by the government of the said place and province: I certify that, in consequence of the superior order issued June 19, 1821, relating to the proceedings made at the request of Mr. James Russell, claiming four thousand acres of land which his deceased father bought of the government, I have made the survey and fixed the boundaries of five hundred and fourteen acres on the west side of the river Halifax, which, with three thousand four hundred and eighty-six acres already surveyed in Graham's swamp, make the complement of the four thousand acres aforesaid; which said tract of five hundred and fourteen acres is *conform* in all its particulars to the following draught, and the original thereof, which remains in my possession. St. Augustine, June 25, 1821.

GEO. J. F. CLARKE.

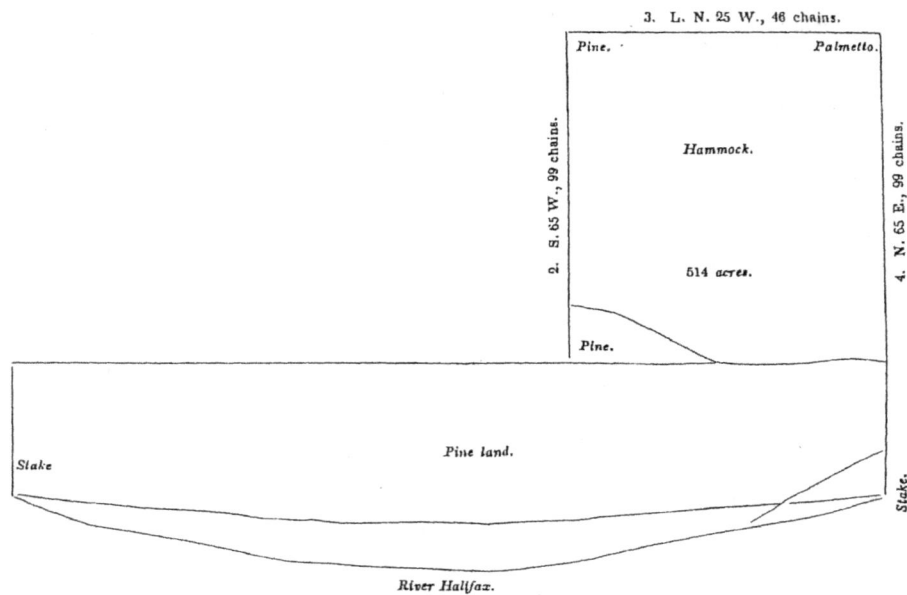

3. L. N. 25 W., 46 chains.

Pine. · *Palmetto.*

Hammock.

2. S. 65 W., 99 chains.   4. N. 65 E., 99 chains.

514 *acres.*

Pine.

Pine land.

Stake   *Stake.*

River Halifax.

Don George Clarke, lieutenant of militia of St. Augustine, Florida, and surveyor general, appointed by the government of this place and province: I certify that I have made the survey and fixed the boundaries of six hundred and seventy-five acres of land in favor of Mr. James Russell; which lands were granted to his deceased father July 28, 1812, and which, in every particular, are *conform* to the following draught, and the original thereof, which remains in my possession.   St. Augustine, June 25, 1821.

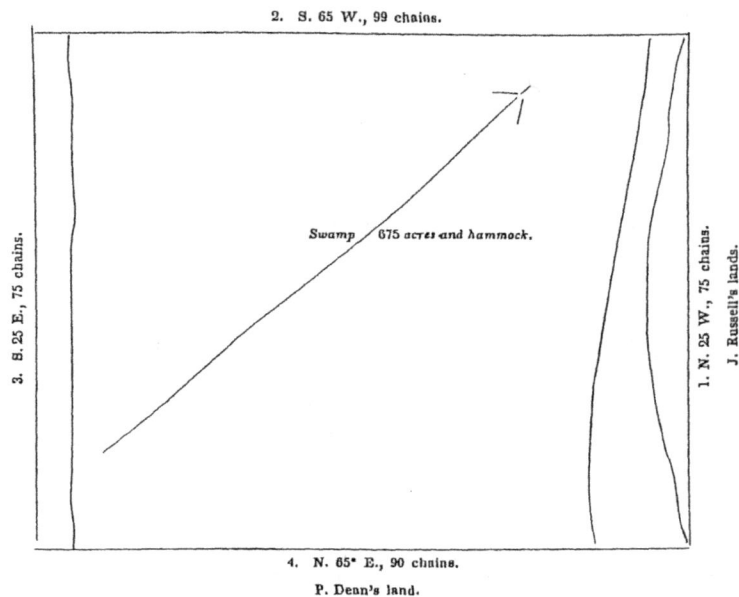

2. S. 65 W., 99 chains.

3. S. 25 E., 75 chains.   1. N. 25 W., 75 chains.   J. Russell's lands.

Swamp 675 *acres and hammock.*

4. N. 65° E., 90 chains.

P. Dean's land.

I certify that the foregoing is a translation from a document in the Spanish language.

F. J. FATIO, *S. B. L. C.*

[Here follows a deed of conveyance from Mary Russell, James H. Russell, William E. Russell, Richard H. Russell, Mary E. A. Russell, and Thomas Philson, heirs of John Russell, deceased, to claimant, dated August 1, 1821.]

ST. JOHN'S COUNTY, *ss:*

This day appeared before the subscriber, a justice of the peace, Joseph Delespine, who, being duly sworn to give testimony in the above case, doth depose and say that he knew John Russell, who had a grant made to him by the Spanish government for the lands above mentioned; that the said John Russell is dead; that the heirs of the said Russell sold the said lands to Charles W. Bulow; left a widow, Mary Russell; daughters, Eliza and Mary; sons, James, Edward, and Henry; that these persons, as far as this deponent knows and believes, are the only legal heirs of the said John Russell.

JOSEPH DELESPINE.

Sworn to before me July 24, 1824.

THOMAS H. PENN, *Mayor of St. Augustine.*

DECREE BY THE BOARD.

Charles W. Bulow's Executors vs. *The United States. For four thousand acres of land; also for six hundred and seventy-five acres of land.*

The board ascertained the above to be valid Spanish grants, and recommend them to Congress for confirmation. September 21.

No. 11.—See REPORT No. 3.

Fernando de la Maza Arredondo vs. *The United States. Claim for fifteen thousand acres of land.*

MEMORIAL.

To the honorable the commissioners appointed to ascertain claims and titles to lands in East Florida:

The petition of Fernando de la Maza Arredondo respectfully showeth: That your memorialist claims title to a tract of land consisting of fifteen thousand acres, situated on the west side of Lake George, in East Florida, bounded and beginning at a palm tree marked +, on the margin of Lake George; thence south 65° west, 400 chains, to a pine; thence north 25° west, 400 chains; thence north 65° east, 400 chains, to a palm tree on the banks of said lake; thence along the meanders of said lake to the beginning; which tract was surveyed by Andres Burgev in August 5, 1819; which title your memorialist derives from a royal title made to him August 9, 1819, by Governor Coppinger, in virtue of the royal order of March 29, 1815, a concession of which was made to memorialist March 24, 1817, as will be seen by a certified copy of royal title herewith submitted. And your memorialist further showeth that he is legally in possession of said lands; that he is a citizen of Spain and resident of Cuba. All of which is respectfully submitted.

F. M. ARREDONDO.

[Translation.]

Don Fernando de la Maza Arredondo, inhabitant of St. Augustine, and actually residing in the city of Havana, through his son, of the same name, residing in this place, to your excellency showeth: That he has the honor of having served his Majesty in different employments and destinations, and particularly in the department of commissary of the Indians, without any salary or any other emolument whatever, for more than twenty years, having discharged the duties of that office with the utmost exactitude to the satisfaction of all the governors of this place, contributing thereby to the peace and harmony which existed with those savages; with which commissior, and that of comptroller *pro tem.* of the royal military hospital of this town, which he likewise discharged for many years without any salary or emolument, which meritorious services have saved to the royal revenue many thousands of dollars, as is well known to your excellency and to the public authorities of this place. Latterly, after obtaining a discharge from the different employments, he separated himself from the service of his Majesty to attend to the discharge of his duty towards his family; he engaged himself in the fatiguing service of patrols and aid-de-camp to the Governor de Estrada, in consequence of the invasion of this province in the year 1812, and for want of officers for that service, in which he was occupied until the year 1813, when, having been elected by a majority of votes, with all the necessary solemnities on the occasion, elector of the parish and district of this said province, he was obliged to go to the city of Havana and remain there as one of the deputies of the provincial junta. To discharge the said duty he was under the necessity, as a loyal subject, to expend large sums, which he willingly did in the service of his King and country, being well persuaded that he would be rewarded for it at a future period. He has been informed that the royal order of his Majesty of March 29, 1815, directs that a remuneration of grants of land be given to all the individuals who were armed in the defence of their country during the insurrection which began in 1812; and as the petitioner is one of them, and is entitled for this reason to said gifts, as also being one of the oldest settlers and having augmented his family and negroes ever since the cession of this province to his Majesty, and one of those whom the royal ordinances and laws recommend that they may be attended to, both in quality of first settlers as also on account of his distinguished services, that he be preferred in the partition of lands; he therefore prays your excellency will be pleased to grant him, in absolute property, thirty thousand acres of land, that is to say, 15,000 acres to the southwest of the large lagoon known by the name of Lake George, which survey may be made that a creek of sweet water situated in that place may occupy the centre of the front thereof, and the remaining 15,000 on the west side of St. John's river; the measurement of which to commence from the old Indian Chacichalty path, opposite the site on which the firm of Panton & Leslie had their store established, known by the name of Upper Store, being at the south side of the large lagoon by the name of Lake George, and thence in a line to run southerly until it completes the number of acres. And as the actual circumstances of the province do not permit at present the measurement and chaining of said lands, and, at the same time, as the survey could not take place for want of surveyors, as Don George Clarke, named by this government, has other occupations which give him no time to attend to it, he therefore hopes, from the justice of your excellency, that you will be pleased to suspend the acknowledgment of the titles of the property whilst the memorialist does not obtain the plats of said lands, in order that their situation and limits may be specified with exactness for perfecting the location and situation of the same. In the meantime the grant which your lordship may think fit to make him may serve as a title under your decree in continuation, for it is the wish of the memorialist that, when the same be given him, it may have all the requisites necessary; a favor which he hopes to receive from the justice of your excellency. St. Augustine, Florida, March 1, 1817.

FERNANDO DE LA MAZA ARREDONDO.

ST. AUGUSTINE, *March* 24, 1817.

In attention to the services which this party specifies, which are manifest and notorious, and making use of the power conferred on me by the laws and the royal will, I administer to Don Fernando de la Maza Arredondo, the senior, the thirty thousand acres of land he solicits, in absolute property, in the places he has designated, without prejudice to a third person, of which titles of dominion will be given as soon as the plats to be made by the surveyor be presented, saving, in the meantime, this decree, and an equivalent in all its parts; which, with the foregoing petition, will be filed in the archives of the notary of government and royal finance. The interested will be furnished with a certified copy of the proceedings, properly authenticated and in due form, in order that this concession may be duly credited, and that he may be able to make use of said lands, and to dispose of them as he may think proper.

COPPINGER.

Before me—   JUAN DE ENTRALGO, *Notary of Government.*

I certify the foregoing to be a true and correct translation from a document in the Spanish language.
F. J. FATIO, *S. B. L. C.*

DECREE BY THE BOARD.

In this case we find that the claimant obtained a concession, without condition, for thirty thousand acres of land from Governor Coppinger, dated March 24, 1817, the fifteen thousand acres being included in said concession, and its location set forth in claimant's memorial to this board. In consideration whereof, we recommend the same to Congress for confirmation. June 5, 1824.

Note.—For further particulars please to refer to the case of Moses C. Levi, for 14,500 acres, reported to Congress the first session.

No. 12.—See Report No. 3.

Juan de Entralgo vs. The United States. For four thousand acres of land.

MEMORIAL.

To the honorable the commissioners appointed to ascertain claims and titles to lands in East Florida:

The petition of Juan de Entralgo respectfully showeth: That your memorialist claims title to a tract of land consisting of four thousand acres, situated on Black creek, and is bounded on the south by Governor's creek; first line runs south 45° west, 170 chains, to a pine tree marked thus ≡; thence south 45° east, 250 chains, to a cypress tree marked ═; which title your memorialist derives from a royal grant made to F. M. Arredondo by Governor Coppinger, in virtue of the royal order of March 29, 1815, who sold the same to your memorialist; a copy of the said grant is herewith filed, as is the deed from Arredondo to your memorialist. And your memorialist further showeth that he is in actual possession of said lands; that he resided in St. Augustine at the change of flags, and now in Cuba.

JUAN DE ENTRALGO,
By GEORGE MURRAY.

Translation of a concession for ten thousand acres, part of which this is, is copied in a claim of John B. Entralgo for four thousand acres, recommended for confirmation.

[Translation.]

Don Andres Burgevin, of this place, and private surveyor: I certify that, by an order of this government, made August 20, 1819, I have measured in favor of Don Fernando de la Maza Arredondo, jr., a piece of land which contains 4,000 acres, which is situated to the west of the river St. John's, on a creek known in English as Black creek, being part of a greater quantity which was granted him on March 20, 1814. And for its confirmation I give these presents, which I sign at St. Augustine, Florida, July 25, 1820.

ANDRES BURGEVIN.

[The plat precedes this.]

I certify the foregoing to be a true and correct translation from a document in the Spanish language on file in the office of the public archives of St. Augustine.

F. J. FATIO, *S. B. L. C.*

[Translation.]

CONVEYANCE.

Be it known that I, Don Fernando de la Maza Arredondo, jr., an inhabitant of this city, do declare that I really sell to Don Juan de Entralgo, notary of government and the public domain in this city, four thousand acres of land, which I hold as my property in this province, situated to the west of the river St. John's, on a creek known in English as Black creek, and having for a boundary another creek named the Governor, known under the following dimensions: the first line runs south 45° west, measures 170 chains, and ends with a pine tree marked ≡; the second runs south 45° east, measures 250 chains, and ends in a cypress marked ═; which 4,000 acres of land, with another portion more, this government granted me in absolute property and dominion, as a reward for services, on March 20, 1817, and for which a full title was given me on the 9th of August last, as appears in the archives of the said notary. And I sell the said 4,000 acres of land under the dimensions and other things which are explained, with all its entrances, outlets, uses, customs, rights, and services, which it has and belong to it, free of all encumbrance, at the price of four thousand dollars, which the purchaser has paid me in ready money; which sum I acknowledge as delivered to my will. I renounce proof, laws of delivery, exception to money not counted, fraud, and everything else in the case, for which I deliver a formal receipt. In virtue of which I separate myself from the right of property, possession, use, seigniory, and all other rights, real and personal, which I had or held to the said 4,000 acres of land; and I cede, renounce, and transfer them to the said Don Juan de Entralgo, and to whoever shall represent his right, that, as their own, they may possess, sell, and alienate it at their will, in virtue of this writing, which I give in their favor as a mark of real delivery, by which it is seen that he has acquired possession without occasion for other proof, from which I release him. And I bind myself to the eviction and guarantee of this sale in sufficient form, and as may be best, in favor of the purchaser, with my property, present and future, power and submission to the tribunals of his Majesty, that they may force me to compliance with it as by sentence confessed and passed in authority of an adjudged case; on which I renounce all laws, customs, rights, and privileges in my favor, and formal exception which prohibit it. And I, the said Juan de Entralgo, being present, accept in my favor this writing, and by it receive, as purchased, the said 4,000 acres of land, at the price and agreement upon which they were sold to me; and I acknowledge them as delivered to my will. I renounce proof, laws of delivery, those of a thing not seen or received, fraud, and everything else in the case, for which I deliver a formal receipt. In testimony of which, this is dated at St. Augustine, Florida, January 5, 1821.

FERNANDO M. ARREDONDO.
JUAN DE ENTRALGO.

I, José Coppinger, colonel of the national armies, military governor, civil chief and sub-delegate of ultramarine possessions for this city and province, do certify that I know the parties who thus *said*, delivered, and signed in my presence, and that of assistant witnesses whom I have chosen for this deed, Don Tomas de Aguilar and Don Antonio Alvarez, there being no other notary in the entire province. The witnesses to this writing being Don José Mariano Hernandez, Don Bernardo Segui, and Don José Bernardo Reyes.

COPPINGER.

Witnesses present:
> TOMAS DE AGUILAR.
> ANTONIO ALVAREZ.

This is conformable to the original which exists in the archives of the said notary of government, to which I refer; and at the desire of the party, sign this present copy, with the assistant witnesses, on two leaves of common paper, stamped not being in use. St. Augustine, Florida, January 5, 1821.

JOSÉ COPPINGER.
TOMAS DE AGUILAR.
ANTONIO ALVAREZ.

I certify the foregoing to be a true and correct translation from a document in the Spanish language on file in the office of the public archives of St. Augustine.

F. J. FATIO, *S. B. L. C.*

DECREE.

Juan de Entralgo vs. The United States.   For four thousand acres of land.

The board having ascertained the above to be a valid Spanish concession made previous to January 24, 1818, and this claim being part thereof, regularly conveyed to claimant, it is therefore recommended to Congress for confirmation. June 30, 1824.

[Nos. 13 to 18, inclusive, were not returned to the General Land Office by the commissioners.]

No. 19.—See REPORT No. 3.

John Forbes vs. The United States.   For seven thousand acres of land.

MEMORIAL.

To the honorable the commissioners appointed to ascertain claims and titles to lands in East Florida:

The petition of John Forbes respectfully showeth: That your memorialist claims title to a tract of land consisting of seven thousand acres, situated on Little St. Mary's, and bounded as follows: first line commencing at a pine tree near Spell's swamp, running north 10° west, 246 chains, to a pine; thence south 80° west, 286 chains, to a pine; thence south 10° west, 246 chains, to a pine; thence north 80°, 286 chains, to the beginning, and containing within the said boundaries seven thousand acres, as appears by a survey made by George J. F. Clarke, and a plat of which is herewith filed, marked B; which title your memorialist derives from a grant made to himself by Governor Kindelan on July 28, 1814, (see document marked A, filed herewith.) And your memorialist further showeth that the said tract of land was surveyed by George J. F. Clarke, above named, on October 23, 1816, as will appear by the paper marked B. Your memorialist further showeth that he is in possession of said lands, and that at the change of flags he was a Spanish subject and resident of Cuba.

JOHN FORBES.

[Translation.]

MEMORIAL.

SEÑOR GOVERNOR: I, Don Juan Forbes, partner of the house of Juan Forbes & Co., successors of Panton, Leslie & Co., merchants of this province, before your excellency, with due respect, appear and say that the aforesaid house of Panton, Leslie & Co. obtained in the year past, of 1799, a concession of fifteen thousand acres of royal lands in the district of St. John's, to employ their negroes in agriculture and pasture their cattle, as appears by the annexed certificate; but at the end of a very little time it was found necessary to abandon them, from their being of an inferior quality, having experienced what commonly happens in this province where the farmer does not succeed in his choice until sad experience; and as it has been seen by many precedents that the government, attending to similar misfortunes, and the injuries and expenses which have been incurred, has had the goodness to allow that they should select lands belonging to the King, always giving up the former concession. Finding myself in this case, and desirous to establish a plantation of rice, which up to this time we find ourselves obliged to bring from abroad, I make from now a surrender of the said fifteen thousand acres of land in favor of his Majesty, (whom God preserve,) praying that you will be pleased to allow it, and, in its place, grant me an equivalent in the district of Nassau river. In virtue of which, he prays your excellency to be pleased to command that the formal surrender which I make shall be allowed, and that, in consequence, there be granted to me ten thousand acres in the said district of the river Nassau, the survey of which I shall present as soon as the province becomes tranquil, and gives an opportunity to effect it; which I will receive as a favor, &c.

JUAN FORBES.

DECREE.

Let the report be made from the comptroller's office.

KINDELAN.

REPORT.

As in this province lands are given gratis, the comptroller's office has not taken cognizance of their distribution, nor to whom; for which reason it is ignorant of the grants and of the lands remaining vacant, and therefore cannot say anything respecting the particular which it is ordered to report. Nevertheless, it appears that the culture of rice crops is useful, for which, according to the statement of the interested, the lands are not fit which were granted to him on August 7, 1799, with the expression of *for pasture*, as the accompanying certificate shows, given by the former secretary of the government, Don Juan de Pierra. St. Augustine, Florida, July 27, 1814.

MANUEL LOPEZ.

St. Augustine, *Florida, July* 28, 1814.

Let this interested party be allowed the formal cession which he makes of the fifteen thousand acres of land which the document accompanying this memorial comprises, and, in their place, let there be granted him, without injury to a third person, the ten thousand acres for the purposes which he solicits in the district or margin of the river Nassau; and in consequence, let the correspondent certificate be issued to him from the secretary's office, that it may serve him for a title in form. This party having to present the plat and demarcation at his own time, and the *proceeding* be placed in the archives of the secretary's office.

KINDELAN.

On this date a copy of this proceeding was furnished to the interested—date as above.

AGUILAR.

I certify the foregoing to be a true and correct translation from a document in the Spanish language on file in the office of the public archives of St. Augustine.

F. J. FATIO, *S. B. L. C.*

[Translation.]

Don George Clarke, lieutenant of militia of the city of St. Augustine, Florida, and surveyor general, appointed by the government of said place and province: I certify that I have measured and laid off for Don Juan Forbes seven thousand acres of land at the head of the Little St. Mary's river, on the banks of the river St. Mary's, to complete ten thousand acres which were granted to him in absolute property by the government, and conformable to the following plat and its copy which I preserve in the book of surveys in my charge. Fernandina, October 23, 1816.

GEORGE J. F. CLARKE.

[Here follows the plat.]

I certify the foregoing to be a true and correct translation from a document in the Spanish language.

F. J. FATIO, *S. B. L. C.*

DECREE.

John Forbes vs. *The United States.   For seven thousand acres of land.*

The above being a valid Spanish concession made previous to January 24, 1818, and this claim being part thereof, it is therefore recommended to Congress for confirmation. July 13, 1824.

No. 20.—See Report No. 3.

John Forbes vs. *The United States.   For three thousand acres of land.*

MEMORIAL.

To the honorable the commissioners appointed to ascertain claims and titles to lands in East Florida:

The petition of John Forbes respectfully showeth: That your memorialist claims title to a tract of land containing three thousand acres, being a part of a tract of ten thousand acres granted to the said John Forbes by Governor Kindelan July 28, 1814, in lieu of the quantity of fifteen thousand acres abandoned by your memorialist on the St. John's river; the said three thousand acres situated in Cabbage swamp, on or near an arm of the little St. Mary's river, and is bounded as follows, as will appear by a survey and plat thereof made by George J. F. Clarke, filed herewith, marked B, and dated October 20, 1816, viz: beginning at a pine tree, and running south 80° west, 195 chains, to a pine tree; south 40° west, 35 chains, to a pine; thence west, 77 chains, to a pine; thence north, 105 chains, to a pine; thence north 80° east, 299 chains, to a pine marked O+|||; thence south, 105 chains, to the beginning. Your memorialist further showeth that he was a Spanish subject residing in Cuba at the change of flags in 1821.

JOHN FORBES.

[Here follows translation of a concession for ten thousand acres to John Forbes, dated July 28, 1814, copied into a claim for seven thousand acres.]

[Translation.]

Don George Clarke, lieutenant of militia of the city of St. Augustine, Florida, and surveyor general, appointed by the government of the said city and province: I certify that I have measured and laid off for Don Juan Forbes three thousand acres of land in Cabbage swamp, near the river St. Mary's, in part of ten thousand acres, which were granted him by the government in absolute property, and agreeable to the following plat and its copy which I keep in the book of surveys in my charge.   Fernandina, October 20, 1816.

GEORGE J. F. CLARKE.

[Here follows the plat.]

DECREE.

John Forbes vs. *The United States.   For three thousand acres of land.*

The board having ascertained the above to be a valid Spanish concession for ten thousand acres made previous to January 24, 1818, do therefore recommend it to Congress for confirmation.   July 13, 1824.

[CASES REPORTED THIS SESSION.]

No. 1 a [2L]—See REPORT No. 3.

Sarah Fish vs. *The United States.   For ten thousand acres of land, Anastasia island.*

MEMORIAL.

To the honorable the board of commissioners appointed by Congress to try the validity of titles to lands in East Florida :

The memorial of the subscriber respectfully showeth—

1. That your memorialist claims title to the island lying in front (*i. e.,* to the east) of the city of St. Augustine, and running south above 18 miles, more or less, along the east bank of the river Matanzas, known by the name of the Island of St. *Anastatia*, supposed to contain ten thousand acres, as belonging to the deceased husband, Jesse Fish, sr., in the year 1763.

2. That in the year 1792 this island was sold at public sale by order of the Spanish governor, Quesada, when her son, the late Jesse Fish, jr., deceased, became the purchaser.

3. That the Spanish governor, Quesada, or his deputy, Morales, from the indisposition of Governor Quesada, with the advice of the King's attorney, Ortega, did then reserve a certain part of the quarry existing in said island; which reservation was made for the sake of the stone only, for the purpose of keeping in repair the King's fortification and other public buildings.   The part so reserved has always been known by the name of the King's quarry and begins at what is called the King's road to the south, and as far as a small distance to the north of the light-house; east and west no further than where the quarry ends, as appears by stakes, and (if not taken away) were planted at the delivery.

All the above explanation will appear by the annexed voucher's delivery of said island, with witness, and Spanish custom, and receipt from the treasurer for the money.

SARAH FISH.

ST. AUGUSTINE, *August* 31, 1823.

[Translation.]

FLORIDA, 1794.

Don José Fish, soliciting from the government that the ten thousand acres of land should be granted to him which his deceased father of the same name possessed at the plantation named the *Orange Grove,* which was sold at public auction.

ST. AUGUSTINE, *Florida, December* 2, 1796.

SEÑOR GOVERNOR AND COMMANDER-IN-CHIEF: Don Jesse Fish, native and resident of this city, presents himself to your excellency with the most profound respect; states that, at the public auction which was made of the property of his deceased father for the payment of his creditors, the memorialist purchased the place called the Orange Grove at $1,700, which sum he only gave with a view to the fruit trees of said place and the wood which is on the land belonging to it, as the land is entirely useless for planting; that he has observed that several residents are cutting the said wood, and therefore he humbly prays your excellency to be pleased to declare him owner of the lands which his said father possessed, annexed to said place of the Orange Grove, which, according to the deeds granted in the time of the British possession, amounted to ten thousand acres, according to what Don John Leslie and Don Manuel Solana can declare, it being well known to them, from their having been here at that time, whether it may be as a new settler of this province or by the right which his deceased father had to them.   Since, if your memorialist does not obtain this favor from your excellency, he will consider himself as at the greatest loss of the part of his purchase, because the lands will not produce crops of any kind, and a great number of the fruit are dried, which is likely to occur to the remainder of them.   A favor which he does not doubt to enjoy from the justice of your excellency.   JESSE FISH.

Let his honor, the assessor general, consult with me.   Thus it is decreed and ordered by Señor Don Juan Nepomuceno de Quesada, brigadier of the infantry of the royal armies, governor, commander-in-chief, vice legal patron and sub-delegate of the royal domain of this city of St. Augustine, Florida, and its province, for his Majesty, who signed it December 15, 1794; which I attest.

QUESADA.

Before me—

JOSÉ DE ZUBIZARETTA, *Notary of Government.*

On the same day this was made known to Don Jesse Fish; which I attest.

ZUBIZARETTA, *Notary.*

I have seen this memorial of Don Jesse Fish, and if it directed itself to the setting forth that he would prevent other persons from cutting wood on his lands, or to recover them according to the titles of his property and the injuries which it had caused or might have caused him, I would consult on the interlocutory decree with your excellency, according to law; but this memorial ending in making out for Fish the boundaries of the lands which his father possessed at the time of the British dominion, which he desires should be granted to him to the same number of acres which he sets forth as annexed to the Orange Grove, which he purchased at public auction held of the property left by the decease of his said father— the said sale, as the present notary states, and setting forth the boundaries of those which this party purchased when he did the Orange Grove, it remains with your excellency to assign him those which he asked for as a new settler, to which the possession of his father, alleged by him, gives him sound right of preference, and the more if he proves it, or to distribute to him those which your excellency thinks. proper, and which may be without injury to another possession; with which hearing in the case it ought to be determined judicially. This is my opinion, which I sign in St. Augustine, Florida, December 15, 1794.

LICENTIATE JOSEF DE ORTEGA.

St. AUGUSTINE, *Florida, December* 15, 1794.

In conformity with the foregoing opinion, let the interested make the proof which announces before the present notary, to whom it is committed, and in sight of it the matter on which it treats shall be decreed upon; for which purpose let the proceedings be brought forward.

QUESADA.

Before me—

JOSÉ DE ZUBIZARETTA, *Notary of Government.*

On the same day, month and year the foregoing decree was made known to Don José Fish; which I attest.

ZUBIZARETTA, *Notary.*

In the city of St. Augustine, Florida, September 22, 1795, before me, the notary, Don Jesse Fish presented as a witness for the proof which he was ordered to give, Don John Leslie, resident, &c., and merchant of this said city, from whom, in conformity with the commission which was conferred upon me, I received the oath which he made in all form of law, under which he promised to tell the truth, to the best of his knowledge, in what should be asked him, and it being done so in consequence of the aforesaid petition presented by the said Fish; that as the person who declares was one of those who, in the time of the British government, valued the lands, houses, and lots which Don José Fish, deceased, had in his possession, and amongst them was the plantation named the Orange Grove, which his son of the same name now claims; which he possessed with lawful titles given in the time of the former Spanish government, and it is known to him that he had the ten thousand acres of land, a little more or less, according to the knowledge and belief of the deponent, in possession of which he remained peaceably while the British government held this province; and answers that what he has said is the truth, by virtue of the oath which he has taken; that he is over twenty-five years of age, and signed this; which I attest.

JOHN LESLIE.

Before me—

JOSÉ DE ZUBIZARETTA, *Notary of Government.*

In the city of St. Augustine, Florida, February 10, 1795, the said Don José Fish presented as a witness Don Lorenzo Llanes, resident of this said city, and a native of it, from whom I, the notary, received the oath which he made by God and the Holy Cross, according to law, under which he promised to say the truth in what he knew and should be asked of him; and it being done so in consequence of the foregoing petition, he said that, as a native, which he is, of this city, having lived in it both during the time of the old Spaniards as well as the greater part of that in which this province was governed by the British arms, he is certain of having always seen the deceased Don Jesse Fish, the father of the memorialist, in possession of the Orange Grove, which, a little more or less, contains the ten thousand acres of land which is stated, which it is also well known to him he possessed, with lawful titles from the old Spanish government; and he answers that this is the truth under his oath; that he is of the age of forty-five years, and signed this; which I attest.

LORENZO LLANES.

Before me—

JOSÉ DE ZUBIZARETTA, *Notary of Government.*

In the city of St. Augustine, Florida, in the same day, month and year, he presented as a witness Don Manuel Solana, native and resident of this said city, from whom I, the notary, received the oath which he made by God and the Holy Cross, according to law, under which he promised to tell the truth, to the best of his knowledge, in what should be asked him, and being so as to the tenor of what the foregoing petition presented by Don José Fish contained, said that, as a native and resident of this said city, in which he has always resided, he is certain that Don Jesse Fish, the person who brings him forward, has possessed in the island called St. Anastasia the plantation called the Orange Grove, in which he lived since the —— of the old Spaniards until they returned to take possession of this province in the year 1784, and since that until 1790 or 1791, when he died, and was buried on the same plantation; and from what the deponent has heard of the result of the survey and valuation, which was generally made before the English had delivered this province to the Spaniards, of the real property of the said Fish, he knows that, at the said plantation, he possessed the ten thousand acres of land, and the deponent corroborates it, a title more or less, from what he has seen on the many occasions when he was at the said plantation, and he answers that this is the truth by virtue of his oath; that he is of the age of forty-six years, and he adds, that he recollects that at the time of the old Spaniards the deponent went with the notary, Don José de Leen, by command of the government, to separate the King's quarries on the said island, in order to grant the remainder of it to Don José Fish, who solicited it after it was actually granted to him, after having made said separation; that, after the Spaniards returned to take possession of the province, by the treaty of peace with the English, who rented it about twenty years, and the second year of possession the government commissioned him, that, with the engineer, Don Manuel de la Roque, and two other workmen, they should designate the old quarries, which they actually did, and they set up four stakes to mark out the lands of the King on the said island, and Fish remained owner of the remainder as he had been; until then he did not sign it, as he said he did not know how to write; which I attest.

Before me—

JOSÉ DE ZUBIZARETTA, Notary of Government.

St. Augustine, Florida, February 12, 1975.

The foregoing proof being completed, and in order to the making a decree, now fully, let the whole be submitted to the collector of the royal treasury, that, as fiscal of it, he may represent as convenient in the discharge of his functions; and, with what he may say, let it be brought forward.

QUESADA.

Before me—

JOSÉ DE ZUBIZARETTA, Notary of Government.

On the same day the foregoing decree was notified to Don José Fish; which I attest.

ZUBIZARETTA, Notary.

On the same date it was communicated to Señor Don Gonzalo Zamorano, collector of the royal treasury, as fiscal of it; which I attest.

ZUBIZARETTA, Notary

St. Augustine, Florida, February 27, 1795.

The collector of the army and the royal domain, as fiscal of it, in the proceedings moved by Don Joseph Fish, on which he was declared owner of the lands which his father possessed annexed to the situation called the Orange Grove, which he bought at auction, and according to the decree of your excellency of the 12th of the present month, in which your excellency was pleased to order that they should be submitted to him, states that, at the sale which was made of the said place, the Orange Grove, to Don Joseph Fish, son of the deceased of the same name, the boundaries of the land were not taken into consideration, and only the valuation of the trees within the precincts of the said grove, without noticing the 10,000 acres of land annexed to it, according to the report of the notary of government and the royal domain, the fiscal minister is of opinion that, although Fish proves by the proofs he has given in that his father possessed, in the time of the British and Spanish government, all that land, he ought to have a right to nothing more than what he proves by the inventory, valuation, and sale which was made of the said Orange Grove; that this land being laid off, the remainder up to the 10,000 acres of land ought to be sold as belonging to his deceased father, and for the benefit of the creditors of his estate, said Fish getting the preference for as much as another would give; that, for the better proof and elucidation of this proceeding, it seems fit to the minister your excellency should be pleased to order that there be annexed to the testimony the inventory, valuation, and sale of the said Orange Grove, which was sold by auction to Fish at the sum of $1,605; and in case that Don Joseph Fish has occasion for public lands, without injury to a third person, the fiscal minister does not find any objection that your excellency should grant them to him as a new settler, according to what his Majesty has commanded of this particular; which is all that offers itself to me for your excellency's information, who will please to determine as appears most just.

GONZALO ZAMORANO.

Let the testimonial which is indicated be placed in continuation, and with it those proceedings returned to the assessor general, that he may consult with me as to what is proper as respects the other points to which the foregoing fiscal representation refers. It is thus decreed and ordered by Señor Don Juan Nepomuceno de Quesada, brigadier of infantry of the royal armies, governor, commander-in-chief, vice royal patron, sub-delegate of the royal domain of this city of St. Augustine, Florida, and its province, for his Majesty, which he signed March 6, 1795; which I attest.

QUESADA.

Before me—

JOSÉ ZUBIZARETTA, Notary of Government.

On the same day the foregoing decree was made known to Don José Fish; which I attest.

ZUBIZARETTA, Notary.

On the same day it was made known to Don Gonzalo Zamorano, collector of the royal revenue, as fiscal of the same; which I attest.

ZUBIZARETTA, Notary.

COMMISSION.

Don Juan Nepomuceno de Quesada, colonel of the royal armies, governor, and commander-in-chief of this city of St. Augustine, Florida, and its province, for his Majesty:

Whereas, in the proceedings which took place in this tribunal, arising from the recovery of the estate which remained by the decease of Don José Fish, resident that was of this city for the payment of his debts, on which the proceedings being opened, several creditors appeared on the memorial of the defender appointed for said estate, Don Fernando Arredondo, I have granted permission that there should be valued and sold at public auction the lands which result in the said proceedings to be the property of Fish, to avoid the deterioration some of them were about to experience, and which would ultimately result to the injury of the creditors, and according to what was resolved in the decree of the 15th of December last, with the houses and lots of the same. Wherefore, according to what has been decreed by me under date of the 16th instant, I have appointed, and do appoint, as said valuators, men skilled in such business, Don Manuel Solana and Don Roque Leonardy, the former of the justice of the peace, and the latter ensign of the local militia of it; that, taking into consideration the boundaries, and whatever else appears on said proceedings, which extract will be placed in continuation, and in presence of the said defender of the estate of Don Vincente Mexias, Don Francisco Revira, as witnesses present, commissioned by the government for want of a notary, let them pass to said places, with proper justice and integrity; for which purpose let the said valuators previously appear before this government, and then proceed, and then begin the commission in the following form:

9*th item*. The place called the Orange Grove, which belongs to the deceased, although the title under which he enjoyed it does not appear in the proceedings; and, when concluded, let it be returned, with their account of what has been done, to this government, to proceed further, as they may think proper. St. Augustine, January 18, 1792.

JUAN NEPOMUCENO DE QUESADA.

VALUATION.

Valuation and survey of the savannas, lands, and lots belonging to the estate of the deceased John José Fish, made by the appraisers appointed, Don Manuel Solana and Don Roque Leonardy, in virtue of a commission by his excellency the governor and commander-in-chief of this city and province for his Majesty, in presence of Don Vincente Mexias and Don Francisco Revira, for want of a notary, and the assistance of the defender, Don Fernando de la Maza Arredondo:

9*th item*. The Orange Grove consists of 540 large orange trees, which are of the best quality, and valued at three dollars, which amount to 1,620 hard dollars; and said property answers to number nine of the commission	$1,620 0
Idem. Three hundred small ones, bearing fruit, at four reals—150 hard dollars	150 0
Idem. Two hundred and fifty orange trees to transplant, at three reals—93 dollars 6 reals	93 6
Idem. Four hundred sour orange trees, at four reals—200 hard dollars	200 0
Idem. One hundred and twenty medlar trees, at four reals—60 hard dollars	60 0
Idem. Seventy-five fig trees, at two reals—18 dollars 6 reals	18 6
Idem. Seventy peach trees, valued at 12 dollars 4 reals	12 4
Idem. Eighty pomegranates, at two reals—20 hard dollars	20 0
Idem. A plantation of lime trees, valued at	25 0
Total	2,180 0

Which valuations the said appraisers appointed declared that they had performed well and faithfully, to the best of their opinions. The first did not sign it, because he said he did not know how to write; the second did it, with the assistant witnesses and the defender. In St. Augustine, Florida, February 3, 1792.

VINCENTE MEXIAS.
ROQUE LEONARDY.
FERNANDO DE LA MAZA ARREDONDO.
FRANCISCO REVIRA.

AUCTION.

In the city of St. Augustine, Florida, January 31, 1792: I, the governor, with the assistance of the collector of the royal revenue, and defender of the estate of the deceased British subject, Don José Fish, and the assistant witnesses, by whom, when it was despatched, for want of a notary, according to what is provided in the decree of said month and year, for the auction and sale of said estate, which remained to be sold at the sound of a drum and by the voice of the free negro Francisco Blasco, who performed the duty of a crier; having called together a sufficient portion of the people, he began in a loud and distinct voice to declare the sale to the best bidder, from eleven in the morning of the said day, stating that it was to be sold without reserve; and several bids and outbids having been made by the meeting, and called for by the crier, without more having been offered, which being finished, the auction, the hour having arrived which was pointed out, was concluded in favor of the individuals, and for the prices which follow: to Don José Fish the Orange Grove was laid off, which answers to number nine of the commission, for the sum of 1,605 hard dollars; and there being no person who would offer a larger sum than the foregoing, the hour pointed out being finished, it was ordered that they should be bid off in favor of the aforesaid, interposing therein my authority and judicial decree, as I can, and of right ought to do, in virtue of which he was declared the purchaser; and there signed with me the collector of the royal domain, and defender of the estate, and the assistant witnesses, for want of a notary.

QUESADA.
ZAMORANO.
FERNANDO DE LA MAZA ARREDONDO.
JUAN FULTON.
JOSÉ FISH.

This is conformable to the commission, ninth clause of it, sixth of the valuation, and that of the auction, which originated from the proceedings of the meetings of creditors caused by the death of the Englishman Don José Fish, which remain in the archives in my charge, to which I refer. And in obedience to orders I have caused the present copy, which I sign and seal in St. Augustine, Florida, March 12, 1795.

JOSÉ DE ZUBIZARETTA, *Notary of Government.*

Having been seen, it was passed over to Don José Fish, and was thus ordered and decreed by Señor Don Juan Nepomuceno de Quesada, brigadier of the infantry of the royal armies, governor, vice royal patron and sub-delegate of the royal domain of this city of St. Augustine, Florida, and its province, for his Majesty, who signed it, with the opinion of his honor the assessor general, March 26, 1795; which I attest.

QUESADA,
LICENTIATE ORTEGA.

Before me—

JOSÉ DE ZUBIZARETTA, *Notary of Government.*

On the same day, month and year, the foregoing decree was notified to Don José Fish; which I attest.

ZUBIZARETTA, *Notary.*

On the same day it was communicated to Señor Don Gonzalo Zamorano, collector of the royal revenue; which I attest.

ZUBIZARETTA, *Notary.*

Don José Fish, a new settler in this province and a subject of his Majesty, in consequence of the proceedings which I am following up, in order to have granted to me the ten thousand acres of land which my deceased father, of the same name, possessed, at the place named the Orange Grove, which was sold at the public auction which was held of all his property left at his decease, before your excellency, in the manner most conformable with law, through the medium of the public solicitor, appears and says that said proceedings shall be delivered to me, to answer the copy which was given me of the representation of the fiscal, informed of the contents of which, and also of the subsequent proceedings of the valuation and auction of the said Orange Grove, the said señor fiscal not giving a solid and convincing reason that his opinion should take effect, contrary to my right and just pretension. And whereas I have sufficiently confirmed it by the proof which I have adduced, proving by it the ancient possession which my father had of said grove, the same for which I have always been anxious, and on which account I have given the excessive price, which the proceedings at auction, copied in the judicial proceedings, show, which sum I would on no account have given for the trees alone, which have been valued much less for the lands which these occupy, in virtue of which, I, submitting to the consideration of your excellency, that I have not enjoyed the least valuable article of the many which my said father left, as even by the possession to which I aspire I injure my interest, giving more for it than it lawfully is worth, solely impelled by the great love I have for that place, in which I have not only been born, but also brought up and educated—the ancient residence of my dear parents and beloved sisters, who are actually under my protection and charge, without any other help to protect them, which I also do for my dear mother, although with very limited means, which can only be obtained from the few trees which have been sold at auction, and to which space only the fiscal pretends to restrict me: Wherefore, and hoping that whatever else may be said in my favor will be taken into consideration, as I cannot express myself properly, from the little knowledge I have in those matters, and for want of directors in them, I ask and pray your excellency to be pleased to grant me the said island as I have solicited; which favor I hope for from the justice of your excellency, swearing that I do not proceed from malice, and what is necessary, &c.

Furthermore, to prove the little value and estimation which the place I claim and bought had, and also my intentions, and that I had given such a large sum, not alone for the trees, but for the land which I have solicited, I pray your excellency to be pleased to order that the present notary place in continuation a copy of the deed which he presented, asking for the island for a valuation, which are united to the principal proceedings of the meeting of the creditors of the estate of my deceased father, and that he may so certify at foot, as, although before it was brought to public sale and auction, there was nothing offered, that all may produce the corresponding effects. I demand justice as above.

JOSÉ FISH.
BARTOLOME DE CASTRO Y FERRER.

The copy which is solicited in the note being placed in continuation, let the whole be passed over to the fiscal representation. It is thus decreed and ordered by Señor Don José de Ortega, advocate of the royal council, lieutenant governor, auditor of war, and assessor general of this city of St. Augustine, Florida, and its province, for his Majesty, who signed it in consequence of the illness of the governor and commander-in-chief April 17, 1795; which I attest.

LICENTIATE ORTEGA.

Before me—

JOSÉ DE ZUBIZARETTA, *Notary of Government.*

On the same day the foregoing decree was made known to Don José Fish; which I attest.

ZUBIZARETTA, *Notary.*

On the same day it was communicated to Señor Don Gonzalo Zamorano, collector of the royal revenue, and attorney for the same; which I attest.

ZUBIZARETTA, *Notary.*

REPRESENTATION.

FLORIDA, *March 22, 1792.*

SEÑOR GOVERNOR AND COMMANDER-IN-CHIEF: Don José Fish, with the greatest respect, states to your excellency that, at the auction which was yesterday made of the property of my deceased father, there was no person who would bid for the island of the Orange Grove; and that being the place which his father inhabited during his life, the possession of it would be the greatest satisfaction to your memorialist, obliging himself to deliver for it $1,605 in government money, in consideration of which, and the said island being abandoned, losing much of its value every day, he prays your excellency to have the goodness to order that he be placed in possession of it. A favor which he hopes for from the benevolence of your excellency.

JESSE FISH.

This is conformable to the original, which is in folio 135 of the proceedings of the meeting of the creditors of the deceased Don José Fish, to which I refer, certifying, as I do certify, that, at the auction which was made March 21, 1792, which runs to leaves one hundred and twenty-nine of the said proceedings, it does not appear that the Orange Grove was brought forward to public outcry and auction; but, from the various memorials which were presented since said auction, soliciting the purchase of some lands, and the plea of the defender of the estate of the said Fish, which runs up to leaves one hundred and forty-two, it is evident that said lands of the Orange Grove had no bidder at that sale at auction. And in conformity with orders I sign and seal these presents in St. Augustine, Florida, April 20, 1795.

JOSÉ DE ZUBIZARETTA, *Notary of Government.*

St. Augustine, *Florida, May* 4, 1795.

The first officer of the chief comptroller's department of the army, who performs the duties thereof, from the occupation of the collector, who is charged with the administration and judicature of the royal revenue, from the illness of his excellency the governor, and as attorney fiscal of the royal revenue, in proceedings moved by Don Joseph Fish, in order that he should be declared owner of the lands which his father, of the same name, possessed, annexed to the situation called the Orange Grove, which was sold at auction, and in consequence of the preceding decree of the 17th of the month before, in which orders were given that he should examine them, states that, by the copy annexed to this proceeding, it is proved that Don Manuel Solana and Don Roque Leonardy were named as appraisers; that, taking into consideration the boundaries which appear in the testamentary proceedings of the deceased Don Joseph Fish, that possession which belonged to him was valued in presence of the defender of the estate, Don Fernando de la Maza Arredondo, of Don Vincente Mexias, and Don Francis Revira, as assistant witnesses, for want of a notary; that, in consequence of this, the said appraisers proceeded only to the valuation of the trees of the said Orange Grove, which amounted to $2,180, without ascertaining boundaries, nor the number of acres of land which these valued trees occupy, much less made mention of ten thousand acres of land as belonging to the estate of the deceased Don Joseph Fish. But what does not admit of doubt is that, in virtue of that valuation of trees, the sale of them at auction was proceeded to, and was made to Don Joseph Fish, son of the deceased of the same name, for the sum of $1,605, a little more than two-thirds of said valuation; and consequently the reason of the fiscal attorney, in his opinion of the 27th February last, is well founded, in considering Don Joseph Fish as owner only of the land and trees which the said valuation occupy, which is what was lawfully sold at auction, because until then nothing appeared of the number of acres of which the said Orange Grove consisted—a defect, in truth, very easy to be remedied by the appraisers, since, it having been promised to them that they should lay off the land, they should have done it with the particular designation of the land which properly belonged to the deceased Fish, from which defect this new appeal arises. Under these circumstances, the fiscal attorney thinks that, in virtue of the proof which Fish has made in these proceedings, he proves that the land or site named the Orange Grove consisted of ten thousand acres of land, and that his intention was, when he bought it, without doubt, under the impression that the ten thousand acres of land which his said father enjoyed would be included in said sale, because, separating the land occupied by the fruit trees which were valued, the remainder is not fit for planting, and as respects the defect, (a negligence of the appraisers, Don Manuel Solana and Don Roque Leonardy, in laying off the boundaries of said ———,) he considers that it ought not to prejudice the right which favors Don Joseph Fish. From all these reflections, to which this proceeding gives rise, the fiscal attorney concludes, and it appears to him that your excellency may order, that the boundaries be marked which correspond to the Orange Grove, to the number of ten thousand acres of land, which he proved belonged to his father, and are annexed to the said Orange Grove; or your excellency will determine what you may think most proper, and with your usual justice.

JOSÉ ANTONIO DE YGUINEZ.

Having examined the proceedings, it was thus decreed and ordered by Señor Don Bartolome Morales, colonel of the infantry of the royal armies, commandant of the third battalion of Cuba, which garrisons this city of St. Augustine, Florida, and political and military governor of it and its province, from the indisposition of the governor, who signed it May 16, 1795; which I attest.

MORALES.
Licentiate ORTEGA.

Before me—

JOSÉ DE ZUBIZARETTA, *Notary of Government*

On the same day the foregoing decree was made known to Don Antonio de Yguinez for his official cognizance; which I attest.

ZUBIZARETTA, *Notary.*

On the same day it was notified to Don José Fish; which I attest.

ZUBIZARETTA, *Notary.*

St. Augustine, *Florida, June* 13, 1795.

To decree more fully, let notice be given to the defender of the estate on Don José Fish, and have the proceedings returned.

MORALES.
Licentiate ORTEGA.

Before me—

JOSÉ DE ZUBIZARETTA, *Notary of Government.*

St. Augustine, *Florida, June* 17, 1795.

Don Rafael Saavedra de Espinosa, attorney general of this city, and defender of the estate of the deceased Don José Fish, who was a resident of this city, and in consequence of the proceedings commenced by Don José Fish, son of the aforesaid deceased, appear before your excellency, and, in the manner most conformable to law, state that I have examined, with all the attention my little capacity allows me, what the son of the said Fish sets forth in favor of his right; and I find that up to this time he proceeded inadvertently to the time when he purchased the place called the Orange Grove at auction, since he ought at that time to have shown clearly and distinctly to what his petition referred; notwithstanding which he now endeavors to remedy his inadvertency by the proof which he has adduced in said proceeding. For all which reasons, and agreeing with the well-founded exposition of the first officer of the royal comptroller's office, Don José Antonio de Yguinez, who performs the functions of his honor the fiscal attorney, which exposition is in folio 47, on which reference is made to the want of precaution with which the appraisers, Don Manual Solana and Don Roque Leonardy, proceeded, who ought to have shown at that time the boundaries which that land had, by adverting to which they would not only have given full effect to their commission, but also obviated the present litigation; and consequently it would have operated with entire effect in the present case, and without waiting for the injury done both the estate and the mover of these proceedings, for which reasons it appears to me that your excellency may grant to Don José Fish the ten thousand acres of land which his deceased father of the same name possessed; and especially your excellency will decree according to what is every day exhibited in your judicial decrees, this being all I have to say as defender of said estate, in compliance with the discharge of my duty.

RAFAEL SAAVEDRA DE ESPINOSA.

Having examined those proceedings, and seen the proof adduced in them by Don José Fish, it appears not only his father, of the same name, possessed, since the time of the old Spaniards, and in that of the British dominion, the ten thousand acres of land, possession of which he claims at the place called the Orange Grove, which he purchased at public auction, but also that he made a bid for the said land, under which his purchase ought to be understood, which defect in not explaining it thus, at that time, should not be prejudicial to him, and has given cause to this litigation. His excellency said that declaring it, as he declared now, he ordered, in consequence, that whether by the right which the burdensome acquisition of the said land gives Fish, which cost him $1,605, which it appears he paid for the purchase of the Orange Grove, or by the right which the ancient possession of his father gives him to the said ten thousand acres of land; or, finally, in consequence of the petition of Fish, that they should be granted to him as a new settler, he be placed in possession of the said land, which it appears his said father possessed, and is already laid off, with the reserve of the quarries, and the remainder which was not granted to his said father, and which the King has reserved, renewing, in case of necessity, at the cost of the interested, the boundaries by said appraisers, Don Manuel Solano, who, at the time of the old Spaniards, and at the new possession by them of the province laid off by order of the governor, the aforesaid quarries, to give possession, as is proven, to the father of the memorialist of the land which he claims, and let them be granted to him on the terms above set forth the present notary, who is commissioned for the purpose, when with the said appraiser, and any other workman that may be necessary, he shall assist at marking the boundary, at which also shall assist, to represent the royal treasury, the person whom the minister of the royal domain may depute for the purpose. All of which shall be made appear on the proceedings with which, and the taxation of the costs, which the interested shall satisfy, this proceeding shall be held as concluded. It was thus decreed and ordered by Señor Don Bartolome Morales, colonel of infantry of the royal armies, commandant of the third battalion of Cuba, which garrisons this city of St. Augustine, Florida, and political and military governor, who signed this, with the opinion of his honor the assessor general, June 19, 1795; which I attest.

BARTOLOME MORALES.
Licentiate JOSEF DE ORTEGA.

St. Augustine, on the same day, month and year the foregoing decree was notified to Don José Fish; which I attest.

ZUBIZARETTA, Notary.

On the same day it was intimated to Don Rafael Saavedra de Espinosa for his cognizance.

ZUBIZARETTA, Notary.

On the same day, month and year it was communicated to the collector of the royal domain for his fiscal cognizance.

ZUBIZARETTA, Notary.

PROOF OF BOUNDARY AND POSSESSION.

Being at the plantation called the Orange Grove, in the island of St. Anastasia, July 10, 1795, in conformity with what is provided in the foregoing decree, we proceeded to the marking the boundaries of the land comprised in these proceedings. Don Manuel Solano, the appraiser appointed for the purpose, passing from said place to where the quarries of the King and of individuals are situated, who, passing along the ancient boundaries with Don José Lorente, chief master of the royal works, who accompanied him, to inform himself; Don Tadeo Arribas, officer of the royal comptroller's office, from the employment of the collector, for his fiscal cognizance, and I, the present notary, went, fixing up stakes, to point out said boundaries, across the island, and separated the said quarries, saying that all besides them was what corresponded to Don José Fish; to whom, being also present, I, the said notary, in discharge of the commission which was conferred upon me, put him in possession of the land pointed out, leading him into it by the hand, and riding together on horseback by various places, until arriving at the dwelling-house; all of which I did as a token of said possession, which he took quietly, peaceably, and without contradiction. In testimony of which, and for the due proof, I have extended the present proceedings, which all signed, with the exception of Solano, who said he did not know how; and all of which I attest.

TADEO DE ARRIBAS.
JOSÉ FISH.
JOSÉ LORENTE.

Before me—

JOSÉ DE ZUBIZARETTA, Notary of Government.

I, Francis J. Fatio, secretary of the board of land commissioners for East Florida, do hereby certify that the foregoing is a true and correct translation from a document in the Spanish language on file in the office of the public archives.

F. J. FATIO, S. B. L. C.

[Translation.]

Having seen that of the justification set forth in these proceedings by Don Joseph Fish, it not only appears that his father, of the same name, possessed since the time of the old Spaniards, and during the British dominion, the ten thousand acres of land, which possession he claims at a place called *Vergel*, which he purchased at public auction, but also he fixed a price to the said land, according to which sale ought to have taken place, which defect, in not making it known at the time of the same, ought not to injure him, and which has given cause to this litigation, his excellency said that, declaring it, as by these presents he does declare, and ordering, in consequence, by the right which the honorable acquisition of the said land, purchased in the sum of $1,605, gives to Fish, as is proven by the sale which he paid for the *Burgal*, or by the right given him by the old possession of his father of the above-mentioned ten thousand acres of land; or, lastly, in consequence of the petition of Fish, that it should be granted him as a new settler, he be put in possession of the same land which is known his father possessed, and is already laid off, with the exception of the quarries, and also what was not granted to his said father, and was always reserved by the King, renewing, if thought necessary, at the expense of the interested, the boundaries by the same skilful person, Don Manuel Solano, who, at the time of the old Spaniards, and the repossession of these of the province, laid off by order of government the aforementioned quarries, to give possession, as was effected to the father of the memorialist of said land, and he is granted on the same terms as above set forth, giving him possession thereof by the present notary, who is commissioned for that purpose, whenever the skilful person named, and some other person that may be named for the purpose of laying off the same, and also the minister of the royal finance, who will attend as representative of the royal exchequer. All of which will be made to appear in the returns, and with the valuation of the costs, which the interested will pay, these proceedings will be at an end. Being thus decreed and ordered by his excellency Don Bartolome Morales, colonel of infantry of the royal armies, commandant of the third battalion of Cuba, which garrisons this city of St. Augustine, Florida, and military governor *pro tem.* of the same and its province, on account of the indisposition of the incumbent; signing it, with the advice of the attorney general, June 19, 1795. I attest.

BARTOLOME MORALES.
LICENTIATE JOSÉ DE ORTEGA.

Before me—

JOSÉ DE ZUBIZARETTA, *Notary of Government.*

NOTIFICATION.

In St. Augustine, on the same day, month and year, I notified the preceding decree to Don José Fish. I attest.

ZUBIZARETTA, *Notary.*

On the same day I addressed Don Rafael Saavedra de Espinosa thereof, on account of his agency. I attest.

ZUBIZARETTA, *Notary.*

On the same day, month and year I made it known to the accountant of the royal finance, Don Gonzalo Zamorano, as attorney of the exchequer. I attest.

ZUBIZARETTA, *Notary.*

Being on the plantation named *Vergel*, situated on the island of St. Anastasia, July 10, 1975, in conformity with what is ordered in the foregoing decree, the measurement of the land comprised in these proceedings was proceeded to, and Don Manuel Solano, a skilful person named for the purpose, proceeded to the place where the quarries of the King and private persons are situated, who, passing along the old boundaries with Don José Lorente, master workman of the royal works, who accompanied him for the purpose of being informed thereon; Don Tadeo de Arribas, officer of the royal accountant office, on account of the occupation of the accountant as attorney of the exchequer, and I, the present notary, placed the stakes for the purpose of pointing out said boundaries, according to the width of said island, separating the said quarries; making known that all the rest was what belonged to Don José Fish, to whom I, the said notary, being likewise present, according to the commission conferred on me, gave him possession of the land pointed out, taking him thereon by the hand, riding together on horseback on different parts, until our arrival at the dwelling-house; all of which he done, as a sign of having taken quiet and undisturbed possession of the same without opposition. In testimony of which, and that it may be duly made known, I made out the present returns, which all signed, except Solano, who said he did not know how; and to all of which I attest.

TADEO DE ARRIBAS.
JOSEPH FISH.
JOSEPH LORENTE.

Before me—

JOSÉ DE ZUBIZARETTA, *Notary of Government.*

According to its original, presented in the proceedings on the subject, to which I refer; and at the request of the party, do seal and sign the present copy on two leaves of ordinary paper, stamps not being used. St. Augustine, Florida, March 29, 1788.

[SEAL.]

JOSÉ DE ZUBIZARETTA, *Notary of Government*

[Translation.]

Don Bartolome Benitez y Galeoz, intendant elect of the province of *Ylocos*, in the Philippine islands, and treasury of the royal finance in this city, received of Don Joseph Fish, resident of this city, 13,880 reals in specie, deposited in these royal chests under my charge, being the amount of a lot opposite Pedro Garcia and the plantation called *The Bergel*, appertaining to the will of his deceased father, which was purchased by him, as is communicated to me from the principal accountant's office in an official letter of the 12th instant. And of the above 13,880 reals in specie, I take charge as a deposit, in virtue of this receipt, of which an account will be taken by the accountant of the royal finance, with the approval of his excellency the governor of this said city and province of St. Augustine, Florida, April 19, 1792, on account of the indisposition of the treasurer and his substitute.

PHILIP DE AGUIRRE.

13,880 reals in specie.

I took an account of the same.

GONZALO ZAMORANO.

Approved.

QUESADA.

A copy from the original on file in this principal accountant's office; and this is made out that it may serve as a security to the interested. St. Augustine, Florida, April 19, 1792.

G. ZAMORANO.

I certify the foregoing to be a true and correct translation from a document in the Spanish language.

F. J. FATIO, *S. B. L. C.*

DECREE.

The board having ascertained the above to be a valid Spanish grant for the 10,000 acres of land, do therefore recommend it to Congress for confirmation. December 16, 1825.

No. 2 *b* [22.]—See Report No. 3.

Teresa Rodriguez vs. The United States. For five thousand five hundred acres of land.

MEMORIAL.

To the honorable the commissioners appointed to ascertain the claims and titles to lands in East Florida:

The memorial of Teresa Rodriguez, widow of Miguel Marcos, for and in behalf of herself, and as guardian to her children, the heirs of the said Miguel Marcos, respectfully showeth: That your memorialist claims title to a tract of land consisting of five thousand five hundred acres, situated on the two margins of a creek running from the west, and empties into the river St. John's, about two miles north of a lake known by the name of Long lake—the mouth of the above creek is called "Big spring;" which said tract of land was granted to the said Miguel Marcos by Governor Estrada October 18, 1815, in virtue of various royal orders, as appears by the original grant in the office of the public records in this city, kept by Wm. Reynolds, and a certified copy herewith presented, which land has never been surveyed. Your memorialist further represents that Don Miguel Marcos was a resident of this province, for many years in the service of his Catholic Majesty, and that he was legally possessed of said tract when this Territory was ceded to the United States. St. Augustine, December 1, 1823.

TERESA RODRIGUEZ,
By her attorney, J. W. SIMONTON.

[Translation.]

Señor Governor: Don Miguel Marcos, first sergeant and sub-lieutenant by brevet of the corps of royal artillery detached to this city, with all respect, states to your excellency that he has served his Majesty for forty-one years in this class, and always commissioned by his chiefs for duty of the highest consideration, which, from his capacity and efficiency, have been placed in his charge; he has, furthermore, been in several actions, and particularly in the invasion of the year 1812, occasioned by the rebels of the province, in which he gave the strongest proofs of his valor, loyalty, and patriotism, always exposing himself to the greatest risks in defence of his King and religion. In attention to all that is set forth, and availing himself of the royal bounty which his Majesty has been pleased to grant to all the officers, sergeants, soldiers, and others who were under arms at that period of 1812, as respects giving them lands gratis in recompense for the proofs of valor and enthusiasm with which they have defended their country; for all which he prays your excellency that, attending to all which has been set forth, and also that he is married and charged with children, you will be pleased to grant him in absolute property five thousand five hundred acres of land, which are vacant, on the two banks of a creek which comes from the west and discharges itself into the river St. John's, about two miles to the north of the lake known as "Long lake" and the mouth of the said creek called "Big spring." A favor which he does not doubt to obtain from the strict justice which your excellency administers. St. Augustine, Florida, October 18, 1815.

MIGUEL MARCOS.

St. Augustine, *Florida, October* 18, 1815.

Let there be granted to the interested, on the terms which he solicits, the lands indicated in this memorial, in virtue of the several royal orders which authorize to that effect; and that he may be able to prove this concession in any event, let the necessary certificates be delivered to him from the secretary's office.   ESTRADA.

I certify the foregoing to be a true and correct translation from a document in the Spanish language on file in the office of the public archives.

F. J. FATIO, *S. B. L. C.*

DECREE.

The board having ascertained that the foregoing is a valid concession for the five thousand five hundred acres of land made to Miguel Marcos, do therefore recommend it to Congress for confirmation. December 16, 1825.

No. 3 *c* [23.]—See Report No. 3.

John W. Simonton vs. The United States. For Cayo Hueso, or Key West.

MEMORIAL.

To the honorable the commissioners appointed to ascertain claims and titles to lands in East Florida:

The memorial of John W. Simonton, a citizen of the United States, respectfully showeth: That your memorialist claims title to a tract of land, being the island of Key West, known by the name of Thomson's island, containing about seven thousand acres of land, situated in East Florida, on the southern coast, about the latitude of 24° 27′ north, longitude 82° 12′ west, from London; which island was granted to Juan P. Salas August 26, 1815, in consideration of services rendered by him to the Spanish government, the grant for which island, signed by Estrada, governor of East Florida, was made in virtue of various royal orders, and is deposited in the office of public archives kept by Mr. Reynolds in the city of St. Augustine, a copy of which is herewith presented. And your memorialist further showeth that he purchased the said island for a valuable consideration of the grantee December 20, 1821, as will appear by the deed of conveyance from Salas and his wife to your memorialist, recorded in the office of public records for the county of St. John's January 23, 1822; that, under the said conveyance, your memorialist took peaceable possession of the said island January 19, 1822, where no living person was on said island, and has ever since held quiet possession of the same; that he has erected many buildings thereon and made many improvements. All of which is respectfully submitted. St. Augustine, Florida, November 25, 1822.

JOHN W. SIMONTON,
By his attorney, JOHN RODMAN

[Translation.]

MEMORIAL.

Señor Governor: Don Juan P. Salas, postmaster of this city, with due respect and submission, states to your excellency that, in consideration of the merits and services which he has performed at different times, both in the corps of royal artillery which garrisons this city, as well as that he has voluntarily and without any gratuity served in the office of the secretary of the government under the command of your excellency, all of which can be proved by legal documents in proper time, and which are well known to your excellency; in virtue of which he humbly prays your excellency to be pleased to grant him, in absolute property, one of the keys, known as Cayo Hueso, situated to the south of Cape Florida. A favor which he does not doubt to obtain from the strict justice which your excellency administers.

JUAN P. SALAS.

St. Augustine, *Florida, August* 23, 1815.

DECREE.

St. Augustine, *Florida, August* 26, 1815.

In virtue of the power by which several royal orders have authorized this government to distribute lands to the inhabitants, subjects of his Majesty, gratis, in this province, let there be granted to the interested in absolute property the key named Hueso, included within the limits of this jurisdiction, without injury to a better right; and, for a proof of this grant at all times, let there be issued from the secretary's office the necessary certificate.

ESTRADA.

I certify the foregoing to be a true and correct translation from a document in the Spanish language on file in the office of the public archives.

F. J. FATIO, *S. B. L. C.*

United States Commercial Agency:

Be it known, on the day of the date hereof, before me, John Mountain, vice commercial agent of the United States of America at Havana, personally came and appeared Don Tomas de Aguilar, who, being duly sworn according to law, upon the solemn oath did depose, declare, and say, that he acted as secretary to the following named governors of East Florida, viz: Don Enrique White, Don Sebastian Kindelan, Don Juan José de Estrada, and Don José Coppinger; that he was acting as the secretary of Don Juan José de Estrada in the month of August, 1815; that some time in the said month of August, 1815, Don Juan P. Salas presented a memorial to Don Juan José de Estrada, who was then acting as governor of East Florida, requesting him, the said Estrada, by virtue of the powers vested in him as the governor of that province, to grant him, the said Salas, the island called Cayo Hueso; that, in conformity to the memorial of the said Silas, Governor Don Juan José de Estrada did grant the said island to the said Salas some time in the said month of August, 1815; that this deponent did put the same on file in the office kept for that purpose. This deponent further states that the consideration of the above grant was, that the said Salas had, in the years 1812, 1813, and 1814, rendered important services in the suppression of an insurrection in the province, and had afterwards faithfully served in various civil capacities, for which he obtained no other remuneration.

TOMAS DE AGUILAR.

Signed and sworn to before me, the said vice commercial agent, to which I have hereunto subscribed my name, and affixed the seal of my office, at Havana, October 30, 1824.

JOHN MOUNTAIN. [L.S.]

Know all men by these presents that we, Juan Pablo Salas, late of East Florida, residing in the city of Havana, Island of Cuba, and Margarita Lorente, the wife of the said Juan, in consideration of the sum of $2,000 to us in hand paid by John W. Simonton, of the State of New Jersey, in the United States of America, the receipt whereof we do hereby acknowledge, have bargained, sold, and quit-claimed, and by these presents do bargain, sell, and quit-claim unto the said John Watson Simonton, and to his heirs and assigns forever, all our and each of our right, title, interest, estate, claim, and demand, both at law and in equity, as well in possession as in expectancy, of, in, and to all that messuage or tract of land called Cayo Hueso or Key West, it being a key or island situated on the south coast of Florida, about the latitude of 24° 27′ N., and longitude 82° 12′ W., from London; which key or island was granted to the said Juan Pablo Salas on August 26, 1815, by his excellency Don Juan Estrada, then governor of East Florida, as will appear by the following copy of memorial and decree of the said governor, viz:

St. Augustin de la Florida, 26 *de Agosto de* 1815.

Señor Governador: Don Juan Pablo Salas, adm'r de correo de esta plaza ante vs. con todo respecto dice; que in atencion a los meritos y servicios que ha contraido en destintas epochas tanto en el real cuerpo de artilleria que guarnece esta plaza con en el que estuvo voluntariamente y sin gratificacion alguna en la secretaria de govierno del mando de vs. como todo puedo acreditarlo con legitimos documentos en tiempo oportuno y que lo son constantes á vs. en esta virtud A. V. S. rendidamente suplica que teniendo en consideracion lo expuesto se seria conceder ne en absoluta propiedad uno de los cayos conosido pr. Cayo Hueso sitnado al sur de Cayo Florida gracio que no duda alcanzar de la recta justicia que vs. administra.

JUAN PABLO SALAS.

St. Augustin de la Florida, 26 de Agosto, 1815.

En virtud de las facultades que autorizan a este gobierno varias reales ordenes sobre repartim: erto de tierra gratis á los habitantes varsalos de S. M. en esta provincia se le concede al interesado en absoluta propriedad el cayo nombrada Hueso, correspondiente á los limites de esta jurisdiccion sin perjuicio de mayor derecho y para que pueda hacer constar esta merced en todo tiempo se le despechara pr. secretaria le necesaria cercificacion.

ESTRADA.

I hereby certify that the foregoing is a true copy of the original, which now remains deposited in the office of the alcalde and notary public of county of St. John's, province of East Florida, William Reynolds, the said Juan Pablo Salas hereby declaring that himself, nor any one for him, has ever disposed of, to any person or persons, any right, title, or interest, ceded to him by the grant of the said Governor Estrada, of which a copy is hereinbefore written, with all and singular the hereditaments and appurtenances thereunto belonging.

In witness whereof, we have hereunto set our hand and seals at Havana this 26th of December, in the year 1821.

JUAN P. SALAS.
MARGARITE LORENTE.

Signed, sealed, and delivered in the presence of—
　　　JOHN MOUNTAIN.
　　　JAMES BURNHAM.

DECREE.

The board having ascertained the above to be a valid Spanish grant for the island in question, made to Juan P. Salas, who sold and conveyed the same to claimant, do therefore recommend it to Congress for confirmation.　December 14, 1825.

[Number four (24) was not returned to the General Land Office by the commissioners.]

No. 5 e [25.]—Report No. 3.

Archibald Clark vs. The United States.　For eighty thousand acres of land.

MEMORIAL.

To the honorable the commissioners appointed to ascertain claims and titles to lands in East Florida:

The petition of Archibald Clark, of the State of Georgia, respectfully showeth: That your memorialist claims title to a tract of land consisting of eighty thousand acres, situated at or near Cape Florida, bounded on the east by the Atlantic ocean, on the south by Black Acres creek, on the west by vacant land, and on the north by the Rio Nueva, as by reference to the plat herewith affixed, with the evidences of title, will more fully appear; which title your memorialist derives from a grant made to John Arrambide by provincial deputation at Havana, Governor Apodaca presiding, December 4, 1813.　And your memorialist further showeth that he is at this time, by his tenants, in actual possession of said lands; that he is a citizen of the United States and resident of St. Mary's, Georgia.　St. Augustine, May 17, 1824.

ARCHIBALD CLARK.

[Translation.]

RECORD.

In the city of Havana, January 12, 1814, I, the undersigned notary public of his Majesty, of the number of this city, in virtue of the orders of Don Ignacio Pedroso, constitutional alcalde of the same, by a decree of this date, made to a memorial presented by Don Juan Xavier de Arrambide, I have recorded in continuation said memorial, with the document accompanying it, which is another presented to the most excellent captain general, superior political chief of the province, and president of the most excellent provincial deputation, asking for a testimonial of the certified act of the same passed on the 4th of December last; which testimonial appears placed in continuation of it by the government notary of this city.　And to attest which, and said documents remaining recorded, I sign these presents, Don Vicente Perez, Don Manuel Farnari, and Don Francisco de Silva, residents, being witnesses.

JOSÉ LEAL.

MEMORIAL.

Señor Constitutional Alcalde: Don Juan X. de Arrambide, a resident of this city, with due respect, states that, requiring that the annexed document be recorded in one of the public offices of this city, in order that the necessary testimonials may be taken from it, he supplicates that you will please to order that it be recorded in the notary's office, where he presents it, and that the copies I require be furnished me.　Havana, January 12, 1814.

JUAN XAVIER DE ARRAMBIDE.

Havana, January 12, 1814.

As he asks for.

PEDROSO.
JOSÉ LEAL.

MEMORIAL.

Most excellent sir, captain general, superior political chief of this island and the two Floridas:

Don Juan Xavier de Arrambide and Goecoechea, native of Puerto Real, and a resident of this city, with due respect, states to your excellency that, on the meeting of the most excellent provincial deputation held on the 4th instant, it was ordered that the honorable council of St. Augustine, Florida, should grant me, say, two leagues to each cardinal point of the compass, in the territory of that province, for the ends contained in my memorial of the 28th of May of that year. Wherefore, I pray your excellency to be pleased to order the person whose duty it is to furnish me with an authorized copy of that act, which he hopes for from the justice of your excellency. Havana, December 9, 1813.

JUAN XAVIER ARRAMBIDE Y GOECOECHEA.

DECREE.

HAVANA, *December* 10, 1813.

Let the memorialist receive a testimonial of the determination stated by him in his memorial.

APODACA.

TESTIMONIAL.

I certify that at the session held by the most excellent provincial deputation the day of the date hereof, presided over by his excellency the captain general, superior political chief of the province, there was read the report of the commission presented on the 15th of the preceding November, on the solicitation of Don Juan Xavier de Arrambide, that there should be granted him in property a certain extent of land in East Florida, with the object of establishing on it mills for sawing timber and of exporting resins, with respect to which Señor Don José Ferrequi said that in the distribution of these lands the letter of the sovereign decree of the 4th of January of this year ought not to be observed, but rather the laws of the Indies in the matter, as that decree applies to the division of vacant and royal lands in the provinces already peopled, in which state the Floridas are not; since, with the exception of a small part of their coasts, the remainder of which, and the entire of the interior, which is of incalculable extent, remains uncultivated and desert. Arrambide ought, therefore, to be considered as one of the settlers of whom the said laws treat, and, consequently, the land granted to him in absolute property should not be limited to the small tracts pointed to in said decree; and having sufficiently discussed the business, the most excellent deputation agreed that in virtue of the conformity manifested by the council of St. Augustine, Florida, in its act of the 16th of August last, with which the deputation resolved in this case, after having consulted the captain general, superior political chief of that province, with a certified copy of the present act, the most excellent deputation were pleased to state to that council that they grant, in property, to Don Juan X. de Arrambide two leagues square to each cardinal point of the compass of the land he may choose, from the mouth of the Rio Nueva, which discharges itself on the coast of East Florida, and the *Punta Larga*, on the south part, following the same course to the seashore, permitting him to cut timber without the square set forth, and, when the bounding lands are not granted to other inhabitants, prohibiting him from burning them and offending the Indians, returning the proceedings to the commission, that they may propose the best mode of distributing the remaining lands, conforming as nearly as possible to the said decree. Havana, December 4, 1813.

TOMAS ROMAY, *Secretary.*

AT FOOT—This is conformable to the original, which I returned to the office of the secretary of government, to which I refer; and, in obedience to orders, I put these presents. Havana, December 14, 1813.

MIGUEL MENDEZ.

This is conformable to the originals, which are recorded with the public instrument in my archives, to which I refer; and, in compliance with orders in the decree made to the memorial first copied, I give these presents. Havana, January 13, 1814.

[A cipher.]
[A SEAL.]
JOSÉ LEAL.

We attest that Don José Leal, by whom the foregoing copy appears authenticated, is notary public of his Majesty, of the number belonging to this city, faithful, lawful, of entire confidence, and to persons such as himself full faith and credit is given both in law and equity; and, to confirm it, we agree to give these presents, which we sign and seal with that of our college. Havana, dated as above.

[A SEAL.]   [A SEAL.]   [A SEAL.]

MAURICIO PERRAS PITA, *Notary of War.*
JOSÉ LORENZO RODRIGUEZ.
ESTABAN ESQUINEZ.

I certify the foregoing to be a true and correct translation of a document in the Spanish language.

F. J. FATIO, *S. B. L. C.*

The most excellent captain general states me, under date of the 10th of December last, that which I copy: "Don Juan Xavier Arrambide having solicited that a certain extent of land should be granted him in East Florida for the reasons and object which he sets forth, I enclose to your excellency a copy of the opinion given me by the most excellent provincial deputation on the subject, which I have agreed to, to the end that, on your part, it may have due course and completion, which I pass over to your honors for your information and consequent ends, accompanied with a certified copy of the opinion mentioned, receipt of which you will advise of. God preserve you many years. St. Augustine, March 16, 1814.

SEBASTIAN KINDELAN.

BAHAMA ISLANDS.

Know all men by these presents that I, John Arrambide, of East Florida, but now in Nassau, New *Province*, have made, ordained, constituted, and appointed, and by these presents do make, ordain, and appoint, James Bixby, of Georgia, (one of the United States of America,) my true and lawful attorney, for me, and in my name and stead, and to my use, to sell all, or any part or parts, of my tracts of land in East Florida, whereon I reside, containing 90,000 acres, or thereabouts; and I do further empower and authorize my said attorney to transfer by deed whatever he may sell as aforesaid, promising and engaging to satisfy and confirm whatever my said attorney may do in the premises.

In witness whereof, I have hereunto set my hand and seal at Nassau, New Providence, this 15th day of July, in the year of our Lord 1817, and in the 57th year of his Majesty's reign.

JOHN ARRAMBIDE.

Signed, sealed, and delivered in the presence of—
    JOSEPH BIXBY.

STATE OF GEORGIA, *County of Camden:*

This indenture, made the 1st day of December, in the year of our Lord 1817, and in the independence of the United States of America the forty-second, between James Bixby, of Camden county, attorney in fact for Jean Arrambide, of Havana, in the Island of Cuba, of the one part, and Archibald Clark, of the county and State aforesaid, attorney at law, of the other part, witnesseth: That the said James Bixby, attorney in fact as aforesaid, for and in consideration of the sum of $20,000 to him, the said James Bixby, attorney in fact as aforesaid, in hand well and truly paid, the receipt whereof is hereby acknowledged, and thereof, and of every part and parcel thereof, doth acquit, exonerate, and discharge the said Archibald Clark, his heirs, executors, administrators, and each and every of them, he, the said James Bixby, attorney as aforesaid, and by virtue of the special powers in him by power of attorney vested, dated and executed July 15, 1817, hath granted, bargained, sold, aliened, conveyed, and confirmed, and by these presents doth grant, bargain, sell, alien, convey, and confirm unto the said Archibald Clark, his heirs and assigns, forever, 80,000 acres of land, being part of that tract of land situated on the coast of East Florida, on New river, containing 90,000 acres, be the same more or less: bounded eastwardly by the Atlantic ocean, westwardly by vacant lands, northwardly and southwardly by vacant lands, at the time of the issuing the royal grant for the same, a description of the aforesaid tract of land being hereunto annexed, and is intended to form a supplementary part of this indenture, and which said grant stands on record in the office of the *scrivana* in the town of St. Augustine, in East Florida aforesaid; to have and to hold the aforesaid 80,000 acres of land, part of the above-described tract, with all the improvements, rights, hereditaments to the same belonging, or in anywise appertaining, unto the said Archibald Clark, his heirs and assigns, forever. And the said James Bixby, as attorney as aforesaid for him, the said Jean Arrambide, doth hereby warrant and defend the premises *aforesaid, the claim or claims* of him, the said Jean Arrambide, his heirs, executors, or assigns, and against the claims of all and every person or persons whomsoever, by virtue of these presents.

In witness whereof, the said James Bixby, as attorney as aforesaid, hath hereunto set his hand and seal, at St. Mary's, in the State and county aforesaid, this 1st day of December, in the year of our Lord 1817, and in the forty-second year of the independence of the United States of America.

JOHN ARRAMBIDE,
By his attorney in fact, JAMES BIXBY.

Signed, sealed, and delivered in presence of—
    AND. ATKINSON.
    R. HOLCOMBE.

DECREE.

The board having ascertained the above to be a valid Spanish grant for the 80,000 acres made previous to January 24, 1818, do therefore recommend it to Congress for confirmation. December 15.

No 6 *f* [26]—See REPORT No. 3.

Joseph Delespine vs. *The United States.   For ninety-two thousand one hundred and sixty acres of land.*

MEMORIAL.

TERRITORY OF FLORIDA, *East Florida:*

To the honorable the commissioners appointed to ascertain claims and titles to lands in East Florida:

The memorial of Joseph Delespine respectfully showeth: That your memorialist claims title, in fee simple absolute, in and to ninety-two thousand one hundred and sixty acres of land, situated and being in East Florida aforesaid. Your memorialist shows that on the 15th day of November, in the year 1813, one Juan Xavier de Arrambide, a Spanish subject, applied to a certain body—a committee called the "Provincial Committee"—then established in the city of Havana, in the Island of Cuba, whose business and duty it was to consider, consult, advise, and determine as to the most proper and advantageous distribution and disposition of the public lands in the Island of Cuba, and also in the then provinces of East and West Florida, over which its authority in this respect extended, for a grant, in absolute ownership and property, of two leagues of land to each point of the compass, for the purpose of erecting saw-mills, making rosin, &c.; that the said committee, at its session on the aforesaid 15th day of November, 1813, at which its president, his excellency the then captain general of the Island of Cuba and of the two Floridas, was present and presided, resolved that the lands solicited by the said Juan Xavier de Arrambide should be granted to him in complete and absolute ownership and property and that his excellency the said captain general, at the said session of the said committee, directed that the act or proceedings of the said committee at their said session, in relation to the said grant of land, should be transmitted to the governor and chief civil magistrate of East Florida, in order that the corporation of the said province might make a grant to the said Juan Xavier de Arrambide of two square leagues of land to each point of the compass, on the spot which he, the said Juan Xavier de Arrambide, might choose, from the mouth of the Rio Nueva, which empties itself on the coast of Florida, to the Punta Larga, on the south side, running said side up to the seashore. Your memorialist further shows that at a regular meeting of the corporation of East Florida, held at St. Augustine, March 22, 1814, at which presided his excellency Don Sebastian Kindelan, then governor and chief civil magistrate of East Florida, a memorial of the said Juan Xavier de Arrambide, dated at the Havana, on the 1st day of February, in the year 1814, was presented, accompanied by an authenticated copy of the aforesaid resolution and act of the said provincial committee, and of the aforesaid order of the captain general; in which memorial the said Juan Xavier de Arrambide, after referring to the said proceedings of the provincial committee and of the captain general, solicited a grant of the said two leagues of land to each point of the compass to the north of the river De los Miamies, which lies on the northwest of Cayo Viscayno; that the said corporation, at its said meeting, resolved to grant, and did grant, to the said Juan Xavier de Arrambide the said lands then solicited by him, in full and absolute property, and directed that a copy of this act and proceedings in relation to the claim of the said Juan Xavier de Arrambide, together with his memorial to said corporation, should be duly authenticated by their secretary, and be directed to him, the said Arrambide, for his security, and as a title to the said land, which was accordingly done; all of which will fully and at large appear by a reference to certified copies of the proceedings and acts hereinbefore mentioned and set forth, now here submitted and filed, and marked exhibit A.

Your memorialist further shows that immediately after the completion of the said grant the said Juan Xavier de Arrambide entered upon and took actual possession of the lands embraced by it, and carried a number of persons with him from the Island of Cuba for the purpose of settling the said lands, and of promoting and proceeding in the purposes he had in view in obtaining the said land; that the said Arrambide for several years prosecuted the settlement and improvement of the said land, and the making of tar and rosin, and the cutting of timber thereon, when he was driven from it, and compelled to abandon his plans founded on the possession of it, by the hostility of the Indians and fugitive negroes who infested that part of the country; that the said Juan Xavier de Arrambide (by his agent, lawfully authorized in that behalf) sold and conveyed the said lands, in absolute property, to one George J. F. Clarke, a Spanish subject, according to the formalities required by the Spanish law, April 29, 1820, as will appear by a certified copy of the said conveyance herewith submitted and filed, and marked exhibit B; that, after the purchase of the said land by the said George J. F. Clarke, that is to say, May 7, 1821, he applied for, and obtained from the then governor of East Florida an order for the survey of the said land, which will appear from a certified copy thereof herewith submitted and filed, and marked exhibit C; that, after the appointment of the surveyor to execute the said order, his acceptance thereof, and preparations made to effect the said survey, it was found that it could not, with any safety, be attempted, on account of the decided and open hostility of the Indians to the whites just at that period, in consequence of which the design to survey the said land at that time was laid aside; that, January 4, 1822, the said George J. F. Clarke sold and conveyed the said lands to one John B. Strong, as will appear by his original conveyance thereof, herewith submitted and filed, and marked exhibit D; and that the said John B. Strong, for a large and valuable consideration paid to him by your memorialist, sold and conveyed the said lands and their appurtenances to your memorialist, in fee simple absolute, February 25, 1822, as will appear by the original conveyance thereof to your memorialist, now here submitted and filed, and marked exhibit E.

Your memorialist further avers and shows that there are a number of families and settlers established on the said land under the title of your memorialist—believes are persons placed on the said lands by the aforesaid Arrambide at the time he attempted to establish himself on it as aforesaid; and that considerable improvements have been made thereon by clearing and cultivating the ground and erecting buildings. All of which is respectfully submitted by your memorialist.

JOSEPH DELESPINE,
By his attorney, JOHN DRYSDALE.

['Translation.]

RECORD.

In the city of Havana, January 12, 1814, I, the undersigned notary public of his Majesty, of the number of this city, in virtue of the orders of Don Ignacio Pedroso, constitutional alcalde of the same, by a decree of this date made to a memorial presented by Don Juan Xavier de Arrambide, I have recorded in continuation said memorial, with the document accompanying it, which is another presented to the most excellent captain general, superior political chief of this province, and president of the most excellent provincial deputation, asking for a testimonial of the certified act of the same passed on the 4th December last; which testimonial appears placed in continuation of it by the government notary of this city, and to attest which, and said documents remaining recorded, I sign these presents; Don Vincent Perez, Don Manual Fornari, and Don Francisco de Silva, residents, being witnesses.

JOSÉ LEAL.

MEMORIAL.

Señor Constitutional Alcalde: Don Juan Xavier de Arrambide, a resident of this city, with due respect states that, requiring that the annexed document be recorded in one of the public offices in this city, in order that the necessary testimonial may be taken from it, he supplicates that you will please to order that it be recorded in the notary's office, where he presents it, and that the copies I require be furnished me. Havana, January 12, 1814.

JUAN X. DE ARRAMBIDE.

Havana, January 12, 1814.
As he asks for.

PEDROSO.
JOSÉ LEAL.

MEMORIAL.

Most excellent sir, captain general, superior political chief of this island and the two Floridas:

Don Juan Xavier de Arrambide and Goecocha, native of Puerto Real, and a resident of this city, with due respect states to your excellency that, on the meeting of the most excellent provincial deputation held on the 4th instant, it was ordered that the honorable council of St. Augustine of Florida should grant me, say, two leagues to each cardinal point of the compass, in the territory of that province, for the ends contained in my memorial of the 28th of May of that year. Wherefore, I pray your excellency be pleased to order the person whose duty it is to furnish me with an authenticated copy of that act; which he hopes from the justice of your excellency. Havana, December 9, 1813.

JUAN XAV. DE ARRAMBIDE AND GOECOCHA.

DECREE.

HAVANA, *December* 10, 1813.

Let the memorialists receive a copy of the decision stated by him in his memorial.

APODACA.

COPY.

I certify that, at the session held by the most excellent provincial deputation the day of the date hereof, presided over by his excellency the captain general, superior political chief of the province, there was read the report of the commission presented on the 15th of the preceding November, on the solicitation of Don Juan Xavier de Arrambide, that there should be granted him in proportion a certain extent of land in East Florida, with the object of establishing on it mills for sawing timber, and of exporting rosins, with respect to which Señor Don José Terragues said that, in the distribution of those lands, the letter of the sovereign decree of the 4th January of this year ought not to be observed, but rather the laws of the Indies on the matter, as that decree applies to the division of vacant and royal lands in the provinces already peopled, in which state the Floridas are not; since, with the exception of a small part of their coasts, the remainder of which, and the entire of the interior, which is of incalculable extent, remains uncultivated and desert. Arrambide ought, therefore, be considered as one of the settlers of whom the said law treats, and, consequently, the lands granted to him in absolute property should not be limited to the small tracts indicated in said decree; and having sufficiently discussed the business, the most excellent deputation agreed that, in virtue of the conformity manifested by the ——— of St. Augustine, Florida, in its act of the 16th August last, with which the deputation resolved, in this case, after having consulted the captain general, superior political chief of that province, with a certified copy of the present act, the most excellent deputation were pleased to state to that council that they grant, in property, to Don Juan Xavier de Arrambide two leagues square to each cardinal point of the compass of the land he may choose, from the mouth of New river, (Rio Nueva,) which discharges itself on the coast of East Florida and the Long Point, (Puerto Largo,) on the south part, following the same course to the seashore, permitting him to cut timber without the square set forth; and, when the bounding lands are not granted to other inhabitants, prohibiting him from burning them, and of offending the Indians, returning the proceedings to the commission, that they may propose the best mode of distributing the remaining lands, conforming, as nearly as possible, to the said decree.

TOMAS ROMAY, *Secretary.*

HAVANA, *December* 4, 1813.

AT FOOT.—This is conformable to the original which I returned to the office of the secretary of government, to which I refer; and, in obedience to orders, I put these presents.

MIGUEL MENDEZ.

HAVANA, *December* 14, 1818.

This is conformable to the originals which are recorded with the public instruments in my archives, to which I refer; and, in compliance with the orders in the decree made to the memorial first copied, I give these presents.

JOSÉ LEAL. [L. S.]

[*A cypher.*]
HAVANA, *September* 17, 1814.

I certify the foregoing to be a true and correct translation from a document in the Spanish language.

F. J. FATIO, *S. B. L. C.*

Don Juan de Entralgo, secretary to the honorable council of the city of St. Augustine, East Florida:

I certify that at an ordinary session held the 22d of March last, at which met Señors Don Sebastian Kindelan and O'Regan, knight of the order of St. James, brigadier of the national armies, military governor and political chief, president; Don José Sanchez, constitutional alcalde; Don Francisco Pons and Den Pedro Rodriguez de Cala, regidores; and Don José Bernardo Reyes, syndic, they resolved, amongst other things, the following act: "Resolution.—At this session the secretary of the council has presented a representation, directed to this honorable body, by Don Juan Xavier de Arrambide under date of the 1st of February last, enclosing a copy of the resolution of the most excellent provincial deputations, respecting the concession of two leagues to each point of the compass, which were made to him with the consent of the most excellent the captain general, political chief of the Island of Cuba and both Floridas, in the territory of the south side of this province, soliciting that this honorable body do despatch to him the title of property of the said two leagues of land to the north of the river Miamies, which are on the northwest side of Cayo Biscayno, and the gentlemen agreeing, having in view the said determination of his excellency, with an authenticated copy of the said most excellent deputation, which was communicated to this council by the president, his excellency the governor, in obedience as well to the resolution of the aforesaid deputation as to the approval of the most excellent captain general, they determined to grant the favor solicited by Don Juan Xavier de Arrambide; for which end, and that he may be able to prove the title of property which he claims, let the present secretary deliver to him an authenticated copy of the said representation and this act, which shall be given him for his security as a title for the grant which is made to him, with the exception of everything which, according to the laws, this body ought to know of the business."

REPRESENTATION.

To the honorable the council:

Don Juan Xavier de Arrambide, with due attention, lays before your honors that, it having been determined by this provincial deputation, as appears from the act of the 4th of December, and is confirmed by the annexed copy, to grant me in property two leagues to each point of the compass, in the territory on the south part of that province, for the purposes set forth in my petition of the 28th May of last year, and what appears likewise from the said act, leaving to my choice the place where I should settle myself, and desiring to effect it two miles to the north of the river of Miamies, which is at the northwest side of Cayo Biscayno, I pray your honors to be pleased to expedite to me the corresponding title of property for the two leagues of land to each point of the compass, agreeably to this situation, reserving to myself to produce the plat of the said lands, and what is made known on the subject, as soon as I find myself prepared to take it out, to commence the establishment which I am to effect.

JUAN XAVIER DE ARRAMBIDE.

HAVANA, *February* 1, 1814.

This is a copy.

JUAN DE ENTRALGO, *Secretary.*

ST. AUGUSTINE, *Florida, June* 3, 1814.

Don Manuel Lopez Garcia, ministerial officer and royal collector of the national chests of this city of St. Augustine, of Florida, and Don José Antonio Yguinez, treasurer *pro tem.* of them:

We certify that Don Juan de Entralgo, by whom the foregoing certificate is signed, is secretary of this honorable council, as he styles himself, and notary *pro him* of the government in this said city, the only one in it and its province; and to such persons as him full faith and credit is given, both in law and equity. To confirm which, we sign these presents at the request of the party in this city of St. Augustine, Florida, June 6, 1814.

MANUEL LOPEZ.
JOSÉ ANTONIO YGUINEZ.

I certify the foregoing to be a true and correct translation from a document in the Spanish language.
F. J. FATIO, *S. B. L. C.*

[Translation.]

POWER.

Be it known that I, Don Juan Xavier de Arrambide y Goecocha, resident in this city, declare that I give my power, full and sufficient, as may be required and necessary in law, to Mr. John B. Strong, a citizen of the United States of America, general, that he may charge, defend, liquidate, sell, and finish whatever affairs may appertain to or concern him in the said States, with a revocation of every other power, particularly that granted in favor of Don John Forbes, as I declare of no value, whatever document may have reference to it, and especially for the sale of the lands I have in East Florida, delivering the respective writings which he may make valid and firm, as if I myself were present in person; and, in case of necessity, sue with writings, witnesses, proofs, other documents and papers, which he may take possession of wherever they shall be found; make protests, citations, and summonses; demand executions, captions, discharges, detention, and releasing of property, sale, sale to pay debts, and auction of what he shall take possession of should it be adjudged to him, and for every kind of proofs the necessary terms, and renounce them; power to delegate; warrants to comply precepts and commissions, which he may cause to be read publicly, and made known to whomsoever and wheresoever he finds it necessary; he may see and examine witnesses presented and sworn on the adverse side, make objections to and find defects in them; be surety for persons, and vouch for depositions; make oaths and recusations; hear and bring to a conclusion judicial decrees and interlocutory and definitive sentences; consent to what is favorable, and petition and appeal to what is adverse; instruct and direct appeals, and whatever competent legal courses he can and ought to pursue; finally, to proceed, act, and do all other matters, judicial and extra-judicial, required in any of my affairs; for which, and all evidences and dependencies, I give this power, without limitation, with free and general administration, power of commencing suits, swearing, sustaining them, and concluding them himself, or compromising them through arbitrations, juries, or friendly references, and exonerating the parties in form; for the firmness and accomplishment of what he shall perform, in virtue of this I bind present and future property, power of tribunals, and renunciation of laws. In testimony of which, this is dated in the city of Puerto Príncipe, January 17, 1820. I, the notary of the council, attest that I know the grantor, who said as is set forth and signed this, there being witnesses present, Don Pedro de Zespedez, Don Pio de Evia, and Don Ramon de la Torre.

JUAN XAVIER DE ARRAMBIDE & GOECOCHA.

Before me—

JOSÉ RAFAEL CASTELLANOS.

This is conformable to the original, to which I refer, and at the desire of the party caused it to be written. Puerto Príncipe, January 20, 1820.

JOSÉ RAFAEL CASTELLANOS.

This is conformable to the originals which exist in the archives in my charge, to which I refer; and by desire of the party, sign and seal the present copy on two leaves of common paper, the stamped not being in use. St Augustine, Florida, April 20, 1820.

JUAN DE ENTRALGO, &c.

I certify the foregoing to be a true and correct translation from a document in the Spanish language.
F. J. FATIO, *S. B. L. C.*

[Translation.]

CONVEYANCE.

Be it known that I, John B. Strong, citizen of the United States of America, at present a resident of this city, and attorney of Don Juan Xavier de Arrambide Goicoechea, resident of Puerto Príncipe, in the Island of Cuba, as appointed by him before the notary of that council, Don José Rafael Castellanos,

January 17 of the present year, a copy of which shall be added in continuation, and is sufficient for what shall be said. I declare that I really sell to Don George Clarke, an inhabitant of this province, surveyor general in it, two leagues of land to each point of the compass, which is in square in the territory on the south side of this province, situated about two leagues to the north of the river Miamies, which is on the northwest side of Cayo Biscayno, and is between the mouth of Rio Nueva, (New river,) which discharges itself on the coast of Florida, and the long point on the south side, following the same course to the sea-shore; which land was granted to me in full property by the constitutional junta of this city, by an act passed March 22, 1814, in virtue of the determination of the most excellent captain general of the Island of Cuba and both Floridas, communicated with an authenticated copy of the opinion of the most excellent provincial deputation. And I sell him the said two leagues to each point of the compass on the terms and under the circumstances on which they were granted to my said principal, Don Juan Xavier de Arrambide Goicoechea, with its pastures, roads, waters, entrances, outlets, uses, customs, rights, and services, in the manner which corresponds to him, and that he may use it for himself and his successors free of all encumbrance, (as I, the notary, certify from the result of my search of the book of mortgages in my charge, which I have made for the purpose,) at the price of $20,000, which the purchaser has paid me in current money, which I acknowledge as delivered to my will. I renounce proof, laws of delivery, exception to money not counted, fraud, and everything else in the case, for which I deliver a receipt in form; in virtue of which I separate my principal from the right of property, possession, use, seigniory, and other actions, real and personal, which he had and held to said lands, as I cede, renounce, and transfer it to the purchaser and his representatives, that, as his own, he may take possession in the manner most convenient to him by virtue of this deed, by which he may dispose at his will of the thing acquired without occasion for further proof, from which I relieve him. And I bind my principal to the execution and guaranty of this sale in sufficient form, and as may best suit, in favor of the purchaser, with the goods of my principal, present and future power and submission to the tribunals of his domicil, that they may compel him to its performance as by sentence consented and passed in authority of an adjudged case, in which I renounce all the laws, customs, rights, and privileges in his favor, and the general law in form which prohibits it. And I, Don William Travers, being present by order of the purchaser, Don George Clarke, accept in his favor this deed, and by it receive as purchased the said lands at the price and agreement on which they have been sold to him, which he gives as delivered to his will, with a renunciation of proof, laws of delivery, those of a thing not seen or received, fraud, and everything else in the case, for which I deliver a receipt in form.

In testimony of which, this is dated in this city of St. Augustine, Florida April 29, 1820. I, the notary, attest that the parties said thus and signed it; there being witnesses, Don Bernardo Segui, who served as interpreter, there being no public one; Don Pedro Miranda and Don Fernando de la Maza Arredonno, jr, inhabitants present.

JOHN B. STRONG.
WILLIAM TRAVERS.
As interpreter, BERNARDO SEGUI.

Before me—

JUAN DE ENTRALGO, *Notary of Government.*

I certify the foregoing to be a true and correct translation from a document in the Spanish language.

F. J. FATIO, *S. B. L. C.*

THE STATE OF SOUTH CAROLINA:

Know all men by these presents that I, John B. Strong, of the city of St. Augustine, in East Florida, but at present in Charleston, in the State aforesaid, for and in consideration of the sum of $20,000 to me in hand paid by Joseph Delespine, of the same place, but at present in the city of Charleston, in the State aforesaid, have granted, bargained, sold, and released, and by these presents do grant, bargain, sell, and release unto the said Joseph Delespine all that certain piece or parcel of land situate, lying, and being in the southern part of the province of East Florida, of two leagues of land to each point of the compass, in the northern part of the river De los Miamies, which lies to the northward of Cayo Viscayno or Key Biscayno, and which said tract contains 92,162 acres, be the same more or less; and which said tract of land was granted to Juan X. de Arrambide by the captain general of the Island of Cuba and of the two Floridas, and confirmed by the governor and corporation of East Florida, and was sold to me by the said Arrambide in Puerto Principé, in the Island of Cuba, in the month of July, 1819; and, for a more particular description of said tract of land and everything relating thereto, more particular reference may be had to the original grant made to the said Juan X. Arrambide, together with all and singular the rights, members, hereditaments, and appurtenances to the said premises belonging, or in anywise incident or appertaining, to have and to hold all and singular the premises before mentioned unto the said Joseph Delespine, his heirs and assigns, forever. And I do hereby bind myself, my heirs, executors, and administrators, to warrant and forever defend all and singular the said premises unto the said Joseph Delespine, his heirs and assigns, against myself and my heirs, and all other persons lawfully claiming, or to claim, the same in any part thereof.

Witness my hand and seal this 25th day of February, in the year of our Lord 1822, and in the 46th year of the independence of the United States of America.

JOHN B. STRONG.

Signed, sealed, and delivered in the presence of—

    Wm. W. Cormick.
    Thos. W. Holwell.

DECREE.

The board having ascertained the above to be a valid Spanish grant for the 92,160 acres, made previous to January 24, 1818, do therefore recommend it to Congress for confirmation. December 14.

GEORGIA, *Camden County:*

This indenture, made June 4, 1822, between George J. F. Clarke, of the province of East Florida, on the one part, and John B. Strong, of said province, on the other part, witnesseth: That the said George

J. F. Clarke, for and in consideration of the sum of one dollar to him in hand paid at and before the sealing and delivery of these presents, the receipt whereof is hereby acknowledged, hath granted, bargained, sold, and conveyed, and by these presents doth grant, bargain, sell, and convey unto the said Strong a quantity of land lying in the southern part of said province, situated two leagues north of the river Miamies, which lies to the northwest of Key Viscayno, and containing two leagues measurement to each wind, as will more fully appear by the grant thereof made by the Spanish government to John X. Arrambide, and which said quantity of land was sold to said Clarke by the said Strong, as the attorney of said Arrambide, as per an instrument executed in the records of St. Augustine, East Florida, April 29, 1820, to have and to hold unto him, the said John B. Strong, his heirs and assigns, the said lands in the same state that he, said Clarke, received them from him; and the said George J. F. Clarke, for himself, his heirs, executors, and administrators, unto the said John B. Strong, his heirs and assigns, will forever warrant the said bargained premises only against themselves.

In witness whereof, the said Clarke hath hereunto set his hand and seal the day and year above written.

GEO. J. F. CLARKE. [L. S.]

Signed, sealed, and delivered in the presence of—
JAMES BENTHAM.
THOS. H. MILLER, *J. J. C. C. C.*

No. 1.—See REPORT No. 4.

Francis Woods vs. The United States. For six hundred and forty acres of land.

MEMORIAL.

To the honorable the commissioners appointed to ascertain claims and titles to lands in East Florida:

The memorial of Francis Woods respectfully showeth: That your memorialist claims title to a tract of land situate on the north side of Mills' swamp, and on the east side of the road formerly called the King's road; which title your memorialist derives from an act of Congress passed and approved May 26, 1824, for such persons as were in the actual occupation of the land. And your memorialist further showeth that he is and has been in the occupation and cultivation of the said tract of land since the year 1812 and 1814; that he does not claim any other tract of land in the Territory of Florida; that he is a citizen of the United States and resident of Florida, and above the age of twenty-one years. All of which is respectfully submitted, &c.

FRANCIS WOODS.

DECREE.

Francis Woods vs. The United States. For six hundred and forty acres of land.

The board having ascertained that the claimant inhabited and cultivated the above land February 22, 1819, do confirm the same accordingly. May 18, 1825.

Francis Woods vs. The United States. For six hundred and forty acres of land.

John Uptegrove sworn:
Question. Do you know one Francis Woods?
Answer. I do.
Question. Is he the head of a family and over the age of twenty-one years?
Answer. He is.
Question. Do you know anything of his settling a tract of land situated on the north side of Mills' swamp, and on the east side of the road formerly called the King's road?
Answer. I do.
Question. When did he first settle this tract of land?
Answer. About twenty years ago.
Question. Has he occupied the land since that time?
Answer. He has peaceably occupied it until a year ago.
Question. Does he claim any other land in the Territory derived either from the British or Spanish governments?
Answer. I am very sure he does not.

JOHN UPTEGROVE.

Before the board in session May 18, 1825.

No. 2.—See REPORT No. 4.

Miguel Papy vs. The United States. For six hundred and forty acres of land.

MEMORIAL.

To the honorable the commissioners appointed to ascertain claims and titles to lands in East Florida:

The memorial of Miguel Papy respectfully showeth: That your memorialist claims title to a tract of land consisting of six hundred and forty acres, situated on Deep creek, about six miles from the St. John's river, a small branch running into Six-mile creek, by virtue of an act of Congress of the United States passed and approved May 26, 1824, granting lands to such persons as were in actual possession and occupation of the same, commenced between February 22, 1819, and July 17, 1821, when Florida was ceded to the United States. And your memorialist further showeth that he was and has been in actual habitation, cultivation, and improvement of said tract of land so situated as aforesaid from February 22, 1819, up to the present period. And your memorialist further showeth that he claims no tract of land in this Territory by virtue of any written evidence of title derived from the British or Spanish governments. And your memorialist further showeth that he is a citizen of the United States and a resident of the Territory of Florida.

MIGUEL PAPY,
By his attorney, B. A. PUTNAM.

[Here follows the affidavit of Bartolome Solana, sworn to before the Hon. William H. Allen, one of the commissioners, May 26, 1825, proving the occupation and cultivation of the above land previous to and since the year 1819.]

Miguel Papy vs. *The United States. For six hundred and forty acres of land.*

The board having ascertained that the claimant did actually cultivate and improve the above land February 22, 1819, do confirm the same to him. August 16, 1825.

No. 3.—See REPORT No. 4.

George Gianoply vs. *The United States. For six hundred and forty acres of land.*

MEMORIAL.

To the honorable the commissioners appointed to ascertain claims and titles to lands in East Florida:

The memorial of George Gianoply respectfully showeth: That your memorialist claims title to a tract of land consisting of six hundred and forty acres, situated and bounded as follows: on the south by land claimed by G. Darling, on the west and north by public lands, on the east by land claimed by John Gianoply, as by a reference to a plat herewith will more fully and at large appear, by virtue of an act of Congress of the United States passed and approved May 26, 1824, granting lands to such persons as were in actual possession and occupation of the same, commenced before February 15, 1819, and continued until July 17, 1821, when Florida was surrendered to the United States. And your memorialist further showeth that he was, is, and has been in actual habitation and improvement of said tract of land, situated as aforesaid, from the year 1818 until the date hereof, and he always, in that time, peaceably enjoyed and improved the same. And your memorialist further showeth that he does not claim title to any other tract of land in this Territory by reason of any title derived from either the British or Spanish governments. And your memorialist further showeth that he is over the age of twenty-one years, and that he is a citizen of the United States. And your memorialist, as is duty bound, will ever pray, &c.

ISAAC N. COX, *Attorney for Petitioner.*

[Plat herewith filed, marked A.]

[Here follows a plat by Gamaliel Darling, dated March 20, 1824.]

DECREE.

George Gianoply vs. *The United States. For six hundred and forty acres of land.*

The board having ascertained that the claimant actually inhabited and cultivated the above land February 22, 1819, do confirm the same accordingly. September 14, 1825.

AFFIDAVIT.

TERRITORY OF FLORIDA, *County of St. John's:*

George Gianoply vs. *The United States. For six hundred and forty acres of land in the Twelve-mile swamp.*

The deposition of John Leonardy, taken before Elias B. Gould, a justice of the peace for the county of St. John's.

John Leonardy, being duly sworn, says that he is acquainted with the claimant, George Gianoply; knows that he settled on a tract of land in the Twelve-mile swamp about eight years ago, and that he was on it and cultivated it at and previous to the change of government in 1821, and had done so from the time of his first settlement. He says that the father of the present claimant has land in the same swamp, but that the land which is now claimed lies to the west of it. The claimant had a house on this tract, and lived in it, and planted corn and pumpkins, and knows that claimant had two or three hands. It is about fourteen or fifteen miles from St. Augustine.

JUAN LEONARDY.

Sworn to before me September 8, 1825.

E. B. GOULD, *Justice of the Peace.*

[Nos. 4 and 5 were not returned to the General Land Office by the commissioners.]

No. 6.—See REPORT No. 4.

Pedro Mestre vs. *The United States. For six hundred and forty acres of land.*

MEMORIAL.

To the honorable the commissioners appointed to ascertain claims and titles to lands in East Florida:

The memorial of Pedro Mestre respectfully showeth: That your memorialist claims title to a tract of land containing six hundred and forty acres, situated on the north of the head of the North river, which tract he claims by virtue of an act of Congress of the United States passed and approved May 26, 1824, granting lands to such persons as were in cultivation and occupation of the same, commenced between February 22, 1819, and July 17, 1821, when Florida was surrendered to the United States. And your memorialist further showeth that he was, is, and has been in actual habitation and cultivation of said tract of land, so situated as aforesaid, for a number of years, and that he does not claim title to any other tract of land in this Territory by reason of any title derived from either the British or Spanish governments. And your memorialist further showeth that he is over the age of twenty-one years; that he is a citizen of the United States and a native of East Florida. And your memorialist prays confirmation of the same.

                                                                                    PEDRO MESTRE.

DECREE.

Pedro Mestre vs. The United States. For six hundred and forty acres of land.

The board having ascertained from the evidence adduced that the claimant is entitled to the above land under the donation act, do therefore confirm it to him. December 2, 1825.

[Nos. 7 to 10, inclusive, were not returned by the commissioners to the General Land Office.]

No. 1.—See REPORT No. 5.

Dorcas Black vs. The United States. For six hundred and forty acres of land.

MEMORIAL.

To the honorable the commissioners appointed to ascertain claims and titles to land in East Florida:

The petition of Dorcas Black respectfully showeth: That your memorialist claims title to a certain tract of land containing six hundred and forty acres, situated in the county of St. John's, on the road called the Crawford road, leading from St. Augustine to the St. John's river, and bounded west by lands of William Hollingsworth, on the south by lands claimed by William Hartley and Bowen, on the east and north by vacant lands. Her house and improvements are known as the improvements and premises of the said Dorcas Black. Your memorialist claims title to the above-named premises by virtue of an act of Congress passed and approved May 26, 1824, granting lands to such persons as were in actual possession and improvement of the same between February 22, 1819, and July 17, 1821, when Florida was ceded to the United States. Your memorialist further showeth that she has been, and now is, in actual possession and improvement of said tract of land, so situated as aforesaid, since the year 1818, and has enjoyed peaceable possession and improved the same. And your memorialist further showeth that she claims no tract of land in this Territory by virtue of any written evidence of title derived from the British or Spanish governments. And your memorialist further showeth that she is a native of the United States, over twenty-one years of age, and the head of a family. And your memorialist, as in duty bound, will ever pray, &c.

                                                        DORCAS BLACK, *by her Attorney, Streter.*

TERRITORY OF FLORIDA, *St. John's County:*

Personally appeared before me John Jones and Emanuel D. Mott, who, being duly sworn, depose and say that they are well acquainted with Mrs. Dorcas Black, and that she has been settled on the place where she now lives for five or six years, and that she has built a house and other buildings on said place, and cultivated said place; and has made a crop this year, and lives there now, and has ever since she first settled said place.

                                                        EMANUEL ⋈ D. MOTT.
                                                               his mark.
                                                        JOHN JONES.

Sworn and subscribed to before me this 21st day of September, A. D. 1826.

                                                        SAMUEL FAIRBANKS, *Justice of the Peace.*

DECREE.

Dorcas Black vs. The United States. For six hundred and forty acres of land.

The board having ascertained that the claimant did actually inhabit and cultivate the land above claimed between February 22, 1819, and July 17, 1821, do report it to Congress under the donation act. May 16, 1825.

TESTIMONY.

Dorcas Black vs. The United States. For six hundred and forty acres of land.

John Black, being sworn, and being asked at what time his mother, the claimant, was in possession of the tract of land, answered, about four years since.

Question. How long was she on the land before the exchange of flags?
Answer. Believes she was a few months.
Question. What improvements did the claimant put on the land claimed?
Answer. She built some houses, and cleared and cultivated some land.
Question. Does the claimant still reside on the land?
Answer. She does.
Question. Has the claimant ever derived any written evidence of title from the British or Spanish governments?
Answer. She never has.
Question. Is the claimant above the age of twenty-one years?
Answer. She is.

                                                                            JOHN BLACK.

David Scurry sworn:

Question. What time did Mrs. Black go on the land now claimed by her?
Answer. It was before the change of flags.

                                                                            DAVID SCURRY.

James Hall sworn:

States that the claimant went on the tract claimed by her previous to the exchange of flags, and made some improvements on the same.

                                                                    JAMES HALL.

Before the board in session May 16, 1825.

No. 2.—See Report No. 5.

John R. Hogans vs. *The United States.   For six hundred and forty acres of land.*

MEMORIAL.

To the honorable the commissioners appointed to ascertain claims and titles to lands in East Florida:

The petition of John R. Hogans respectfully showeth: That your memorialist claims title to a tract of land consisting of six hundred and forty acres, situated on the north side of the river St. John's, bounded east by lands of Hudnall, west by Hogans' land, north by public lands, and south by the creek entering in the St. John's river; which title your memorialist derives from possession before January 24, 1818   And your memorialist further showeth that he is in actual possession of the said land; that he is a citizen of the United States and resident of the Territory of Florida.   All of which is respectfully submitted.

                                                            A. BELLAMY, *Attorney.*

DECREE.

John R. Hogans vs. *The United States.   For six hundred and forty acres of land.*

The board finding by the evidence adduced that the claimant did actually inhabit and cultivate the above land between February 22, 1819, and July 17, 1821, do report it to Congress under the donation act.   August 30, 1825.

TESTIMONY.

John R. Hogans vs. *The United States.   For six hundred and forty acres of land.*

Zachariah Hogans sworn:

Question. About what time did claimant settle the land below Jacksonville?
Answer. The latter part of the year 1820.
Question. How long has he resided on the land?
Answer. About three years.
Question. Does he still claim the land?
Answer. Yes, if he has not sold it.

Cross-examined.

Question. Is it public land?
Answer. It was always considered so.
Question. Is claimant above the age of twenty-one years?
Answer. He is.
Question. Is he the head of a family?
Answer. He is.
Question. Has he ever received any written evidence of title from either the British or Spanish governments?
Answer. He never has to my knowledge.]

                                                                    Z. HOGANS.

Before the board in session May 16, 1825

No. 3.—See Report No. 5.

Levi Sparkman vs. *The United States.   For six hundred and forty acres of land.*

MEMORIAL.

To the commissioners appointed to ascertain claims and titles to lands in East Florida:

The memorial of Levi Sparkman, of full age, showeth: That your memorialist claims title to six hundred and forty acres of land in East Florida, lying on Little Trout creek, adjoining the road leading from Jacksonville to Camp Pinckney, and above the road; which said tract of land your memorialist claims title to by virtue of an actual settlement made thereon by himself, and habitation and cultivation of the same in the year 1819, and ever since by himself and family, or by his tenant, and by virtue of the act of Congress approved May 24, 1824, for the benefit of actual settlers in Florida. Your memorialist further shows that he has no claim for lands in Florida derived to him by any grant from the British or Spanish governments.   He prays that it may be confirmed to him for the benefit of Arthur Birney.   All of which is respectfully submitted.

                                                            LEVI SPARKMAN.

DECREE.

Levi Sparkman vs. *The United States.   For six hundred and forty acres of land.*

The board finding by the evidence adduced that the claimant did actually inhabit and cultivate the above land between February 22, 1819, and July 17, 1821, do report the same to Congress under the donation act.   August 30, 1825.

TESTIMONY.

Levi Sparkman vs. The United States.   For six hundred and forty acres of land.

Isaac Carter, sworn on the part of the claimant, states that Levi Sparkman settled a place very early in the spring of the year 1819 on Little Trout creek, joining the main road; thinks that he, the claimant, settled on the land in the month of March or April of the same year; the claimant is the head of a family, and over the age of twenty-one years; that he had a cowpen on the land the next year, and had a black-smith's shop on the same; claimant left the land last year in the possession of another person.

ISAAC CARTER.

Seymour Pickett, sworn, states that in the spring of 1820 he got a ploughshare sharpened at claim-ant's blacksmith's shop, and the improvements indicated that he had been settled there some time.

SEYMOUR PICKETT.

Before the board in session May 19, 1823.

No. 4.—See REPORT No. 5.

John D. Bludworth vs. The United States.   For six hundred and forty acres of land.

MEMORIAL.

To the honorable the commissioners appointed to ascertain claims and titles to lands in East Florida:

The memorial of John D. Bludworth respectfully showeth: That your memorialist claims title to a tract of land consisting of a tract of land situated near the public road, at the head of Deadman's swamp; which title your memorialist derives from an act of Congress passed May 26, 1824, for the relief and benefit of actual settlers. Your memorialist further states that he is in actual possession of said tract of land, and has been since 1820; that he is a citizen of the United States and resident of the Territory. All of which is respectfully submitted.

A. BELLAMY, *Attorney.*

DECREE.

John D. Bludworth vs. The United States.   For six hundred and forty acres of land.

The board finding by the evidence adduced that the claimant did actually inhabit and cultivate the above land between February 22, 1819, and July 17, 1821, do report it to Congress under the donation act. May 18, 1825.

TESTIMONY.

John D. Bludworth vs. The United States.   For six hundred and forty acres of land.

Question. Do you know the claimant?
Answer. I do.
Question. Do you know him to be the head of a family, and above the age of twenty-one years?
Answer. I do.
Question. Do you know at what time he first occupied the land?
Answer About the fall of the year 1820.
Question. Did he build houses and cultivate the land?
Answer. He did.
Question. Do you know whether Mr. Bludworth claims title to any other tract of land in the Territory derived either from the British or Spanish governments?
Answer. Not to my knowledge.
Question. Where is the tract of land situated?
Answer. At the head of Deadman's swamp, near the road formerly called the King's road.

JOHN UPTEGROVE.

Before the board in session May 18, 1825.

No. 5.—See REPORT No. 5.

Heirs of John Carter, deceased, vs. The United States.   For six hundred and forty acres of land.

MEMORIAL.

To the honorable the commissioners appointed to ascertain claims and titles to lands in East Florida:

The memorial of William, Caleb, and Elizabeth Carter, infants and orphans of John Carter, deceased, respectfully showeth: That your memorialists are the legitimate issue and sole heirs of John Carter, deceased; that they claim title to six hundred and forty acres of land lying on Trout creek, and the south side thereof, at a place called the Cold Hill, to include the improvements which were there made, and in the habitation and cultivation of their said deceased father at the time of his death; which said tract of land your memorialists claim by virtue of a settlement purchased thereon by their aforesaid deceased father, John Carter, or his agent, in the year 1809—possession whereof had been held from that time until his death, which happened in December, 1824—and by virtue of the act of Congress approved May 26, 1824, for the benefit of actual settlers in the Territory of Florida. They further say their deceased ancestor, nor any of them, never had any claim to lands in Florida derived from any British or Spanish grant. All of which is respectfully submitted.

WILLIAM CARTER,
CALEB CARTER,
ELIZ'H CARTER,
Infants of Jno. Carter, deceased,
By ISAAC CARTER, *their next friend.*

DECREE.

John Carter's heirs vs. The United States.

The board finding by the evidence adduced that John Carter, deceased, did actually inhabit and cultivate the above land between February 22 1819, and July 17, 1821, do report it to Congress under the donation act.   August 29, 1825.

No. 6.—See REPORT No. 5.

Isaac Carter vs. The United States.   For six hundred and forty acres of land.

MEMORIAL.

To the honorable the commissioners appointed to ascertain claims and titles to lands in East Florida:

The memorial of Isaac Carter respectfully showeth: That your memorialist claims title to six hundred and forty acres of land at the place where he now resides, on Nine-mile creek, about half a mile from the road leading from Jacksonville to Camp Pinckney, and below the place where said road crosses said creek, to include said improvements whereon I reside, and to run down the creek twice the length of its breadth, beginning on William Monroe's east line; which said tract of land your memorialist derives claim to by actual settlement made in the year 1803 by his father-in-law, whose possession was surrendered to him in the year 1819, which he has ever since maintained, and by virtue of an act of Congress approved May 26, 1824, for the benefit of actual settlers in the Territory of Florida. All of which is respectfully submitted.

ISAAC CARTER.

DECREE.

Isaac Carter vs. The United States.   For six hundred and forty acres of land.

The board finding by the evidence adduced that the claimant did actually inhabit and cultivate the above land between February 22, 1819, and July 17, 1821, do report it to Congress under the donation act.   August 29, 1825.

TESTIMONY.

Isaac Carter vs. The United States.   For six hundred and forty acres of land.

John Silcock sworn:
Question. Are you the father-in-law of claimant?
Answer. I am.
Question. Do you know the place on which he resides on Nine-mile creek?
Answer. Yes; I first settled it.
Question. Will you state the time you first settled it?
Answer. About the year 1803.
Question. Will you state the circumstances of giving possession of the same to Mr. Carter?
Answer. I lived on and cultivated it for seven years, when I was obliged to abandon it on account of the troubles of this then province. I again moved on it, and lived thereon six or eight months, and was obliged to leave it again; after which I gave it to Mrs. Carter and her children. The claimant has been residing on the land ever since I gave it to his wife and children.

Cross-examined.

The claimant still resides on the land. Witness further states that, to the best of his knowledge, claimant does not hold any land derived either from the British or Spanish governments.

JOHN SILCOCK.

Seymour Pickett, sworn on the part of claimants, states that he first saw Mr. Silcock, the father-in-law of claimant, on the land, about the year 1804, and also in 1809. When witness moved on Nassau he saw him on the land. Witness first saw claimant on the land in the year 1820 or 1821, but is not certain. The land was cultivated by Mr. Silcock in the year 1819, when he built a house on the same and resided thereon.

SEYMOUR PICKETT.

Before the board in session May 19, 1825.

[No. 7 was not returned to the General Land Office by the commissioners.]

No. 8.—See REPORT No. 5.

John G. Brindley vs. The United States.   For six hundred and forty acres of land.

MEMORIAL.

To the honorable the commissioners appointed to ascertain claims and titles to lands in East Florida:

The memorial of John G. Brindley respectfully showeth: That your memorialist claims title to a certain tract of land consisting of six hundred and forty acres, situated on the north side of Black creek. His house and improvements are known as the improvements and premises of the said John G Brindley, in the county of Duval, by virtue of an act of Congress of the United States passed and approved May 26, 1824, granting lands to such persons as were in actual settlement and improvement of the same, commenced between February 22, 1819, and July 17, 1821, when Florida was ceded to the United States.

And your memorialist further showeth that he is in actual possession and improvement of said tract of land, so situated as aforesaid, since the year 1819 until the date of this memorial, and has peaceably enjoyed, possessed, and improved the same. And your memorialist further showeth that he claims no tract of land in said Territory by virtue of any written evidence of title derived from either the British or Spanish governments. And your memorialist further showeth, agreeably to the statute in such case made and provided, that he is over the age of twenty-one years, and that he is a citizen of the United States. And your memorialist, as in duty bound, will ever pray, &c.

JOHN G. BRINDLEY,
By his attorney, JOHN M. FONTAINE.

TERRITORY OF FLORIDA, *St. John's County:*

Personally appeared before me, Samuel Fairbanks, esq., one of the justices of the peace for said county, William Molphos, who, being duly sworn, deposeth and saith that in the year 1818 or 1819 he helped to build a house on Little Black creek, and helped to plant some peas and corn, and knew John George Brindley to live on said place; and last year he was at Brindley's house, and knew him to have a good crop of corn at the same place; and this deponent helped J. G. Brindley to dig his potatoes last fall.

his
WILLIAM ⋈ MOLPHOS.
mark.

Sworn and subscribed to before me this 16th day of August, A. D. 1824.

SAMUEL FAIRBANKS, *Justice of the Peace.*

TERRITORY OF FLORIDA, *St. John's County:*

Personally appeared before me, Samuel Fairbank, esq., one of the justices of the peace for said county, Hannah Nobles, who, being duly sworn, deposeth and saith that she is well acquainted with John George Brindley, and that he settled at a place at Little Black creek in January, 1820, with his family; and that he had a house and land cleared at said place.

her
HANNAH ⋈ NOBLES.
mark.

Sworn and subscribed to this 18th day of August, 1824.

SAMUEL FAIRBANKS, *Justice of the Peace.*

DECREE.

John G. Brindley vs. *The United States. For six hundred and forty acres of land.*

The board finding by the evidence adduced that the claimant did actually inhabit and cultivate the above land between February 22, 1819, and July 17, 1821, do report his claim to Congress under the donation act. August 29, 1825.

[Nos. 9 to 13, inclusive, were not returned to the General Land Office by the commissioners.]

No. 1.—SEE REPORT No. 6.

John Bachelot vs. *The United States. For a small island of marsh.*

MEMORIAL.

To the honorable the commissioners appointed to ascertain claims and titles to lands in East Florida:

The petition of John Bachelot respectfully showeth: That your memorialist claims title to a tract of land consisting of a small island of marsh, situated near that of the Doctor; which title your memorialist derives from a concession made to him November 29, 1800, by Governor White, in virtue of the royal order of 1790, a certified copy of which concession is herewith presented. And your memorialist further showeth that he is in actual possession of said lands, and was so at the cession; that he is a citizen of the United States, and resident of St. Mary's, in Georgia. He prays confirmation of title, &c.

JOHN BACHELOT.

CERTIFIED COPY.

Don Juan de Pierra, lieutenant of the infantry regiment of Cuba and secretary of the government: I certify that, to a memorial presented by John Bachelot, soliciting a small marsh island, which is near that of the Doctor, for pasturage for his cattle, the following decree was this day made: "Let there be granted to this party the land which he solicits, without injury to a third person.

"WHITE."

And that it may serve as a security to the interested, I give this in St. Augustine, Florida, November 29, 1800.

JUAN DE PIERRA.

I certify the foregoing to be a true and correct translation from a decree made by Governor White, in the Spanish language, on file in the office of the public archives.

F. J. FATIO, *S. B. L. C.*

DECREE.

John Bachelot vs. *The United States. For a small island of marsh.*

The above being a valid Spanish grant, but undefined in quantity, the board do report it to Congress accordingly. September 29, 1825.

No. 2.—See Report No. 6.

The heirs of Thomas Travers vs. The United States.   For one thousand acres of land.

MEMORIAL.

To the honorable the commissioners appointed to ascertain claims and titles to lands in East Florida:

The petition of the heirs of Thomas Travers by one of them, William Travers, respectfully showeth: That your memorialists claim title to a tract of land consisting of one thousand acres, situated at a place called the Old Savannas, where Mr. Mann had a rice plantation, (see an accurate description of the said land and its marks and boundaries in the grant filed herewith;) which title your memorialists derive from a grant made to them by Governor Coppinger, in virtue of the royal order of 1790. The said grant or royal title is dated July 9, 1819, and is founded upon a transfer of concession made by the heirs of Isnardy, with consent of government, August 31, 1805, as will be seen by the accompanying documents. And your memorialists show that they are in actual possession of said lands; that they resided in Florida at the change of flags, and still do so.

GEORGE MURRAY, for Memorialists.

[Translation.]

Señor Governor: Don Miguel Isnardy, an inhabitant and merchant of this city, with due respect, states to your excellency, as, by the annexed memorial and decree of your excellency's predecessor, it is evident that he is in possession of the land cited in it until the royal command; and understanding that his Majesty has resolved to distribute lands to the inhabitants of this province, he prays your excellency to be pleased to grant him and ratify the said concession, from its being certain that your memorialist has been the due time in possession of it in proper form, a favor which he hopes to merit from the justice of your excellency. St. Augustine, January 3, 1791.

MIGUEL ISNARDY.

St. Augustine, October 19, 1791.

Let it be granted to this party in the place in which he is established until, at the survey of the lands, the quantity corresponding to his family be surveyed to him, without injury to a third person.

QUESADA.

I certify the foregoing to be a true and correct translation from a document in the Spanish language on file in the office of the public archives of St. Augustine.

F. J. FATIO, S. B. L. C.

[Translation.]

Señor Governor and Commander-in-chief: Don Miguel Isnardy, an inhabitant of this city, with all due respect, states to your excellency that the officer commissioned for the survey of lands having arrived in the neighborhood of those he possesses on the North river, as he has proved by the preceding memorial which he presented, and by it asked that there should be surveyed for him one hundred acres in the said place; and, besides this, that he shall be put in possession until the complete extension of his family, which is composed at present of twenty-one persons, including himself, in the place known as the Old Savannas, and its vicinity, where rice was planted by a former English inhabitant, Mr. Mann; he prays your excellency to be pleased to grant his petition, and command what is proper for the purpose, in order that they may be surveyed for him in the places already mentioned, a favor which he does not doubt to receive from among the many which your excellency distributes daily. Florida, April 26, 1793.

MIGUEL ISNARDY.

St. Augustine, May 10, 1793.

Let this be placed with the foregoing, and confirming by them the possession which the party has in the lands which Don Pedro Marrot refers to—this decree not opposing the former which he has from this government; and let him proceed to the survey of the hundred acres on the North creek, and the remainder, to complete what his family is entitled to, at the Old Savannas.

QUESADA.

I certify the foregoing to be a true and correct translation from a document in the Spanish language on file in the office of the public archives of St. Augustine.

F. J. FATIO, S. B. L. C.

[Translation.]

Be it known that I, Don Francisco Rovira, attorney and agent of the widow of Don Miguel de Isnardy, and charged by the said widow and the tribunal to adjust and liquidate the accounts which were pending by the death of said Isnardy, having examined the accounts pending between Dr. Don Thomas Travers and the deceased, it results in the property which I administer owing to the said Don Thomas the sum of four hundred dollars; in virtue of which and the said doctor having proposed to me that he would take in payment of the balance in his favor a piece of land which the said Isnardy obtained and cultivated, situated on the Little beaches of Santa Lucia, and having been informed by men who have a knowledge of the said land that it is well paid for at that sum, I have agreed, in the name of the said widow and the other heirs, to sell them; and by this document which, until the government permits a deed of sale to be made in form, shall serve as a title, I sell him the above-named piece of land for the precise sum of four hundred dollars—all accounts at both sides being settled and paid up to this date, without any claim remaining on either side. And I, Don Thomas Travers, acknowledge myself satisfied with the settlement of accounts above mentioned, and receive in payment of the above balance in my favor the lands mentioned, and which I consider as delivered to me; and to confirm all, we sign this in St. Augustine, Florida, August 31, 1805.

THOS. TRAVERS.
FRANCISCO ROVINA,
For Donna Juana de la Torre, and as her Attorney.

I certify the foregoing to be a true and correct translation from a document in the Spanish language on file in the office of the public archives of St. Augustine.

F. J. FATIO, *S. B. L. C.*

[Here follows translation of a survey dated April 25, 1819, and a royal title dated July 9, 1819.]

EAST FLORIDA, ST. AUGUSTINE, *St. John's County:*

This day personally appeared before me, the subscriber, one of the justices of the peace of the county aforesaid, Bartolome Leonardy, who, being duly sworn, doth depose and say that he was well acquainted with Don Miguel de Isnardy, and recollects of his planting for many years up the North river, at a place called the *Old Savannas,* distant about fifteen miles north from St. Augustine, and adjoining to the north by the place now in the occupation of this deponent; that he has always understood that the land in question belonged to said Miguel Isnardy; that he never heard it disputed to the contrary.

BARTOLOME LEONARDY.

Sworn to before me July 20, 1824.

BERNARDO SEGUI, *J. P.*

DECREE.

Heirs of Thomas Travers vs. *The United States.   For one thousand acres.*

The board having ascertained the above to be a valid Spanish concession, but the quantity of land being, in their opinion, undefined, they report the same accordingly for the consideration of Congress. September 27, 1825.

No. 3.—See REPORT No. 6.

Bartolome Mestre vs. *The United States.   For three hundred acres of land.*

MEMORIAL.

To the honorable the commissioners appointed to ascertain claims and titles to lands in East Florida:

Bartolome Mestre, jr., for his mother, Mariana Mestre, respectfully represents: That your memorialist claims title to a tract of land consisting of three hundred acres, situated on Thompson's branch, on the opposite side of the Matanzas river from the Little bar, which has not been surveyed; that the same was granted to her husband, Bartolome Mestre, without specifying the number of acres, but according to the number of his family, which consisted of himself, his wife, and three children, and to take possession in one month; which conditions were performed. And your memorialist states that the said Bartolome Mestre afterwards abandoned his family, and left his children with the said Mariana, who has supported them for many years, and ever since the said Bartolome abandoned his wife and family; which title your memorialist derives from a grant made to the said Bartolome Mestre by Governor White, in virtue of the royal order of 1790, June 28, 1796, as appears by the memorial and decree herewith presented. And your memorialist further showeth that the said Mariana Mestre is in legal possession of said lands, and was at the time of the cession, and has been ever since the grant; that she is a citizen of the United States and resident of Florida.   St. Augustine, October 11, 1823.

JOHN B. STRONG, *Attorney for Claimant.*

[Translation.]

To the Governor:

Bartolome Mestre, an inhabitant of this city, with due respect, submits to your excellency that, finding himself obliged to attend to the daily support of his family, and not having the means to do it in this city without the greatest toil, by reason of his not meeting with a vacant place in which to employ himself; and as he has always lived desirous of complying with his duties, he desires to employ himself in some honest calling which, by its produce, may lead to this intent; and finding himself well acquainted with country labor, which he has exercised for some time, as his Majesty has deigned to grant to the inhabitants of this province lands in proportion to the family which each person may have, embracing this favor he has solicited a piece of land on which to settle himself—he met one in front of the Little bar, on the river Matanzas, named Thompson's branch, which no person is in possession of.   Wherefore, he supplicates your excellency to be pleased to grant him the said land until the survey and distribution of lands already commenced, which has been put a stop to by the declaration of the last war; he followed up a request which he promises himself from the goodness of your excellency.   Florida, June 21, 1796.

The memorialist not knowing how to write his name, I sign for him at his request.

JOSÉ DE ZAVALIA.

DECREE.

ST. AUGUSTINE, *June* 23, 1796.

Let the commandant of engineers report if the land asked for, being settled, would embarrass the defence of this city and province.

WHITE.

REPORT.

All the uncultivated land from the tower of Matanzas to the south would be very useful for the support of the province, the cultivation of it not being in any respect prejudicial to the defence of the city or province; and as the land which the memorialist asked for is comprised in that part, there being no objection to your excellency's granting it, it being on the main land, at a small distance; and opposite the Little bar there is a small island named the Rock, or Large bar, where the predecessor of your excellency permitted the inhabitants to make lime, but ascertaining that his partner, Bike, raised some stone from the borders of the bar in order to sell it to individuals of the city, with manifest injury to the entrance of vessels by it, it being now capable of admitting small canoes, deponent was ordered by the government to quit that post, and not use the license granted to him. If the land which the party asks for is at the said Large bar, and if it be on the main land, there is no inconvenience in your excellency's granting it, if it be your pleasure, for the purpose he pretends, which is all I can report to your excellency in compliance with your preceding decree. St. Augustine, Florida, June 27, 1796.

PEDRO DIAZ BERRIO.

CONCESSION.

ST. AUGUSTINE, *Florida, June* 28, 1796.

The land asked for not being that referred to in the foregoing report, let it be granted to the petitioner, without injury to a third person, and on the conditions allowed to other settlers or inhabitants.

WHITE.

Licentiate ABREU.

Certificate is granted.

PENGIL.

I certify that the foregoing is a true and correct translation from a document in the Spanish language on file in the public archives of St. Augustine.

F. J. FATIO, *S. B. L. C.*

TERRITORY OF FLORIDA, *County of St. John's:*

Francis Pelliser, jr., being duly sworn, doth depose and say that he was acquainted with Bartolome Mestre, of this county; that about twenty years ago, or something more or less, he settled a tract of land on the Matanzas river, west of the Matanzas fort, and is the same tract of land for which he obtained a grant from the Spanish government about that time. This deponent knows he was there making improvements for some time, but cannot say precisely how long; he had a wife and several children; his wife's name is Mariana Mestre, and now resides in the city of St Augustine. The said Bartolome Mestre, some time after, left his said wife and family, and has never afforded them any support for many years, his wife having supported and raised the children. The said Bartolome went to Darien, and has there lived with a colored woman, by whom he has had children, as this deponent has been informed and believes. The tract of land above alluded to is said to contain about three hundred or three hundred and fifty acres.

FRANCIS PELLISER, JR

Sworn before me April 26, 1825.

W. H. ALLEN.

DECREE.

Bartolome Mestre vs. *The United States. For three hundred acres of land.*

The board having ascertained the above to be a valid Spanish concession, but undefined in quantity, do therefore report it to Congress. June 14, 1825.

No. 4.—See REPORT No. 6.

Jehu Underwood vs. *The United States. For six hundred acres of land.*

MEMORIAL.

To the honorable the commissioners appointed to ascertain claims and titles to lands in East Florida:

The memorial of Jehu Underwood, a citizen of the United States, residing in the county of Camden, in Georgia, showeth: That your memorialist claims title to a tract of land situated in the county of Duval, on a creek called Black creek, containing six hundred acres, lying in the following form, to wit: the first line running east twenty chains; second, south eighty-six chains; and the third, west twenty chains, bounded, as your memorialist believes, on all sides by vacant lands; which said tract of land your memorialist claims as follows: first, under a concession made to him on May 20, 1805, granting him the privilege of building a mill thereon, and cutting timber, which said concession is hereunto annexed, marked A; that, in virtue of said concession, shortly thereafter the said Jehu Underwood went into possession of said tract of land, namely, the same year, and built a saw-mill on said Black creek, and continued in the possession of the same until 1812, when the said mill was burnt down by the Indians, and he was driven off by them; that as soon as with safety he could, which was some years after, he went on to said tract of land again, and recommenced another saw-mill, which he shortly thereafter completed, in consideration of which, on February 20, 1821, he obtained a royal title to six hundred acres of land as above described, which said tract of land he was in actual possession of on the day East and West Florida were transferred to the United States. Your memorialist refers, as evidence of such royal title, as per exhibit marked B, which he hereby introduces, not as direct evidence of the derangement of the title, but as collateral evidence, to establish the fact of the quantity of land he was in possession of by virtue of the concession marked exhibit A, at the time of the transfer of this Territory to the United States. All which is humbly submitted to your consideration. August 27, 1823.

BELTON A. COPP.

A.— [Translation.]

To the governor:

Don Jehu Underwood, inhabitant of this province, to your excellency respectfully showeth: That in April, 1804, he swore allegiance to his Catholic Majesty; that in December last he began to cultivate a tract of land, which he has hired on the river St. John's, with fourteen negroes and six white laborers, where has the pleasing prospect of an abundant crop of provisions; that his intention was, from the moment of his arrival in this province, to ask of the government, for the purpose of cultivating them, but has neglected doing so until the present moment; that the government could not doubt his intention of establishing himself in this province; that, lastly, being convinced of the abundance of timber therein, he has determined to erect two saw-mills on the banks of the river St. Mary's, on two creeks, the one called Dunn's creek the other Deep run; the first is situated three miles west from Pigeon creek, appertaining to Don Thomas Travers, bounded on the north by the river St. Mary's, and on all other sides by vacant lands; the last mentioned is situated about ten miles from the first; its front is bounded by the river St. Mary's; on all other sides by vacant lands; the intention of your memorialist being that of erecting the said two saw-mills immediately, with a part of his said laborers, and thirty new negroes, for whom he has written, and expects them very soon. He therefore prays your excellency will be pleased to grant him your superior permission for that purpose, conceding him the land sufficient, that the said two saw-mills may have sufficient quantity of pine timber for their use in their respective neighborhoods. St. Augustine, Florida, May 20, 1805.

JEHU UNDERWOOD.

St. Augustine, *May* 20, 1805.

Agreeably to his request, without injury to a third person, give him the corresponding license from the secretary's office.

WHITE.

I certify the foregoing to be a true and correct translation from a document in the Spanish language on file in the office of the public archives.

F. J. FATIO, *S. B. L. C.*

[Translation.]

In the city of St. Augustine, Florida, May 16, 1818, before his excellency, Don José Coppinger, colonel of the royal armies, political and militay governor of this city and its province, appeared Don George Fleming, captain of militia, with the rank of provincial in this city, and planter, native of Ireland, of the married state, from whom his excellency, in virtue of the information moved for by Don Jehu Underwood, received the oath which he made, according to law, under the obligation of which he promised to tell the truth to the best of his knowledge, in what should be asked him; and, having been questioned as to the tenor of the memorial, said that he knows positively that Don Jehu Underwood built the water saw-mill to which he refers in his representation, in virtue of the permission granted by this government, in which he invested, according to the opinion of the deponent, about eight or ten thousand dollars, which water saw-mill remained working until the year 1812, when the insurrection of this province took place; at which time the deponent knew, by persons worthy of credit, that the said Underwood was ruined, because of fire having been set to the said water saw-mill, and he lost what he had there; that all that he has set forth is amply public, and well known, as also that Underwood was one of the faithful subjects at the time of the said insurrection; so that, to avoid following the course of the malcontent inhabitants of the province, he absented himself from it for the United States, after having been harassed by the said insurgents; and that, further to confirm the deponent that the said saw-mill was in operation at the period referred to, he obtained from it quantities of lumber, which he bought for his own use; further, he does not know that, at the present day, what Underwood says is right, because he has not been at that place since said rebellion, and he answers that all is truth, by virtue of his oath; that he is of the age of sixty years; that the exceptions of the law, which he was made acquainted with, do not affect him. And having been also apprized of the contents of this, his declaration, he signed it with his excellency; which I attest.

[*A signet.*]   JORGE FLEMING.

Before me—

JUAN DE ENTRALGO.

On the same day, month, and year, Don Jehu Underwood, for the information which he is giving, presented as a witness Don Fernando de la Maza Arredondo, jr., native, resident, and planter in this city, from whom his excellency, before me, the notary, received on oath, which he made according to law, under the obligation of which he promised to tell the truth, to the best of his knowledge, in what should be asked him; and, examining the tenor of the foregoing memorial, said that it is very certain, public, and notorious, that Don Jehu Underwood built a water saw-mill on the place pointed out in his representation, where the deponent was with the schooner Palafox, in the year 1810, to load her with lumber, which he effected, carrying it to the Havana; that said mill was in full operation, and very effective; since, for its establishment, the said Underwood expended about ten thousand dollars, which accounts the deponent had in his hands, as they came through those of his father, Don Fernando, is in said Havana; but that, in the year 1812, said mill was destroyed by the fire which the Indians put to it—the said Underwood having been ruined, having lost what he had there, being, as he was, a faithful inhabitant, who did not meddle in said insurrection; that he does not know if said water saw-mill has been actually re-established, because he has not been since at that place; and answers that all is the truth, by virtue of his oath; that he is thirty years of age; not affected by the exceptions of the law; and he signed this, with his excellency; which I attest.

[*A signet*]   FERNANDO DE LA MAZA ARREDONDO, Jr.

Before me—

JUAN DE ENTRALGO.

On the same day appeared before his excellency Eleazer Stafford, an inhabitant of this province, and laborer in it, native of South Carolina, of the married state, from whom his excellency, before me, the notary, received the oath, which he made in form of law, promising to tell the truth, to the best of his knowledge, in what should be asked him; and being so, in the same manner with the former, he said that, since the year 1805, when he was established in this province, he saw that Don Jehu Underwood built a water saw-mill on Black creek, which he put in good order in every respect, and had it working until 1812, when the insurrection of this province took place, at which time said water saw-mill was destroyed and burned by the Indians, by which Underwood suffered losses which left him unable to rebuild said mill, which he has now returned to re-establish, although not with all perfection; but as the deponent lives near the said establishment, he has seen that it has been sawing for these six months; and that, according to the declaration of the deponent, he has sawed since last spring about 100,000 feet of lumber, being at present fit to continue if the waters permit; and answers that all is the truth, by virtue of this oath; that he is of the age of forty-five years, and that the exceptions of the law, which were explained to him, do not affect him. And, being informed of what is contained in this declaration, he said that it was faithfully written; and signed it, with his excellency; which I attest.

[A signet.]

ELEAZER STAFFORD.

Before me—

JUAN DE ENTRALGO.

I certify the foregoing to be a true and correct translation from a document in the Spanish language on file in the office of the public archives.

F. J. FATIO, S. B. L. C.

B.

[Here follows the translation of a royal title made by Governor Coppinger, dated February 17, 1821, for six hundred acres of land.]

DECREE.

Jehu Underwood vs. *The United States. For six hundred acres of land.*

The board find the above to be a valid Spanish concession, the conditions of which have been complied with; but as the quantity of land is undefined by it, and the royal title confirming and ascertaining the quantity is dated after January 24, 1818, they report to Congress for decision. September 27, 1825.

No. 5.—See Report No. 6.

Francis P. Sanchez vs. *The United States. For six hundred acres of land.*

MEMORIAL.

To the honorable the commissioners appointed to ascertain claims and titles to lands in East Florida:

The memorial of Francis P. Sanchez respectfully showeth: That he claims title in and to a tract or parcel of land consisting of six hundred acres, situated and being in East Florida aforesaid; that the said tract of six hundred acres is part of a grant of two thousand acres originally made to one Roque Leonardy, now deceased, by three several concessions, one of which was made on December 24, 1792, and one on April 11, 1793, by Governor Quesada, the governor of East Florida, and the other on January 3, 1799, by Governor White, the governor of East Florida; which several concessions were made under and in virtue of a royal order of the King of Spain, bearing date October 29, 1790—all which will fully appear by a reference to a certified copy of the said concession now here submitted and filed, and marked exhibit A; that the said Roque Leonardy, upon the obtaining said concession, took immediate and actual possession of the lands, and improved and cultivated them, and remained in the actual possession and occupancy of them till his death, which took place about the year 1803, and that his heirs are now in the actual occupancy of this part of the said lands now sold to your memorialist; that the said lands were surveyed very soon after their concession by the surveyor general of the province of East Florida, Pedro Marrot, but this plat having been lost, application was made by the heirs of the said Leonardy for a resurvey of them, which was ordered April 5, 1819, as will appear by a reference to a certified copy of the application and order for the said resurvey herewith submitted and filed, and marked exhibit B; that the said concession of two thousand acres were located by the said Roque Leonardy in two distinct tracts—one of which consisted of one thousand four hundred, and the other of six hundred, the latter of which is that claimed by your memorialist, as appears by the certified copies of the plat thereof now submitted and filed, and marked exhibits C and B; that the said tract of six hundred acres is situated on the North river, about sixteen miles from the city of St. Augustine, between the road to San Vincent Ferrer and lands of John Andrew, and has the following lines and dimensions, that is to say: the first line begins at a pine marked +, and runs north 77° east, 60 chains, to another pine, marked +; the second line runs north 13° west, 100 chains, to another pine marked +; the third line runs south 77° west, 60 chains, to another pine marked with a +; the fourth runs south 13° east, 100 chains, to the place of beginning. The said land was, at the time of the survey thereof, bounded on the south by lands of the heirs of Thomas Travers, on the north by vacant lands, on the west by the road to San Vincent Ferrer, as will more distinctly appear by the plat thereof contained in exhibit D. Your memorialist further shows that, May, 25, 1821, a grant in absolute property of the aforesaid tract of six hundred acres of land was made by Don José Coppinger, the governor of East Florida, to the heirs of the said Roque Leonardy, as will appear by a certain certified copy thereof now herewith submitted and filed, and marked exhibit E; and that Bartolome Leonardy, Juan Leonardy, and Maria Ugarti, the heirs of the aforesaid Roque Leonardy, afterwards, that is to say, March 20, 1822, for a valuable consideration paid to them by your memorialist, conveyed to your memorialist in fee simple absolute the said tract or parcel of six hundred acres of land, and its appurtenances, as will appear by original conveyance thereof to your memorialist, now herewith submitted and filed, and marked exhibit F. And your memorialist further avers and shows that the said Roque Leonardy was, at the time the said six hundred acres of land were conceded to him as aforesaid, and at his death, an inhabitant and settler of East Florida, and a subject to the King of Spain; and that his heirs were, at the time of their father's death, also settlers of East Florida, and subjects of the King of Spain, and were settlers of East Florida at the time they conveyed the said land to your memorialist; that your memorialist was, at the time of the cession of this Territory to the United States, an inhabitant and settler of East Florida, and has so continued ever since. Wherefore, he prays confirmation of his title to the said six hundred acres of land and its appurtenances, &c.

FRANCIS P. SANCHEZ,

By his attorney, JOHN DRYSDALE.

[Translation.]

MEMORIAL.

Señor Governor: Don Roque Leonardy, an inhabitant of this city, with due respect, states to your excellency that about fifteen miles to the north of this city there is a piece of land belonging to the King, which in former times was planted by a certain Mr. Menn, and at present, for want of a person to possess it, is uncultivated. Wherefore, he prays the goodness of your excellency to be pleased to grant him the said land, by which he will receive a singular favor, which he hopes from the well-known justice of your excellency.

ROQUE LEONARDY.

St. Augustine, *December* 24, 1792.

As he requires, without injury to a third person, let this party be permitted to establish himself where he solicits until the commissioners appointed for the general survey of lands shall assign him those which correspond to his family.

QUESADA.

MEMORIAL.

Señor Governor and Commander-in-Chief: Don Roque Leonardy, resident of this city and inhabitant of the province, with all respect, states to your excellency that his only business being that of a laborer, by which he has to maintain his large family, and for this same reason your excellency having done him the favor to grant him the plantation called Mr. Menn's, agreeably to the distribution of lands to the other inhabitants, and having resulted to be in possession of another individual by a former decree and disposition of the superior government. Wherefore, he prays your excellency to be pleased to grant him three hundred acres of land, the boundary of which, to the north, is where the cutting of wood for the King takes place, without injuring in any manner said place for cutting wood, the land being open and worked for a few years, and in the whole there is scarcely wood of any consideration; furthermore, those which your excellency should think proper to grant him four miles more to the north of that place at the Rice plantation, so called, as your memorialist has family and slaves enough for the cultivation of said lands, and the three hundred acres which he has set forth not being sufficient, which is a favor he hopes for from the justice of your excellency.

ROQUE LEONARDY.

St. Augustine, *April* 11, 1793.

If the lands which this party solicits be not destined for the King's woods, nor previously to any other inhabitant of the province, the captain, Don Pedro Marrot, commissioned for the general distribution of them, shall assign those which correspond to him in the places which he points out.

QUESADA.

MEMORIAL.

St. Augustine, *January* 3, 1799.

Señor Governor and Commander-in-Chief: Don Roque Leonardy, inhabitant of this city, with due respect, states to your excellency that when the lands were surveyed there remained a piece near his plantation, and to the south of it, which bounds that of Don Teresa Gill; this said piece of public land consists of a scrub, very thick, and full of palmettos, although there is a small part a little cleared; but, although that which corresponds to him of the uncleared is but small, he receives much injury from the vicinity of it to the house of your memorialist. He humbly prays your excellency to be pleased to give him a piece of land, good and bad, that, by this means, he may lessen the increased damages which he receives in clearing and cultivating it, a favor which he hopes to receive from the equitable charity of your excellency.

ROQUE LEONARDY.

St. Augustine, *January* 3, 1799.

Let the commandant of engineers report.

St. Augustine, *January* 3, 1799.

Señor Governor: The lands on which the petitioner has his plantation correspond to those of North creek, and he sees no objection that the lands which he solicits shall be increased in his possession and placed in cultivation, it being not only useful to shun the damages which the thickness of the woods occasions him, but also advantageous to the improvement of the agriculture of the province, which is all he has to inform your excellency of in compliance with the foregoing decree.

PEDRO DIAZ BERRIO.

DECREE.

St. Augustine, *January* 3, 1799.

Let there be granted to this party, without injury to a third person, the lands he solicits until, agreeably to the persons he may have for its cultivation, the corresponding quantity be assigned him.

WHITE.

I certify the foregoing to be a true and correct translation from a document in the Spanish language.

[Translation.]

The legitimate heirs of Don Roque Leonardy and Don Aguida Coll, now deceased, with due veneration, represent to your excellency, through the medium of Don José M. Urgarte, as husband of Donna Maria

Leonardy, one of them, and the only one present, that there belonging to them by concessions, which the annexed documents prove, as also long possession and constant cultivation for more than twenty-six years, the following lands, to wit: beginning by a line which should run east and west from that of their bounding neighbors; on the south, the heirs of Francisco Aman; on the creek named the King's landing, distant twelve miles to the north of this place; on the margin of the West river, until it terminates to the north, with the lands and appurtenances of the old plantation named Mesta Man, as all must run under the same lines, and amongst them the said possession of Menn, three hundred acres marked out from the said boundary of Aman to the land also granted January 3, 1799; also what is called the Rice plantation, distant sixteen miles, on the said North river, from this place, also to the west, which, with their appurtenances, as well one as the other, have been formerly surveyed and laid off, except the scrub under the commission of Captain Don Pedro Marrot at that time placed in the general plan of surveys of this province, the place of deposit of which is unknown, and is wanting to the injury of the memorialists. Wherefore, they pray your excellency to have the goodness to permit that the private surveyor, Don Andres Bergevin, may pass to said lands to make new surveys of them under the regulations established in such cases; and that being effected, the corresponding documents be delivered to them to proceed to prove the other circumstances which consolidate the right of property which they ought to enjoy from having complied with the conditions imposed by the regulations of this government on this matter, they being ready to pay in full the expenses due.   St. Augustine, Florida, April 3, 1819.

JOSÉ MARIA UGARTE.

DECREE.

St. Augustine, *April* 5, 1819.

Let it be granted as asked for, agreeably to the forms of law, and with notice to the bounding neighbors.

COPPINGER.

St. Augustine.

On the same day, month and year the foregoing decree was made known to Don José Maria Ugarte; which I attest.

ENTRALGO.

On the same day Don Andres Bergevin was notified of the appointment made of him as surveyor, and, on being informed of it, said that he accepted of it, and promised under oath, in due form, well and faithfully to discharge the duties intrusted to him according to the best of his knowledge and understanding, and signed it; which I certify.

ANDRES BERGEVIN.

Before me—   JUAN DE ENTRALGO, &c.

I certify the foregoing to be a true and correct translation from a document in the Spanish language.
F. J. FATIO, *S. B. L. C.*

[Translation.]

Don Andres Burgevin, as surveyor appointed by government by decree made on the 5th instant in favor of the interested: I certify that I have measured and laid off for the heirs of Don Roque Leonardy and Don Aguida Coll a piece of land which contains six hundred acres, situated on the western bank of the North river, twelve miles from this city, beginning on the southern boundary with the north line of the heirs of Don Francis Aman, ending to the north with the first salt creek to the east of said river, and to the west with vacant pine land, and being in its other circumstances conformable to the following plat, to confirm which I give these presents; which I sign in St. Augustine, April 28, 1819.

ANDRES BURGEVIN.

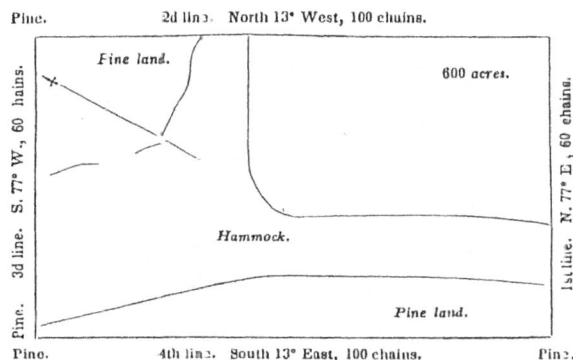

I certify the foregoing to be a true and correct translation from a document in the Spanish language.
F. J. FATIO, *S. B. L. C.*

[Here follows a deed of conveyance from the heirs of Roque Leonardy to claimant, dated March 21, 1822.]

DECREE BY THE BOARD.

The claimant, in support of his title, exhibited in evidence three concessions of different dates made to Roque Leonardy, deceased; the last of which, by Governor White, is dated January 3, 1799, the quantity of land conceded not specified nor defined in the second concessions. The board not being authorized to decide finally on claims when the amount claimed is undefined, they order that all the documents filed in this case be forwarded to Congress for their determination. April 14.

No. 6.—See Report No. 6.

Gabriel W. Perpall vs. *The United States. For six hundred and forty acres of land.*

MEMORIAL.

To the honorable the commissioners appointed to ascertain claims and titles to lands in East Florida:

The petition of G. W. Perpall showeth: That your memorialist claims title to a tract of land consisting of a mile square, (640 acres,) situated on the river St. Sebastian, about one mile in a southwest direction from this city; bounded on the east by the river Matanzas and St. Sebastian; on the south by a little creek called Jula; on the north by another creek called Gonzalez; and on the west by the pine barren; which title your memorialist derives from a judicial sale by Governor Quesada to Thomas Travers, and by him sold to George Taylor, who, by his attorney, F. M. Arredondo, sold to your memorialist. And your memorialist further showeth that he is in actual possession of said lands; that he is a citizen of the United States and resident of St. Augustine. November 10, 1823.

G. W. PERPALL.

[Translation.]

JUDICIAL SALE.

Don Juan Nepomuceno de Quesada, colonel of the royal armies, governor, and commander-in-chief of this city and province of St. Augustine, Florida, for his Majesty, says that an official letter was transmitted to me from the accountant's office of the royal ———— of this said city, dated 9th October of the year last past, 1790, showing me that, by the decease of Don Jesse Fish, of the English nation, under which Protestant religion he died, there remained a piece of cultivated land called the Grove, and that a son of the said deceased had retired to the dominions of his Britannic Majesty, and that the laws of these kingdoms forbid that foreigners should hold real property unless they are established in our dominions, soliciting said minister that thus the said landed property, as well as whatever others are found in this province and belong to said Fish, their rents and arrears, should belong to his Majesty, requesting me, at the same time, to take the necessary measures for the investigation of this business. In virtue of which, by a judicial decree of the same month and year, I ordered that, being included in one of the resolutions which the said official letter from the accountant's office points out in law 34th, book 2d, and chapter 32 of the recopilatos (abridgment) of these kingdoms, to give completion to the said estate, testimony is to be taken by the notary of the testamentary disposition of Fish, or any other under which he may have died, informing his executors or other persons; certifying also, and warning the tenants previously to anything else, that they have to account to the royal administration for the rents; that it ought to be made known that, unless lawful creditors appear, the King, our sovereign, is to enter subsequently into possession of the whole. In attention to which the said notary, having a copy of the will annexed, certified that the property of which he had notice, what the said Fish left, besides what the said will contained, consisted of copies of deeds which he produced; in which stage the executors, Don Thomas Travers and Don John Leslie, presented themselves, setting forth the just reasons which hindered them from soliciting a writing of inventory, and referring to the property in the said notice which the notary presented—they asked for a postscript, "that many of the goods were of these that were purchased (servando servare non passunt) and others, as the houses which were every day losing their value for the want of repairs, so that their total ruin was to be dreaded in a little time, to the injury of the creditors or his Majesty. I did order, having previously, according to law, received information of it, that all should be valued and sold regularly; that the proceeds might be placed or deposited in the royal coffers until the issue; and, by a decree of the 6th of November of said year ago, I ordered that the master carpenter and masons should proceed to a valuation of the houses which were pointed out; also explaining, by a sworn return, what they think as to the necessity for selling them, and that, along with what the accountant's office had to say, whose duty it is to interfere in said business, there shall be a decree. In attention to which the valuation and survey of the houses and lots was proceeded to, the said master's swearing in due form that, in the state in which they found this property, it was threatened with entire ruin; that the sale of it would be favorable, since, if not, they would be exposed to the loss of their value, which, being seen by the accountant's office of the royal domain, it was their opinion that the said sale should be proceeded to, and by a decree of the 15th December of the said year I ordered that the sale should be proceeded to; for which purpose handbills were posted up at the public places for the lawful time, and the day of the sale being made known, it was carried into effect at the gates of this government house in legal form; and various bids, offers, and outbids being made for said goods, the hour appointed for its conclusion having arrived, the said auction was concluded of the houses and lots referred to, by various individuals. In consequence of which, by a decree of January 3, 1791, I ordered that what is contained in the proceedings at auction, being prepared, let each person deposit, respectively, the sums which correspond to him, and in its virtue they shall prove the production of the said sums, as appears from the letters of payment which they produced, made by the royal treasury of this place, with the intervention of the accountant's office of the royal domain, and my approval thereof. By my decree of the 17th of February of the said year, 1791, I commanded that there should be delivered to each purchaser a competent deed of property, and concluded with the corresponding note in the proceeding that may be brought, said deeds being executed as well for the houses and lots referred to, as also the negroes belonging to said estate, which were also auctioned with due solemnity to several individuals, depositing also its proceeds in the royal coffers. I commanded, by a decree of the 2d April of the said year, there shall be given to each interested the copy which he requires, he paying the proper cost, and at the same time the cost of the judicial decrees, and its amount be paid out of the proceeds of the auctions deposited in the royal coffers, and, when done, let it be brought forward, that what is necessary may be decreed in this stage; and various creditors of the said deceased having come forward claiming his credits, and as the tribunal has been informed that there are several others having presented what Don Thomas Travers and Don Juan Leslie in their representation in the 8 volio of the said proceedings, and having in every respect to act according to law, I have commanded that the proceeds of the whole sale being presented, as it was in the royal coffers until another thing is determined on testimony of the accounts of the debts which are pointed out in said 8 volio, and, in every case, that Don Manuel Fernandez Bendicho be presented, who was named as defender of said estate, that, having previously accepted and taken the oath, he shall explain what is necessary of the state and nature of the cause, calling together the present creditors by handbills; and, as respects the absent in the city of Havana and the Island of Cuba, a despatch shall be forwarded to the captain general, to the end that he may order edicts to be posted up that, by themselves or their attorneys, they appear within the term of six months to allege their debts, and in the meanwhile everything shall remain suspended, with the exception of whatever the said defender may move, who renounced the charge, for which purpose he presented a representation, setting forth in it that he did not consider himself to possess the necessary information for this delicate affair; that he found it necessary to give his attention to various business now pending of the rents of the post office which he administered, on views of which I have admitted the said renunciation, and in consequence name in his place Don Fernando de la Maza Arredondo, to whom, having previously notified said appointment, and taken his oath, the above-mentioned judicial decrees shall be handed over: all being concluded, and the new defender having accepted of and sworn to his charge, he came forward representing and saying in his petition of the 2d July of the same year of 1791, that, having examined attentively the steps taken in the said decree, and in as far as they have proceeded all appears to have been very regular, and that he agreed to the whole; but, as many individuals who have to appear at said meeting may delay some time in coming or presenting their powers, he judged that, until they appeared, it would be proper not to cause them any delay afterwards, and to prevent every contingency of damage of the property which remains, that it be valued in due form, and auctioned as the former, passing the proceeds to the deposit before provided, setting forth at the same time, in addition, that, inasmuch as the place named the Grove belonged to the deceased, although it does not appear in the deed of title with which he enjoyed it, being certain that he had an immemorial possession, I should be favored by having it ordered that the trees and buildings should be valued, and that they should go to auction with the rest, determining on what may be most correct as to the land. To all which I have acceded by my decree of the said month and year commanding that all should be done as required and in proper form, which proceeding has been delayed some time by the great business of the notary, and sometimes by sickness, which prevailed at that time. The said defender represented again, stating that, from the well-known injury sustained by the property of the deceased, Fish, from want of a master who would take care of it as his own, he prayed that I would order that, without loss of time, the valuation should be made, and the sale provided for; explaining by an addition, for the better understanding, that inasmuch as by the deed of property of the possession of the said Don Juan Eligu de la Puenta had not sold them under any survey, only marking the limits with creek, salt marshes, roads, and other marks, which are yet in being; in virtue of which he asked that two measurers or surveyors should be hired, and it would be sufficient to name only two skilful persons, who, informed of the places more or less advantageous, and instructed of what lands produce in this country, should value said possession, accompanied by the individuals who may find it convenient to choose, that, in the place of a notary, supposing there was not one, if said valuation should be presented—it being well understood that the lots which were within the city were to be measured and valued without fail, in the regular form, for which he asked for the judicial and final decrees by my decree of the 16th January of the present year—I commanded, among other things, that, it resulting that the valuation and sale referred to had not had effect, it should be proceeded to in presence of the said defender of Don Vicente Maria and Fran. Rovira, for want of a notary, and Don Manuel Solana and Don Roque Leonardy, who were named as skilful men; that the boundaries being regulated according to what is certain from the deeds of sale of the land, they may proceed to its valuation, having first performed the customary forms, and may successively make the sale of the whole at public outcry in favor of the best bidder, for which purpose the corresponding commission shall be expedited with an insertion of the lands which ought to be valued, with the boundaries assigned, that orders may be complied with; which being done, it being added to the judicial decrees on the business to confirm them; and as respects what relates to the lot, it may be done as the said defender proposes; in consequence of which, the said commission was delivered, and the said valuation made as was ordered. I commanded him to show it to the office of royal accountant general, to say if there was anything to be said relative to the royal interests; and in order that, in the accustomed manner, the survey and valuation of the lots should be proceeded to with its knowledge, which, notwithstanding, resulted without this circumstance, and, in consequence, to the sale of all, naming as master carpenter John Purcell, and mason Joaquin Sanchez, who, in compliance with orders, and by virtue of the concurrence of the said royal accountant general's office communicated in the opinion of the 11th February, they proceeded to the sale at auction, which was done in form of law, and various bids, offers, and out-bids having been offered, the hour appointed for its conclusion having taken place, there remained auctioned in favor of Don Thomas Travers the savannas of St. Sebastian, which are situated at the distance from this city, to the southwest, of more than a quarter of a league on the west side of the river of this name of St. Sebastian; and the said savannas, from a creek which leaves said river and turns to the west, which is called Gonzalez Mendez, runs to the south more than a quarter of a league on the banks of the salt marshes this way, which runs towards the bar at Matanzas until it bounds with other salt marshes which divide the savanna of Brioso, which is the last of St. Sebastian, with another which is called de Jula. The breadth of said savannas is, from east to west, more than a quarter of a league; the boundaries of which are: on the north of the said creek of Gonzalez Mendez; on the west by a pine barren and a gravelly place, from which proceeds a branch which runs to the south; on the south, the said salt marsh of Jula; and on the east, said river St. Sebastian and its salt marshes, and that which communicates, as is already set forth, with the bar of Matanzas; which sale was verified in favor of said Don Thomas Travers for the sum of fifty dollars, there being no person who would give more, and I have approved it in favor of the aforesaid; and by my decree of the 22d of March, I have ordered that it should be notified to those contained in the proceedings of sale, that within three days they should each produce into the accountant general's office the sum which respectively corresponds to them, that it might be deposited in the royal coffers, placing a note to that effect on the judicial decrees, and, that being done, I would give a provisional judgment; after which, and having continued in various other proceedings relating to the said property, some of it being already sold, that they have not had a bidder for the former; and having already decreed, provisionally, on various memorials of some creditors to the said property, Don Felipe de Aguirre, one of the purchasers, presented himself, praying me to order what may be convenient, in order that a deed or document of property should be delivered to him, which would accredit what had been performed relative to the land referred to, called the Five Miles, and as he had satisfied the amount and presented the receipt for payment, which prove it, to the notary; in attention to which, by my decree of the 28th July, that it being certain that the said amount was satisfied, the corresponding deed should be formed, which was solicited, and the same to other persons in a similar case. In virtue of which, and there being no person to represent the rights of the said Fish, with the exception of the said defender, given officially, with whose concurrence said sale was carried into effect, and that the said Thomas Travers may have a legitimate title to the said property or land sold to him at auction, and my orders the due effect, I declare by these presents, in the name of his Majesty, (whom God preserve,) and of his royal justice, which I administer, that I sell, and give in absolute sale forever, to the said Don Thomas Travers, for himself and his heirs, the said lands of the savannas of Sebastian, free of all tribute or mortgage, at the price of the said fifty dollars, which he gave in silver, paid and deposited in the royal treasury of this city, for which there was given a receipt of payment, and, it being necessary, let it be given anew, with the renunciation of the laws which may be necessary; and from hence and for the future I take from him, the said Jesse Fish, the power, and separate him from the right which he, his heirs, or other persons, may have to the possession, property, seigniory, title, power, appeal, and any other right which appertained or belonged to said savannas; since I cede, renounce, and transfer it all to the said purchaser and his representatives, that, as their own, they may possess, sell, and alienate the said savannas at their will, in virtue of this deed, which I deliver in their favor, by which they can take and acquire the possession when it best suits them; and for its better validity and firmness, I interpose my authority and judicial decree, as I can and of right ought to contribute thereby to the good administration of justice; and I deliver these presents in this city of St. Augustine, Florida, November 22, 1792, there being witnesses, Don Manuel Rengil, Don Thomas Aguilar, and Sylvester Miranda, inhabitants present, and his excellency signed it, and whom I, the undersigned notary, know, and hold as such governor and commander-in-chief of this said city and its province, he as such exercising the administration of the royal justice in it. All of which I attest.

QUESADA.

Before me—

JOSÉ DE ZUBIZARETTA, *Notary of Government.*

I certify the foregoing to be a true and correct translation from a document in the Spanish language on file in the office of the public archives of St. Augustine.

F. J. FATIO, *S. B. L. C.*

I, William Reynolds, keeper of the public archives, do hereby certify that, on August 29, 1803, Thomas Travers sold and conveyed to George Taylor a tract of land, situated on St. Sebastian river, containing an undefined number of acres, being the same which he bought at government sale March 21, 1792, all which appears on record in my office. In testimony whereof, I hereunto set my hand and seal of office, at the city of St. Augustine, this 7th day of September, 1824.

[L. S.]   WILL. REYNOLDS, *Keeper of the Public Archives.*

[Translation.]

GENERAL POWER.

Be it known that I, George Taylor, a new settler of this province, received under the protection of his Catholic Majesty, declare that I give all my full, ample, and sufficient power, as may be required in law and necessary, to Don Fernando de la Maza Arredondo, of this place, that, in my name, and representing my proper person, rights, and actions generally, he may have, demand, receive, and recover, judicially or extra-judicially, of all and every person, of whatever state, quality, and conditions they may be, all the sums of money, gold, silver, jewels, slaves, merchandise, goods, property, and effects, of whatever kind or quality they may be, which may be owing to me, and may be due to me henceforward, in virtue of public or simple instruments, and without them, all the debts, persons, cause or reason of proceeding, quality, quantity, time, form, or other circumstances necessary in law, are not declared, because, under the generality of this clause, I have comprised whatever particularity may arise; and that he may demand and take accounts of my debts, and give them to the persons who may owe me, and make charges, and allow their acquittances, with the approval or contradiction of the terms, until the conclusion or liquidation of the balances which he may receive and recover agreeably to the same; and, in case of doubts or differences arising which cannot be conveniently adjusted, he may refer them to judges in arbitration, friendly referees, and umpires, that in arbitrating, adjusting, and compounding, they may decide and determine them, obliging myself to stand and abide by their decision. That he may be able to administer all and every my goods, real and personal, movable and immovable, sell some and buy others, rent and mortgage them, for the prices and terms which he may adjust and agree to, delivering the deeds, receipts, and letters of payment necessary, which I approve and ratify, as if I myself were present at the delivery; and that he may defend me in all my lawsuits, causes, and business, civil and criminal, ordinary and executive, moved and to be moved, with all persons whatsoever, demanding and defending, presenting petitions, deeds, witness, testimonials, certificates, proofs, bonds, accounts, balances, and other instruments, see presented, sworn to, and consented to those on the contrary side, make objections and find defects, guarantee depositions and persons, hear judicial decrees and sentences, interlocutory and definitive, consent to what is favorable, and appeal from what is adverse, and petition when he can and ought lawfully to do so, follow the course of law or desist from it, refuse judges, lawyers, notary, and other law officers, proving the causes of his refusals, or withdrawing himself from them as may best suit, and finally proceed, act, and do whatever may be in my favor, so that, for want of my power, clause, requisites, or precise circumstance, he may fail to act, since, in every respect, I give him full power, without limitation, with free, open, and general administration, incidences, and dependencies, power to prepare causes for judgment, to swear, omit, and substitute, make substitutes, and name others with substitution in form; and for the fulfilment of what he shall perform, I bind myself, with my property, present and future power, and submission to the tribunals of his Majesty, that they may compel me to its performance, as by sentence consented to and passed in authority of an adjudged case; on which I renounce all laws, customs, rights, and privileges, in my favor, and the general in form which prohibits it. In testimony of which, this is dated in the city of St. Augustine, Florida, February 18, 1804. I the notary, attest that I know the grantor who signed this, being witness, Don Francisco Rovira, Don Juan de Entralgo, and Don Bernardo José Segui, inhabitants present.

GEORGE TAYLOR.

Before me——

JOSÉ DE ZUBIZARETTA, Notary of Government.

I certify the foregoing to be a true and correct translation from a document in the Spanish language on file in the office of the public archives of St. Augustine.

F. J. FATIO, S. B. L. C.

[Translation.]

CONVEYANCE.

Be it known that I, Don Fernando de la Maza Arredondo, merchant of this city, general attorney of Don George Taylor, who is absent, and which power he has conferred on me before the present notary, February 15, 1804, which power has not been revoked, and is sufficient for what shall be said: I declare that I really sell to Don Gabriel G. Perpall, also of this place, certain savannas belonging to my principal, known by the name of St. Sebastian, and which are situated to the southwest of this city, at the distance of a quarter of a league, on the west side of the river of St. Sebastian, which, from a creek which it forms and turns to the west, called Gonzalo Mendez, runs to the south more than a quarter of a league on the bank of salt marshes on this course to the bar of Matanzas, which divide the savanna of Briesto, which is the last of St. Sebastian, with another called Juta, having a breadth east and west a little more than a quarter of a league, whose boundaries are on the north of said creek of Gonzalo Mendez, on the west the pine barren and a gravel bank, from which arises a creek, turning to the south on this side the said salt marsh of Juta, and on the east the said river St. Sebastian and its salt marshes, and of that which communicates, as said before, with the bar of Matanzas, which said savanna my principal had and bought from Don Thomas Travers, deceased, by deed, which he made in these archives August 29, 1803; and I make him the said sale, with all its entrances, outlets, uses, customs, rights, and services, which belong and appertain to the said savannas, and free of all encumbrance, as I, the said notary, certify, from the results of the book of mortgages in my charge, which I have searched for the purpose, at the price of six hundred and fifty dollars, which the purchaser has paid me in cash, which sum I acknowledge as delivered to my will; on which I renounce proof, laws of delivery, exception to money not counted, fraud, and everything else in the case; for which I separate my said principal from the right of property, possession, use, seigniory, and other rights, real and personal, which he had or held to the said savannas of St. Sebastian; that I cede, renounce, and transfer them to the purchaser, and his representation, that, as his own, he may possess, sell, and alienate them at his will, in virtue of this writing, which I deliver in his favor as a token of real delivery, by which it is seen that he has acquired the possession, without occasion for further proof, from which I release him, and oblige myself to the eviction and guarantee of this sale in due form, and as may best suit, in favor of the purchaser, with my property, present and future power, and submission to the tribunal of his Majesty, that they may force me to compliance, as by sentence consented to and passed in authority of a thing adjudged, on which I renounce all laws, customs, rights, and privileges in my favor, and everything in form which prohibits it. And I, the said Don Gabriel W. Perpall, being present, accept in my favor this writing, and by it receive as purchased the said savannas of St. Sebastian, at the price and agreement on which they were sold to me, and I acknowledge them as delivered to my will. I renounce proof, laws of delivery, those of a thing not seen or received, fraud, and everything else in the case; for which I deliver a receipt in form. In testimony of which, this is dated in the city of St. Augustine, March 18, 1809. I, the notary, attest that I know the parties who signed this, being witnessed by Don Juan de Entralgo, Don Bernardino Sanchez, and Don Bernardo José Segui, inhabitants present.

FERNANDO DE LA MAZA ARREDONDO.
GABRIEL G. PERPALL.

Before me——

JOSÉ DE ZUBIZARETTA, Government Notary.

I certify the foregoing to be a true and correct translation from a document in the Spanish language on file in the office of the public archives of St. Augustine.

F. J. FATIO, S. B. L. C.

DECREE BY THE BOARD.

The claimant in this case exhibited a judicial or government sale of the land by Governor Quesada to Thomas Travers, which sale we ascertain was made in conformity to the laws and usages of the late Spanish Government, and dated November 22, 1792. An abstract from the office of the public archives was also exhibited, by which it appears that Travers sold and conveyed the land to George Taylor, by his attorney, Fernando de la Maza Arredondo, who sold and conveyed the same to the claimant. The board having ascertained from the exhibits offered that the quantity of land claimed is undefined, they order that this case be reported to Congress for their determination. April 14.

No. 7.—See REPORT No. 6.

Robert Gilbert vs. The United States. For one hundred acres of land.

MEMORIAL.

To the honorable the commissioners appointed to ascertain claims and titles to lands in East Florida:

The memorial of Robert Gilbert respectfully showeth: That your memorialist claims title to a tract of land consisting of one hundred acres of land, situated on the Matanzas river, and has not been surveyed, the original documents of which are in the office of the archives, as is supposed, and a certificate of which from the government secretary is herewith presented, dated March 1, 1798; which title your memorialist derives from a grant made to him by Governor White, in virtue of the royal order of 1790; and your memorialist further showeth that he is not in actual possession of said lands, they not having been set off to him by the government, but were granted to him on account of grievances which he had suffered by the government; that he is a citizen of the United States and resident of Florida.

JOHN B. STRONG, *Attorney for Claimant.*

St. Augustine, *November* 24, 1823.

[Translation.]

Don Juan de Pierra, sub-lieutenant of the fourth company of the third battalion of the infantry regiment of Cuba, and secretary of this government, and commanding general: I certify that a memorial presented by Robert Gilbert the 27th of last month, soliciting, in virtue of the definitive sentence in the decrees against various inhabitants for the crime of rebellion, lands which are vacant in the place named Mosse, this day the following decree was made: "This party having made it appear that the lands which he solicits are not in Mosse, but in Matanzas, this error originating from the mistake of the writer, let those he solicits be granted him, without prejudice to a third person, until, according to the persons he may have for its cultivation, the corresponding quantity is assigned. This writing having to be passed to the military assessor in order that it may be united to the proceedings instituted against the petitioner for the crime of rebellion, and that it may serve for the interested, I give these presents at St. Augustine, Florida, March 1, 1798.

"JUAN DE PIERRA."

I certify that the foregoing is a true and correct translation from a document in the Spanish language.

F. J. FATIO, *S. B. L. C.*

DECREE OF THE BOARD.

The claimant exhibited to the board a certified copy of concession for the land by Governor White to him, dated March 1, 1798; quantity undefined. The board not being authorized to decide finally on claims of this nature, they therefore order that the documents accompanying the memorial be forwarded to Congress for their determination. December 1.

No 1.—See REPORT No. 7.

William Travers vs. The United States. For four hundred and twenty acres of land.

MEMORIAL.

To the honorable the commissioners appointed to ascertain claims and titles to lands in East Florida:

The petition of William Travers, son of Thomas Travers, late of St. Augustine, deceased, for himself and the other heirs of the said Thomas Travers, respectfully showeth: That your memorialist claims title to a tract of land containing four hundred and twenty acres, situated about two or two and a half miles west of St. Augustine, and bounded as follows: beginning at a pine marked with a cross; running thence north 63° east, 70 chains 71 links, to a pine marked with a Roman number XII; thence south 27° east, 52 chains, to a pine marked with a cross; thence south 74° west, 24 chains, to a pine with III; thence north 34° west, 12 chains, to a pine with III; thence north 63° west, to a pine with a cross; thence north 27° west, to the beginning; which title your memorialist derives from a sale made to Joseph Peavitt, May 18, 1779, by Henry Skinner, of the said land; and your memorialist further showeth that the said Peavitt cultivated the said lands, and had possession of them up to the time of his death, when they came legally into possession of Maria Evans, wife of the said Peavitt, who, by her last will and ——, *devised* them to your memorialist's father, Thomas Travers. Your memorialist further shows that he is in actual possession of said land, and that he is an American citizen, and a resident of St. Augustine.

WILLIAM TRAVERS.

[Here follows a mutilated instrument of writing, purporting to be a lease from Henry Skinner to Joseph Peavitt for one year, dated May 17, 1775; also a mutilated release in fee, dated May 18, 1779, and also an order of survey directed to Benjamin Lord by Governor Pat. Tonyn, dated March 10, 1783.]

[Here follows the translation of the certificate and plat of survey, by A. Burgevin, of the 428 acres, dated December 20, 1819.]

East Florida, *St. John's County:*

This day personally appeared before me, the subscriber, one of the justices of the peace for the county aforesaid, Gabriel Triay, who, being duly sworn, doth depose and say that he has resided in and about St. Augustine near fifty-five years; that he knew Joseph Peavitt as early as 1779, and remained acquainted with him up to the time of his death: that Peavitt remained here after the cession of the country by Great Britain to Spain in 1784, and became a Spanish subject; that he, this deponent, was employed by Peavitt, whilst the British had possession of the country, to build houses, &c., upon a plantation belonging to the said Peavitt, at a place about two miles west from St. Augustine, at a place called Peavitt swamp; that Peavitt retained possession of the said lands up to the time of his death, which took place some time after the Spaniards came into the country; that he never heard the right of Peavitt's heirs to this property questioned. The improvements made upon this plantation were burnt by the Indians, and the plantation broken up many years ago. A man by the name of Penman had a plantation about a mile and a half to the northward of the place described by this deponent. Deponent knows that Joseph Peavitt had negroes upon Penman's place for several years, and cultivated that place at the same time that he planted the plantation in Peavitt's swamp. Deponent does not know how much land Peavitt owned in the swamp, but always thought the whole belonged to him. Deponent knew Maria Evans, the wife of Peavitt, well; after the death of Peavitt she married a man by the name of Hudson, who died here some time since— some time before the death of Maria Evans. Peavitt had no children, and, after his death, his wife had possession of all his property to the time of her death. The house built by Peavitt was from thirty to thirty-five feet long, and sixteen or seventeen broad; he had about twenty-eight negroes, workers, and all necessary houses for them, and had about forty or fifty acres cleared and in cultivation for them, besides a considerable quantity of pine land.

GABRIEL + TRIAY.
his
mark.

Sworn to before me July 19, 1824.

BERNARDO SEGUI, *J. P.*

EAST FLORIDA, *St. John's County :*

This day personally appeared before the subscriber, one of the justices of the peace for the county aforesaid, Nicholas Estefanopoly, who, being duly sworn, doth depose and say that he has resided in St. Augustine for many years; that he was acquainted with Joseph Peavitt before and after the cession of this country by Great Britain to Spain, and knew of the said Joseph Peavitt becoming a Spanish subject; that he, this deponent, was employed by Peavitt at sundry jobs at said Peavitt's plantation, situated about two miles west from St. Augustine, and at a place called Swamp—this ——— whilst under the government of Great Britain; but that he knows Peavitt remained cultivating the said land up to the time of his death, and that he has not a doubt his widow continued in possession for many years after and planted the same; that he never heard the right of Peavitt's heirs to this land questioned. Deponent knew Maria Evans, the wife of Peavitt; after the death of Peavitt she married a man by the name of Hudson, who died here some time before the death of Maria Evans.

NICHOLAS + ESTEFANOPOLY.
his
mark.

Sworn to before me July 21, A. D. 1824.

BERNARDO SEGUI, *J. P.*

DECREE BY THE BOARD.

In this case we ascertain that the land was originally granted to one Skinner by the British government; that he conveyed it by deed to Joseph Peavitt; that Peavitt, after the cession of this country to Spain, continued to occupy and cultivate it; that he became a Spanish subject, and died without issue; that his wife continued to occupy, and cultivated the same until her death; that in her last will and testament she bequeathed the land to Thomas Travers, deceased. We confirm the title to claimant. April 15.

[Nos. 2, 3, 4, 5 were not returned to the General Land Office by the commissioners.]

No. 6.—See REPORT No. 7.

Charles W. and Geo. J. F. Clarke vs. *The United States. Claim for three hundred acres of land.*

MEMORIAL.

To the honorable the commissioners appointed to ascertain claims and titles to lands in East Florida :

The petition of Charles W. and George J. F. Clarke respectfully showeth: That your memorialists claim title to a tract of land consisting of three hundred acres, situated on the Matanzas river, at a place called Worcester; the first line beginning at a stake, and running west, forty-seven chains, to a pine; second line, south, fifty-five chains, to a blank corner; the third, east, sixty-seven chains, to a pine; fourth line formed and bounded by the marshes of Matanzas river; which title your memorialists derive from a British title made to Thomas Clarke, their father, by Governor Grant, as will appear by an original grant accompanying this petition. The original instrument showing the Spanish recognition of this title has been already presented to your honorable board by George J. F. Clarke in another petition. And your memorialists further show that they are in actual possession of said lands; that they are natives and residents of Florida. Your petitioners will, as in duty bound, forever pray, &c.

GEO. J. F. CLARKE,
For CHARLES AND GEORGE CLARKE.

[Here follows a grant of the British governor, James Grant, to Thomas Clarke, dated April 2, 1776.]
[Here follows a recognition of the above grant by the Spanish government, dated November 15, 178-.]

Charles W. and George J. F. Clarke vs *The United States. Claim for three hundred acres of land.*

The board having ascertained that the above is a valid British grant, and that it has been duly recognized by the Spanish authorities, and that the claimants are the legitimate heirs of the grantee, do confirm it to them accordingly.

No. 7.—See REPORT No. 7.

James and George Clarke vs. *The United States. Claim for five hundred acres of land.*

MEMORIAL.

To the honorable the commissioners appointed to ascertain claims and titles to lands in East Florida :

The petition of James and George J. F. Clarke respectfully showeth: That your memorialists claim title to a tract of land consisting of five hundred acres, situated on the west of Matanzas river; first line, south sixty-six degrees west, eighty-two chains, from a pine to a pine; second line, north twenty-four degrees west, sixty-one chains, to a stake; third, south sixty-six degrees west, eighty-two chains, to a stake; fourth, twenty-four degrees east, sixty-one chains, to the pine of beginning; which title your memorialists derive from a British title made to Honoria Clarke, their mother, by Governor Tonyn, as per original grant herewith presented; the recognition thereof will be found in a Spanish original instrument already presented by George J. F. Clarke in another memorial. Three hundred and fifty of these five hundred are the property of said James Clarke, of the Spanish army in Europe, and the remaining one hundred and fifty are that of your petitioner present. And your memorialists further show that they are in actual possession of said lands. Both your petitioners are natives of East Florida, and the present a resident. Your petitioners will, as in duty bound, pray, &c.

GEO. J. F. CLARKE,

For JAMES AND GEORGE CLARKE.

[Here follows a grant of the British governor, Patrick Tonyn, to Mrs. Honoria Clarke, dated September 29, 1780.]

[Here follows a recognition of the above grant by the Spanish government, dated November 15, 1787.]

DECREE.

James and G. J. F. Clarke vs. The United States. For five hundred acres of land.

The board having ascertained that the above is a valid British grant, and that it has been duly recognized by the Spanish authorities, and that the claimants are the legitimate heirs of the grantee, do confirm it to them accordingly. October 10, 1825.

[No. 8 was not returned by the commissioners to the General Land Office.]

No. 1.—See REPORT No. 8.

Farquhar Bethune vs. The United States. For a lot in Fernandina.

MEMORIAL.

To the honorable the commissioners appointed to ascertain claims and titles to lands in East Florida:

The memorial of Farquhar Bethune respectfully showeth: That your memorialist claims title to a lot in the town of Fernandina, designated on the plan of said town by the number seven of the ninth square, measuring in front seventeen varas, and in depth thirty-four, bounded on the north by White street, on the east by another lot belonging to your memorialist, on the south by Joseph Gantt's lot, and on the west by Joseph Hernandez's lot; which title your memorialist derives from a grant in fee simple made to George Atkinson by Governor Kindelan, August 16, 1814. Your memorialist further showeth that he is in possession of said lot, and was so at the time of the cession. That he is an inhabitant of Florida, and a resident of Amelia island, having purchased said lot from George Atkinson September 1, 1814. The bill of sale, marked A, is annexed, as also the grant marked B. All of which is respectfully submitted, &c.

FARQUHAR BETHUNE.

[Here follows the translation of the royal title made by Kindelan to George Atkinson for the lot of land, dated August 16, 1814.]

[Here follows the translation of a sale from Atkinson to claimant, dated September 1, 1814.]

DECREE.

The board ascertain this to be a valid Spanish grant made previous to January 24, 1818, and confirm the title to claimant. April 25.

No. 2.—See REPORT No. 8.

Farquhar Bethune vs. The United States. For a lot of land in Fernandina.

MEMORIAL.

To the honorable the commissioners appointed to ascertain claims and titles to lands in East Florida:

The memorial of Farquhar Bethune respectfully showeth: That your memorialist claims title to a lot of land in the town of Fernandina, number five of the ninth square, bounded on the east by Daniel Hurlbert's lot, on the south by Josiah Grey's, on the west by your memorialist's lot number seven, on the north by White street, and contains in front seventeen varas, and in depth thirty-four; which title your memorialist derives from a grant made to Andrew Atkinson October 2, 1811, by Governor Estrada, from whom your memorialist purchased it September 1, 1814. Your memorialist further showeth that the said lot was improved in compliance with the conditions imposed by the order of May 10, 1811, by the first occupant and by your memorialist; that he has been in possession of said lot since the year 1814, and is so now; that he is an inhabitant of Florida and resident of Amelia island. All of which is respectfully submitted.

FARQUHAR BETHUNE.

[Here follows the translation of a grant by Governor Estrada of the lot of land to Andrew Atkinson, dated May 2, 1811.]

[Here follows the translation of a sale of the lot from Atkinson to claimant, dated September 1, 1814.]

DECREE.

The board ascertain this to be a valid Spanish grant made previous to January 24, 1818, and confirm the title to claimant. April 21.

No. 3.—See REPORT No. 8.

Zephaniah Kingsley vs. The United States. For a lot in Fernandina.

MEMORIAL.

To the honorable the commissioners appointed to ascertain claims and titles to lands in East Florida:

The petition of Zephaniah Kingsley, by George Gibbs, attorney in fact, respectfully showeth: That your memorialist claims title to a lot of land consisting of seventeen varas in front and thirty-four varas in depth, situated in the town of Fernandina, Amelia island, bounded on the north by the marsh of Egan's creek, on the south by a lot of John McClure, on the east by the street Pasco de las Damas, on the west by a lot of Philip R. Yonge; which title your memorialist derives from a royal title made to your memorialist by Governor Estrada July 7, 1815, marked A, herewith submitted. And your memorialist further showeth that he is in actual possession of said lot; that he is now a citizen of the United States and resident of the Territory of Florida.

ZEPHANIAH KINGSLEY,
By GEORGE GIBBS, *Attorney in fact.*

[Here follows the translation of the royal title made by Governor Estrada for a lot, dated July 7, 1815.]

DECREE.

The board ascertain this to be a valid Spanish grant made previous to January 24, 1818, and confirm the title to claimant. April 26.

No. 4.—See REPORT No. 8.

Zephaniah Kingsley vs. The United States. For a lot.

MEMORIAL.

To the honorable the commissioners appointed to ascertain claims and titles to lands in East Florida:

The petition of Zephaniah Kingsley, by George Gibbs, attorney in fact, respectfully showeth: That your memorialist claims title to a tract of land consisting of about one hundred and seventy feet north and south, situated in the town of Fernandina, about ninety-three feet from east to west, which is equal to about fourteen hundred and seventy square yards, bounded on the north by a creek called Egan's creek, on the east by vacant marsh, on the south by other lands belonging to your memorialist, and on the west by the canal belonging to Hibberson and Yonge, being from north to south forty-seven varas, and from east to west thirty-four varas; which title your memorialist derives from a royal title made to your memorialist by Governor Coppinger, per memorialist's decree dated July 8, 1815, marked A, herewith enclosed, and reference to the documents in the office of the archives of the Territory will more fully appear. And your memorialist further showeth that he is in actual possession of said lands; that he is now a citizen of the United States and resident of the Territory of Florida.

ZEPHANIAH KINGSLEY,
By GEORGE GIBBS, *Attorney in fact.*

[Here follows translation of a royal title made by Governor Coppinger, dated March 27, 1817.]

DECREE.

Zephaniah Kingsley vs. The United States. For a marsh lot in the town of Fernandina.

The board ascertained this to be a valid grant made to memorialist previous to January 24, 1818, and therefore confirm the same to claimant. April 29, 1825.

No. 5.—See REPORT No. 8.

Farquhar Bethune vs. The United States. For a lot in Fernandina.

MEMORIAL.

To the honorable the commissioners appointed to ascertain claims and titles to lands in East Florida:

The memorial of Farquhar Bethune respectfully showeth: That your memorialist claims title to a lot of land in the town of Fernandina, designated in the plan of said town by number nine of the ninth square, containing in front seventeen varas, and in depth thirty-four, bounded on the north by White street, on the east by another lot of your memorialist, on the south by Damian Rainey's lot, and on the west by Joseph Bergallos; which title your memorialist derives from a grant made to Francis Entralgo January 31, 1811, by Governor White. Entralgo dying without heirs, said lot became his mother's, Catalina Hijuelos, according to Spanish laws, who sold said lot to Francis Marin, by his attorney, John Entralgo, from which Marin your memorialist purchased said lot. At the time of issuing this grant there was no regularly laid out town, but, May 10, 1811, orders were had for forming a regular plan, and decree passed that those who should build and improve on said new plan should be entitled to a grant in fee simple, which was not previously the case. Your memorialist further showeth that the said lot has been duly improved by the first occupants and by himself; that he is now in possession of said lot, and was so at the time of the cession; that he is an inhabitant of Florida and a resident of Amelia island. All of which is respectfully submitted, &c.

FARQUHAR BETHUNE.

[Here follows translation of a concession made by Governor White January 31, 1811, to Francis de Entralgo.]
[Here follows translation of a conveyance from Catalina Hijuelos, legal heiress of Francisco de Entralgo, to Francisco Marin, dated December 28, 1816.]
[Here follows translation of a conveyance from Francisco Marin, by his attorney, Pedro Pons, dated September 12, 1818.]

DECREE.

Farquhar Bethune vs. The United States. For a lot in Fernandina.

The board having ascertained the above to be a valid Spanish concession, and the deraignment to claimant being regular, the same is confirmed accordingly. April 29, 1825.

No. 6.—See REPORT No. 8.

George Fleming's heirs vs. The United States. For a lot in Fernandina.

MEMORIAL.

To the honorable the commissioners appointed to ascertain claims and titles to lands in East Florida:

The petition of the heirs of George Fleming, deceased, by Sophia Fleming, widow and relict of said decedent, respectfully showeth: That your memorialists claim title to a tract of land consisting of one lot, situated in the town of Fernandina, designated as lot number seven; which title your memorialist derives from a concession made to George Fleming May 2, 1811, by Governor Estrada, which is herewith exhibited, marked B. And your memorialists show they are in actual possession of said lot, and were so by *themselves ancestor* before the cession of this Territory to the United States by *Spain, as well as that time,* and ever since; that they are citizens of the United States and residents of East Florida. They pray confirmation of title, &c. All of which is submitted, &c.

SOPHIA FLEMING,
For herself and the heirs of George Fleming.

[Here follows the translation of a decree of concession by Governor Estrada, dated May 2, 1811.]

DECREE.

George Fleming's heirs vs. The United States. For a lot in Fernandina.

The board having ascertained the above to be a valid Spanish concession to George Fleming, deceased, do confirm it to his heirs accordingly. April 29, 1825.

No. 7.—See REPORT No. 8.

William Hobkirk vs. The United States. For a lot in Fernandina.

MEMORIAL.

To the honorable the commissioners appointed to ascertain claims and titles to lands in East Florida:

The petition of William Hobkirk respectfully showeth: That your memorialist claims title to a tract of land consisting of a town lot, situated in the town of Fernandina, numbered square eighteen, and lots three and four in the plan of said town, measuring seventeen varas front and thirty-four varas in depth; which title your memorialist derives from a royal title made to memorialist by Governor Coppinger, a copy of which said royal title is herewith filed, dated January 13, 1816, marked A; and your memorialist further showeth that he is legally seized and ——— *possession* of said lands; that he is a citizen of the United States and resident of East Florida, and was so at the time and before the cession of this province. *He prays* confirmation of title, &c.

WILLIAM HOBKIRK.

[Here follows translation of a royal title from Governor Coppinger, dated January 13, 1816.]

DECREE.

William Hobkirk vs. The United States. For a lot in Fernandina.

This being a valid Spanish title, made previous to January 24, 1818, it is therefore confirmed. May 30, 1818.

No. 8.—See REPORT No. 8.

George Atkinson vs. The United States. For a lot in Fernandina.

To the honorable the commissioners appointed to ascertain claims and titles to lands in East Florida:

The petition of George Atkinson, by George Gibbs, attorney in fact, respectfully showeth: That your memorialist claims title to a lot consisting of seventeen yards in front, and thirty-four in depth, situated in the town of Fernandina, bounded on the north by San Fernando street, on the east by the lot of the black woman Flora, on the south by the lot of Henry Quible, and on the west by the lot of Anna Wiggins; which title your memorialist derives from a grant made to your memorialist by Governor Coppinger, May 7, 1817, as will more fully appear by reference to the said grant, herewith exhibited, of the above date, marked P. And your memorialist further showeth that he is in legal possession of said lot; that he is a citizen of the United States and resident of Darien, Georgia.

GEORGE ATKINSON,
By GEORGE GIBBS, Attorney in fact.

[Here follows translation of a royal title by Governor Coppinger, dated May 7, 1817.]

DECREE.

George Atkinson vs. *The United States.   For a lot in Fernandina.*

This being a valid Spanish title made previous to January 24, 1818, it is therefore confirmed. June 6, 1825.

No. 9.—See Report No. 8.

John Middleton vs. *The United States.   For a lot.*

MEMORIAL.

To the honorable the commissioners appointed to ascertain claims and titles to lands in East Florida:

The memorial of John Middleton, by his attorney, Farquhar Bethune, respectfully showeth: That your memorialist claims title to a lot in the town of Fernandina, known in the plan of said town by the number six of the first square, containing in front seventeen varas, and in depth thirty-four, bounded on the north by Mrs. Jane Sibbald's lot, on the east by William Hall's, on the south by Constitution square, and on the west by Joseph Arredondo's lot; which title your memorialist claims from a grant in fee simple made to James Cashen by Governor Kindelan on the thirtieth March, one thousand eight hundred and fourteen, and by said Cashen conveyed to Middleton and Sibley by the deed bearing date November 20, 1817; and your memorialist further showeth that he is in actual possession of said lot, and was so at the time of the cession; that he is a citizen of the United States and resident of Fernandina.   The title above referred to, marked A, and the deed, marked B, accompanies this memorial.   All of which is respectfully submitted.
                                                    JOHN MIDDLETON,
                                        By his attorney, FARQ. BETHUNE.

[Here follows translation of a royal title, dated March 30, 1814, made by Governor Kindelan to James Cashen.]

[Here follows a conveyance from James Cashen and Susannah, his wife, to John Middleton and John Sibley, dated November 20, 1817.]

DECREE.

John Middleton vs. *The United States.   For a lot in Fernandina.*

The board having ascertained the above to be a valid Spanish grant made to James Cashen, and by him conveyed to John Middleton and John Sibley, the same is confirmed to them accordingly.   May 12, 1825.

No. 10.—See Report No. 8.

George Atkinson vs. *The United States.   For a lot in Fernandina.*

MEMORIAL.

To the honorable the commissioners appointed to ascertain claims and titles to lands in East Florida:

The petition of George Atkinson, by his attorney, George Gibbs, respectfully showeth: That your memorialist claims title to a tract of land consisting of a lot of land in Fernandina, situated in Amelia island, containing seventeen yards in front, and thirty-four yards in depth, bounded on the north by a lot belonging to memorialist, on the east by a lot of Joseph Alvarez, on the south by a lot of George Clarke, and on the west by Constitution square; which title your memorialist made to him by Governor Kindelan August 16, 1814, as will more fully appear by reference to the grant herewith exhibited, of the above date, as marked below.   And your memorialist further showeth that he is legally in possession of said lands or lot called No. 11, per exhibit G A, No. 11; that he is a citizen of the United States and resident of Darien, Georgia.
                                                    GEORGE ATKINSON,
                                        By GEORGE GIBBS, *Attorney in fact.*

[Here follows translation of a royal title by Governor Kindelan, dated August 16, 1814.]

DECREE.

George Atkinson vs. *The United States.   For a lot in Fernandina.*

The board having ascertained the above to be a valid Spanish title to claimant, do confirm the same accordingly.   July 8, 1825.

No. 11.—See Report No. 8.

George Atkinson vs. *The United States.   For a lot in Fernandina.*

MEMORIAL.

To the honorable the commissioners appointed to ascertain claims and titles to lands in East Florida:

The petition of George Atkinson, by George Gibbs, his attorney in fact, showeth: That your memorialist claims title to a tract of land consisting of seventeen yards in front and thirty-four in depth, situated in the town of Fernandina, bounded north by the lot of José M. Arguelles; east by the lot of Felicia, a free woman of color; on the south by White street; and on the west by the lot of Charles Clarke; which title your memorialist derives from a grant made to him by Governor Coppinger May 7, 1817, as will more fully appear by reference to the said grant herewith submitted, of the above date, marked R. And your memorialist further showeth that he is in legal possession of said lot; that he is a citizen of the United States and resident of Darien, Georgia.

GEORGE ATKINSON,
By GEORGE GIBBS, <i>Attorney in fact.</i>

[Here follows translation of a royal title made by Governor Coppinger, dated May 7, 1817.]

DECREE.

George Atkinson vs. The United States.   For a lot in Fernandina.

The board having ascertained the above to be a valid Spanish title, do confirm the same accordingly. July 8, 1825.

No. 12.—See REPORT No. 8.

Lindsay Todd's executors vs. The United States.   For a lot in Fernandina.

MEMORIAL.

To the honorable the commissioners appointed to ascertain claims and titles to lands in East Florida:

The petition of the executors of Lindsay Todd, by George Gibbs, attorney in fact, showeth: That your memorialists claim title to a tract of <i>lot</i> consisting of seventeen yards in front and thirty-four yards in depth, situated in the town of Fernandina, bounded on the north by the lots of Diana Domingo, on the east by Commandant street, on the south by White street, and on the west by the lot of Maria Clark; which title your memorialists derive from a grant made to ———— by Governor Kindelan, in virtue of ————, June 7, 1814, as will more fully appear by a reference to the grant herewith submitted, of the above date, marked W.   And your memorialists further show that they are in actual possession of said lot; that they are citizens of the United States and residents of Darien, Georgia.

GEORGE ATKINSON,
DAVID KIDD, } <i>Executors,</i>
By GEORGE GIBBS, <i>Attorney in fact.</i>

[Here follows translation of a royal title made by Governor Kindelan, dated June 7, 1814.]

DECREE.

Executors of Lindsay Todd vs. The United States.   For a lot in Fernandina.

The board having ascertained the above to be a valid Spanish title made to Lindsay Todd, deceased, do confirm the same to his executors.   July 8, 1825.

No. 13.—See REPORT No. 8.

Henry Yonge vs. The United States.   For a lot in Fernandina.

MEMORIAL.

To the honorable the commissioners appointed to ascertain claims and titles to lands in East Florida:

The petition of Henry Yonge respectfully showeth: That your memorialist claims title to a tract of land or lot consisting of seventeen yards in depth and the same number in breadth, situated in the town of Fernandina, bounded on the north by the street of St. Fernando, on the east by another lot belonging to Henry Yonge, on the south by another lot belonging to John Forbes, and on the west by Marine street; which title your memorialist derives from a grant made to Henry Yonge by Governor Kindelan, who sold the same to your memorialist; which grant is dated January 31, 1814, as will more fully appear by reference to the said grant and transfer herewith exhibited, of the above date, marked X.   And your memorialist further shows that he is in actual possession of said lot; that he was a subject of Spain and resident of the United States.

HENRY YONGE,
By GEORGE GIBBS, <i>Attorney in fact.</i>

[Here follows translation of a royal title by Governor Kindelan, dated January 31, 1814.]

DECREE.

Henry Yonge vs. The United States.   For a lot in Fernandina.

The board having ascertained the above to be a valid Spanish title to claimant, do confirm it to him accordingly.   June 11, 1825.

No. 14.—See REPORT No. 8.

Hibberson & Yonge vs. The United States.   For a lot in the town of Fernandina.

MEMORIAL.

To the honorable the commissioners appointed to ascertain claims and titles to lands in East Florida:

The petition of Hibberson & Yonge, by their attorney, George Gibbs, respectfully showeth: That your memorialists claim title to a tract of land consisting of a lot of land situated in the town of Fernandina, Amelia island; which said lot extends two hundred feet northeast from their storehouse, thence to the southwest; which title your memorialists derive from a license made to them to build a wharf by Governor Estrada, December 4, 1811, as per exhibit U, as by reference to the said grant, herewith submitted, will more fully appear. And your memorialists further show that they are legally in possession of said lands; that they were subjects of Spain and residents of the United States.

HIBBERSON & YONGE,
By GEORGE GIBBS, *Attorney in fact.*

[Here follows translation of a concession by Governor Estrada, dated December 4, 1811.]

DECREE.

Hibberson & Yonge vs. The United States. For a lot in Fernandina.

The board having ascertained the above to be a valid Spanish concession do confirm the same accordingly.   July 11, 1825.

No. 15.—See REPORT No. 8.

Hibberson & Yonge vs. The United States. For four and a quarter acres of land.

MEMORIAL.

To the honorable the commissioners appointed to ascertain claims and titles to lands in East Florida:

The petition of Hibberson & Yonge, by George Gibbs, attorney in fact, showeth: That your memorialists claim title to a tract of land consisting of one and three-quarters acre of high land and two and a half acres of marsh, situated in the town of Fernandina, on the north by Egan's creek, on the east by Amelia street, lots of different individuals, and marshes of the said creek, on the south by San Fernando street, and west by the lots of James Cavedo and James Cashen, Estrada street and swamp; which title your memorialists derive from a grant made to them by Governor Coppinger, in virtue of ————, February 1, 1816, as will more fully appear by reference to the said grant herewith submitted, of the above date, marked Z. And your memorialists further show that they are in legal possession of said lands; that they are subjects of Spain and residents of the United States.

HIBBERSON & YONGE,
By GEORGE GIBBS, *Attorney in fact.*

[Here follows translation of a royal title by Governor Coppinger, dated February 1, 1816.]

DECREE.

Hibberson & Yonge vs. The United States. For four and a quarter acres of land.

This being a valid Spanish title made previous to January 24, 1818, it is therefore confirmed.   July 11, 1825.

No. 16.—See REPORT No. 8.

Hibberson & Yonge vs. The United States. For thirty-four yards of marsh land.

MEMORIAL.

To the honorable the commissioners appointed to ascertain claims and titles to lands in East Florida:

The petition of Hibberson & Yonge respectfully showeth: That your memorialists claim title to a lot of land consisting of thirty-four yards of marsh land, situated in the town of Fernandina, *on the north by a marsh* granted to D. la M. Arredondo, on the east by Marius tract, on the south by vacant marsh, and on the west by the river; which title your memorialists derive from a grant made to them by Governor Coppinger February 1, 1816, as will more fully appear by reference to the grant herewith exhibited, of the above date, marked Y. And your memorialists further show that they are in actual possession of said lot; that they were subjects of Spain and residents of the United States.

HIBBERSON & YONGE,
By GEORGE GIBBS, *Attorney, &c.*

[Here follows translation of a royal title by Governor Coppinger, dated February 1, 1816.]

DECREE.

Hibberson & Yonge vs. The United States. For thirty-four yards of marsh land.

The board having ascertained the above to be a valid Spanish title, do confirm the same accordingly. July 11, 1825.

No. 17.—See REPORT No. 8.

Hibberson & Yonge vs. The United States. For a lot.

MEMORIAL.

To the honorable the commissioners appointed to ascertain claims and titles to lands in East Florida:

The petition of Hibberson & Yonge, by George Gibbs, attorney, respectfully showeth: That your memorialists claim title to a tract of *lot* consisting of thirty-four yards of marsh land, situated in the town of Fernandina, *on the north by vacant marsh*, on the east by Marius tract, on the south by Sommeruelos street, and on the west by the river; which title your memorialists derive from a grant made to them by Governor Coppinger, in virtue of the royal order, February 1, 1816, as will more fully appear by reference to the said grant herewith exhibited, of the above date, marked H. And your memorialists further show that they are in actual possession of the said lot; that they were subjects of Spain and residents of the United States.

HIBBERSON & YONGE,
By GEORGE GIBBS, Attorney in fact.

[Here follows translation of a royal title by Governor Coppinger, dated February 1, 1816.]

DECREE.

Hibberson & Yonge vs. The United States. For a lot in Fernandina.

The board having ascertained the above to be a valid Spanish title, do confirm the same accordingly. July 11, 1825.

No. 18.—See REPORT No. 8.

Domingo Fernandez vs. The United States. For a lot in the town of Fernandina.

MEMORIAL.

To the honorable the commissioners appointed to ascertain claims and titles to lands in East Florida:

The memorial of Domingo Fernandez respectfully showeth: That your memorialist claims title to a lot of land in the town of Fernandina, designated in the plan of said town by the number four, of square twenty-three, measuring in front seventeen varas, in depth thirty-four varas, bounded on the north by John Moore's lot, on the east by William Garvin's lot, on the south by White street, and on the west by your memorialist's lot; which title your memorialist derived from a grant in fee simple made to him by Governor Coppinger April 10, 1817. Your memorialist further showeth that he is now in possession of said lot, and was so at the time of the cession; that he is an inhabitant of Florida and a resident of Amelia island. All of which is respectfully submitted, &c.

DOMINGO FERNANDEZ,
By his attorney, FARQUHAR BETHUNE.

[Here follows translation of a royal title made by Governor Coppinger, dated April 10, 1817.]

DECREE.

Domingo Fernandez vs. The United States. For a lot in the town of Fernandina.

The board having ascertained the above to be a valid Spanish grant, do confirm the same accordingly. August 9, 1825.

No. 19.—See REPORT No. 8.

Domingo Fernandez vs. The United States. For four half lots in Fernandina.

MEMORIAL.

To the honorable the commissioners appointed to ascertain claims and titles to lands in East Florida:

The memorial of Domingo Fernandez, by his attorney, Farquhar Bethune, respectfully showeth: That your memorialist claims title to four half lots in the town of Fernandina, known in the plan of said town by the numbers five, six, seven, and eight, of square number twenty-three, and containing in front seventy-eight varas, in depth seventeen varas, bounded on the north by St. Fernando street, on the east by John Moore's and John Lofton's lots, on the south by White street, and on the west by New street; which title your memorialist derives from a grant made to him by Governor Coppinger April 10, 1817; which grant is hereunto annexed, marked A. Your memorialist further showeth that he is an inhabitant of Florida and a resident of Amelia island. All which is respectfully submitted, &c.

DOMINGO FERNANDEZ,
By his attorney, FARQUHAR BETHUNE.

[Here follows translation of a royal title by Governor Coppinger, dated April 10, 1817.]

DECREE.

Domingo Fernandez vs. The United States. For four half lots in Fernandina.

The board having ascertained the above to be a valid Spanish title, do confirm the same accordingly. August 9, 1825.

No. 20.—See REPORT No. 8.

Domingo Fernandez vs. The United States. For a lot in the town of Fernandina.

MEMORIAL.

To the honorable the commissioners appointed to ascertain claims and titles to lands in East Florida:

The memorial of Domingo Fernandez, by his attorney, Farquhar Bethune, respectfully showeth: That your memorialist claims title to a lot in the town of Fernandina, designated in the plan of said town by the number two, of square number eighteen, containing in front seventeen varas, and the same in depth, bounded on the north by John Sharp's lot, on the east by Commandant's street, on the south by William Hobkirk's lot, and on the west by Zephaniah Kingsley's lot; which title your memorialist derives from a grant made to him by Governor Coppinger, March 27, 1819, in consequence of your memorialist's having complied with the conditions on which such grants were made, as appears from the certificate of the surveyor general, dated June 1, 1817, referred to in the title. Your memorialist further showeth that he is now in possession of said lot, and was so at the time of the cession; that he is an inhabitant of Florida and a resident of Amelia island. The grant above referred to is annexed to the memorial. All of which is respectfully submitted.

DOMINGO FERNANDEZ,
By his attorney, FARQUHAR BETHUNE.

[Here follows translation of the certificate of George J. F. Clarke, surveyor general, accrediting the compliance with the conditions prescribed by the government, and stating the boundaries, dated June 1, 1817.]

[Here follows translation of a memorial to the governor, with his decree granting the prayer of the same, that a royal title should be given for the above lot, dated March 27, 1819.]

[Here follows translation of the royal title, dated March 27, 1819, by Governor Coppinger.]

DECREE.

Domingo Fernandez vs. *The United States. For a lot in the town of Fernandina.*

The board having ascertained that the title to the above was a valid Spanish concession made previous to January 24, 1818, and that the necessary proceedings were afterwards taken in confirmation thereof, do confirm it accordingly. September 2, 1825.

No. 21.—See Report No. 8.

Joseph Allen Smith vs. *The United States. For a lot of land in St. Augustine.*

MEMORIAL.

Territory of Florida, *East Florida:*

To the honorable the commissioners appointed to ascertain claims and titles to lands in East Florida:

The memorial of J. Allen Smith respectfully showeth: That your memorialist claims title to a certain lot or parcel of ground situated and being in the city of St. Augustine, in East Florida aforesaid, having the following lines, dimensions, and boundaries, that is to say: the north line thereof is ninety varas long, and is bounded by lands belonging to George J. F. Clarke; the east line is eighty-four varas long, and is bounded by the head of Matanzas river; the south line is eighty varas in length, and at the time of the survey thereof was bounded by lands of the King; and the west line thereof is two hundred and seventy-five varas in length, and is bounded by the road or street which leads from the powder-house to the city. The said lot of ground is situated near the southern extremity of the boundaries of the city called Sully's Buildings Stand; which said lines and several boundaries will fully appear by a reference to the description of the said lot, as it is contained and set forth in the royal title to the same granted March 9, 1818, which is of record in the office of the keeper of the public archives of East Florida. Your memorialist further shows that the said lot of land was originally granted in or about the year 1793, to one José Ximenes, under the royal order of the King of Spain of March 29, 1790; that possession of said lot was actually taken and kept by the said Joseph Ximenes until his death; that the original grant or concession to the said José Ximenes has been lost, and appears to have been lost before the royal or absolute title thereto was granted; that Catalina Acosta, after the death of her husband, the said José Ximenes, applied for said royal title, alleging the loss of the original concession, making proof of its existence, the possession and actual occupancy of the said lot of land from about the year 1793, by her husband and his family, and after his death by herself; and of the cultivation thereof, and her right to an absolute title: Whereupon, an absolute or royal title was made to the said Catalina Acosta, the widow and heir of the said José Ximenes, March 9, 1818, and the said allegations with respect to the right of the said Catalina Acosta will appear by a reference to the said original grant, of record as aforesaid. Your memorialist further shows that the ancient concession and grant of the said lot of ground to the said José Ximenes is further proved by the original plat and certificate of the first survey of the same for the said José Ximenes made in the year 1797, which is of record in the office of the keeper of the public archives, and to which your memorialist prays a reference; that the said lot of land and its appurtenances were, on the 12th of March, conveyed by the said Catalina Acosta to the late Michael Crosby, deceased, and by the said Michael Crosby to your memorialist on June 25, 1821, for a valuable consideration paid to him by your memorialist, as will appear by a reference to the original conveyances of record in the office of the keeper of the public archives, since which your memorialist has erected three large dwelling-houses, and otherwise improved the said lot of ground, and the said houses are occupied by tenants of your memorialist. Your memorialist further shows that the said José Ximenes, and Catalina Acosta, and Michael Crosby, were severally, at all the times herein mentioned, inhabitants and settlers of East Florida and Spanish subjects; and that your memorialist was a resident of East Florida at the time of the conveyance to him of the said lot, and at the cession of this Territory to the United State. Wherefore, your memorialist prays confirmation of his title to the said lot of land and its appurtenances; and he will ever pray, &c.

J. ALLEN SMITH,
By his attorney, JOHN DRYSDALE.

[Here follows the translation of a certificate of survey, dated January 3, 1797.]

[Here follows the translation of an order from Governor Coppinger, directing a royal title to be issued for the above, dated March 8, 1819.]

[Here follows the translation of a royal title to Catalina Acosta by Governor Coppinger, dated March 9, 1819.]

[Here follows the translation of a conveyance from Catalina Acosta to Miguel Crosby, dated March 12, 1819.]

[Here follows the translation of a conveyance from Miguel Crosby to Joseph Allen Smith, dated June 25, 1821.]

DECREE.

Joseph Allen Smith vs. The United States.   For a lot of land in St. Augustine.

The board having ascertained the above to be a valid Spanish grant, and the deraignment to claimant regular, do confirm the same accordingly.   September 6, 1825.

TESTIMONY.

J. Allen Smith vs. The United States.   A lot of land in St. Augustine.

John Drysdale, being sworn on the part of claimant, states that it is within his knowledge that the buildings which now stand on the lots claimed by the memorialist were erected by Chester Sully, as the agent for claimant, soon after the purchase of the property; that from that time until Mr. Sully left this city, which was about eighteen months ago, *had* charge of the property as agent for the claimant; that at the time when Mr. Sully left this, this deponent was appointed the agent of Mr. Smith for the purpose of taking care of said property; and that said property now belongs, as the deponent believes, to claimant; and that one of the houses on the said lot is now occupied.

JOHN DRYSDALE.

Before the board in session September 6, 1825.

No. 22.—See Report No. 8.

J. Allen Smith vs. The United States.   For seven and a quarter acres of land.

MEMORIAL.

Territory of Florida, *East Florida:*

To the honorable the commissioners appointed to ascertain claims and titles to lands in East Florida:

The memorial of J. Allen Smith respectfully showeth: That your memorialist claims title in and to a certain lot of ground in the city of St. Augustine, in East Florida aforesaid, containing seven acres and a quarter, and rather more; that the said lot of ground was originally granted, or many years ago belonged, to one Martin Floriand; and that the said lot was, in the year 1809, sold by the order of the Spanish government of East Florida at public sale, to raise certain duties which were due and owing by the said Martin Floriand to the Spanish government; at which sale one Francisco Rovira became the purchaser, as will fully and at large appear by reference to the proceedings under which the said lot of ground was sold, and of the sale thereof, which are of record in the office of the keeper of the public archives of East Florida; that the said Francisco Rovira afterwards, to wit, on October 21, 1810, conveyed the same to one Joseph Sanchez, as will appear by a reference to the original conveyance to the said Joseph Sanchez, of record as aforesaid; and that the said Joseph Sanchez, on October 3, 1821, for a large and valuable consideration paid by your memorialist to the said Joseph Sanchez, conveyed the said lot of ground and its appurtenances in fee simple absolute to your memorialist, as will appear by a reference to a recorded copy of the said original conveyance in the office of the clerk of the county court; that the said lot had, at the time of the survey thereof, the following boundaries, that is to say: it was bounded on the north by a lot belonging then to Francisco Perez, now to Josiah Smith, on the south by a lot belonging to Don Bartolome de Castro y Ferrer, on the west by the Ferry river, and on the east by lands belonging to the estate of Mr. William Lafont and to John Geiger; and that the said lot of land has been in the actual possession and occupancy of the aforesaid persons, under whom your memorialist claims title, for a great many years past, and has been in the occupancy of the agent of your memorialist ever since his purchase thereof; that the aforesaid Rovira and Sanchez were, at the times they respectively acquired the said lot, Spanish subjects, and inhabitants and settlers of East Florida; and that the said Sanchez was, at the time of the cession of this Territory to the United States, and at the time he conveyed the said lot to your memorialist as aforesaid, an inhabitant and settler of East Florida; and that your memorialist is a citizen of the United States, residing in Charleston, South Carolina.   Wherefore, he prays a confirmation of his title to the said land and its appurtenances.

J. ALLEN SMITH,
By JOHN DRYSDALE, his Attorney.

[Here follows translation of a conveyance made by Francisco Rovira to José Sanchez, dated August 21, 1810.]

[Here follows a conveyance from José Sanchez to J. Allen Smith, dated October 3, 1821.]

DECREE.

J. Allen Smith vs. The United States.   For seven and a quarter acres of land.

The board having ascertained that a judicial sale in due form was made of the above land on October 27, 1809, at which Francisco Rovira was the purchaser, and the deraignment being clear from him to the claimant, the same is confirmed accordingly.   September 14, 1825.

TESTIMONY.

J. Allen Smith vs. The United States.   For a lot of land at the back part of St. Augustine.

G. W. Perpall, sworn on the part of the claimant, states that the lot in question has been known as private property for forty years; that Joseph Sanchez was the owner of it about eight or ten years ago, and cultivated the same, and had people living on the same until he sold it to Mr. Sully, which was about the exchange of flags. Since that period Mr. Sully has had the management and care of it.

G. W. PERPALL.

Before the board in session September 14, 1825.

No. 23.—See Report No. 8.

The wardens of the Roman Catholic church of St. Augustine vs. The United States. For thirty-one and a half acres of land.

MEMORIAL.

To the honorable the board of land commissioners appointed to ascertain claims and titles to lands in East Florida:

The memorial of the wardens of the Roman Catholic church of St. Augustine, incorporated by law, respectfully showeth: That your memorialists claim title to a tract of land containing thirty-one and a half acres, situated at the point called Esperanza, within the limits of the city of St. Augustine, bounded on the north by the lands of the heirs of B. Segui, deceased; on the south and west by St. Sebastian's river; and on the east by the creek called Bridge creek; which title your memorialists derive, as wardens of said church, from the will of the late Maria Evans, deceased, as will be seen by a reference to the third section of said will on record in the office of the public archives. And your memorialists further show that they will produce further evidence of title when required by the board.

For the board of wardens:

F. J. FATIO, *Secretary of Board of Wardens.*

[Here follows translation of an extract from the will of Maria Evans, deceased, dated July 29, 1792.]
[Here follows a conveyance from Alexander Todd to Joseph Peavett, esq., dated September 16, 1782.]

DECREE.

Wardens of the Roman Catholic church of St. Augustine vs. The United States. For thirty-one and a half acres of land.

The board having ascertained the above title to be a valid British one, and recognized by the Spanish government, and that the deraignment to claimants is regular, do confirm the claim accordingly. October 26, 1825.

TESTIMONY.

The wardens of the Roman Catholic church of St. Augustine vs. The United States. For thirty-one and a half acres of land.

Charles W. Clarke, being duly sworn, doth depose and say that he was acquainted with Mrs. Peavett; that he knew her to have a framed house between Maria Sanchez's creek and St. Sebastian's river on the point, which she resided in for some time; she had, also, negroes planting there for some years, with the knowledge and acquiescence of the Spanish government. And further this deponent saith not.

CHARLES W. CLARKE.

Before me this 21st September, 1825.

DAVIS FLOYD.

No. 24.—See Report No. 8.

The wardens of the Roman Catholic church vs. The United States. A lot of land in the city of St. Augustine.

MEMORIAL.

To the honorable the commissioners appointed to ascertain claims and titles to lands in East Florida:

The memorial of the wardens of the Roman Catholic church of St. Augustine respectfully showeth: That your memorialists claim title to a lot of land situated in the city of St. Augustine, on the north side of the public square, and upon which the church and school-house now stand, bounded on the west by St. George's street, on the east by the custom-house and the Marquis Fougere's lots, on the south by the public square, and on the north by the lots of Joseph M. Hernandez and the heirs of Peso de Burgo, measuring 72½ varas, Spanish yards, front on the square, and 58½ varas in depth; which title your memorialists derive from a judicial sale executed on April 12, 1793, as will more fully appear by a certified copy of the same herewith filed. And your memorialists, on behalf of the said church, pray confirmation of title to the said lots.

On behalf of the wardens of said church:

F. J. FATIO, *Secretary.*

[Here follows the translation of deed of sale dated April 12, 1793.]

DECREE.

The wardens of the Roman Catholic church of St. Augustine vs. The United States. For a lot of land in the city of St. Augustine.

It appearing in evidence before this board that this was a valid British grant confirmed by the Spanish government, and regularly conveyed by deed, bearing date April 12, 1793, to the King, in trust for the Roman Catholic congregation of St. Augustine, for the purpose of building a church thereon, it is therefore confirmed to said wardens in trust for said congregation. October 29, 1825.

The wardens of the Roman Catholic church of St. Augustine vs. *The United States.   For a lot of land in St. Augustine.*

G. W. Perpall, sworn and examined on the part of claimants, says that Mrs. Humbert, who, by her attorney, M. Lazaga, sold the lot on which the Roman Catholic church and the new city council chamber stands, was the sister of the witness; and that the whole of said lot was at the time of said sale an orange grove, that is, from St. George's street to the late custom-house square.   Witness says that the whole of the lot was sold for the purpose of building the church.   The house of the city council was then a dwelling-house, and was intended for a parsonage house, but as the parsons or priests usually had houses of their own in which they preferred living, the house on the lot was used for the purpose of a public school.   The members of the Catholic church, at the purchase of the lot, and the commencement of building the present church, raised sums as large as they were able, by subscription, for the purchase of the lot and building of the same; but as they were unable to complete the said church, Governor Quesada made a representation to the King of Spain, who directed that the church should be finished at the King's expense.

G. W. PERPALL.

Before the board in session October 27, 1825.

No. 25.—See Report No. 8.

Antelm Gay vs. *The United States.   For two lots of land in St. Augustine.*

MEMORIAL.

To the honorable the commissioners appointed to ascertain claims and titles to lands in East Florida:

The memorial of Antelm Gay, a citizen of the United States, and resident of the city of St. Augustine, in East Florida, respectfully showeth: That your memorialist claims title to two lots of land in the city of St. Augustine, which your memorialist purchased of Don Bartlome de Castro y Ferrer, on January 26, 1822—one of which said lots is bounded west on the street which passes to the east of the convent or barracks of St. Francis, on the east by the bay, on the south by the public land, and on the north by a lot the property of the said Bartolome de Castro y Ferrer; the other of the said lots is bounded west by the said street, on the east by the bay, on the north by the lot of Mariano Serra, and on the south by the lot of the heirs of Salvator Martin; which said two lots were purchased by the said Bartolome de Castro y Ferrer of Antonio Vallejo and his wife, at which time there were houses on the said lots, but which have been since destroyed, the said Antonio Vallejo having purchased one of the said lots of Miguel Rodriguez, as appears by the original deed deposited in the public archives, executed June 14, 1803; and the other lot was bought by Antonio Peter's wife of the said Antonio Vallejo of Pedro Fornells, as appears by a deed deposited in the public archives, executed April 10, 1799.   Both of the aforesaid lots fell to the domain of the King of Spain after the evacuation of the British, but were delivered to the purchasers and occupants, and confirmed to them by a decree of the Spanish government of June 17, 1801; all which will more clearly appear by the certificate of José de Zubizaretta, the public escribano, dated July 30, 1812, herewith presented; and your memorialist has been in possession of said lots since his purchase, as before mentioned.

In confirmation of his title, the following documents are herewith respectfully presented:

1. Certificate of the above-mentioned of the public escribano, (deed from Don Bartolome de Castro y Ferrer to your memorialist,) recorded in the public office of records in St. Augustine, January 6, 1802. All which is respectfully submitted.

ANTELM GAY,
By his attorney, JOHN RODMAN.

St. Augustine, *August 20, 1823.*

[Here follows translation of the grant to Bartolome Cartado, dated November 17, 1792, by Governor Quesada, and a translation of a transfer to Pedro Fornells, dated April 14, 1795.]

[Here follows translation of a deed of conveyance from Pedro Fornells to Antonio Petrus, dated April 10, 1799.]

[Here follows translation of a concession to Bartolome Cartado by Governor Quesada, dated January 13, 1794, and a transfer to Pedro Fornells, April 14, 1795.]

[Here follows translation of a deed of conveyance from Bartolome Cartado to Pedro Fornells, dated April 14, 1795.]

[Here follows the translation of a deed of conveyance from Pedro Fornells to Miguel Rodriguez, dated November 6, 1799.]

[Here follows the translation of a deed of conveyance from Miguel Rodriguez to Antonio Vallejo, dated June 14, 1803.]

[Here follows translation of a deed of conveyance from Antonio Vallejo and Antonio Petrus, husband and wife, to Bartolome de Castro Ferrer, dated April 2, 1807.]

[Here follows deed of conveyance from Bartolome de Castro y Ferrer to Antelm Gay, dated January 26, 1822.]

DECREE.

Antelm Gay vs. *The United States.   For two lots of land in St. Augustine.*

The board having ascertained the above to be founded on valid Spanish concessions, and the deraignment being regular, do confirm the same accordingly.   October 29, 1825.

[Nos. 26, 27, and 28, were not returned to the General Land Office by the commissioners.]

[Note.—The commissioners returned no papers with report No. 9.]

No. 1.—See Report No. 10.

George F. and Oliver Palmes vs. The United States. For nine hundred and ninety-nine and three-quarters acres of land.

MEMORIAL.

To the honorable the commissioners appointed to ascertain claims and titles to lands in East Florida:

The petition of George F. Palmes and Oliver Palmes respectfully showeth: That your memorialists claim title to a tract of land consisting of nine hundred and ninety-nine and three-fourths acres of land, situated at the place called Turnbull, on both sides of Spruce creek, in the territory of Mosquito, bounded on the north by pine lands, on the south by lands belonging to William Williams, on the east by marsh; for which an absolute title was made to Robert McHardy by Governor Estrada July 3, 1815; which title your memorialists derive from a grant made to Robert McHardy July 21, 1803, by Governor White, in virtue of the royal order of October 29, 1790, who sold the same to Paul Dupon, by deed dated June 2, 1818, which is herewith submitted, who holds the same in trust for memorialists, as will be seen by bond filed in their claim for 245 acres. And your memorialists further show that they are legally seized and possessed of said lands by the trustee aforesaid, and were so at the time of cession; that they are citizens of the United States and residents of Savannah, in the State of Georgia. They pray confirmation of title, &c. All which is respectfully submitted, &c.

GEORGE F. PALMES.
OLIVER PALMES.

[Translation.]

Title of property in favor of Don Robert McHardy. For one thousand acres of land.

Don Juan José de Estrada y Toro, lieutenant colonel of the royal armies, &c., &c., &c.:

Whereas, by a royal order communicated to this government October 29, 1790, by the captain general of the Island of Cuba and the two Floridas, it is provided, amongst other things, that lands shall be laid off gratis for those foreigners who, of their own free will, present themselves to swear allegiance to our sovereign, in proportion to the number of laborers each family may have; that Don Robert McHardy having presented himself as one of those, he solicited from the government, and there were granted to him July 21, 1803, one thousand acres of land at the plantation named *Dr. Trumbul,* situated towards a part of the river Mosquito, and at both sides of the creek named Spruce, as appears from the certificate which was issued on the same date by the secretary, and is annexed to the proceeding moved for, soliciting that the corresponding title of property to said lands should be delivered to him, the boundaries of which are as follows: on the north and west with pine lands, on the south by lands of the heirs of Don William Williams, and on the east by marsh, as the said proceeding sets forth. And as there has not been delivered to the said Don Robert McHardy any title for the security and confirmation of his dominion to the said land, in the form in which it has been granted to others who have already passed more than ten years of uninterrupted possession to obtain the useful and direct dominion to the said lands, made buildings upon them, cultivated them, and complied with the other conditions established by the government for concessions and grants of this nature existing in the titles delivered to other settlers in the proceedings set forth: Wherefore, and in consideration of everything, I have granted unto the said Don Robert McHardy the 1,000 acres of land, for himself, his heirs and successors, in absolute property; and in expediting to him, as by these presents I do, the corresponding title by which I separate the royal domain from the right and dominion it had to said lands; and I cede and transfer it to the said McHardy, his heirs and successors, that, in consequence, they may possess it as their own, use and enjoy it, without any encumbrance whatsoever, with all its entrances, outlets, uses, customs, rights, and services, which it has had, and in fact and law belong and appertain unto it; and, at their will, sell, cede, transfer, and alienate it as may best suit them. To all of which I interpose my authority, as I can and of right ought, in virtue of the sovereign will.

Given under my hand, and countersigned by the undersigned notary *pro tem.* of government and the royal domain, in the city of St. Augustine, Florida, July 3, 1815.

JUAN JOSÉ DE ESTRADA.

I certify the foregoing to be a true and correct translation from a document in the Spanish language.
F. J. FATIO, *S. B. L. C.*

[Translation.]

CONVEYANCE.

Be it known that I, Don Robert McHardy, an inhabitant of this province, declare that I really sell unto Paul Dupon, a new settler in it, nine hundred and ninety-nine and two-thirds acres of land, situated in the territory of Mosquito, in this province towards the river, at a place called Dr. Turnbull, and at both sides of a creek called Spruce, bounded on the north and west with pine lands, on the south by lands belonging to the heirs of Don William Williams, and on the east by a swamp, which lands are the same that were granted to me by the government July 21, 1803, and for which a title of absolute property was expedited to me to the number of 1,000 acres of land July 3, 1815, remaining only with one-quarter of an acre for my use and dominion, and I sell him the other 999¾, with all its entrances, outlets, uses, customs, rights, and services, which it has and belong to it, free from all encumbrance (as I, the said notary, certify, from the result of my search of the book of mortgages which I have made for the purpose,) at the price of one thousand five hundred dollars, which the purchaser has paid me in cash, which I acknowledge as delivered to my will. I renounce proof, laws of delivery, exception to money not counted, fraud, and anything else in the case, for which I grant a receipt in form. In virtue of which, I separate myself from the right of property, possession, use, seigniory, and other actions, real and personal, which I had and held to the said lands, all of which I cede, renounce, and transfer to the purchaser and his representatives, that, as their own, they may possess, sell, and alienate it at their will, in virtue of this deed which I grant in their favor as a token of real delivery, by which it is seen that he has acquired the possession without occasion for further proof, from which I relieve him, and oblige myself to the eviction and guarantee of said sale in due form, and as may best suit the purchaser, with my property, present and future, power and submission to the tribunals of his Majesty, that they may compel me to compliance as by sentence consented to and passed in authority of an adjudged case, on which I renounce all the laws, customs, rights, and privileges in my favor, and the general law in form which prohibits it. And I, the said Don Pablo Dupon, being present, accept in my favor this deed, and by it receive as purchased the said lands at the price and agreement on which they were sold to me, and I acknowledge them as delivered to my will. I renounce proof, laws of delivery, those of a thing not seen or received, fraud, and everything else in the case, for which I deliver a receipt in form. In testimony of which, this is dated in this city of St. Augustine, Florida, the second of June, one thousand eight hundred and eighteen. I, the notary, attest that I know the parties who signed this, there being witnesses present, Don José Mariano Hernandez, Don Eusebio Maria Gomez, and Don José Maria Bousquet, inhabitants present.

ROBERT McHARDY.
P. DUPON.

Before me—

JUAN DE ENTRALGO, Notary of Government.

I certify the foregoing to be a true and correct translation from a document in the Spanish language.
F. J. FATIO, S. B. L. C.

DECREE BY THE BOARD.

The claimant exhibited to the board a royal title made by Governor Estrada to Robert McHardy for the land for headrights, dated July 3, 1815, who sold and conveyed the same to Paul Dupon in trust for claimants, as per bond referred to and filed in the claim of Miss Palmes for 245 acres. The board having ascertained that the title of the claimants is interfered with by British titles, under which the heirs of Turnbull claim, they therefore order that the documents accompanying the memorial in this case be reported to Congress for their determination. September 24.

No. 2.—See REPORT No. 10.

John Bunch vs. The United States. For two thousand one hundred and sixty acres of land.

MEMORIAL.

To the honorable the commissioners appointed to ascertain claims and titles to lands in East Florida :

The petition of John Bunch respectfully showeth: That your memorialist claims title to a tract of land consisting of two thousand one hundred and sixty acres, situated on the waters of Mosquito or Halifax river, and is bounded as follows, (as by survey herewith filed, marked B:) beginning at a cabbage tree near a marsh, and running west, 98 chains, to a pride of Egypt; thence north 80° west, to a pine; thence along the public road south 50° east, to a stake; thence east, 100 chains, to Tomoka river; thence with said river to its mouth; thence with Haulover river to the beginning; which title your memorialist derives from a grant made to him by Governor White, in virtue of the royal order of 1790, for headrights, on August 11, 1804, (see order of concession, marked A, filed herewith;) and your memorialist further showeth that he has, since the 11th day of August, been in actual possession of said lands; that he has cultivated them up to the present period, and still continues to do so. Your memorialist further shows that he was, at the change of flags, a Spanish subject, and that he intends residing at Tomoka, his present home, in future. Your memorialist therefore prays that his title may be confirmed; and he will ever pray, &c.

JOHN BUNCH,
By his attorney, GEORGE MURRAY.

[Translation.]

Don Juan de Pierra, lieutenant of grenadiers of the third battalion of the regiment of Cuba, and secretary of the government: I certify that to a memorial presented by Don Juan Bunch, soliciting that there should be granted to him in the territory of Mosquito the lands which corresponds to him, his wife, sixty-two negroes of more than twenty years, and thirty-four from eight to sixteen, which, in the time of the British dominion, were possessed by Moultrie and Moncrief; these, which were granted to Don Nicolas Turnbull, who did not take possession of them in due time, the following decree was made: " Let there be granted to the interested two thousand one hundred and sixty acres of land in the place which he solicits, without injury to a third person, and those are what he is entitled to; and until, according to the number of laborers he may have, when the general survey takes place, those which correspond to him be surveyed, he being bound to take possession of the said land within the term of six months."

WHITE.

And that it may serve for a security to the interested, I give these presents at St. Augustine, Florida, August 11, 1804.

JUAN DE PIERRA.

NOTE.—That by a decree of April 11, 1808, there were —— to Don Samuel Bunch, son of him contained in this certificate, 240 acres of land on the river St. Mary's, for nine negroes over sixteen years, and one of thirteen years; which number of acres are to be deducted from the two thousand one hundred and sixty of his father, on account of those which correspond to his son's ten negroes being included to this number of acres.   PIERRA.

I certify the foregoing decree and note are true and correct translations from their originals on file in the office of the public archives of St. Augustine.

F. J. FATIO, S. B. L. C.

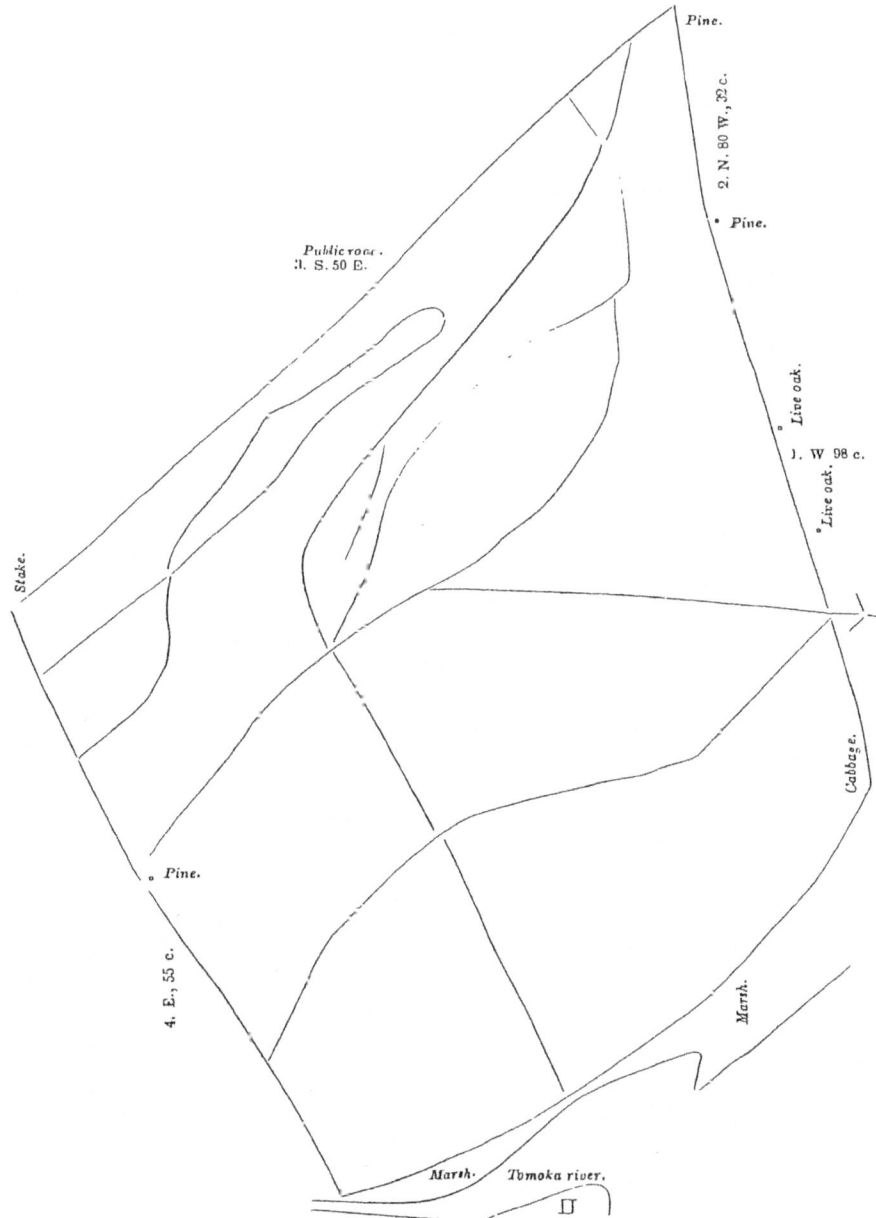

DECREE BY THE BOARD.

The claimant in this case produced a certified copy of concession for the two thousand one hundred and sixty acres of land, dated August 11, 1804, made by Governor White to him for "headrights." It appeared further to the board that the claimant occupied and cultivated the land ever since it was granted to him; but having ascertained that his title is interfered with by a British title, under which the heirs of Turnbull claim, we do therefore order that the documents accompanying the memorial be forwarded to Congress for their determination.   October 11.

John Bunch vs. *The United States.   For two thousand one hundred and sixty acres of land.*

Horatio S. Dexter, being sworn, states that in the year 1813 he was at the said tract of land occupied by Mr. Bunch, who had a considerable quantity of stock, and above forty negroes, and that it was a matter of general notoriety under the Spanish government that said tract of land was the property of said Bunch.

HORATIO S. DEXTER.

Before the board in session October 11, 1824.

G. W. Perpall, being sworn, states that he recollects Mr. Bunch having obtained possession of the above tract about a week after the grant was made him by the Spanish government, and has continued cultivating the same to the present period, and that the said Bunch has had continually on the place from thirty to forty negroes.

G. W. PERPALL.

Before the board in session October 11, 1824.

No. 3.—See Report No. 10.

Zephaniah Kingsley vs. The United States. For two thousand acres of land.

MEMORIAL.

To the honorable the commissioners appointed to ascertain claims and titles to lands in East Florida:

The petition of Zephaniah Kingsley, by his attorney, George Gibbs, respectfully showeth: That your memorialist claims title to a tract of land consisting of two thousand acres, more or less, situated on the island called Drayton island, at the entrance of Lake George, bounded on all sides by the river St John's and Lake George, it being an island, as per royal title, certified by Juan de Entralgo, government notary, dated July 27, 1821, per exhibit K, to which, and to other documents in the office of the archives of the Territory, will more fully appear by reference to the same; which title your memorialist derives from a title made to George Sibbald for part by Governor Kindelan, in virtue of the royal order of October 29, 1790, who sold your memorialist fifteen hundred acres of the said island, being all his interest and right in the same; and the rest and residue of the said island was granted to your memorialist by the same Governor Kindelan, as per the aforementioned title—reference to the documents in the office of the public archives—will more fully appear. And your memorialist further showeth that he is in actual possession of said lands; that he is now a citizen of the United States and resident of St. Augustine.

　　　　　　　　　　　　　　　　　　ZEPHANIAH KINGSLEY,
　　　　　　　　　　　　　　　　By GEORGE GIBBS, *Attorney in fact.*

[Translation.]

Title of property in favor of Don Zephaniah Kingsley, of Drayton island.

Don Sebastian Kindelan and O'Regan, knight of the order of St. James, brigadier of the royal armies, political and military governor of the city of St. Augustine, Florida, and its province:

Whereas, in a royal order communicated to this government October 29, 1790, by the captain general of the Island of Cuba and two Floridas, it is provided, amongst other things, that lands should be granted and surveyed gratis to those foreigners who, of their own free will, offer themselves to swear allegiance to our sovereign, in proportion to the number of workers each family may have; that Don George Sibbald having presented himself as one of them, he solicited from the government, and had granted unto him, fifteen hundred acres of land, October, 5, 1804, in the island called Drayton, at the entrance of Lake George, in the river St. John's, which he ceded to Don Zephaniah Kingsley, with all its improvements, to whom it was adjudged in *solutune*, in virtue of the agreement of the parties authorized by a decree of this said government July 18, 1811; and afterwards, by a decree of the 4th of September of the same year, there were granted to the aforesaid Kingsley five hundred acres more, which were vacant in the said island, which in all may contain about two thousand acres, more or less, as appears more at length from the documents and certificates which are annexed to the proceeding moved by the said Kingsly, soliciting that there should be issued in his favor the corresponding title for the lands which the said island of Drayton contains: Wherefore, and considering that he has already passed more than ten years of an uninterrupted possession to obtain the useful and directed dominion to the said island of Drayton, made buildings on it, cultivated it, and finally complied with all the other conditions established by the government for grants and concessions of this nature existing in the titles delivered to other settlers, as is set forth and proved in the said proceeding, I have granted, as in the name of his Majesty I do grant, unto the aforesaid Don Zephaniah Kingsley the said Drayton island, for himself, his heirs and successors, in absolute property; and in despatching to him, as by these presents I do, the corresponding title, by which I separated the royal domain from the right and dominion it had to said land; and I cede and tranfer it unto the said Kingsley, his heirs and successors, that, in consequence, they may possess it as their own, use and enjoy it, without any encumbrance whatsoever, with all its entrances, outlets, uses, customs, rights, and *services*, which it has had, has, and of custom and by law belong and may appertain unto it; and, at their will, sell, cede, transfer, and alienate it as may best suit them. To all which I give the sanction of my authority, as I can and of right ought to do, in virtue of the sovereign will.

Given under my hand, and countersigned by the undersigned notary of government and of the royal domain, in this said city of St. Augustine, Florida, January 7, 1815.

　　　　　　　　　　　　　　　　　　SEBASTIAN KINDELAN.

By command of his excellency:
　　JUAN DE ENTRALGO, *Notary of Government pro tem.*

I certify the foregoing to be a true and correct translation from a document in the Spanish language on file in the office of the public archives.

　　　　　　　　　　　　　　　　　　F. J. FATIO, *S. B. L. C.*

DECREE.

The board having ascertained that this claim is covered by a British grant, they therefore order that it be reported to Congress for their determination. December 15.